THEORETICAL PSYCHOLOGY

THE MEETING OF EAST AND WEST

PATH IN PSYCHOLOGY
Published in Cooperation with Publications for the Advancement of Theory and History in Psychology (PATH)

Series Editors:
David Bakan, *York University*
John Broughton, *Teachers College, Columbia University*
Miriam Lewin, *Manhattanville College*
Robert Rieber, *John Jay College, CUNY, and Columbia University*
Howard Gruber, *Rutgers University*

WILHELM WUNDT AND THE MAKING OF A SCIENTIFIC PSYCHOLOGY
Edited by R. W. Rieber

HUMANISTIC PSYCHOLOGY: Concepts and Criticisms
Edited by Joseph R. Royce and Leendert P. Mos

PSYCHOSOCIAL THEORIES OF THE SELF
Edited by Benjamin Lee

DEVELOPMENTAL APPROACHES TO THE SELF
Edited by Benjamin Lee and Gil G. Noam

THEORETICAL PSYCHOLOGY: The Meeting of East and West
A. C. Paranjpe

A CRITICAL PSYCHOLOGY: Interpretation of the Personal World
Edmund V. Sullivan

THEORETICAL PSYCHOLOGY

THE MEETING OF EAST AND WEST

A. C. PARANJPE

Simon Fraser University
Burnaby, Bristish Columbia, Canada

PLENUM PRESS • NEW YORK AND LONDON

Library of Congress Cataloging in Publication Data

Paranjpe, A. C.
Theoretical psychology.

(PATH in psychology)
Bibliography: p.
Includes index.
1. Psychology—Philosophy. 2. East and West. I. Title. II. Series.
BF38.P33 1984 150.19 83-24546
ISBN 0-306-41400-7

A Division of Plenum Publishing Corporation
233 Spring Street, New York, N.Y. 10013

Printed in the United States of America

To my revered guru,
to the late Śrī Gurujī,
and to all my teachers

PREFACE

This book is an outcome of my bicultural experience as a student and teacher of psychology in India and North America. As a student in India, the psychology I learned in the classroom was totally Western in its perspective. A book on Indian economics, called *Bhāratīya Arthaśāstra,* written by the late Paṇḍit Dīndayāl Upādhyāya, inspired me to look into the sources of the Indian intellectual tradition for an indigenous perspective within the discipline of my training and research. The late Bāḷśāstrī Hardās suggested K. K. Kolhaṭkar's *Bhāratīya Mānasaśastra,* a book that translates and comments on Patañjali's Yoga sūtras in Marāṭhī, as a sourcebook of psychological concepts of Indian origin. My response to this initial exposure to Yoga as a system of psychology was one of bewilderment. Having been trained in psychology with Woodworth and Schlosberg's *Experimental Psychology* as the textbook of psychology, I could not comprehend how ideas so diverse as those of Patañjali and Woodworth and Schlosberg could be designated by a common label—psychology! Obviously, it was necessary to sort out psychology's *meaning* in different sociocultural contexts, beginning with the most fundamental notions on which psychological concepts are based. This book represents an attempt to understand psychological concepts, especially those relating to consciousness and the self, as they developed in the different intellectual traditions and cultural contexts of India and the West.

More than two decades have passed since I began the intellectual journey that brought me to the set of ideas presented here. Many teachers, friends, and well-wishers have encouraged me at various stages of this enterprise. Foremost among them are Professors Gardner Murphy, Cora DuBois, Stanley Milgram, Willard Day, Erik Erikson, Durganand Sinha, Paul Bakan, McKim Marriott, David Bakan, Yujiro Ikemi, and Dr. George V. Coelho. In their own ways, all these people have given valuable support; I am extremely grateful to all of them. The following persons read small or large sections of the manuscript and offered useful comments and constructive criticism: Drs. Ashok and Vidyut Aklujkar, Swami Asesananda, Drs. David Bakan and Barry Beyerstein, Swami Bhaskarananda, Mr. Stuart Bush, Swami Dayananda Sarasvati, Drs. John R. M. Goyeche, Ron Laye, James Marcia, Basil McDermott, Norman Sjoman, S. R. Talghatti, and Harold Weinberg, and Lolita Wilson. I have been able to avoid many errors and incorporate innumerable good points into the manuscript as a result of their astute suggestions. Doctor Goyeche and Professor Wilson went through the entire manuscript with a fine-toothed comb and helped me improve the book in form and content. Dr. Rosemary Carter helped edit an earlier draft of the first five chapters. While I must give all of them credit for various strengths of the book, I am responsible for its numerous shortcomings. I have no words to express my gratitude to Professor Wilson, who, in addition to reading the entire manuscript, taught me innumerable nuances of the English language and Canadian culture, prepared an index, and showered me with affection and appreciation.

This book could not have seen the light of the day without the help of Drs. David Bakan and Robert Rieber of the PATH in Psychology series. I wish to express my indebtedness to both of them, and also to Professors Durganand Sinha, Yujiro Ikemi, and J. B. P. Sinha for their valuable help in seeing this work into publication.

Various sections of this book have been read by and discussed with a number of students. In fact, several themes have evolved during the course of discussions during the past several years in my seminars in social psychology, personality, and the history of psychology at Simon Fraser University. It is impossible to list the large number of students who have contributed good points to the discussion of various issues, prompted me to elaborate when necessary, and assisted in bringing clarity to my thought and expression. I am thankful to all of them. Coleen Melsness, Ray Davison, Joan Foster, and Anant Vaze helped me deal with the computer, which continued to pose problems every now and then. Quite certainly, I am indebted to my wife Meena, and sons Prasad and Shreyas who suffered because of my absorption in work at times when I should have been attending to my duties at home.

Finally, I wish to thank the members of the President's Grants Committee at Simon Fraser University, who sanctioned appropriate funds to pay for certain costs in preparing the manuscript.

A. C. PARANJPE

PRONUNCIATION AND TRANSLITERATION OF SANSKRIT TERMS

The transliteration of Sanskrit used in this book follows the most commonly used format. What follows is a general guide (rather than a strict phonetic account) of Sanskrit terms transliterated in the text.

The vowels are described thus:

a	as *u* in cut
ā	as *a* in far
i	as *i* in fit
ī	as *ee* in tree
u	as *u* in put
ū	as *oo* in root
ṛ	somewhat like *r* in bird
l, ḷ	somewhat like *l* in bottle
e	as *ay* in say
ai	somewhat like *ai* in aisle
o	as *o* in go
au	as *ou* in out
ṁ	nasalizes the preceding vowels
ḥ	sounds like *h* with a sharp exhalation of air

The consonants are generally similar to English with a few exceptions. There is a series of "alviolars" (t, th, d, dh, n) produced with the tip of the tongue touching the gum ridge, and a series of retroflex sounds (ṭ, ṭh, ḍ, ḍh, ṇ, ḷ) produced by curling the tongue backward. The ṣ is a similar retroflex. The c sounds like *ch* in chair, j as *j* in jug, ś like *sh* in shirt, ñ like the Spanish señor, and ṅ like *n* in king. The aspirates (kh, gh, ch, jh, th, ṭh, dh, ḍh, ph and bh) are pronounced with a clearly audible release of breath following the consonant, for example, ṭh as in ant-hill, and dh as in bald-head.

A Note on Sources

Sanskrit sources cited in this book are indicated by the name of the author, followed by the chapter number, section number where applicable, the verse or aphorism number. Different works of the same author are distinguished by lower-case alphabets in the same way as references. Classics such as the *Bhagavad-Gītā* or the epic *Mahābhārata* are referred to by their titles. The year of publication of the Sanskrit works is not given because the exact dates of publication for most of the old sources are either unknown, or known only approximately.

CONTENTS

1

INTRODUCTION

Some Converging Trends

During the past few years there has been growing interest in psychological concepts and phenomena such as samādhi, satori, meditation, gurus, and others which originated in such Eastern traditions as Yoga and Zen Buddhism. In the West, Yoga is no longer restricted to exercises at the Y.M.C.A., to such popular movements as Transcendental Meditation, or to a few secluded Ashrams run by "gurus" imported from the East. Interest in psychological concepts of Eastern origin is spreading among university students and teachers. Systematic theoretical and experimental work is being published in psychological and medical journals ranging from the *Journal of Humanistic Psychology* to *E.E.G. and Clinical Neurophysiology*. Charles Tart's book, *Altered States of Consciousness* (1969/1972), which includes several papers on meditation and yogic states, has become popular among students of psychology. This book has been followed by another volume edited by Tart (1975), called *Transpersonal Psychologies*, which brings together contributions on the psychologies of Yoga, Buddhism, and Sufism. Robert Ornstein's *Psychology of Consciousness* (1972) represents a serious attempt to integrate concepts from the East into the mainstream of modern psychology.

Recent publications attempting to link Eastern and Western approaches to psychological issues are too many to mention here. This healthy trend in publication deserves a warm welcome. For a world that is shrinking in its dimensions due to faster means of communication, such a trend is, in fact, overdue. There is no reason why anyone should deprive himself of knowledge or techniques on the basis of their time

Notes for Chapter 1 are on p. 53.

and place of origin. During the long history of the Indian continent, many men have asked themselves the same types of questions that have intrigued their Western counterparts. Sometimes thinkers separated by time and place have arrived independently at similar answers to the same questions. Sometimes those in the East have arrived at solutions that have eluded Westerners, sometimes the reverse. For want of better communication and comparative study we may unnecessarily tread paths proven fruitless elsewhere, or keep asking questions which have already been satisfactorily answered. A preliminary acquaintance with the histories of Eastern and Western thought indicates that psychological insights of Yoga have much to contribute to the understanding of the higher reaches of human experience and potential. These contributions may prove to be a valuable complement to the excellence of Western psychologies in analytical rigor, meaurement, experimentation, and technology. An integration of the right aspects of both traditions should give us a broader and more comprehensive view of man, and more viable psychology. In this book I propose to present a modest attempt at converging Indian and Western thinking on a few issues in psychology.

An attempt to integrate two different traditions requires a systematic comparison of the contributions of both to some common issues. Such a comparison has more to it than simply retrieving valuable insights attained in the past that might otherwise be lost. An attempt to compare two different systems necessitates "stepping out" of both systems now and then, since this enables us to assess each of them as a whole. Temporary distancing from a system of ideas enables us to stop and question whether things which we have taken for granted are indeed unconditionally true. Thus, our *implicit assumptions* become *explicit* in the process of comparison. A continual comparison of diverse systems usually accentuates the differences between them. Problems which are brushed aside as unimportant in one system are sometimes found to be legitimate and important issues in the other system. A "blind spot" in one tradition turns out to be one which is illuminated in the other system. We tend to exaggerate our strengths and discount our weaknesses when working within only one system, while a comparative perspective enables us to see the strengths and weaknesses of our own as well as other systems in their real proportions.

Before starting on a comparative study, we may wish to know briefly what the Indian tradition may have to offer for the student of psychology. Certainly it has much more to offer than the little that psychologists in India or elsewhere have been able to translate into modern terminology. First, there is a vast literature on various systems of philosophy that involves critical thinking concerning the mind. Second, there is a centuries-old, living tradition that has transmitted techniques such as meditation and breathing exercises which can help one reach higher states of consciousness. This means that there are persons living today who have acquired traditional techniques through apprenticeship or other forms of learning. Such persons can demonstrate that what is written in books is not merely words or hollow ideals, but something that is actually practiced. Third, in India today there are social institutions using highly developed methods of counseling to help individuals toward personality growth. These methods could be developed into techniques which would be useful in psychological counseling throughout the modern world.

In other words, the Indian tradition has the following main ingredients that are required to make a comprehensive system of psychology: an elaborate conceptual framework comprising a worldview, a theoretical analysis of the structures and processes relating to human personality, a normative account defining the nature of higher and lower levels of the functioning of personality, a set of techniques designed to help the not-so-well-developed individual reach more desirable levels of development, and a set of social institutions within which growth of personality can be facilitated.

I am well aware that a statement like the one above, asserting the existence of a system of psychology of Indian origin, is bound to raise doubts and questions, not only outside India but also among psychologists at the universities of India itself. If India has had a psychology of its own, how is it that even the Indian universities do not teach courses based on it? The answer to this question is simple. In India, as in many other countries, separate departments devoted to teaching and research in psychology were started in opposition to philosophy, the "mother discipline" of psychology. In the process of growing up, psychology has often taken a rebellious stand against mother philosophy, and many psychologists have neglected the historical roots of their thinking. In many Indian universities, the new departments were staffed by scholars trained in England or the United States, and American textbooks have long dominated the psychology curricula. As a result, most of the psychology taught in India today is another edition of Western psychology. Durganand Sinha, a senior Indian psychologist, has castigated his compatriots for turning their backs on their own rich tradition. He has rightly ascribed the neglect of their own cultural roots to bedazzlement by the scientific psychology of the West and to the antiphilosophical stance of psychology in general (see Sinha, 1965). A mature approach to psychology, however, cannot afford to neglect the philosophical underpinnings of contemporary theories, nor their historical roots.

It must be granted that a separate, independent academic discipline called psychology is not very old, either in the East or in the West. Only recently have there been books labelled "textbook of psychology" or a community of people who call themselves psychologists. Psychology, as a formal, independent academic discipline, is a relatively recent phenomenon. Patañjali did not call himself a psychologist, nor did he label his *Yoga Sūtras* a textbook of a psychology. But the absence of a label does not alter the content, which is obviously psychological. A common belief among psychologists is that psychology was born in Germany with the founding of Wundt's laboratory between 1875 and 1879. What began with Wundt, however, was not psychology itself, but the application to psychology of the method of experiment developed by the natural sciences. It is, of course, not necessary to belabor this point, since many historians of Western psychology, such as Brett (1912/1962), the Murphys (1968), and Watson (1978) begin their accounts of psychological thought with such ancient Greek philosophers as Aristotle.

The historical roots of Indian psychological thought can be traced back to the Upaniṣads, the mystical and philosophical discourses which were composed from approximately the 8th Century B.C. onward. The most important source of the psychological concepts of India is Pantañjali's well known text of aphorisms on Yoga. Dating such texts from the Indian tradition is a historian's nightmare since historical record-keeping was one of the neglected aspects of Indian culture. There are differences of opinion among scholars about the date and author of the full text, but Patañjali's text seems to have been completed no later than the 5th Century A.D. Philosophically, Pantañjali's Yoga is closest to the Sāṅkhya system, a dualistic philosophy that is one of the oldest known. But the Advaita, or non-dualistic system, particularly as interpreted by Śaṅkara (788–820 A.D.), is the most dominant school of Indian philosophy. However the Advaita conception of the psychic apparatus, as noted by Hiriyanna, the well-known historian of Indian philosophy, closely resembles that of Pantañjali (Hiriyanna, 1932, p. 341).

There are six major and several minor systems of Hindu philosophy besides the separate and well developed systems of Jainism and Buddhism. Each of these schools has contributed in its own way, to a greater or lesser extent, to thinking about perception, the nature of self, and other psychological issues. Psychologically significant material can also be found in the numerous texts written by religious communities that are known by the name "Tantra," a word that means, literally, "a device or technique," and often refers to their spiritual practices. There are also several texts describing elaborate techniques of breathing and bodily posture in the tradition set forth by Patañjali's old text. There are treatises that describe in detail the nature of gains resulting from the practice of breathing exercises. Some texts speculate on the physiological underpinnings of the yogic techniques. It must also be noted that India's indigenous system of medicine, called Āyurveda, deals with various forms of psychopathology and suggests ways of treating them. Taken together, these sources represent a vast field that is worth exploring for phenomena, concepts, and techniques relevant to psychology.

The initial development of psychological thought in the West occurred in the context of philosophical speculation, and the same is true in the case of Indian thought. Modern Western psychology developed under the influence of the natural sciences, mainly biology and physiology, in the university setting. A second source of influence was medicine (as in the case of Freud who developed psychoanalysis in the therapeutic context). In India however, psychology developed primarily (although not exclusively) in the context of what is called adhyātma, a Sanskrit word meaning "pertaining to the ātman" or the self. The word ātman is alternatively translated as "soul." As in the West, the Indian quest for the nature of the soul has been associated with man's search for immortality and existence after death. The attempt to liberate the soul from the continuous cycle of birth, death, and rebirth has been the preoccupation of Indian religions, just as the Judeo-Christian religions have been interested in the salvation of the soul.

But here the similarity between the Western and Indian traditions ends. In the West, especially under the influence of the Roman Catholic Church during the medieval period, organized religion claimed authority over everyone's soul, and theologians monopolized the quest for the nature of the individual self. In India, however, the clergy could not claim such monopoly. The sphere of adhyātma, the domain of man's quest for the nature of his self and his effort to attain whatever heights he is capable of attaining, developed autonomously, free from the influence of priests, deities, and rituals. As an example, we may refer to the concept of a guru, which, despite its apparently religious character, has social and psychological significance in the sphere of adhyātma, and not in the domain conventionally associated with priesthood. Thus, a guru is not a priest, but a spiritual guide who facilitates the disciple's spiritual development. Any person who aspires to enlightenment and spiritual progress may seek guidance from the guru who seems most suitable to his idiosyncratic needs without obstacles arising from differences in social background between himself and the guru. Discrepancies in age, sex, wealth, status, and even caste do not pose a barrier between the aspirant and his guru, although such differences prove to be formidable barriers in almost all other types of social relationships. The guru is not an agent of an organized religion guaranteeing a place in heaven for the follower after his death, but a person, who, somewhat like a modern therapist, provides personal counseling.[1] I cannot elaborate on the East–West differences at this stage, but I wish to emphasize that the context of adhyātma has influenced the development of Indian psychology in a way that stands in sharp contrast to the continual conflict between science and religion in the development of psychological thought in the West. The nature of the influence on Western psychology of this long and bitter conflict is an important issue, so far as the comparison of Indian and Western psychologies is concerned. I shall deal with this issue in the latter half of this chapter.

As a consequence of the opposition between organized religion and science in the history of Europe, many students of Western psychology tend to avoid anything that seems associated with religion—whether it is the concept of a soul or spiritual progress, meditation, or Yoga. This being the case, it might be useful to point out that we are not concerned here with Yoga or Vedānta as religious doctrines, but as philosophical viewpoints involving a "theory of personality." Besides the association of Yoga with religion, there is another aspect of Yoga that has negative connotations for many psychologists today. This concerns Patañjali's reference to such phenomena as extrasensory perception, clairvoyance, and telepathy, considered taboo in modern psychology. Certainly, Patañjali indicates the powers that can be attained through the practice of Yoga, and it is true that many people are attracted to Yoga as a tool in their pursuit of power. Patañjali (3.37), however, has clearly stated that these powers are but obstacles in the way of the attainment of the desirable state of samādhi. This is an important point because (as I shall argue later at greater length) the de-emphasis on power, wealth, and control is a value of the Indian tradition which contrasts sharply with the dominant Western values. It is important to note this contrast in values because it has led to the growth of divergent psychological thought. Whether or not the claims to extrasensory powers of perception are valid is a separate issue, with which I shall not deal in the present work. The emphasis here, as suggested earlier, is on the system of psychology implicit in the Yoga and Vedānta traditions.

It has been fashionable in recent psychological writings to refer to Eastern psychologies as esoteric. The dictionary meaning of the word esoteric is "designed for or understood by the specially initiated alone," or "relating to knowledge that is restricted to a small group." In addition, the image of Yoga as a secret doctrine is associated with magic. Since many self-proclaimed yogis are found demonstrating their extraordinary powers and performing magical feats, Yoga appears mysterious and even dangerous. The English expression "mystical experience," often associated with descriptions of Yogic and other "religious" pursuits, refers to a psychological phenomenon, such as a highly pleasureable experience, that is considered beyond description. But the word "mystic" has other connotations, including "occult," "mysterious," "obscure," or "having magical properties." This is an unfortunate situation, and unnecessarily adds to suspicion and fear. It must be noted that, so far as psychological theories such as Patañjali's are concerned, nothing is secret or inaccessible: the original texts and their numerous commentaries and translations are available on book stands all across the globe. One is extremely unjustified in calling such publicly available theories esoteric, and the English expression "mystical experience," as we have seen, lumps together a broad range of phenomena which have been assigned distinct terms in Sanskrit, much as we use the word "snow" to refer collectively to the varieties of precipitation labeled distinctively by the Inuit languages. As we begin to explore the terrain charted by students of Yoga, we will begin to adopt the existing labels from Sanskrit (just as we use the German term "Gestalt" for want of an English equivalent), or perhaps coin new words. Once this is done, we need not be trapped by the incidental connotations of the word "mystic." A proper understanding of the goals of Yoga will enable us to assign to the Yogic "feats" their legitimate place, which is one of minimal importance.

Once, as I was lecturing to a certain class of North American students, one cried out in the middle of my introduction to the Indian psychology: "You are converting us from our Catholic background." This reaction is hardly surprising in an atmosphere of rivalry among religious groups that places volunteers at busy street corners in most neighborhoods with signs and pamphlets that promise salvation *only* if you accept their own particular creed. The Western world is influenced by religious creeds that seek converts and even proselytize. Those exposed to such creeds may find it hard to appreciate the fact that there are religions that do not seek converts. Although Yoga is associated with Hinduism and is theistic, it is a system of philosophy in its own right. It need not arouse suspicion as a religious creed in disguise any more than do the philosophies of Descartes, Kant, and Kierkegaard, all of whom believed in the existence of God. It is also necessary to note that when a yogi concentrates on the image of a deity or God, the implicit meaning and function of this variety of theism is radically different from that in the West. Geraldine Coster (1934/1972, pp. 82–83) has put it well:

"Here again we have a reversal of values between east and west. The western mystic sets high value on one-pointedness because it leads the soul to God; the eastern yogi sets high value on the conception of God because it leads to one-pointedness." One-pointedness here implies extreme concentration of attention, which is considered a necessary step in controlling psychological processes such as ideation and thinking so as to enable the individual to attain states considered superior to normal. The image of God is often used as an object upon which attention is concentrated and, as such, serves as a means to an end—self-realization.

There is a sphere of life in which psychology, religion, and philosophy overlap: call it the search for happiness, fulfilment, growth of personality, self-actualization, self-realization, understanding the meaning of life, or what you will. Certainly, most modern psychologists tend not to focus on this common sphere, or to consider the field of psychology a science independent of religion and morals. Some may even consider psychology and religion to be opposed in many respects. The antireligious stance of psychologists and their scientists is partly a product of the legitimate disillusionment of modern man regarding churchmen who have spread wars in the name of universal brotherhood. Notwithstanding the context of antagonism between the Church and science within which modern psychology was born, a continual interaction between psychology and the Judeo-Christian tradition has been maintained. Despite Freud's antireligious views, for instance, the father of psychoanalysis transformed several aspects of the Jewish mystical tradition into a secular, "scientific" format (see Bakan, 1958). The similarity between the cathartic effect of the Catholic confession and psychoanalytic free association is well known. Pastoral counseling overlaps with secular psychological counseling in many ways: both try to allay the anxiety, fear, and guilt of their clients, and both types of counselors have borrowed directly and indirectly from each other. A clear example of the mutual influence of psychology and religion in more recent times is the development and widespread use of T-groups, sensitivity training, and other such techniques in secular as well as religious settings in the West. It has been pointed out, for instance, that the technique of using "negative feedback" from peers to recognize the hidden aspects of one's social image in order to improve one's understanding of oneself is borrowed by psychologists from the ritualistic method of open mutual criticism of members of a congregation used by certain church groups. The technique of negative feedback has now become part of the standard package used by group leaders in psychological laboratories that train T-group leaders. Certain church organizations have been sponsors and users of T-group methods. It is not an accident that Carl Rogers, a renowned psychologist and a leader of the encounter group movement, happened to be a student of theology before he turned to psychology. Whether the fields of psychology and religion should encroach upon one another is a matter of opinion; that the two overlap is a matter of fact.

With reference to Indian psychological concepts that are couched in old, religio-philosophical contexts, some readers may ask: In what ways are such concepts relevant to modern, scientific, and secular interests? The answer is that they are relevant in several ways. First, the concept of self is as relevant and central to psychology today as it has always been. The Indian approach to this concept is different than the approaches of most modern schools of psychology. Being different, it avoids the danger of pursuing just one more version of the existing Western models. Moreover, the Indian view of the self promises to be a valuable complement to Western views. We shall examine the Indian and Western approaches comparatively in a separate chapter. Second, the Indian tradition has much to contribute to the study of states of consciousness, a topic to which many psychologists have returned with a revitalized interest in the past few years. Third, ideas concerning the philosophy of the mind directly influence the nature of psychological theory, and the Indian thought has much to offer in this area. Fourth, the Yogic methods of controlling the body and the mind involve voluntary control of functions normally considered to be under the influence of the autonomic nervous system, and such control has already become an object of study by physiological psychologists and medical men. Fifth, finding ways to improve the human condition is a perennial theme for psychologists and philosophers, ancient as well as modern. The traditional and contemporary interests converge on this common focus. There are other questions which some readers may ask. Is an attempt to compare and integrate Indian and Western systems of psychology particularly relevant now? Has it not already been done? If some work has already been done, is it inadequate? If it is adequate, why has it been neglected for so long? These are relevant questions and they can be reasonably answered.

The exposure of Western audiences to Indian thought is certainly not new. British officers and missionaries in India began to translate important philosophical and religious texts into English during the early days of British influence on the Indian continent. The Indian spiritual leader and missionary, Vivekananda, introduced Yogic and Vedāntic concepts to the United States in the 1890s. The theosophical movement involved Europeans and Americans interested in the study of the "occult" phenomena associated with yogic practices. It helped promote the dissipation and integration of ideas across the continents. In the year 1926, Radhakrishnan, an Indian philosopher, was invited to deliver the Upton Lectures at Oxford University (published as *The Hindu View of Life*), an indication of early recognition of Indian philosophy in Western academic circles. In fact, certain German, British, and American universities had much earlier started publication of standard translations of basic philosophical texts of India in comprehensive series. The Harvard Oriental Series, for instance, published James Woods's translation of Patañjali's aphorisms as early as 1914. It has certainly been a long time, however, since translations of the basic sources of Indian psychological thought have been available in English, French, and German.

It is important to note that in the West, acquaintance with Indian thought was initially limited to indologists and philologists, and later spread to the field of philosophy. James Woods, the translator of Patañjali, was a philologist, not a psychologist. Since the subject matter of the text is basically psychological in nature, someone trained in psychology and Sanskrit could have produced a better translation. It is also important to remember that in 1914 when Woods's translation was published at Harvard, psychology was a brand new discipline trying to establish its independent existence as a university department. The writing of William James, the father of American psychology, shows the transition of psychological thought from its philosophical roots to the modern scientific format. Thus, James in his long chapter on the self (*Principles*, 1890), reviews the most important contributions of Western philosophy, from Locke through Kant and J. S. Mill. Here he indicates no familiarity with Indian philosophy, although in his *Varieties of Religious Experience* (1902) he once makes reference to Vivekananda, the Indian missionary who had lectured at Harvard in 1896. In the same book there are also a few references to Ramakrishna, the great mystic, saint, and spiritual guide (guru) of Vivekananda. These references show James's awareness and appreciation of Indian thought.

A disciple of Vivekananda, Swami Akhilananda, stayed in the United States for a length of time on behalf of the Ramakrishna Vedānta Society and wrote two books attempting to integrate Indian and Western views on a few topics in psychology and mental health (Akhilananda, 1948, 1952). Without trying to review these works at length, it may be noted that the author was well versed in Indian thought but was handicapped by a lack of formal training in Western psychology. Also, whatever their merit, these works did not seem to reach a broad audience in psychology, and are quite outdated in view of developments in Western psychology. More recently, Gardner and Lois B. Murphy edited a volume called *Asian Psychology* (1968) in which they excerpted translations of selected passages from the Indian texts of the ancient *Ṛg Veda*, through the Upaniṣads to Patañjali. These selections offer a glimpse into the typical Indian way of thinking regarding psychological issues, but they do little in the way of concentration on specific topics of common interest, or of a systematic integration of Indian and Western ideas.

Like William James, Sigmund Freud also seems to have been aware of Yoga and of certain concepts of Indian origin, as stray references in his writings indicate. But some of the references suggest that he was neither very much interested nor, perhaps, much impressed by what he had heard (see, for example, Freud, 1930/1961, pp. 72–73). Jung, however, was very much interested in Eastern philosophy, had read several works in this field, and had even journeyed to India. To some readers in the West he may appear to be the only well-known psychologist to have attempted an integration of psychological concepts of Eastern and Western origin. Undoubtedly he may be credited with popularizing terms such as *maṇḍala* and arousing curiosity about Eastern concepts among his readers. Many of Jung's readers who have good acquaintance with Indian literature, however, question the quality of Jung's work. It is small wonder that he evaluates psychological concepts of Yoga from his own psychoanalytical point of view. Thus, in a paper on the *Tibetan Book of the Great Liberation,* he admits that consciousness is inconceivable without the ego. He says, "I do not doubt the existence of mental states transcending consciousness," but concludes that consciousness that transcends the ego must only be "unconscious" (Jung, 1939/1958, p. 484). One can understand the difficulties in trying to interpret higher states of consciousness without extending the psychoanalytical framework. However, when Jung goes on to suggest that "to the West . . . samadhi is nothing but a meaningless dream state" (p. 492), he shows that he has misunderstood and misinterpreted some very basic concepts of Yoga. The problem with Jung does not end with such misconceptions. Note, for instance, the following statement from this presumed integrator of Eastern and Western psychologies: "You cannot mix fire and water. The Eastern attitude stultifies the Western, and vice-versa" (p. 483). Now take another statement of his: "Critical philosophy, the mother of modern psychology, is foreign to the East as to medieval Europe" (p. 475). These very brief quotations should indicate Jung's typical bias.

Luckily, the Jungian type of bias is not commonly found in the published literature. More common, of course, is lack of interest in, and information about, the older systems. This is true in India as well as elsewhere. Part of the problem is language. The original sources of the Indian systems are in Sanskrit, a language which is as difficult and unknown to many modern Indians as are Greek and Latin to most Euro-Americans. Those, like Geraldine Coster (1934/1972), who rely on consultants to translate original works for them, may find the help unreliable.[2] But language need no longer be a major obstacle, as many more original works are now translated than were available in Coster's time, and some of the translations are better than the previous ones. Yet, translations do not always prove adequate. Although the study of Sanskrit appears to be declining, scholars well trained in Sanskrit texts are still not rare. In fact, dependable Sanskritists are now available not only in India but also in many North American universities.

There is another field of study related to Indian psychology which does not depend on the interpretation of old texts since it focuses on such phenomena as breathing exercises and their directly observable physiological effects. Interest in the study of physiological aspects of Yoga goes back to the early days of the British rule in India, when British doctors came across yogis who claimed to bury themselves alive in pits for long periods of time, voluntarily control their breathing, or perform similar feats that seemed humanly and medically impossible. Serious experimental testing of such claims and recording of physiological phenomena associated with Yogic states, however, did not begin until the early 1930s. One of the pioneers in this field was K. T. Behanan, an Indian student pursuing graduate studies in psychology at Yale University, who in 1931 obtained a fellowship to study Yoga in a modern institute of Yoga near Bombay. As part of his doctoral work he studied the physiological aspects of breathing exercises, such as the rate of oxygen consumption, and, on the experiential side, reported a condition of "extreme pleasantness" as a result of the exercises. His experimental observations and impressions about certain Yogic practices were later published in the form of a book entitled *Yoga: A Scientific Evaluation* (Behanan, 1937/1964).

Around 1935, Therese Brosse, a French cardiologist, visited India to study certain physiological aspects of Yoga. In a paper published in English in 1946, Brosse reported a yogi who, while under medical observation, buried himself for a period of ten hours. She conducted several studies using electrocardiographic and pneumographic recording of yogis and reported finding them to be "incontestable masters" of bodily functions such as blood circulation and rate of metabolism. She remarked that a yogi could voluntarily put his body "in a state of slowed-up life comparable to that of hibernating animals" (Brosse, 1946, p. 82). In the mid-1950s, Wenger, a physiological psychologist from the University of California at Los Angeles, conducted electroencephalographic studies of Yogic states at Kaivalyadhāma (the Yoga institute where Behanan and

Brosse had experimented) and at other places in India. One of his studies concerned voluntary control of the heart and pulse, as did Brosse's earlier study (Wenger, Bagchi and Anand, 1971). Another study dealt with the electrical activity of the brain during certain yogic exercises (Bagchi and Wenger, 1957/1971). A similar study by Anand, Chhina and Singh (1961) reports that when a yogi reached the ecstatic state of consciousness called samādhi, his brain produced alpha waves (electrical waves of a frequency ranging from about 8 to 12 cycles per second) persistently and with greater strength (increased amplitude). In Japan, Kasamatsu and Hirai (1972) reported similar findings (along with some other observations) with practitioners of Zen meditation.

The claim of the electrophysiological studies of Anand, Kasamatsu, and others that meditative states are associated with high alpha activity of the brain has attracted the attention of a great number of people. Anyone who has heard of the fabulous "high" the yogis are said to reach would be attracted to studies of the samādhi states. Since these studies found something "concrete"—curves inscribed by a machine—that could be associated with ecstatic states heretofore described in the most abstract and obtuse terms, they have appeared as a significant landmark in the understanding of complex psychological phenomena. Further, Joe Kamiya's experiments in Chicago and San Francisco demonstrated that subjects could easily be trained to voluntarily produce high alpha activity of the brain (Kamiya, 1972). In this technique, called biofeedback training, a subject hears a beep produced by electronic equipment as soon as a scanning mechanism identifies wave forms within the alpha range of frequency produced by the electrical activity of the subject's brain. Most subjects readily learn to get the instruments to react with a beep by increasing the alpha output of their brains, although most cannot say how they accomplish this task. Since the state of the subject when he produces high alpha waves is considered to be one of pleasant relaxation, biofeedback has attracted many psychologists interested in a technique by which to help subjects relax, reduce tension and acquire a state of well-being. Biofeedback has appealed to some psychologists as a breakthrough in methodology, opening new avenues in brain–behavior research. To many people biofeedback is a quick road to "instant samādhi," a short-cut to the fabled goal of Yoga. Notwithstanding the cheap popularization of biofeedback and the faddishness of its fans, it is true that electrophysiological studies of Yoga and Zen meditation have led to a new field of collaborative psychological research in the United States, India and Japan.

"Maharishi" Mahesh Yogi's Transcendental Meditation is a popular movement that has induced some psychophysiological research related to the "TM" brand of meditation techniques. A typical piece of research of this type is R. K. Wallace's doctoral study in physiology at the University of California at Los Angeles. Wallace studied various physiological effects of the practice of Transcendental Meditation over long and short periods of time. He found that TM produces a rapid decrease in oxygen consumption, decreases heart rate, cardiac output, and acidity of the blood, and increases the intensity of alpha waves produced by the brain. After comparing the physiological correlates of the meditative states of TM practitioners with normal characteristics of wakefulness, deep sleep, and dreaming, Wallace concluded that "transcendental meditation produces a fourth major state which is physiologically and biochemically unique" (Wallace, 1970, p. 36).

The Wallace study illustrates an expanding trend in the research started by Behanan and Brosse which conjoins Western techniques and Eastern concepts. While such convergence is welcome as a sign of East–West cooperation, decreasing prejudices, and expanding frontiers of psychological research, the findings of this research must be examined with care. It is dangerous to assume, for instance, that Wallace's study helps explain the "Fourth State" (turiyā avasthā) about which the yogis have spoken. First, there is no specific claim by Wallace that he is referring to anything like the samādhi experience, although the fourfold classification used closely resembles the traditional Indian view. Second, he says little about the nature of the experience of the meditators during the experiments, although a pleasant character is alluded to by the description of the TM technique as being "easy and enjoyable." Third, given the fact that many of Wallace's subjects had practiced meditation for very short periods, it is difficult to believe that they have attained the Fourth State of Consciousness described by Vedānta. (See Wallace, 1970, p. 45, for data on duration of practice among Wallace's subjects.) The convention suggests that the pathway to such "superior" states of consciousness is a difficult path on which aspirants make very slow progress. Fourth, and the most important reason for caution in evaluating the merit of the psychophysiological studies of Wallace and others, is their common explicit or implicit assumption that all states of consciousness, including the higher states described by Yoga, have a definite biochemical base. Such studies are based on the implicit assumption that there are two independent worlds of reality, mind and matter, so that the experiences of the mind have definite correspondence with states of the material body. The assumption that every experiential state can be reduced to an electrochemical state of the brain is an axiomatic principle or an untested (and perhaps untestable) assumption derived from an ontological theory in the Cartesian tradition. The Vedāntic concept of the Fourth State of Consciousness is not based upon such a Western theory of reality. To say the least, it is essential that the fundamental assumptions on which Western methods are based must be examined carefully before they are used in interpreting concepts based on different and perhaps contradictory assumptions about reality. A close examination of the electrophysiological approach to the studies of the Fourth State of Consciousness will be undertaken in Chapter 3.

For many people the convergence of East and West in psychology means the application of the techniques of modern science to the study of phenomena described by Yoga or Zen Buddhism. In 1948, Gordon W. Allport sounded a note of caution about such applications. In his brief introduction to Swami Akhilananda's book, *Hindu Psychology,* Allport says that he is convinced that American psychology would improve in richness and wisdom if it took into account the phenomena related to meditation. But he says he is not sure about the more "occult" manifestations of mental powers associated with Hindu psychology. "Whether the occult in Hindu psychology stems from its relative lack of acquaintance with what we in the West call 'scientific method' or whether this Western 'scientific method' is nothing but a narrow cult that blinds itself to uncongenial phenomena, I am not at this moment prepared to say. Perhaps concessions are needed to both sides" (Akhilananda, 1948, p.x).

Allport's words of caution are well taken. About three decades have passed since he expressed his doubts about the use of scientific method. We are now in a better position to understand the nature of this issue in light of the problems in cross-cultural understanding, which have been discussed from a variety of angles over the past several decades. The cultural limitations of psychological knowledge have been recognized. It has long been recognized, for instance, that Freud's views of the role of guilt in neurosis were partly a result of the "Victorian morals" of the patients he observed in his clinic. A large number of cross-cultural studies have been conducted wherein Western psychological concepts and techniques have been carried across the world; and while examining their observations and comparing them across cultures, many psychologists have become aware of the limitations on the cross-cultural applicability of psychological models (Berry, 1969; Paranjpe, 1975). Sociologists like Mannheim and others have pointed out that the pursuit of scientific knowledge is a social undertaking that is usually guided and sometimes constrained by the needs, goals, and ideologies of the scientists' communities. The historian of science, Thomas Kuhn (1970), has suggested that communities of scientists share sets of assumptions, values, model methods or exemplars, or frameworks of ideas (usually called paradigms) to which they are committed as a group. Such commitments are not universal and everlasting, but vary across groups and cultures, and are revisable from time to time. Further, Alan Buss (1975) has suggested that a new field of study he calls "the sociology of psychological knowledge" is now emerging. What this means is that there is a growing concern about the social context of psychological theories and the nature of its influence on what we know about psychological phenomena.

All the developments referred to in the previous paragraph are of relatively recent origin. The recent awareness of the sociocultural context of psychological inquiry and of the restrictive influence of that context has led many students of Western psychology to be receptive to perspectives from distant places. Ornstein (1972, p. 8) mentions the popularity in the United States of the "esoteric" disciplines of the East, such as Zen Buddhism, Tibetan Buddhism, Sufism, and Yoga, as one of the factors leading to an extension of the scope of psychology. He mentions the following aspects of the changing American culture as additional factors contributing to this extension: the emergence of a "counter cultural" community opposed to "science," which exhibits a distaste for rational thought and its products, such as machines, computers, and technology in general; a widespread interest in consciousness-altering or "psychedelic" drugs; and, at the same time, the development of research tools such as electroencephalography that have made it possible to study sleep, dreams, hypnosis, and other states of consciousness. Such states were formerly considered purely "private" phenomena, no aspect of which was accessible to recording and "scientific" study. Now that recordings of phenomena such as the rapid eye movements during dreams are possible, the scope of psychology has been extended to the study of dreams. In other words, a variety of events has induced an extension of conventional perspectives in Western psychology.

At the same time in India, too, the blinding influence of Western psychology in the universities, which had led Indian psychologists to turn their backs on their Indian heritage, is gradually receding. Several Indian psychologists are looking for psychological concepts rooted in their own native tradition. Indian books on Yoga, for instance, are no longer the monopoly of philosophers, philologists, or Hindu missionaries: psychologists trained in India are gradually turning their attention to this field which they had neglected for so long. (See, for example, Joshi, 1967; Kulkarni, 1972; Ramachandra Rao, 1962; and Safaya, 1976.) Then again, outside the field of psychology there is a renewed interest in mystical experience, a topic that is of central importance in Indian psychology (Bharati, 1976; Scharfstein, 1973/1974; and Staal, 1975). The study of mysticism has so far been largely influenced by students of religion, but some of them are now turning to psychology for help in understanding the nature of mystical experience. Frits Staal, a scholar of the Sanskrit language and Eastern religions has recently surveyed psychological and physiological studies of mysticism. Although he concludes that psychological studies are unsatisfactory and that they reveal the limitations of present-day psychology, he thinks that the future outlook for the psychological study of mysticism is not bleak, but "very promising." Staal stresses, however, that the prospects for such study will be bright if "psychology would be deepened and widened so as to be in a position to take account of these particular aspects of the mind" (Staal, 1975, p.118). Widening the scope of modern Western psychology to enable us to account for such phenomena as mystical experience can be meaningfully done by incorporating into its mainstream perspectives from Indian psychology which have been well developed.

From the foregoing paragraphs it will be clear that the time is now right for extending the scope of psychology by integrating ideas from the Indian and Western traditions. Before taking a step in that direction, it would be useful to try to define the common ground between the two traditions. One way of exploring common ground would be to compare and contrast major cultural themes that have molded psychological thought in India and the West. We shall turn to such cultural themes in the next chapter. Before starting with that issue, however, it would be useful to examine certain specific aspects of the development of psychology as a *science*, more particularly as a natural science, since such development is peculiar to Western psychology. The remainder of this chapter is devoted to such an examination.

Some Implications of the Development of Western Psychology as a "Science"

There is a popular belief that science is a product of Western civilization alone. What we see by way of science and technology in Asia today is considered to be only an imported product, not of indigenous origin. This view is based partly on an implicit definition of science as natural science, and partly on ignorance of the significant Indian contributions to mathematics, linguistics, medicine, psychology, and the other sciences. It is of course true that many developments in the natural sciences, such as Newtonian physics, which led successively and successfully to technology and industrial revolution, are exclusively the gifts of European countries to the rest of the world. There is another popular belief that the West is materialistic and that the East is spiritual. This, however, is mostly a myth: materialistic philosophy is not unknown to the East, and Asians have never stopped pursuing material goals; nor has the West been spiritually naïve. It is certainly important to avoid such stereotypical generalizations of "the East" and "the West."

It may seem rather incongruous that the author of the previous lines uses the expression "Western psychologies." It is recognized that broad generalizations about vast segments of the world population into hemispheric blocks can be dangerous. Certainly there is considerable diversity within each country, let alone across entire continents. One does not need much knowledge of psychology to recognize that, at least in some respects, two single persons are quite different from one another. What is the justification, then, for putting together all the psychologists and psychologies in the whole of the West and contrasting them with those of a large continent such as India? The answer to this question is that, despite diversities within the continents of the Western Hemisphere and the subcontinent of India, it makes sense to study Western philosophy as a field distinct from Indian philosophy. Although there has been some communication across continents over the past centuries resulting in some mutual influence, the Western philosophies have retained certain characteristics that differ from those of the Indian philosophies. For centuries, generations of Indian thinkers have been receiving sets of ideas mainly from past thinkers of their own continent and, except for the past century or so, there has been little influence from the West. Despite the fact that Buddhist thinkers were opposed to Hindu thinkers, and despite the incessant quarrels between the dualists and the non-dualists, followers of each school of thought were generally well exposed to the rival viewpoints. Exposure to the traditional debates within the Indian tradition has led to the sharing among Indian intellectuals of certain common themes that are distinct from those shared in the West. In the history of philosophy in Europe and America too, we can find certain common themes and threads of continuity through periods of time stretching over centuries. As each generation benefits from the legacy of the past and tries to correct earlier errors, issues such as the mind–body problem or freedom versus determinism cannot be understood without taking into account a series of arguments and counterarguments that span several generations of thinkers. A comparison of the Indian tradition with that of the West thus requires the identification of common issues within the two traditions without disregard for the diversity of opinion within each tradition. It also requires that we avoid stereotypical generalizations without losing the unifying themes within each tradition.

One distinctive feature of the Western tradition is the dual legacy of ancient Greece and the long and uninterrupted growth of the Judeo-

Christian faith. Among the Greek philosophers the influence of Plato alone is so great that the Anglo-American philosopher, Whitehead, once remarked that "Twenty-five hundred years of Western philosophy is but a series of footnotes to Plato."[3] The two traditions possess some very distinct characteristics. The essence of the Hellenic spirit is primarily a spirit of reason. As in the life and work of Plato, the rational, analytic approach sets out in search of the *essence* of all objects. The emphases are on abstraction and ideas. The dominance of the analytic approach in the Greek mode of thought is reflected in Aristotle's invention of logic, and in the elevation in Greek thought of mathematics to an almost sacred status. The Greek thinkers emphasized the general over the particular; the problems of man *qua man* seemed more important to them than the problems of particular persons in their particular predicaments. Here the abstract notion of essence is placed over existence; the rational ability of man is separated from his intuitions and feelings.

By contrast, the Hebraic spirit places emphasis on the concrete man in his wholeness. Passionate involvement of man with his mortal existence is important. The man who loves his family, offspring, and his particular community is committed to the protection and survival of his tribe. He cannot detach himself from his surroundings and find solace in abstract principles, forms, and ideas. Involvement in practical human affairs requires action, and the concern about right and moral action overrides logical analysis and abstraction. The ideal man of Hebraism is the man of faith, not the man of reason cherished by Plato and Aristotle. Western civilization has preserved both the Hellenic and Hebraic spirits. At times the two streams ran parallel and the best in each buttressed the other. The vitality of these two strands of Western civilization seemed to weaken after the 5th Century A.D. during the several centuries of the Dark Ages. Toward the end of the Middle Ages, St. Thomas Aquinas attempted to combine the best in both traditions by synthesizing Aristotelian philosophy with Christian thought. However, despite such attempts to benefit from the strengths of both streams, the differences between the rational and "irrational" elements have proven to be too great to reconcile. In fact, the history of Western thought is fraught with numerous controversies, sometimes leading to open conflict, between irreconcilable positions following from the pagan Greek heritage on the one side and the religious Hebraic heritage on the other.

A serious conflict between the rational view of the world and the traditional view guided by faith in Biblical precepts erupted in 17th-century Europe. It would be useful to briefly outline the history of this conflict, since it led to the Cartesian formulation of the "mind–body problem" and eventually helped shape the schools of contemporary

Western psychology. Also, since the newly emerging science had to establish itself in the teeth of opposition by the Catholic Church, an antireligious stance became ingrained in the world view of science in general, and of psychology in particular. To enable us to appreciate the significance of the historical background of Western psychology in its length and breadth, let us note certain events that followed Copernicus' revolutionary formulation of a heliocentric view of the universe.

Galileo Galilei (1564–1642) openly upheld the Copernican theory that the earth moved around the sun and not vice-versa. Since the Copernican view contradicted the Ptolemaic geocentric view of the universe, Galileo was made to appear before the court of the Inquisition by the Church of Rome. Under threat of torture in the prisons of the Inquisition, Galileo abjured his views publicly, although he was convinced about the validity of Copernicus' logical conclusions. René Descartes (1596–1650), a junior contemporary of Galileo, was attracted to the newly developing sciences of astronomy, mathematics, and physiology. He originated the Cartesian coordinates, founded analytical geometry, and wrote a book called *L'Homme* (1664/1967), which is considered the first textbook of physiology. Psychology owes him much, since Descartes is not only the first one to arrive at the concept of reflex action, but is also rightly recognized as one of the founders of physiological psychology. Although himself a devout Catholic, Descartes openly wrote that the question of God and the soul should be matters of philosophical speculation rather than theological opinion. He held certain other views that were clearly antitheological. He held, for instance, that the Earth rotates and that the universe is infinite. Becoming anxious about the reaction of the clergy, Descartes, when he heard of the Inquisition of Galileo, fled to Holland, hoping for protection under a government that had proclaimed a policy of religious toleration. One of the important names in the history of psychology was thus saved from the hands of fanatic churchmen.

The development of anatomy was stifled because the Church was opposed to dissection. The Church believed that the human body contained an indestructible bone with which resurrection begins. (Russell, 1935a, p. 102). Vesalius (1514–1564) who pioneered anatomy through his dissections of dead bodies got away with his sacrilegious act because he was a favorite personal physician of Emperor Charles V. Upon questioning, it was revealed that he had found no such special bone. But after the death of his mentor, the churchmen persecuted him. Once, as he was examining a dead body with the consent of the relatives, his enemies claimed that the heart under his knife showed some signs of life. He was then accused of murder and called before the judges of the

Inquisition. Vesalius was saved only because he died of natural causes before the inquiry began. The development of physiology and thus the growth of knowledge was hampered by similar opposition from the clergy.

Disease was usually taken as punishment for previous sin. Even after the invention of chloroform as an anaesthetic, its use to relieve a woman's suffering during childbirth was opposed. As a justification the clergy quoted the Bible: "In sorrow shalt thou bring forth children" (Gen. 3:16)[4]. One of the chief obstacles in the development of methods of treatment for mental disorders was the belief that insanity was the result of diabolical possession. The stories of cruelty in the name of exorcism are too well-known to mention.

The latest and most important round of conflict between science and religion came after the end of the Middle Ages. Darwin's theory of evolution was as great a threat to theology as Copernicus' theory had been. The ideas in Darwin's *Origin of Species* (1859/1966) directly contradicted the Biblical account of creation. During the year following publication of Darwin's book, Bishop Wilberforce proclaimed that the principle of natural selection was absolutely incompatible with the word of God. Luckily for Darwin, the great power of the institution of the Inquisition had considerably eroded by this time. Although there was considerable uproar against Darwin (even Carlyle called him an "apostle of dirt-worship") it was the ancient doctrine that suffered more than the theory of evolution. Nevertheless, the old guard tried hard to prevent the new ideas from spreading. As late as the second decade of this century, the state of Tennessee in the United States had laws against the teaching of Darwin's theory. In a notorious case in 1925, John T. Scopes, a public school teacher was prosecuted in Dayton, Tennessee, for teaching the theory of evolution.

Modern psychology developed against a backdrop of such bitter conflict. It is small wonder that a strong antireligious feeling was expressed in the early writings of modern psychology. Max Meyer wrote a textbook of psychology popular in the United States during the 1920s. In it, Meyer said: "Thruout [sic] history we find religion being spread by fire and sword, by torture and death . . . Innumerable human lives were sacrificed in order that souls be saved" (Meyer, 1922, p. 410). There is nothing wrong with Meyer's historiography. But why would a psychologist indulge in material such as this, outside his field? The reason for such an excursion is not difficult to understand if we note the intellectual climate of his time and the place where he published his book, namely the southern state of Missouri in 1922. We need only remember that the abovementioned Scopes was prosecuted in the southern state of Tennessee only three years later. What is of particular note in this context is the manner in which the sociohistorical background molded Meyer's view of psychology. Meyer expresses his views in the paragraph that immediately follows the above quotation:

> Now assume, for comparison, the attitude of the modern psychologist. He will make no attempt at proving to you that you have no soul. Your soul and the question of its existence are your own business. Because your soul is your own business, can never be any other's experience or business, and must therefore be forever mysterious, forever closed to the inductive methods of science, closed to the infinitely repeatable sensory-motor test of scientific procedure, therefore the psychologist minds his own business and leaves your soul alone. Your religion is to him a set of peculiar reactions of your body. . . . The psychologist is much interested in these actions of your body. (Meyer, 1922, pp. 410–411)

Meyer's attitude seems to be one of calling a truce between psychology and religion. Centuries earlier Descartes, himself torn between Catholicism and science and threatened with the possibility of inquisition, created his two-world theory by assigning the body to the world of matter and the psyche or soul to the nonmaterial world. Such division could, hopefully, establish two separate domains so that an anatomist would be free to dissect the material body, while the soul was assigned to the clergy. The scientist and the priest could thus each work in his own way without treading on the other's feet. The agreement appears simple, but the two-world theory born under such circumstances has proven to be a knotty problem for subsequent generations of philosophers. Ever since Descartes, psychologists have been forced to take a stand on the body–mind issue. Under the pressure of peculiar historical circumstances psychologists like Meyer, who asked to be free to deal with the body, seemed to sign away their right to deal with whatever there is to human beings other than their bodies. Meyer's declaration that every other person's experience must remain mysterious and be forever closed to methods of science is not borne out by a fresh new discovery in the 1920s. The problem of each person having privileged access to his own feelings and thoughts is not a new one, but it did acquire a new dimension in the sociohistorical context of Meyer's time. It became an important tenent of methodological behaviorism and contributed to the genesis of what is called the "black box model" of psychology which avoids any reference to experiences, feelings, intentions and other "mental" phenomena. This is not to suggest, of course, that the relationship with religion was the sole factor leading to the emphasis on the inaccessibility of other minds. Psychology in the United States during Meyer's time was also reacting to the failure of Titchener's method of introspective analysis of ideational phenomena. The issue is complex. We shall examine the implications of the failure of Titchener's structuralism and the rise of behaviorism in the Chapter 3.

The point is not simply that ignoring the soul, psyche, or mind creates a "mystery complex,"[5] from which modern psychology is said to suffer. "Self" is another common synonym of the word *soul*, and counting the soul out of the jurisdiction of psychology has resulted in banishing the self as well. Note that the title of Max Meyer's text is *Psychology of the Other-one.* For those who may think that I am giving undue importance to an obscure historical text, I must only point out that the exclusion of the topic of self is not a characteristic of a single old textbook such as Meyer's, but a common feature of a good number of modern psychology textbooks. The neglect of the concept of self was recognized as a major deficiency in American psychology by D. O. Hebb (1960) who, in his presidential address to the American Psychological Association meeting in 1960, called for an "American revolution" to correct it. It must be recognized that such neglect is not common to all types of modern psychological theories; it is characteristic of behaviorism, the most dominant school of Anglo-American psychology. There are modern theorists such as Rogers, Allport, Maslow and others who did consider self an important concept. But none of them was a behaviorist. Carl Rogers had theological training, and Allport wrote an entire book on the psychology of religion. The point is that behaviorists, who consider psychology a natural science and derive their philosophical basis from positivism (which, in turn, belongs to the Hellenic tradition), have no interest in the study of the self. It would also make sense, again, that the major self theorist, Carl Rogers, derives his philosophical base from phenomenology a discipline closely related to existential philosophy and, as noted by William Barrett (1958), belonging to the Hebraic tradition.

Once psychology considers the self to be outside its scope, it becomes a psychology of "the other one"— as it did for Max Meyer. The implications of this stance are far-reaching. First, the psychologist, as a concrete, single individual with his own self-definition, motives, goals, feelings, intentions and other aspects of his own self, disappears from the scene. The psychologist is no longer a particular person but a scientist *qua scientist*, an abstract entity that deals with generalizations, not with particular instances. Second, the psychologist assumes that, as long as he plays the impersonal role of the scientist, his expectations about the outcome of his study, as well as his values and goals, are not going to affect his pursuit of truth. This, we now know, is a myth, thanks to the work of Orne (1962) and Rosenthal (1966) who have pointed out that "experimenter bias" is a pervasive phenomenon. Third, the "others," who are the objects of his study, are conceived of as entities devoid of self-image, motives, or feelings. They are black boxes that can be observed as dispassionately as rocks, trees, or animals. The psychologist assumes that he can predict and control behavior, just as a physicist can predict the course of a trajectory and control it. While trying to control and modify his subjects' behavior, he often seems to forget that, unlike the physical objects studied by the natural scientist, his subjects are far from passive. Here again we must recognize our indebtedness to recent research on the social psychology of experiment which has shown that, in a situation where the psychologist is observing other persons, neither the experimenter nor the subject is a passive participant. Their active interaction is shown to systematically affect the outcome of the experiment. The patients, students, criminals, or others whose behavior is observed are not only aware of being observed, but are also capable of uniting against the observing "authorities" to establish their own systems of counter-control. The physicist may be accidentally killed by the atom or other source of energy which he is trying to control, but he need not be afraid of an organized uprising among the objects of his study. Also, no natural scientist needs to be afraid of being accused of ulterior motives by the objects of his study. The psychologist is obviously open to such accusations.

The impersonal role of the psychologist as scientist is deeply rooted in a rationalist tradition that advocates the pursuit of knowledge for its own sake and the strict separation of the field of science from that of religion. For long periods in the history of Western civilization, the sphere of morals was within the authority of the Church. Throughout the Middle Ages the task of moral philosophy was to systematize the various commandments of scripture as interpreted by the Church fathers. After the Middle Ages, as science began to establish its own existence apart from religion, attempts were made to derive moral sanctions from a source independent of the Church. Locke (1632–1704), for instance, tried to put morality on a rational basis. Good and evil, he said, are nothing but pleasure and pain. A rational man should be able to sort good from bad as simply as he distinguishes pleasure from pain. David Hume (1711–1776), however, argued that morality cannot be grounded in reason. In his view, reason judges matters of fact or points out relations among what is observed; it cannot tell us what men ought to do. He separated the domain of facts sharply from that of values. Hume's statement on the distinction between "is" and "ought" has given rise to a long controversy in Western philosophy. Although we need not concern ourselves with the arguments for or against Hume's thesis, it is necessary to note that as the battle between science and religion continues, the scientists have assigned themselves to the Humean domain of facts, leaving the theologians and politicians to deal with morals and values.

Psychologists, in particular, have been overly concerned with the separating facts from values. The psychologist is supposed to keep his value judgments outside the laboratory and assume a value-neutral role as he slips into his sterilized lab coat. We insist that the student refer to himself anonymously as *E* (for experimenter) and write his journal report in the third person. He must report exactly what transpired between the *E* and the *S* (subject), meticulously avoiding any reference to opinions or values. While we strive to maintain the value-neutral format, the content of psychological research reflects the fact that moral behavior is a neglected field of study. Kohlberg-type studies regarding moral behavior are still relatively rare and have become popular only very recently. Even in such studies, the emphasis is primarily on moral *reasoning*, not on moral action. Moreover, the thrust of Kohlberg's (1971) work lies in trying to derive the "ought" from "is," that is, in showing how the forms of reasoning, which, "by nature" appear later in the course of development, are superior to the primitive forms of reasoning that appear in early years of life. This is a good illustration of the psychologist's impulse to restrict himself to the sphere of facts even as he studies moral reasoning.

Notwithstanding the negative aspects of this neglect of the role of values in psychology, the separation of science from values does make sense. It makes sense in the same way it is desirable to maintain the independence of the judiciary from the executive branch of government. As long as the Church (or party bosses in a totalitarian society) decide what the scientists ought to do, what kind of research he will do, or what conclusions he must draw from his investigations, there is no hope for an impartial search for truth. But if the scientist, while seeking to maintain his freedom from control from outside forces, decides not to be concerned with moral issues, a number of problems arise. First, knowledge is power, and usually there are a number of possible applications of knowledge of the way things work. Technology, the systematic application of scientific knowledge, is a double-edged weapon. Whether it is a simple device such as the wheel, or the complex technology of inducing nuclear fission, what one accomplishes depends on the intentions of the user. The wheels that can carry a seriously ill patient to the hospital can also be used to carry guns, and nuclear power that can be used to generate electricity for peaceful purposes can also be used for the destruction of mankind. The scientist can hardly remain neutral concerning use of the results of his research. The scientists involved in research in physics that led to the atom bomb were indeed concerned about its use. Likewise, the behavior therapist can use his technology to stop a child from bedwetting, but could also use his techniques for the brainwashing of his enemies if he so desired. So he cannot afford to remain neutral about how his techniques are used. Second, modern science is not a hermit's quest for his own salvation, which he can carry out on his own. Science is largely a state-subsidized enterprise. Funds go where the granting agencies want them to, for purposes defined by the policies of the politicians in power. The more a scientist decides to be value-neutral, the more apathetic he becomes about where his research is going to lead. The scientist committed to a value-free science is more easily used by a government than one who faces up to the issue and asks himself what science is ultimately for.

It is necessary to note here that, even within the scientific enterprise itself, it is important to keep values from interfering with the search for truth. Commitment to values or goals sometimes leads one to interpret one's observations in a manner that fits one's values. Thus, a white-supremacist is likely to interpret the data of IQ tests to mean that black people are intellectually inferior, while the equalitarian is likely to find fault with the tools, refusing to admit even the possibility of real racial differences. The recent controversy in the United States over genetics and IQ following the publication of Jensen's paper on racial differences in IQ scores, has shown us how deeply psychologists are committed to either side of the issue of racial equality. The idealization of democracy and the often unwarranted vilification of "authoritarian" personality and leadership is another instance; many more can be easily pointed out (see Brown, 1965). No one can deny the importance of avoiding bias and the distorting effect of values on the research process.

The influence of values on science is not restricted to the possible distortion of truth in the interpretation of research data; it begins even before research is started. What the scientist chooses to study depends on what he considers important. Thus, his values are brought into play the moment he chooses his topic. What the scientist avoids as unimportant equally reflects his values. Consider, for instance, the relative neglect of religious or mystical experience in Western psychology. William James (1902/1958), Carl Jung (1958) and Gordon Allport (1950) are perhaps the only well-known psychologists who wrote book-length works on the psychology of religion or religious experience. Given the conflict between science and religion, it is small wonder that psychologists who derived inspiration from the successful natural sciences considered religious experience an unimportant phenomenon. It may be pointed out in this connection that sociology and anthropology, which are also young sciences, have given much more attention to the study of religion than has psychology. This, too, makes sense, for, unlike psychology, sociology and anthropology developed as social sciences and have felt little affinity with the natural sciences. Here one may ask: "How do we explain the newly emerging interest in the study of mysticism among psychologists who have neglected it for so long? In response one may suggest that such an emergence of interest reflects changing values in the community of psychologists. After all, the period of developing interest in mysticism in the United States has not been a period of idealization of sciences and technology, but rather of questioning the uses of technology—for mass destruction in Vietnam and rampant pollution in prosperous industrial centers. Mysticism, which was believed to be inimical to the spirit of science, is no longer completely taboo.

The negative value attached to mysticism in Western psychology is not restricted to the association of mysticism with religion, the "enemy" of science. Devaluation of mysticism goes back to the age-old rivalry between rationalism and irrationalism. For ages, logic has been considered one way of searching for knowledge, intuition and mysticism another. The two are not considered complementary but opposed to each other. Partisans of one approach have denounced those using the other approach. Bertrand Russell (1921) has given a historical account of the rivalry between the two in his essay called "Mysticism and Logic." He notes that in the early Greek period, Plato represents the rationalist spirit and Heraclitus that of mystical thinking. After the Middle Ages, Hume, in Russell's opinion, stands for the scientific impulse, while Blake is given as an example of one who had profound mystical insights along with hostility to science. The contemplative, mystical approach emphasizes the direct experience of reality without mediation of the logical, analytic process. The scientific approach is said to start with elements of sensory data and to develop propositions regarding the nature of reality by attempting to systematically arrange the elements into patterns. While the analytic process of science approaches various aspects of reality piece by piece, the mystic attempts to comprehend the reality as an undivided whole.

In the essay mentioned above, Russell suggested that great philosophers have felt the need for both science and mysticism, as "the attempt to harmonize the two was what made their life, and what always must, for all its arduous uncertainty, make philosophy, to some minds, a greater thing than either science or religion" (Russell, 1921, p.1). Despite such lofty idealization of the need for the convergence and integration of scientific and mystical ways of thinking, Russell, in a later essay called

"Philosophy in the Twentieth Century," takes a partisan position. Instead of trying to paraphrase his ideas in my words, I will quote a rather long paragraph from Russell.

> Traditional mysticism has been contemplative, convinced of the unreality of time, and essentially a lazy man's philosophy. The psychological prelude to the mystic illumination is the "dark night of the soul," which arises when a man is hopelessly balked in his practical activities, or for some reason suddenly loses interest in them. Activity being thus ruled out, he takes to contemplation. It is a law of our being that, whenever it is in any way possible, we adopt such beliefs as will preserve our self-respect. Psycho-analytic literature is full of grotesque examples of this law. Accordingly the man who has been driven to contemplation presently discovers that contemplation is the true end of life, and that the real world is hidden from those who are immersed in mundane activities. From this basis the remaining doctrines of traditional mysticism can be deduced. Lao-Tze, perhaps the first of the great mystics, wrote his book (so tradition avers) at a custom-house while he was waiting to have his baggage examined; and, as might be expected, it is full of the doctrine that action is futile . . . The mystic is usually a temperamentally active man forced into inaction; the vitalist is a temperamentally inactive man with a romantic admiration for action . . . Their temperamental basis is boredom and skepticism, leading to love of excitement and longing for an irrational faith–a faith which they found ultimately in the belief that it was their duty to make other people kill each other. (Russell, 1935b, pp. 46–47).

The above passage came in the course of a criticism of the intuitionist philosopher, Bergson, who was his senior contemporary. In Russell's opinion, Bergson's philosophy was "merely traditional mysticism expressed in slightly novel language." I have no quarrel with his interpretation of Bergson. But while commenting on the intuitionist's claims about the pure memory of moments of intuition, Russell adds: "To recover the pure memory of intuition is a matter of self-discipline. We are not told how to do it, but one suspects something not unlike the practices of Yogis . . . If one might venture to apply to Bergson's philosophy so vulgar a thing as logic . . ." (p. 47). The slanted references to Lao-Tze and the yogi are transparent enough to reveal underlying stereotypes and prejudices. Russell's reasoning is something like this: To contemplate is to be inactive, which means to be lazy. Bergson, Lao-Tze, as well as the yogi, all emphasize intuition and contemplation, therefore they must all be lazy. To contemplate means to avoid being analytical and logical, and therefore every mystic must be irrational. Since many mystics belonged to one religion or another, and since many people in the past have killed others in the name of religion, everyone associated with religion and mysticism must be inciting his followers to kill his "enemies."

A mystic who goes in search of the experience of the highest truth or self-realization can hardly afford to be lazy. In fact, those that are serious in attaining self-realization cannot afford to be impersonal about their undertaking, as can a scientist. They have to lay their very lives on the line. Granted, some mystics take to hermitages and pursue an inactive life, but not all mystics do so. Śaṅkara, one of the greatest mystics of India, was an exceptionally active man. Although he had renounced a life of family and children, wealth and power, he roamed over the entire subcontinent, debating with learned people of his time, and wrote many volumes before dying at the early age of 39. Although a mystic, he was not averse to logical analysis. In fact, he would be considered one of the greatest of analytical minds of all time. What Śaṅkara and many other mystics have said is that there are limitations to analytical reasoning when it comes to the knowledge of the self. To speak of the comprehension of truth which is *beyond* the ability to reason is not to be irrational or illogical. Again, it is important to distinguish between a mystic and a priest. Certainly there have been intolerent clergy in all religions and many of them are culpable for inciting wars. But most mystics have been "peaceniks" and a genuine mystic is usually a man of saintly compassion.

Russell's name is well established in the history of Western philosophy. Therefore, I do not expect to be accused of trying to create a straw man so as to fell him easily. I do not claim to be a logician, but my understanding of social psychology tells me that Russell's writing, quoted above, displays partisan zeal and stereotypical thinking. Mysticism and logic are conceived of as opposite categories, black and white. One is idealized, while the other is vilified to the same degree. Such stereotyping, I suspect, is widespread, and belongs to the same category as Jung's statements about the East and the West being hard to mix, like fire and water. Many scientists, psychologists among them in particular, insist that scientific considerations are amoral, equally unconcerned about the moral and the immoral. But they seem unable to consider a non-rational sphere of life, one which is beyond reason. The dichotomous distinctions between rational and irrational, logic and mysticism, are often drawn too far. Russell is not an isolated instance. He seems to represent a widespread trend of thought comparable to the history of conflict between science and religion in the Western hemisphere. The wounds are too deep to heal quickly. The influence of this historical clash on Western psychological thought is broad and deep.

It would be useful to contrast the development of psychological thought in India, so that we may appreciate the nature and extent of the effects of social history on the direction of its development. As mentioned before, Indian psychology developed in the context of adhyātma, which is different and independent from both religion and science. Throughout the history of India there has been no conflict between religion and science. It is true, of course, that natural sciences did not develop in India at the rate and in the form they did in Europe from the 16th century. The findings of modern natural science were introduced to India by the British, starting around the late 19th century. When these scientific concepts reached the Indian intelligentsia, they met no opposition from a religious viewpoint. First of all, the scientific theories did not shatter any of established myths of the culture, as the Copernican and Darwinian theories did in Europe. Second, the nature of Hinduism differs from the monotheistic religions of the West: its relevant aspects may be noted here insofar as they relate to the science–religion relationship.

Hinduism is a name given to a conglomeration of diverse sets of religious beliefs and practices that originated and survived on the Indian subcontinent. Unlike Christianity, Islam, or Buddhism, there was no single person who was responsible for the founding of a religion called Hinduism. In fact, the name *Hindu* comes from the river Indus: those who came from abroad referred to the religious practices of the Indus valley as the religion of the Hindus. This label has come to stick since those to whom it was applied did not reject it. Despite great diversity among them, there are certain common features of the belief systems of most of the Hindu sects. These common features involve cultural themes, some of which will be discussed in the next chapter. One need not believe in God, worship any deity, or accept any particular authority to call oneself a Hindu. With respect to belief systems, Hinduism follows a complete *laissez-faire* philosophy. Since acceptance of any particular creed is not the criterion for being a Hindu, adopting any set of beliefs, scientific or otherwise, leads neither to a special bonus, nor to a threat of expulsion. Since there is no organized Church based on a particular creed, there has never been a powerful institution such as the Inquisition to discipline the "heretics."

The above account of Hinduism may give the impression that the Hindus have no social regulatory mechanism— and I do not wish to convey such an impression. The *Manu Smrti* is a book that codifies the ethical conventions of Hinduism; it has been influential in providing guidelines for conduct in the areas of marriage, caste, various rituals relating to religious rites, and so on. The de facto regulators of social conventions, however, were not the priests but caste councils. The role of the priest has mainly been to help perform rituals in worship, marriage, funeral, and other occasions. The caste system was rigid, and the caste councils quite powerful for centuries. For a variety of reasons (which we need not examine here), the influence of caste has turned to secular and political activities over the past few decades. I do not wish to convey the false impression that the Hindus have been the most tolerant of people on earth. They have exhibited more than their share of dogmatism and intolerance. Intolerance seems to have been strongest in the sphere of rituals in general, and those associated with the caste system in particular. Untouchability and other practices placed those on the lower rungs of the hierarchy in humiliating conditions. Such practices were founded on the basic principle of karma, a belief that implies, "as you sow, so you reap." The plight of the untouchable was rationalized with the argument that *he* was responsible for the situation as dues for his own bad deeds (karma) in the previous incarnation of the soul. Whatever the other implications of the principle (some of which will be examined in the next chapter), generations of Hindus stuck to such an interpretation of the principle at the cost of human dignity for those who were born in the "lower" castes.

Notwithstanding such negative aspects of the Hindu dogma, it remains that the field of adhyātma was open to everyone, irrespective of caste status, although it was mainly the path of devotion (bhakti) rather than that of jñāna, or knowledge, that was open to them. Despite great socioeconomic handicaps and general cultural deprivation, some members of the lower castes were able to go a long way toward self-realization. Some of them were recognized as saints and could become spiritual guides (gurus) for members of the higher castes. Since holding particular beliefs was no prerequisite for spiritual progress, even non-Hindus such as the well known Saint Kabir could attain great spiritual heights. The Hindus have traditionally revered such non-Hindu saints as they have Hindu saints.

As psychological concepts and techniques developed mainly in the sphere of adhyātma, religious and social barriers such as sectarian forms of worship, caste, or even religion did not adversely affect the development of psychology in India. There were all sorts of rivalries among the worshippers of gods such as Śiva and Viṣṇu, among philosophical systems such as the dualist and non-dualist, and among major religious sects such as Jainism, Buddhism and others. Rivals fought bitterly on such trivial issues as whether the sacred mark on the forehead should have horizontal or vertical stripes (the views of the worshippers of Śiva and Viṣṇu respectively). Nonetheless, techniques of breathing and other aspects of Yoga with psychological significance were developed and used by worshippers of Śiva as well as Viṣṇu, by non-dualists, Jains, Buddists, and Hindus of all persuasions. The cultish nature of their religions or philosophies did not seem to prevent them from borrowing from and contributing to a common source of knowledge and the "know-how" of all brands of Yoga.

Whatever the similarities and differences between other aspects of the Indian and Western traditions, the absence and presence, respectively, of the science–religion type of conflict is a major contrast between them. As such, it should be easy to appreciate that the dichotomy between science and religion and between logic and mysticism, or the issue of value-free science, have not influenced Indian psychological thought as they did in the West.

The foregoing discussion leads to the point that sociocultural and historical background is an important determiner molding psychological thought and that sociology of knowledge is a discipline that tells us how and how far knowledge of all types is determined by the society in which it develops. In the remainder of this chapter we shall discuss certain ideas from the sociology of knowledge insofar as they are relevant to psychological theories.

The Nature of Science and the Sociology of Knowledge

The development of science in 17th-century Europe radically transformed the world view of many Western thinkers. Science replaced religion as a central and dominant force in the lives of many people, particularly the intelligentsia. The promise of heaven became unnecessary as a balm to soothe the miseries of life, for the industrial application of scientific knowledge promised wealth and glory on earth. The 18th-century French mathematician, Condorcet (1743–1794), for instance, wrote a book called *Sketch for a Historical Picture of the Progress of the Human Mind,* in which he depicted a secular, this-worldly heaven to be attained with the help of new instruments, machines, and looms. As for enlightenment, not only theology but even philosophy seemed useless, for the methods of science began to be considered the only reliable source of attaining knowledge. In the early 19th century, the French philosopher, August Comte (1798–1858), proposed his famous law of the three stages of the development of knowledge. This law stated that "each branch of our knowledge passes in succession through three different theoretical states: the theological or fictitious state, the metaphysical or abstract state, and the scientific or positive state." It was implied that the successive stages superceded the previous ones, and that science represented the ultimate state of human knowledge. Comte believed his law of three stages to be "a great fundamental law, to which the mind is subjected by an inevitable necessity" (Comte, 1830/1970, p. 1).

As noted earlier, Darwin's theory of evolution proved to be a major blow to the religious domination of Western man's world view. The writings of Ernst Haeckel (1834–1919), an early German advocate of Darwin's theory, reflect the impact of science on the new world view. According to Haeckel, science had proven beyond all doubt that the universe was eternal, infinite, and filled with energy and matter in eternal motion. Countless organic forms were supposed to gradually emerge in an unbroken course of development. He believed that everything could be explained in terms of the evolutionary development of material substance. Haeckel's reaction to the traditional concept of God and morality was expressed in the following words:

> Monistic cosmology proved . . . that there is no personal God; comparative and genetic psychology showed that there cannot be an immortal soul; and monistic physiology proved the futility of the assumption of "free will." Finally, the science of evolution made it clear that the same eternal iron laws that rule in the inorganic world are valid, too, in the organic and moral world. (Haeckel, 1900/1968, p. 349)

The point in quoting the above is not to raise issues of the existence of God, or the assumption of free will to which Haeckel refers; it is to note how a certain theory about the nature of reality (in this instance, the theory of material monism) is taken as a fact or a final truth established by the methods of natural science. Here the zeal for science does not reflect the spirit of doubting and free inquiry, but reflects a feeling of conviction similar to that of a narrowly conceived religious faith. Science, to some people, thus became the be-all and end-all. Sometimes there is a tendency to identify the spatiotemporal manifold with *ultimate reality* and to consider contemporary theories of science as the ultimate truth. Such a tendency may be called scientism rather than science, and may turn out to be a blind faith in an implicit view of the world.

Toward the end of the 19th century, advances in biology led some scientists to believe that, ultimately, life could be completely explained in physicochemical terms. Like Haeckel, many began to believe that the laws of behavior of animals, including human beings, could be unequivocally explained in terms of the laws of physics and chemistry. The work of Jacques Loeb (1859–1924) on the movement of phototropic organisms toward the source of light was a serious attempt to show that the behavior of organisms could be explained in physicochemical terms. Notwithstanding the merits of Loeb's contribution, along with some genuine advances in learning, such studies introduced a strong tendency among psychologists to "reduce" psychology to biology and chemistry, and, ultimately, to physics. Implicit in such reductionism is the ontological theory of material monism, a belief in "determinism," and the view that moral principles have no meaning, since all behavior is strictly controlled by the "iron laws" of physics and chemistry. Quite often such a view is entertained with the zeal of scientism rather than the spirit of science.

Criticisms of reductionism are not new to Western psychology and it is unnecessary to repeat them here. The influence of positivism on modern Western psychology, particularly on behaviorism, is well known, and critiques of positivism are well known also. Comte's influence on Western psychology is seen in many ways, including the antitheological and antimetaphysical stance common among psychologists. There is a common belief that physics dispossessed metaphysics, just as chemistry expelled alchemy. In the same vein, it is held that the physiology of the brain will replace the philosophy of mind, and that theories of perception will make epistemology obsolete. Note, for example, the following lines from a paper entitled "Does Psychology Need Its Own Philosophy of Science?" published in the *American Psychologist* in 1971.

> Perhaps the questions about whether we perceive what we perceive, which traditionally formed the epistemology branch of psychology, could be dealt with with more success by the science that studies human perception. Were, indeed, Hume, Kant, Nagel, Schopenhauer, Mach, and Ryle better prepared to find out how we perceive than, let us say, von Bekesy (1967), Corso (1967), Gibson (1966), Gregory (1966), and Helson (1964)? Why should one assume that someone sitting at his desk knows more about the moon than people who landed there? . . . And how do epistemological essays compare to experimental studies in sensation and perception? (Wolman, 1971, p. 883)

The question that compares the man sitting at the desk to the men who reached the moon makes all the "thinking" scientists who planned the moonshot appear "dumb" in comparison to the "smart" astronauts. The implicit argument is too simple-minded to take issue with; but the author of the above lines is not the only psychologist who is bedazzled by such feats of modern technology and logistics as the voyage to the moon. The mood of the lines quoted above reflects the fairly widespread feeling among psychologists that natural science is the only model to which they must look, and that philosophy, epistemology, ontology, and similar fields are substandard pursuits fit for lesser minds. Wolman graciously grants the philosopher of science a role in the knowledge enterprise, one of offering an "ex post facto critique of scientific procedures;" considers it similar to that of a literary critic who is incapable of producing a literary work of his own. Wolman's views apart, the influence of the Comtean theory of the progress of knowledge is not restricted to stray authors, but is quite widespread in modern psychology.

Here it is necessary to note, however, that the overenthusiastic modeling of psychology after the natural sciences has not gone without sharp criticism in the Western hemisphere. Abraham Maslow and other "humanistic" psychologists in the United States, and the existential psychologists in Europe have pointed out the "dehumanizing" influence on psychology following from an attempt to develop entirely along the lines of the natural sciences. However, Maslow's "Third Force" is pretty weak in comparison to the large following of a positivist viewpoint. It may be noted that existential psychology represents the irrationalist trend in the history of Western thought, as opposed to the rationalist trend. One may also remember that the antiphilosophical stance is partly a result of positive gains from the use of the experimental method in psychology over the "armchair speculation" it successfully replaced.

Max Scheler, a pioneer in the field of the sociology of knowledge, has suggested that Comte's view of the growth of knowledge is based exclusively on the European experience of the previous few centuries, and that it is erroneous to derive a universal statement about the nature of growth of knowledge on such limited grounds. He considers theological, metaphysical, and scientific knowledge as *kinds* rather than stages of knowledge, all of which are "essential to the human mind." In Scheler's view, the three types of knowledge rest on three different motives and aims, three different "groups of acts of the knowing mind," and they are relevant to three different personality types. The religious type of knowledge, which aims at salvation of a person or a group, is motivated by an urge for mental self-preservation; involves the hoping, fearing and loving mind in addition to the knowing mind; and has as its leading personality type the "homo religious" or saint. Metaphysical knowledge, on the other hand, aims at wisdom; is motivated by wonder and an urge for the knowledge of essences; involves reasoning of the "essence-visioning" type; and has as its leading personality an intellectual type of sage. In contrast to these two types, the scientific type of knowledge aims at identifying relationships among observed phenomena, usually with the purpose of directing and controlling nature; involves acts of observation and experiment, induction, and deduction; and has as its leading personality type the scientist, who is not particularly interested in "wisdom" or saintliness (see Scheler in Curtis and Petras, 1970).

Scheler has added that science never aims at a complete, conspective view of nature, reality, or existence, but only at an understanding of one specific aspect of nature at a time. Science progresses by division of labor: each type of specialist focuses on narrower and still narrower sets of phenomena. International communities of scientists use basically the same "language." Scientific work proceeds impersonally and continuously. Starting from an earlier stage, each step devalues the previous stage which then becomes obsolete, making cumulative progress all along. Metaphysics, however, cannot progress by division of labor. Insofar as it aims at knowing essences that are supposed to be "world constants," metaphysics does not depend upon the observation of specific phenomena and the building of propositions by the inductive process. Although Descartes and Kant may have benefited from Plato, they did not render obsolete Plato's metaphysical system, as Ptolemy's astronomy and Newton's physics were rendered obsolete by later developments.

The Indian philosopher, B. G. Tilak (1915/1956), has offered a critique of Comte's theory of the growth of knowledge that is somewhat akin to that of Scheler. Like Scheler, he disputes Comte's view of the superiority of scientific knowledge, and considers metaphysical and natural sciences as different kinds rather than different stages of knowledge. Tilak has suggested three traditional Indian terms, namely ādhidaivika, adhyātmika, and ādhibhautika to refer respectively to theological, metaphysical, and scientific types of knowledge. Unlike Scheler, however, Tilak considers the ādhidaivika (theological) type of knowledge to be inferior to the other types, for he considers it similar to animism, which assigns different spirits or "deities" to animals, rivers, clouds and other natural phenomena. Tilak's distinction between the ādhibhautika and adhyātmika types of knowledge is similar to Kant's. The natural sciences study phenomena, that is, objects as they *appear* to our sensory experience, whereas Kant's metaphysics deals with "noumena," or things-in-themselves, that is, with *reality*. The task of natural science is to identify relationships among observed phenomena, and, as noted by Scheler, the knowledge of such relationships is useful in controlling nature. For Tilak, the seeking of scientific knowledge and its use in controlling nature seemed legitimate in itself, but was not sufficient for pursuit of this type of knowledge alone. Moreover, like Scheler, Tilak considered the human urge to seek knowledge of reality beyond mere appearance as natural and important. While Kant (1781/1966, p. 201) considered the knowledge of *noumenon* or the thing-in-itself as beyond the grasp of the human mind, Tilak noted that, according to the Indian tradition, such knowledge is attainable.

In order to help understand the typical Indian view of the uses and limitations of various types or "levels" of knowledge, it is useful to refer to certain conventional concepts. In India there is a traditional distinction between parā vidyā or the knowledge which is *beyond* the power of the senses and reason, and aparā vidyā which is within the reach of reason. Parā vidyā, which refers to the knowledge of the Individual Self (ātman) and that of the Universal Self (Brahman), is considered attainable in a special or superior state of consciousness. Such knowledge is believed to help the individual in the attainment of a permanent or final release from the miseries of life (sā vidyā yā vimuktaye), and, as such, is considered to be a superior type of knowledge. Knowledge based on sensory experience (or, in other words, empirical or "scientific" knowledge) is definitely considered useful; it is said to be inferior only in the sense that it is not enough for the attainment of self realization or the "ultimate" release from miseries, which is the highest goal of life.

The schematic accounts of Scheler's and Tilak's views of types of knowledge indicate that they differ from each other in the use of such labels as theological and metaphysical. But it may also be clear that both of them are addressing the question, "Knowledge for what?" and both see reasons for seeking knowledge other than those of prediction and control of natural phenomena. Now the relevance of the above discussion to psychology should be obvious. Excepting the minority of existential psychologists, and a few others such as Abraham Maslow and those from his Third Force in the United States, the dominant view in the West is that psychology is a natural science aimed at the prediction and control of behavior. As mentioned before, Indian psychology, by contrast, seeks adhyātmika knowledge, aiming at liberation (mukti) and has developed techniques for self-realization. Such differences in the Western and Indian psychologies arise from historical and social factors.

Many psychologists have recently become interested in the historical aspects of the growth of psychological knowledge. This is particularly apparent in the various attempts to examine the history of psychology in the light of Kuhn's (1970) thesis that sciences often progress through periodical "revolutions" or major revisions in their fundamental principles. In a recent controversy over the applicability of the Kuhnian view of progress-through-revolution, arguments and counter-arguments have been made to support or oppose the thesis that a Kuhnian revolution is currently under way in the field of psychology (Palermo, 1971; Warren, 1971; Briskman, 1972; Lipsey, 1974; Weimer and Palermo, 1973). Throughout the controversy it is taken for granted that psychology is (perhaps nothing but) a natural science, and even the Comtean view of natural science as a superior stage of knowledge seems implicit. Alan Elms (1975) has suggested that such discussion serves mainly to express wishful thinking, and may be paraphrased somewhat like this: 'Now that we have a real crisis, and since Kuhn has told us sciences advance through crises, psychology must really be a science.' After all, only the hope of progress following the current crisis could validate our status in the community of natural scientists!

Whether science progresses through a process of cumulation or through abrupt, revolutionary spurts is a controversial issue. Even if one is convinced that progress comes through the revolutionary restatement of basic assumptions of the science, how does one bring about a revolution to ensure progress? In fact, the more important aspect of Kuhn's analysis is the point that science is a social enterprise and that sciences acquire many arbitrary features as a consequence of the historical, social and cultural milieu of the scientists' communities. This point is not new. It is borrowed from the field of sociology of knowledge, pioneered by German thinkers like Max Scheler and Karl Mannheim. We have seen how Scheler considered Comte's ideas to be determined by the history of Europe, where science developed in opposition to theology. Mannheim persuasively argues in his well known work, *Ideology and Utopia,* (1929/1936) that the process of knowing does not follow only from the "nature of things" or from "pure logical possiblilities," but also from extratheoretical factors such as collective purposes, experiences, and ideologies shared by the seekers of knowledge as members of a community. Human interests, argued Mannheim, often lead to more or less conscious deception. He tried to explain how biasing factors enter into the process of seeking knowledge and proposed a methodological strategy to identify and minimize the limitations on knowledge imposed by social factors. Since Mannheim's approach to the sociology of knowledge is obviously relevant to a comparative study of theories born in diverse social and cultural traditions, it would be reasonable to briefly outline some of his main points.

The process of obtaining knowledge in any field, such as in any particular science, has a history of its own. In most cases, the formulation of a problem by anyone is based on the precedence of someone else having faced the same or a similar problem. So each generation inherits a set of problems as formulated by the previous generation. The problems, as well as the data in light of which they are to be examined, are selected from among many that are known or available. The selection is normally based on experiences and values in the life of the investigator. The problem is seen in a certain "perspective," composed of the axiomatic assumptions and *a priori* categories with which an investigator begins to analyze a problem. These categories are independent of the nature of the data to be examined, and often predetermine the nature of the conclusions the investigator may draw. Usually the perspective of an investigator or "knower" is based on his social position. Certainly there are problems, such as "How much is two plus two?" where the social position of the knower is of no consequence. A question of this type may arise in counting bananas, cows, or rocks, and the social position of the farmer, cowboy, or geologist who asks it would not alter either the question or the answer. In many other types of questions, however, the type of questions asked, as well as the answer given, may depend on what type of a person asks the question. The perspective on a social or psychological question such as "Are all men equal?" may depend on the knower's background. Christians, communists, capitalists, rich, or poor—all are likely to see the problem in a different light.

How does this relate to the study of psychological issues? A paper by Allan Buss (1976) provides a good example. Buss has suggested that Galton's pioneering studies of individual differences were prompted by the democratic, liberal, capitalistic and individualistic ideology of the late 19th-century England, where individuals were held to be equal before the law, and the promotion of diversity among individuals was necessary to promote an industrial capitalist economy. Galton's formulation of the problem of the origin of individual differences was conditioned by the ideas of his half-cousin Charles Darwin, namely the ideas of inheritance of physical traits, natural selection, and so on. Further, it is not an accident that Galton, who was a member of the aristocratic elite, considered heredity to be a particularly important determinant of individual differences. I may add here that the typical American deemphasis on heredity and overemphasis on environmental factors makes sense when compared to the British situation, for the elite ruling class was of much less importance in the New World than in the Old World. In another paper, Buss (1975) presented several examples of ways in which social and ideological factors have influenced various trends of thought in psychology. Citing several recent publications that try to relate various ideas in psychology to the ideologies of the societies in which they arose, Buss argues that such publications show that there has emerged a new field of study within psychology which he has christened *the sociology of psychological knowledge*.

Against the backdrop of the rise of Marxist and other sociopolitical ideologies in the Europe of his day, Mannheim emphasized the biasing influence of such ideologies on knowledge. When Mannheim referred to social position in this setting, he meant membership in a socioeconomic class such as Galton's aristocratic family background. But Mannheim's point about social position may be, and has been, interpreted to mean social position by religion, occupation, sex, age, and similar other categories as well. The way in which the occupational status of the psychologist influences his perspective is of particular interest to our purpose. As is well known, psychoanalysis arose in the medical–therapeutic context, while behaviorist psychology developed in the academic–scientific establishment. Freud saw patients suffering from anxiety, and many of them were members of the Victorian middle class who were burdened by social mores restricting the expression of their sexual impulses. As a consequence, his image of man involves a guilt- and anxiety-ridden individual. The behaviorists, impressed by the advances in biology since Darwin, saw man as an animal, and their laboratory experiments on rats led them to formulate what Arthur Koestler (1967) has called a "ratomorphic" view of man. It is a patent observation that many psychologists, being college teachers, found it easy to use college sophomores as their subjects and created what is called a "sophomore psychology." The influence of the vocation of the theorists on the theories of their creation is clearly reflected in the fact that psychoanalysis focuses on pathology and on the restoration of mental health, while behaviorism emphasizes mainly such things as learning and prediction of performance. By contrast to both of these theories, the originators of Indian psychological concepts were primarily spiritual aspirants or philosophers. They were not attached to the modern type of academic establishment or clinic. It is not surprising, then, that their perspective on psychological issues is different from that of Western psychologists.

The sociologist of knowledge tries to relate the nature of a theory to the social position of the theorist, as shown by examples above. Mannheim (1929/1936, p. 284) recommends a useful strategy for examining the relationship between a theorist and his social position. First, he suggests, the sociologist of knowledge should start with a deliberate suspicion that any assertion might represent "merely a partial view" of the field of investigation. Second, the suspicious examiner should acquire an overall view of the theory in question from a distance, as it were, without getting involved in the ideas and perspectives of the theorist under examination. If the examiner does not try to view the theory from the outside, the danger is that he may find himself wrapped up in the theory and fail to see its limitations, as did the original theorist. How does one step out of the perspective of the original theory and develop a different, overall perspective of his own?

Here Mannheim gives the analogy of the son of a peasant from a village who goes to the city. If the young man looks back on his early years after having adapted to city life over a period of time, he begins to realize what his native, rustic perspective was like. He would never have been able to identify the characteristics of his native perspective without being "detached" from his original surroundings. This analogy makes a certain amount of sense, but hardly specifies exactly how a sociological analysis of knowledge can be carried out. How should a psychologist proceed with a sociological analysis of the theories he has known? Can he take a trip to a distant land, for instance, and hope to acquire a perspective on psychology as did Mannheim's rustic peasant? Well, that is exactly what happened to several psychologists who took psychological concepts and techniques developed in their native cultures and tried to apply them to persons from alien cultures. Those involved in cross-cultural studies in psychology have, in fact, recognized the limitations of psychological concepts that arise from the influence of the culture of their origin. This is a complex issue and needs to be discussed at some length. We shall turn to it shortly.

One does not necessarily have to move out of one's culture to develop an "outside" perspective. According to Mannheim (1929/1936, p. 282), it happens naturally within one and the same society when "two or more socially determined modes of interpretation come into conflict and, in criticizing one another, render one another transparent and establish perspectives with reference to each other." Such mutual criticism has occurred in the recent years in the United States. A case in point is the ongoing conflict between psychoanalysis and behaviorism and, even more particularly, the mutual criticism, between behaviorism and phenomenology. In a symposium organized at Rice University, advocates of behaviorism and phenomenology were brought together and the critiques and counter-critiques from both sides published in the form of a book (Wann, 1964). As mentioned before, there have been attempts in the past to evaluate Indian theories from a Western viewpoint (Coster, 1934/1972; Behanan, 1937/1964) and vice-versa (Akhilananda, 1948, 1952). Although such critiques have helped develop "outside" perspectives with reference to various Indian and Western theories of psychology, they were not intended as exercises in the sociology of knowledge and have accomplished only a small part of what a systematic, sociological analysis promises to do. As a guideline for systematic research in the field of sociology of knowledge, Mannheim has proposed a two-step technique which is worth describing briefly at this point.

The first step involves the reconstruction of integral styles of thought and perspective, starting from single expressions and relating them to a central world-view or Weltanschauung which they collectively express. This means that the underlying unity of outlook, which may be implicit, must be explicated. One tries to reconstruct central themes or "ideal types" in a certain trend of thought. Ideal types identified in this manner are indispensable hypotheses formed in the first step of analysis. The second step, then, proceeds to explore the extent to which particular assertions and theories are influenced by the hypothesized ideal types of thinking. In the following chapter, I shall follow this Mannheimian procedure to reconstruct "ideal types" of Western and Indian thinking on the basis of historical accounts of Western and Indian philosophies, and then relate the major themes in the hypothesized ideal types to particular ideas in the psychological theories of India and the West. Given the length and breadth of two traditions, both are rich in content and full of controversies, the identification of unitary influential themes cannot be expected to be an easy task. Some very broad generalizations are inevitable. Yet, where contrasts in the two systems of thought are conspicuous, the identification of implicit unity is not too difficult. Also, historians of Western as well as Indian thought have identified distinct trends within each tradition. The rationalistic thought of the Greek heritage and the "irrationalist" influence of the Judeo-Christian tradition are good examples of separate trends within the Western hemisphere. That these traditions have inspired the behaviorist and existential psychologies in the West is a well-known thesis that follows from the application of the basic principle of sociology of knowledge to the Western tradition. More recently, psychological thoughts that were embedded in writings of various schools of Indian philosophy have been extracted from their original textual sources to provide a systematic, integrated overview of the broad field of Indian psychology. The work of Raghunath Safaya (1976) is particularly notable in this respect. Such accounts have made it easier to identify the common themes that run across the various schools, as well as the disagreements among them. By carefully comparing histories of Indian and Western psychology, it should be possible to identify the prominent areas of agreement and difference across the two traditions. However, the cultural themes that influence the specific psychological concepts must be located beyond the technical and philosophical literature—in religion, folkways, technology and other aspects of culture. Reconstructing the Weltanschauung, which expresses itself through such themes, is a more difficult task, for which it is not easy to find any rules-of-thumb. Here one must rely on one's wits and leave the readers to judge whether or not the author's analysis has been on the right track.

Cultural Relativity of Psychological Theories: A Perspective from Anthropology and Culture-and-Personality Studies

The main thesis of the sociology of knowledge is that the nature of human understanding is socially relative. Mannheim and other pioneers in the field of the sociology of knowledge realized the importance of relativity in the context of a clash between conservative and radical political ideologies in Germany between the World Wars. Before publication of the systematic formulation of the principles and methods of the sociology of knowledge in such treatises as Mannheim's *Ideology and Utopia,* (1929/1936), psychologists had begun to realize that their theories were subject to cultural limitations. This realization resulted from the attempt of anthropologists to carry European psychological concepts around the globe to study people of diverse cultural backgrounds. A major landmark in this respect was Malinowski's *Sex and Repression in Savage Society* (1927). In this book, Malinowski persuasively argues that Freud's concept of the Oedipus complex was not universally applicable across cultures. This "complex" is said to result from two opposing tendencies within the growing child: a feeling of hatred for the father, who often frustrates the child he tries to discipline, and, simultaneously, a feeling of adoration for the father whose power, authority, and privileges within the family appear so enviably great. Every growing child is said to be in conflict due to these ambivalent feelings. Malinowski pointed out that only children raised in patriarchal families would have to face such inner conflicts; those raised in matriarchal families may not see the father as a threatening disciplinarian and, hence, need not hate him. The concept of the Oedipus complex was the cornerstone of psychoanalytic theory since the resolution of the inner conflict of opposing feelings for the father was conceived of as nearly the sole determinant of the adult character. Malinowski's attack, therefore, proved to be the starting point of a major controversy in the field of study called "culture and personality"— a field that stands midway between anthropology and psychology.

Another move in the same direction was made by the anthropologist Margaret Mead (1928/1968) when she challenged the psychologist G. Stanley Hall's view that adolescence is universally a period of "storm and stress" or emotional disturbances. Hall had assumed that the process of development of an individual member of the human species (ontogeny) is a quick recapitulation of the development of the entire human species through stages of savagery and barbarism to higher levels of civilization. This, he thought, was a biological principle universally applicable to human beings. Mead showed that in the "primitive" society of the island of Samoa, adolescence was not characterized by the typical storm and stress described by Hall and argued that Hall had erroneously generalized his American observations to the rest of the world.

The contributions of Malinowski and Mead were early indications of the ways psychologists might implicitly assume that the particular conditions in society they observe must prevail everywhere else, and go on to construct elaborate theories of human experience and behavior based on their culturally limited perspectives. The recognition of such ethnocentric bias immediately led to the suggestion of specific strategies to correct the bias. Malinowski, for instance, concluded that it is essentially wrong to judge the nature of conduct of alien peoples from the point of view of one's own culture. The right way of studying cultures, he suggested, was to grasp the "native's" point of view or to realize his vision of the world.

As can be easily seen, Malinowski's solution results in a total submission to endless cultural relativism, for if every culture must be understood only in its own terms, any attempt to arrive at a universal generalization has to be considered entirely out of the question. The anthropologist Goldschmidt (1966) has called this predicament "the Malinowskian dilemma." A closer examination of this dilemma indicates that it arises from the implicit assumption that every culture is unique and therefore can be understood only from its unique view of the world. This assumption makes comparison meaningless. Switching the focus for a moment from the study of cultures to the study of persons, we can see that the psychologist can land himself in the same type of dilemma as the anthropologist. There has been an old argument to the effect that the reason a particular person behaves in a particular manner can be understood properly only if we can view the situation from the individual's own point of view. This argument makes the same kind of sense as Malinowski's suggestion that every culture must be understood in its own terms. Given the uniqueness of individual viewpoints, study of persons, too, would appear to be as much a false enterprise as the study of cultures.

Kluckhohn and Murray (1953, p. 53) noted a simple truism about the nature of individual variation. "Every man is, in certain respects," they said, "a. like all other men, b. like some other men, and c. like no other man." Every person is unique in certain ways, making every single person to some extent incomparable to all others. But individuals are not unique in every conceivable aspect of their personalities. Within our respective communities we speak the same language and share similar ways of looking at the world. Without such sharing, social life would be impossible. Moreover, despite the great degree of cultural variation, every man has a brain, grows up in the course of time, tends to avoid pain, and shares many other properties that are universal within the human species. It is the universal biological principles, again, that account not only for our species-wide similarities (such as having vertebrae and erect posture), but also for common characteristics such as skin color and physiognomic features shared within genetic pools, as well as entirely unique features of every individual such as our finger prints. We must assume that there are psychological principles analogous to biological principles that would account for universal, shared, and unique aspects of experience and behavior of persons. This is a cardinal assumption. We must either begin with such an axiom or give up the study of persons as a false enterprise.

For some early anthropologists the range of cultural variation appeared overwhelmingly great. During the early 1950s, however, a few anthropologists suggested that cultural variation is not really as boundless as it appears, and started to search for common threads across cultures by which meaningful comparisons could be made. Florence Kluckhohn (1953), for instance, suggested that there are certain basic human problems for which "all peoples at all times and in all places must find some solution." The following, she thought, were the common problems: (1) What are the innate predispositions of man? (2) What is the relation of man to nature? (3) What is the significant time dimension? (4) What is the valued personality type? (5) What is the dominant modality of the relationship of man to other men? Further, she suggested that the range of solutions to the problems is not unlimited, and that different cultures emphasize one or the other solution along the limited range of possible solutions. It is not possible to elaborate on Kluckhohn's ideas here, nor is it possible to maintain that her thesis is *entirely* defensible. However, the strategy for the identification of a common thread across cultures does make sense. It makes sense to assume, for instance, that all human beings must adapt to their natural habitats, and that there are relatively few basic approaches to solving the problem of man's relation to nature: they may try to master nature's forces, choose to be subdued by them, or learn to live in some kind of harmony with nature. Given these three main ways in which man can relate to nature, we can meaningfully compare cultures in terms of their *dominant* mode of relating to nature. In the next chapter I shall use a similar strategy for comparing the Western and Indian cultures while trying to identify the dominant cultural themes that have influenced their methods of dealing with psychological issues.

Like Florence Kluckhohn, the anthropologist Clyde Kluckhohn addressed himself to the problem of cultural variation. He posed the question in the following manner: "Are there fairly definite limits within which cultural variation is constrained by panhuman regularities in biology, psychology, and the processes of social interaction?" (Kluckhohn, 1953 (b), p. 507). To this question we may add: "Can we identify the specific *aspects* of human personality which are a. universal, b. shared within a culture only, and c. unique to every individual?" If we can answer this last question, the universal categories can be left to general psychology, the unique characteristics to the personologist, and the cross-cultural psychologist can confidently address himself to the meaningful task of comparing those aspects of individuals that are neither unique nor exactly the same across mankind. Although the questions posed above are important, they have not been solved to any level of satisfaction. The lack of solutions has not deterred the cross-cultural psychologist, however. Virtually every theory, concept, or technique has been dragged out of its culture of origin and has been used in communities around the globe, with little thought being given either to the comparability of the phenomena being studied or to the cross-cultural applicability of the methods of its study.

It is small wonder, then, that despite the large number of papers published every year, the field of cross-cultural studies in psychology has come to a theoretical impasse. I am not here speaking about the age-old problems of culture-and-personality research, such as problems concerning the usefulness of the concepts "national character," or "modal personality," and so on. Nor am I referring to the special methodological problems of cross-cultural research, such as problems of translation of tests or of adapting methods of investigation to specific cultural settings. The problem I am referring to is reflected in the proliferation of cross-cultural studies that report and compare sets of scores, T1 and T2, on test X in cultures Y and Z, and so on. Many such studies do not bother to examine whether the phenomenon under investigation (authoritarianism, intelligence, oral personality type, or whatever) is universal, culturally relative, or unique. Usually, little attention is given to the examination of how the phenomenon, the technique of its study, or the theory on which it is based, is viewed by the people to whom the test is administered. In light of the preceding discussion, the problem involved in such studies can be seen to be two-tiered. First, it involves the issue of comparability of phenomena. This is the issue Kluckhohn and others were concerned with; it refers to the need for ensuring that unique, non-comparable aspects of cultures or individuals are not involved in cross-cultural studies. The second tier of the problem involves the cultural limitations of the theories of the type with which sociologists of knowledge have been concerned. At this level we must avoid the dangers involved in examining psychological phenomena in terms of culturally limited concepts. In other words, we must avoid the kind of problems Malinowski pointed out in relation to the concept of the Oedipus complex.

The ideas of John Berry (1969) are relevant to problems regarding cross-cultural studies. He criticized cross-cultural studies of the type that report that 'in culture X, they score Y on test Z' as being "mere anecdotal" studies since they can "tell us nothing about the relationship between behavior and cultural, social, or ecological variables." He recognized the problem of comparing the incomparables which are often involved in such studies, and suggested a way out. Here he followed the solution of the Malinowskian dilemma attempted by Goldschmidt (1966) for making legitmate and meaningful comparisons of social institutions across cultures. Goldschmidt has argued that, although social institutions (such as family, kinship organization, and the like) are not consistent from culture to culture, there are recurrent, common problems that different peoples try to solve. As such, he thought, those aspects of social institutions that are designed to solve common problems (such as raising children) can legitimately be compared, although they may initially be understood only in the respective culture's own terms, as Malinowski recommended. (This solution, we may note, is similar to Florence Kluckhohn's approach to the comparison of cultures insofar as she insists on comparing only those aspects of cultures that are related to the solution of universal human problems.) Reasoning in the same fashion, Berry proposed that "aspects of behaviour occurring in differing behavioural settings may be compared only when they can be shown to be *functionally equivalent* in the sense that the aspect of behaviour in question is an attempted solution to one of Goldschmidt's 'recurrent problems' " (emphasis original, p. 122). Now it would appear that the concept of intelligence would be potentially universally applicable insofar as it can be defined as the ability to adapt to one's environment, which is a recurrent, common problem for all human beings. Yet, since the physical and cultural aspects of environments differ from place to place, different skills are required for adapting to different environments. Therefore, what is considered intelligent behavior in one culture may not be considered intelligent in another culture. This is a well-known argument which is as old as the early attempts to use intelligence tests developed in literate societies to measure intelligence in non-literate societies. A similar argument is made in relation to the use of IQ tests designed by white Americans to test black American children, who do not find the tests meaningful. First, the scholastic tasks in the test are not useful in adapting to their ghetto lives. Second, the ghetto children are less anxious to do well in the test, since a high IQ score does not promise better opportunity in the future, nor does a low score threaten their status among their peers. What Berry points out in relation to this issue is that no meaningful comparisons of test scores across cultural groups are possible unless a thorough investigation is made of the cultural and ecological demands of each situation and it is established that skills measured by the test are indeed response to a *shared problem.*

In relation to the cultural limitations of the theories (i.e., with reference to the second tier of the problem of cross-cultural studies mentioned above) Berry suggests that one must inevitably start with a descriptive framework arising from an examination of behavior from within one and the same culture. Is it not natural, after all, that one begins with the perspective of a culture in which one is raised? Berry names such limited, unicultural, "inside" views as the "emic" approach, following the distinction in linguistics between phonemics, which focuses on sounds in a particular language, and phonetics, which studies sounds from all languages. The "etic" approach, by contrast to the "emic" approach, then, studies behavior from a position "outside the system," examines and compares many cultures, and is presumably universal. The aim, obviously, is to create an "etic" framework for psychology. How does one attain it though, if one is doomed to start with a unicultural emic approach? Berry's suggestion is that, to begin with, the descriptive categories based on the emic be *tentatively* applied to an alien behavior system (so that the emic becomes an "imposed etic" for the time being). In this situation, the categories should be examined from the point of view of the second system (which is another emic) and be modified if necessary. The shared categories can then be used to build further categories which are valid for both systems, thus extending the conceptual frame until it attains universality. The making of an etic framework can thus be seen as a long, hard process in which one can take only a very small step with each major comparative study!

Now we may ask, How does Berry's approach relate to the present task of comparing and integrating Indian and Western systems of psychology? In response to this question we may first note that the various systems of psychology (psychoanalysis, behaviorism, existential psychology, and the Yoga and Vedānta systems) can be considered as emics insofar as these systems developed in response to the specific cultural settings of their origins. They cannot be considered etic or universally applicable without a demonstration of their utility in diverse cultural settings. Since we are bound to strive for universally applicable theories, the least we can do is critically examine them in the context of diverse cultures. If we begin the task of comparing theories of diverse cultural origin, we shall begin to recognize limitations arising from their specific cultural origins. We can then try to rectify their shortcomings and thus move a small step toward the distant goal of arriving at an etic. Granted that the etic will never be attained so as to make it fully comprehensive (by extending it to *all* cultures), it is certainly desirable to try to transcend the limitations of the conventional theories with which we are now familiar. Those parts of Berry's prescription which deal with the need for demonstrating functional equivalence of tasks and for developing test items relevant to such tasks are not applicable here, however. This is because, at this stage, no empirical study is planned which requires specific tasks, such as making and administering an intelligence test. This is not to say that empirical testing of cross-culturally relevant propositions is not important. The task set for the present is limited to an examination of the conceptual frameworks that have developed independently in diverse cultural traditions. To this end it is sufficient to examine those phenomena, concepts, or methods that appear in certain Indian and Western theories in relation to selected common issues.

Even a preliminary examination of Indian and Western psychological thought shows the following things: they have studied phenomena such as waking, dreams, sleep and other states of consciousness; they have introduced the concept of the self, although it is defined in different ways in the different systems within India and in the Western countries; many Indian as well as Western psychologies have devised various techniques to help ameliorate undesirable aspects of experience and behavior, and to attain more desirable states of individual existence. If the phenomena they commonly refer to were not universal, and if the concepts and techniques they have developed were not addressed to shared problems, how would they appear in common in thought systems that developed independently in remote places and different periods of history?

Let us now return to Berry's suggestion that each behavior system must be looked at from "outside" the system so as to extend a narrow, emic perspective to approximate a universal, etic perspective. The reader may recognize that this prescription is the same as Mannheim's suggestion that one detach oneself from a culture-bound perspective—like a rural boy who moves to a city and looks back at his former, rural perspective. Although Berry has not referred to Mannheim or other sociologists of knowledge, he has followed their footsteps in recognizing and trying to correct the cultural limitations of psychological theories. With this in mind, we should now terminate our excursion into the problems of cross-cultural research, and return to certain issues relating to the sociology of knowledge which we could not discuss before.

Certain Criticisms and Limitations of the Sociology of Knowledge

The sociology-of-knowledge approach has met with much criticism since the time it emerged in Germany during the 1920s. Mannheim, in some of the early statements of his position such as his *Ideology and Utopia* (Mannheim, 1929/1936), has responded to some of these criticisms. During the past four decades theoretical and empirical work in the field of the sociology of knowledge has grown widely—and so have the criticisms. It is neither possible nor necessary to account for the numerous critiques and counter-critiques of the field. (There are several sources available for the interested reader, e.g.: Barnes, 1972;, Merton, 1973; Remmling, 1973; Barber and Hirsch, 1962; Curtis and Petras, 1970). It would be useful, however, to briefly examine certain criticisms of the sociology-of-knowledge approach that may be relevant to the present work.

One of the oldest criticisms of the doctrine of social relativity of knowledge suggests that the sociology of knowledge lapses into absolute relativism, thus destroying the hope of a universally valid knowledge of any kind. To this criticism, Mannheim responded with the argument that social relativism does not signify that there are no criteria for rightness and wrongness. It does not imply that all assertions must always be arbitrary, but only that "it lies in the nature of certain assertions that they cannot be formulated absolutely, but only in terms of the perspective of a given situation" (1929/1936, p. 283). It must be emphasized that here relativity is ascribed to *certain types* of assertions, not to all. Mannheim stressed that it is important to *relate* an assertion to the social position of the assertor, insofar as the assertion may have a specific meaning or intent in light of the ideology of the assertor. He insisted on calling his approach "relationism," thus emphasizing the need to examine the context of the assertion and also de-emphasizing the apparent philosophical relativism. It must be noted, however, that despite vocal opposition to philosophical relativism, sociologists of knowledge are heirs to Immanuel Kant, who asserted that there is no such thing as a scientific inquiry free from any kind of presuppositions. No one can start from nothing; every system of inquiry is equipped with a set of presuppositions that are *not* subject to empirical testing. Kant called such presuppositions *a priori* categories. Insofar as the validity of propositions is subject to such untested (and perhaps untestable) categories, all knowledge is relative, and no sociologist of knowledge may deny the charge of being relativist in this sense.

The charge of relativism assumes a sharper edge if and when the sociologist of knowledge begins to imply that the social position of an assertor must always affect what he believes and that the effect must be biasing. Further, anyone who finds his theory being analyzed by an "outside" perspective may feel uneasy about such an examination, for it starts with the assumption that every theorist must be *biased* one way or another. The deliberately suspicious eyes of the socioanalyst are ready to "impute" motives to the assertor, so his searching looks appear threatening and thus arouse resentment among those whose ideas are so analyzed. To appreciate the strength of such resentment, just drop a hint while having a discussion with anyone coming from a different social background that his statement reflects a typical bias shared by his country, class, religion, or sex. I would be surprised if your statement were not greeted with a negative tone. Let me go one step further by noting that whenever I am able to get this point across to my students and they begin to examine the psychological theories in terms of their Western biases, some react as if the ground under their feet is shaking. How do we deal with such reactions?

First, it must be asserted that it is wrong to begin with the assumption that every statement of any theorist must always be biased by his social position. Some sociologists of knowledge may carry it too far, giving the idea that either deliberate or inadvertant deceptions resulting from socially shared ideologies are fairly common. If "socioanalysis" of any field of knowledge involved merely accusing and being suspicious, it would become simply destructive, and the resentment against it would be legitimate. What is of paramount importance is the genuine desire to acquire a broad universal perspective that is as unbiased as possible. Those who share this desire need not be unduly suspicious, nor should one be frightened of shaky ground, for none of the sociologists of knowledge is advocating absolute relativism.

In the course of sociological analysis of knowledge, old justifications of existing theories or established epistemological doctrines are bound to be questioned. This does not mean that those who do such an analysis do not accept any type of epistemology, nor that they expect to supplant all epistemological inquiry (Mannheim, 1929/1936, p. 287). The sociologist of knowledge has the role of a critic of existing knowledge rather than a creator of new knowledge. Mannheim has noted that sociological analyses "do not by themselves fully reveal the truth because the mere delimitation of the perspectives is by no means a substitute for the immediate and direct discussion between the divergent points of view or for direct examination of facts" (Mannheim, 1929/1936, p. 285).

The scope and limitations of the work I propose to accomplish in this book may be outlined in light of Mannheim's point. In the next chapter I plan to attempt the examination of Indian and Western "perspectives" which influence psychological theories, using the Mannheimian two-step procedure. After that, however, I shall turn to a direct comparison between divergent points of view, switching only occasionally to an examination of the relationship between specific ideas and the respective cultural perspectives. I shall compare divergent points of view on issues relating to the nature of consciousness (in Chapters 3 and 4) and relating to the concept of self (in Chapter 5). To some extent I shall try to propose integrated perspectives of my own, derived from combining certain select aspects from both traditions. Such integration can very well be considered a kind of syncretism. I do not propose to develop a new theory or examine new data, which is an obvious limitation of the present work.

Before turning to the next chapter, however, we must examine a few more points relating to the criticism of the sociology of knowledge approach.

It has been argued by Popper (1945/1967, p. 216) that the sociology of knowledge is self-destructive since the socioanalysts "invite the application of their own methods to themselves." Since the sociologist of knowledge cannot go without an ideology of his own, how can anyone expect him to be any more objective than those whose biases he attempts to uncover? And what of the social position of the sociologist himself? The suggestion that sociologists of knowledge be free-floating intellectuals only "loosely anchored" in society has come under even heavier attack. Assigning such a special position to themselves is construed as being of the same variety as those who say "My doxy is orthodoxy and your doxy is heterodoxy."

I cannot respond to such criticisms by pretending to be a spokesman for the sociologists of knowledge. I can only respond to the implications of such criticism insofar as they apply to my effort in examining Indian and Western theories in their cultural and social contexts. Certainly I do not wish to claim to have no ideology, perspective, or social position of my own. As a migrant from India now settled in the Western world, I have a "marginal" position with respect to both cultures which provides me with opportunities to become "involved" in both worlds and also to feel "detached" at the same time. Indeed there is no guarantee that either such "loose anchors" or the use of the specific techniques of the sociology of knowledge will lead to an unbiased perspective. Also, the world is too big to expect universality of coverage. No one can expect to attain an etic perspective on psychology by examining a few Indian and Western theories on certain select topics. What is important at this point is to ensure that, however small a step one wishes to take, it be in the right direction. All that can be said is that trying to uncover biases and to discover limitations is better than trying to gloss over them—or worse, trying to hide or rationalize them.

Objectivity, impersonality and detachment are different names for the same guiding principle, one which helps avoid pitfalls in the search for knowledge. In Western psychology we are familiar with the principle of objectivity. The importance of avoiding narrow, subjective biases cannot be overstressed. An impersonal attitude is the hallmark of the spirit of dispassionate "objective" analysis pased on to us through the rationalist tradition of the West, and as long as impersonality does not become only a facade to hide one's selfish interests and implicit values, it will help avoid bias. Detachment, the key recommendation of the sociology of knowledge, is one of the basic canons in the Indian tradition. Detachment (vairāgya) is considered a prerequisite for one who sets out in the search of truth, particularly for those interested in the knowledge of the Self. The loosely-anchored intellectual is a role recommended by the sociologist of knowledge. The Indian ideal is: padmapatramivāṁbhasā, "being in water, but untouched by it"—like a lotus leaf!

Notes

1. The role of the guru is somewhat similar to that of psychologists who try to facilitate the growth of the human potentials in the client's personality. But the role of the modern professional therapist is different from that of a traditional Indian guru in many other respects. The nature of the similarities and differences between the two roles is an important and complex issue which will be discussed in Chapter 6.
2. Frits Staal (1975, pp. 116–117), who has reviewed some literature on Yoga has rightly pointed out several errors in interpreting Patañjali's aphorisms as found in Geraldine Coster's 1934 book called *Yoga and Western Psychology*.
3. This quotation from Whitehead is borrowed from William Barrett's *Irrational Man*. See Barrett (1958, p. 79). The nature of the influence of the rival forces of Greek and Hebraic legacy has been described and evaluated by many historians of Western philosophy. But I have found Barrett's account of it (1958, Chapter 4) very useful and wish to acknowledge the influence of his ideas on my writing.
4. This quotation from the Bible is borrowed from Bertrand Russell's account of the conflict between science and religion through centuries of European history. This is to acknowledge that my account of this issue owes a great deal to Russell (1935a).
5. I am borrowing the term "mystery complex" from David Bakan's paper, "The mystery–mastery complex in contemporary psychology" (Bakan, 1965). In this paper Bakan has argued that in contemporary psychology there is a pervasive sense of mystery about the psyche and a lack of interest in exploring this inner region, and that this "mystery complex" has grown hand-in-hand with an interest in controlling the "outer" world of nature. We shall return to this "mystery–mastery complex" in Chapters 2 and 3.

2

SEARCH FOR COMMON GROUND

The tasks I plan to undertake in this chapter include: (a) an attempt to identify certain themes from the Indian and Western traditions of thought, which, as aspects of dominant world views adopted by peoples of these traditions, seem to have influenced their psychological theories; and (b) to explore the extent to which such themes may have influenced particular aspects of psychological theories in the two traditions. As noted in the previous chapter, these tasks correspond to the two steps suggested by Mannheim for sociohistorical analysis of knowledge in any field. Such attempts to relate psychological theories to their cultural contexts should help us identify the implicit assumptions borrowed from the prevalent *Weltanschauung* used by the theorists as axioms on which to base their conceptual superstructure. We should also be able to identify the values borrowed from the cultural milieu that determine the goals which the psychologists strive to attain. We can expect to find a common ground for the convergence of psychological theories to the extent to which they are based upon similar axiomatic assumptions. Thus, while similarity in assumptions and values would suggest the possibility of convergence or integration, their divergence would mark the limits beyond which common ground may not extend.

The natural starting points for the identification of dominant themes of the Indian and Western *Weltanschauungen* are the historical accounts of Indian and Western philosophy. Among the many standard works available in this field I have found those of Russell (1945) and W. T. Jones (1969 ed.) useful for Western philosophy, and those of Dasgupta (1922), Hiriyanna (1932), and Radhakrishnan (1929) for Indian philosophy. There are many works which have elaborately analyzed the phil-

Notes for Chapter 2 are on p. 113.

osophical bases of Western psychological theories, but there is a lack of similar work on the Indian side. This gap in the Indian literature is partially filled by a recent book by Safaya (1976) which does a thorough job of identifying specific original sources of psychological thought rooted in the vast literature on Indian philosophy. For our present purpose the identification of the roots of psychological thought in formal philosophical principles is essential, but it is not enough. As suggested in the Chapter 1, not only the formal principles of philosophy, but the entire cultural milieu influences every field of knowledge. For instance, the conflict between religion and science in the history of Europe is just one of the numerous aspects of the development of Western civilization that have influenced psychological thought. There are various other aspects of culture which influence psychological thinking just as philosophical doctrines do. These include technology and a myriad of myths and folklore, folkways, religious practices, and various other aspects of society, in which the cultural anthropologists specialize. These influence psychological as well as other theories in ways that are more subtle than the clear and direct influence coming from tenets of philosophy. It is not easy to identify all of the aspects of culture that may have direct or indirect influence on psychological thought. Adequate analysis of the relationship between psychological theories and the various aspects of culture is too large and difficult a task to undertake in the present study. The only sources of influence outside philosophical doctrines with which I shall be able to deal are the differences between Indian and Western cultures in their attitudes regarding man's relation to nature. We shall return to this topic shortly.

The Western and Indian traditions are so rich and so full of diverse and complex ideas that it is impossible to start an inquiry such as this without feeling overwhelmed. The situation is the same as that in the Malinowskian dilemma mentioned earlier: the range of cultural variation is so great that any generalization appears out of the question. Here we can seek inspiration from the anthropologists and, like Florence Kluckhohn (1953a), start with the assumption that the range of variation is not unlimited. It should be possible to identify common, "universal" issues all people must face, and the various cultures may be seen as adopting solutions within a relatively limited range of possibilities. In a way, our problem is relatively simpler than that of the anthropologists who try to deal with the folklore and folkways of hundreds of cultures around the world. In the present work, the focus is only on Indian and Western *theories of psychology* as they are influenced by the cultures of their origin, not on a broad range of patterns of behavior of people in innumerable cultures and all kinds of situations the anthropologists are hoping to explain. Perhaps we can make our task of examining the cultural themes of the Indian and Western traditions a little easier if we can identify issues wherein the interface of a psychological theory and its cultural milieu is likely to be very critical.

After a long period of pondering over this problem, I have come up with the following list of issues[1] which may be regarded as critical areas of cultural influence on psychological thought:

1. The assumption of the lawfulness of nature.
2. Assumptions or ontological propositions borrowed from philosophy.
3. Attitudes about the relation of man to nature.
4. Assumptions about human nature.
5. Assumptions about the human condition.
6. Values concerning the desirable human condition.

In formulating this list of issues, I am clearly influenced by Florence Kluckhohn's approach. In fact, this list is a variation of Kluckhohn's list (cited in the previous chapter) of basic human problems for which "all peoples at all times and in all places" must find a solution. As in the case of Kluckhohn's list of problems, it is a tentative list; these issues are not considered the only aspects in which culture influences psychological theory. I must acknowledge one more of Kluckhohn's ideas which I find useful. She has suggested that, in view of the interaction between cultures, such as the Spanish-speaking Americans versus the mainstream culture of the majority of the United States population, the degree of assimilation of any subculture with the mainstream will "in large part depend upon the degree and goodness of fit of the group's own basic value orientations with those of the dominant . . . culture" (Kluckhohn, 1953, p. 354). Following this hypothesis regarding the assimilation of one culture by another, I would suggest that, in an analogous manner, the degree to which any theories can be integrated into a broader, inclusive framework is the degree and goodness of fit of the basic assumptions and dominant values underlying the theories.

It must be clarified that the emphasis here is on the *dominant* values and assumptions of a given culture or world view. This means that a certain range of variation in values and beliefs held by persons (including theorists) in any society is taken for granted. In fact, some variation within the groups of theorists, such as behaviorists or Vedāntic psychologists, in their values and assumptions is also taken for granted. Such labels as "psychoanalysts" or "Indians" or "Western man" refer to groups of theorists or members of cultures who can be identified in terms of the dominant values or beliefs of their respective communities.

It is assumed that it is possible as well as reasonable to identify dominant values, assumptions, or themes in general, in small or large communities, although such identification necessarily involves very broad generalizations.

I would maintain that certain broad generalizations about shared beliefs, values, and themes considered dominant in vast populations are useful, and that they make sense even if they appear to be "sweeping" generalizations. For instance, it does make a good deal of sense if I say "the idea that God created man in His own image, and the myth of the Day of Judgment are themes common to Judaism, Christianity, and Islam, the three religions of Semitic origin that dominated Western civilization through millennia." It makes sense particularly when it is noted that this theme is *not* shared by hundreds of millions of people in the East who followed Hinduism, Jainism, and Buddhism, which are religions of Indian origin. Such a generalization stands irrespective of the fact that any number of individuals in the West may not have held these views. It also stands notwithstanding the fact that there have been Jewish, Christian, and Moslem minorities on the Indian subcontinent for centuries. Moreover, the opinions of such minorities have not influenced the psychological theories of Indian origin to any perceptible degree, and, as such, their presence may be neglected so far as our particular sociohistorical analysis is concerned.

No matter how defensible such generalizations about dominant themes in culture may be, one may still ask: Is the identification of such themes relevant to the understanding of psychological theories? And the answer is yes, they are relevant. As is patently known, the Darwinian revolution challenged the established Judeo-Christian myth of the genesis, and, as we saw earlier, the conflict between them has deeply influenced psychological theory in the West. However, the implication for psychological thinking of the myth of the Day of Judgment may not be so clear. This latter myth has provided for innumerable generations of Western men the hope that justice will finally be done, no matter how inequitable the social conditions may appear at any given time. This view implies, in turn, that there is order in the universe—in its moral realm, that is. It is arguable that such beliefs contribute to a view of the world as an orderly rather than a chaotic place, and that such a view of the world is a prerequisite for any scientific inquiry.

A comparison of the Indian tradition with that of the West with respect to beliefs on similar issues will further illustrate the utility of our approach. By contrast to Judaism, Christianity and Islam, the Eastern religions do not have any myth similar to that of the Day of Judgment. However, the Hindus, Buddhists and Jains share a view about orderliness in the moral realm, called the Law of Karma. The Law of Karma states that every man will inevitably face the consequences of his good deeds as well as his bad deeds. As you sow, so you reap. If the account is not settled by the end of the present life cycle, the balance will be carried forward to the next incarnation of the soul. Nobody waits until the day of judgment fixed by God's calendar; there is a continuous chain of the effects of karma or action which can be cut short as soon as a person attains knowledge of his real self. The concept of reincarnation has provided a sense of hope for Indians in the same way the concept of the Day of Judgment has for the Westerners. The Law of Karma has also provided the basic rationale for the social organization of the Hindus, namely the hierarchical structure of the caste system. The social status of members of "lower" castes has been explained as being the result of a person's own karma from his previous incarnation(s). Persons born into lower caste families were reconciled to their inferior position as long as the basic ideas were not questioned. The basis ideas as well as the hierarchical social structure remained in force for over two thousand years. Moreover, as we shall see in later chapters, the concept of karma, and the view of the inevitability of the consequences of karma has deeply influenced the psychological theories of India.

In the remainder of this chapter I shall attempt a similar comparison of the Indian and Western traditions of thought while focusing on the issues considered to be critical in studying the influence of culture on psychological theories. I shall start with the issue of the assumptions regarding lawfulness of the universe and then move to the other issues listed above.

Assumptions Regarding the Lawfulness of the Universe

Any systematic inquiry must begin with the fundamental assumption that the universe is a cosmos and not chaos. Unless one is convinced that events in the universe are lawful, one would not bother to study nature. Before such an assumption is generally accepted, events are ascribed to the capricious wishes of deities, demons, or to any variety of animistic and magical forces. Animistic thinking characterizes the first step in the development of civilization.[2] Both the Western and Indian civilizations passed this stage at least two thousand years ago. The Roman philosopher Lucretius (*ca.* 99–55 B.C.) was convinced of the uniform operation of universal laws without interference from any deities (Jones, 1969, Vol. 1, p. 80). Several centuries before Christ the Upaniṣadic philosophers had conceived of a universal principle which regulates such natural phenomena as day and night, seasons and rivers. Although the general assumption of uniformity and lawfulness of nature has been widely recognized for a long time, it has been interpreted differently and has undergone different courses of history in the West as compared to India.

Men have sought lawfulness in the mental and moral, as well as the physical world. The Greek atomist thinkers postulated orderliness in the physical world. Lucretius, who followed the Greek atomists, insisted that God could not have created the universe out of nothing, nor could he interfere with the operation of universal laws. This spirit of firm belief in the orderliness of nature continues until today. It is a gut-level conviction about the operation of universal laws that was reflected in Einstein's famous quip: "The Lord God does not throw dice." Einstein's belief in the intelligibility of phenomena was so strong that he was never willing to accept the idea that chance plays a fundamental role in the scheme of things, as the persuasive arguments of Niels Bohr and other quantum theorists had tried to show with the help of the laws of probability.[3]

In Western civilization the place of God in relation to the law of nature has been a controversial issue. In the Judeo-Christian view, God created the world out of nothing, and, as such, He stands over and above the laws of physical nature and so may interfere with the operation of the physical world. He can, for instance, bestow supernatural powers on saints, who are citizens of His Kingdom. However, He is supposed to guarantee order in the moral realm. On the Day of Judgment, He rewards those who have obeyed His commandments and punishes those who have disobeyed.

Unlike their Greek predecessors, the Christians were mainly interested in the moral order of the universe. Saint Augustine (354–430 A.D.) was critical of the Greeks, who tried to discover the hidden laws of nature and were even able to foretell the eclipses of the sun and the moon. He dismissed their pride in their knowledge of nature as "impious" (Jones, 1969, Vol. 2, p. 132). After all, God had himself condemned Adam for eating the fruit of the tree of knowledge! The conflict between understanding nature and science on the one side, and religion and morals on the other, is indeed deeply rooted in the history of Western culture.

As indicated in the previous chapter, the Indian tradition contrasts sharply in this respect. No one has ever been persecuted for trying to discover the laws of the physical, mental or moral world. Although theists and atheists have engaged in controversies regarding the place of God in the creation of the universe, they have been unanimous in assuming that the universe is lawful. It is true that the pantheistic Hindu tradition allows for the worship of as many deities as anyone can imagine; in the folk religion any odd tree or rock may be assumed to possess magical powers. But the tolerance of such beliefs among the masses does not imply their acceptance in philosophical inquiry. The plethora of Vedic deities was replaced by a single abstract principle (commonly called Brahman) by the early Upaniṣads, and Buddha dismissed the concept of God altogether. Almost all schools of philosophy, theists and atheists, Hindus, Buddhists, as well as Jains, accepted the concept of karma and developed theories about it. Most of these theories recognize the rule of law not only in nature, but also in the world of the mind and morals. The universe is assumed to be lawful to the core. For the theists, God is not someone who grants mokṣa, or liberation, at will, or keeps you waiting until the Day of Judgment. He is only a supervisor of the Law of Karma (karmādhyakṣa). Karma is a sovereign principle and refers to an ongoing natural process. (Radhakrishnan, 1926/1969, pp. 52–53)

The fact that the Western as well as Indian traditions have accepted the fundamental assumption of the lawfulness of the universe serves as an important base for the convergence of their psychological theories. But the sharp separation of the material sphere from the moral sphere in the Western way of thinking, and their implicit continuity in the Indian theories, poses a difficult problem in the attempt to integrate Indian psychological concepts with those of the West. The concept of karma literally means actions, taken in a mechanical as well as a moral sense. The theory of karma implies that human behavior is lawful in every way. It is controlled by laws of physical nature which nobody can violate; each action is systematically related to the individual's entire past; and finally, in a moral sense, no one can escape experiences of joy or suffering as the fruits or consequences of his own past action. Such a view of human experience and behavior forms the very basis of the psychological theories of India. This contrasts sharply with Western theories. As noted in the previous chapter, the long history of conflict between science and religion has led to a strict separation of moral considerations from scientific inquiry. Science, we are told, must restrict itself to the field of facts, to whatever there *is*, and leave the issue of what *ought* to be to the nonscientist.[4]

Whether or not the assumption of moral order or ultimate establishment of justice is valid is not the issue here. This assumption is not a testable proposition, and, as such, we need not examine its validity. The issue relevant to our purpose relates to the difficulties in convergence of psychological perspectives of India and the West that arise from the strictly nonevaluative or "objective" view of behavior adopted by most Western theories. It is a complex issue which cannot be adequately discussed within the limited scope of this book. It may simply be noted at this point that the Indian psychological theories are inseparable from the spiritual goals the theorists set out to pursue. Even brief accounts of Indian concepts often lead us to the values and ethical issues that legitimize their goals. The convergence of Indian concepts with Western theories becomes problematic because several Western theories tend to meticulously avoid ethical issues in general and spiritual considerations in particular.

Assumptions about the Nature of Reality: Ontological Presuppositions

All psychological theories are based on presuppositions about the nature of reality borrowed from ontological theories of one of the schools of philosophy. The philosophical roots of modern Western theories are in Descartes' dualistic theory. As mentioned in the previous chapter, René Descartes (1596–1650), caught in the conflicting world views of Christian dogma and the newly emerging natural science of Copernicus and Galileo, proposed that there are two types of substances: matter or corporeal substance that has extension in length, breadth and depth, and the soul, which is unextended substance. He held that human beings have a soul or mind (both together called *l'ame* in French) as well as a body made of material substance, and that the two substances interact with each other. Animals, he contended, have no souls; they are simply automata governed by the laws of physics. Descartes considered the human body to be a machine which obeys the laws of physics just as animal bodies do. The soul, which perceives and wills, is not made of material substance and so is free from laws that govern the material world (see Boring, 1950, pp. 160–165).

The Cartesian theory of mind–body dualism has set the tone for the development of various systems of psychology in the West. Philosophers have proposed various solutions to the mind–body problem, ranging from the materialistic monism of Haeckel (which asserts that everything that exists, including "mental" phenomena, can be reduced to matter) to the spiritual monism of Berkeley which recognizes no material substance. Then again there are dualistic theories that accept the duality of body and mind, and suggest specific ways in which the two are related. For example, there is Spinoza's psychophysical parallelism, which accepts the duality of mind and body but rejects their interaction, and there is Russell's double-aspect view, which rejects the theory of two substances but accepts material and mental domains as two *aspects* of the same underlying reality. Modern psychologists have explicitly, or at least implicitly, adopted some such philosophical position on the mind–body problem. Most behaviorists, for instance, have implicitly adopted materialistic monism; and psychophysiologists who have used electroencephalographic or other bodily measures to study Yogic phenomena seem to have implicitly adopted either psychophysical parallelism or the mind–body identity theory. (We shall examine the psychophysiological studies of Yoga in Chapter 3.) The importance of the mind–body problem is such that it is virtually impossible to make sense of the differences between the major systems of modern psychology without knowing their positions on this issue. We shall examine the psychological implications of certain positions on the mind–body issue in the following chapters.

Psychological thought in India has also developed in the context of monistic and dualistic metaphysical theories. The Sāṅkhya philosophy, for instance, is dualistic, and the Advaita branch of the Vedānta school is non-dualistic. There are certain similarities between Cartesian and Sāṅkhya dualism. Descartes, for instance, contrasts the free souls with the determinist material world and, similarly, the Sāṅkhya system contrasts the free Puruṣa or soul with Prakṛti or the material world to which the body belongs. Here I must hasten to add that, despite such apparent similarities, the form and content of the two dualist doctrines are very different, as are their psychological implications.

Although it is not possible to offer a detailed outline of the Indian philosophical doctrines, a brief, rough sketch is in order at this point. This is particularly important insofar as Yoga, the comprehensive system of psychological thought in India, developed against the background of the metaphysical dualism of the Sāṅkhya philosophy, just as Western psychology developed against the background of Cartesian dualism.

According to the Sāṅkhya philosophy, Prakṛti is the uncaused, eternal and pervading principle of the universe. It is the substance of which all things are just different configurations; it accounts for the continual flux of the world wherein things grow and decay. Space and time are specific modifications of Prakṛti. This principle has three invariable components of intertwining "strands" called guṇas. *Sattva* represents whatever is fine, light, luminous; *tamas*, whatever is course, heavy, dark; and *rajas* represents activity. Although each guṇa must be present at all times in anything that exists in the world of Prakṛti, one may dominate the other when their equilibrium is disturbed. When things are at rest, tamas predominates; rajas is predominant in moving things while the other two guṇas remain latent. A person experiences happiness when sattva is dominant, and he may be involved in feverish, restless effort when rajas takes over.

Puruṣa is the principle that represents immutable, ever-present light, the inactive and nonparticipating witness of the incessant flux of Prakṛti. There are many Puruṣas, one associated with everything that has life in it. All Puruṣas are identical in nature, none being limited by size or other qualities of the being in which it resides.[5]

Certain similarities as well as differences between Cartesian and Sāṅkhya dualism may be apparent from the above descriptions. Both Cartesian matter and Sāṅkhya Prakṛti represent the corporeal, tangible substance of which human bodies and other objects are made, but the three Cartesian orthogonal dimensions (of length, breadth, and depth) are far different from the Sāṅkhya guṇas. While Descartes ascribes such psychic activities as willing and feeling to the nonmaterial domain, the Sāṅkhya theory ascribes them to the material Prakṛti and not to Puruṣa, which is only a passive witness. For Descartes, animals do not possess souls, but the Sāṅkhya view ascribes a Puruṣa to each one of the living beings, non-human as well as human. This view illustrates the pan-Indian assumption of continuity within the entire animal kingdom.[6]

Both Sāṅkhya and Cartesian principles arise from metaphysical speculation. Let me make it clear that our purpose here is not to judge their value or relative superiority as metaphysical explanations. They are important for our purpose of comparing psychological theories because they have become the starting points for several generations of psychologists in India and the West. Each generation benefitted from earlier work in its own cultural tradition. The legacy of theoretical advances, when combined with different themes borrowed from the respective cultural trends, has led to vastly different formulations of certain common psychological issues. Most major Western and Indian views about the nature of consciousness, for instance, are based on assumptions derived from the Cartesian and Sāṅkhya forms of dualism, and we shall discuss them at length in Chapters 3 and 4, respectively.

Man's Relation to Nature

Assumptions relating to the lawfulness of nature and ontological presuppositions underlying psychological theories are often explicitly stated and are reasonably well known among psychologists. Discussion of the assumption of lawfulness of events, for instance, is commonplace in textbooks of psychology, and most books on the history and systems of Western psychology discuss the mind–body issue. The themes discussed in the subsequent sections are usually much less explicit when compared with assumptions concerning the lawfulness of nature and the philosophical assumptions discussed earlier. Psychologists like Bakan (1965) and Buss (1975), who adopt, either implicitly or explicitly, a sociology-of-knowledge viewpoint, have drawn our attention to the cultural themes and values implicit in psychological theories. Bakan has pointed out, for instance, that the "Protestant ethic" has been associated with the thrust in the Western countries to master the world through science and industry. He has further claimed that this thrust, as manifest in the American way of life, has resulted in creating a "mastery complex" (or an obsessive concern with prediction and *control* of human behavior) and has interfered with proper understanding of human nature. I think that Bakan is quite right in pointing out this relationship between American psychological themes and their cultural background. He has shown great insight in noting the systematic relationship between the cultural themes like "man in relation to nature" on the one hand and certain characteristics of psychological theory on the other. I propose to follow Bakan's lead and go a step further. I suggest that it would be useful to examine the nature of the influence of such cultural themes on psychological theories in a broader perspective of cross-cultural comparison. Here the psychologist can benefit from anthropologists, who have tried to identify major themes in cultures on the basis of comparative analysis of a broad range of cultures across the globe. As mentioned earlier, I use Florence Kluckhohn's (1953) essay entitled "Dominant and Variant Value Orientations" as my starting point.

Kluckhohn has suggested the following three major variations in the man–nature relationship: Man Subjected to Nature, Man In Nature, and Man Over Nature. She has identified the Anglo-American culture as typifying the Man Over Nature attitude and contrasted it to the Man Subjected to Nature attitude of the typical Spanish-American sheepraisers, who have a fatalistic attitude toward storm, drought, and illness, seeing those as being God's will. It appears that the Anglo-American attitude of "Man Over Nature" became particularly strong during the Age of Reason or the period of Enlightenment that dominated European thinkers toward the end of the 18th century. Newtonian physics gave confidence in the uniformity of nature, and the knowledge of the laws of motion enabled scientists to harness natural forces for human use. The Industrial Revolution brought the early fruits of prosperity and promised much more from the future development of science and industry.

Natural science and the technology based on its discoveries have come a long way since their beginnings in Europe's Age of Reason. The taming of nature seemed to promise endless power, growth, and glory until the ominous effects of atomic power began to raise questions about the Man Over Nature attitude. By the 1970s the destructive effects of the exploitation of nature, ranging from urban industrial pollution, the depletion of natural resources, and the impending doom of nuclear holocaust, have led to searching criticism of the Man Over Nature attitude. This issue, too, is too well known to need elaboration.

When we speak of the Man Over Nature attitude of the Anglo-American culture, we speak of an ideal-typical mode of man's being in the world, which manifests itself not only in building dams on the rivers, highways on the mountains, and satellites in space, but a lot more. It also implies the attitude that man can and should gather material and energy resources from all over the world, and perhaps even from the moon. If the weather is cold, one should not simply wear warm clothing or sit next to a small hearth burning wood, but rather heat the entire home and insulate all the walls, no matter how much it takes in terms of materials, energy and human effort to accomplish this. What is of particular interest to us is that this type of attitude is now so pervasive that it influences the way the psychologist does his research and how he conceives his subject matter. Note, for instance, that the typical American way of studying animals is to study them in cages, where they are placed in man-made, artificial environments. (Many laboratories are air-conditioned, and the animals use slot machines to obtain their food, just as their masters do.) Contrast this approach to the ethological approach in which animals are studied in their natural habitats where they eat, mate, raise their offspring, or migrate as they have always done. Time and again the question has been asked whether the principles of psychology based on laboratory observations can be used to understand the problems of organisms in nature. Without going into this controversial issue, it may simply be noted that the thrust of some arguments of the apologists of laboratory studies is that, at least in principle, the whole of nature can be mastered to create controlled conditions, just as in the laboratory. If the laboratory can be extended to the world, why worry about problems of extending the laboratory findings to the real world?

Certainly there have been advocates of the study of Man In Nature among Western psychologists. It is also true that there is a trend in the West, which is opposed to the Man Over Nature attitude. Poets like Wordsworth and Keats, for example, extolled the glory of nature; the return to nature was a basic theme of the Romantic movement of late 18th century Europe. In the United States, Henry David Thoreau (1817–1862) was a naturalist who despised the tools of technology. He thought that "modern improvements" such as the telegraph and the railways were improved means to unimproved ends. For some time he left urban industrial living and chose to live in a handcrafted log cabin close to nature. He wrote his famous *Walden, or Life in the Woods* to express his views regarding life and nature (Thoreau, 1854/1970). It is obvious, however, that neither the beautiful poetry of the Romantic poets nor the equally beautiful prose of Thoreau could convert the majority of Western men. The dominant theme of the civilization of the modern West has been Man Over Nature.

The influence of this dominant view of psychological thinking is quite clear. It is clearest in behavioristic psychology which aims at prediction and control of behavior, just as the natural sciences aim at prediction and control of all sorts of natural phenomena. It appears that B. F. Skinner was so inspired by Thoreau's experiment of living in the woods that he named his utopian novel *Walden Two* after Thoreau's book mentioned above. Yet, among the principles of the original *Walden* that are conspicuously omitted in its Skinnerian version is the love of nature. It is indeed a paradox verging on satire that Skinner is the arch-technologist of psychology. He has invented tools such as the "Skinner box" to experiment with laboratory animals, as well as the concept of "teaching machines" for the classroom. Perhaps Skinner did not care much for Thoreau's view that the ends were more important than the tools. While Thoreau wanted to leave the gadgets and tools behind so as to be free to live in harmony and close contact with nature, Skinner is concerned with converting the entire society into a testing ground of the new behavioral technology!

The attitude of Man Over Nature implies a man in conflict with his environment. The image of man which consonant with this view is the image of a man who stands apart from his environment, not of one who is willing to be part of something greater than himself. It makes sense that two of the major systems of modern psychology, namely psychoanalysis and behaviorism, involve views of man which share these characteristics. As is well known, Freud saw man as continually involved in conflict with his environment—both material and social. Of particular concern to the behaviorists is the adaptation to and mastery of the environment, which is usually considered inimical to the organism. To say the least, the behaviorist view of man seems to imply some kind of a barrier that separates man from his environment. Some versions of the behaviorist model are rightly described as an input–output model, implying that whatever comes in or goes out must cross a "boundary." Allport (1960) complained that many contemporary Western theories of psychology conceptualized personality as something "integumented," more like a "closed system" than an "open system."

While it is easy to identify the typical Anglo-American attitude toward nature, it is not so easy to say which is the most typical Indian attitude toward nature. On the one hand it may appear that for long the Indian people have allowed themselves to be subjugated by floods, famines, locusts, epidemics and other such natural calamities. On the other hand, it is also true that the Indians have built bridges, dammed rivers, have developed an elaborate and sophisticated system of medicine—which are obviously attempts to master natural forces. It may also be noted in this regard that the Indian folklore idealizes those who have conquered nature. Rāma, the hero of the epic Rāmāyana, for instance, is said to have built a bridge to Sri Lanka, and the mythical Bhagīratha is idealized for having diverted the river Ganges from heaven to earth (or was it from Tibet to India?). Notwithstanding these mutually contradictory aspects of the Indian culture, the most typical Indian attitude toward nature is neither Man Subjugated to Nature, nor Man Over Nature. Moreover, it makes some sense to consider Man In Nature as the most typical Indian attitude. It is reflected in a number of different aspects of the Indian culture. For well over two millennia the Indian life style was mainly agrarian/rural; the peasant and the artisan lived closely bound to the seasons and the flora and fauna of the region. The Indians seemed to feel close to the animals; the cow was almost a member of the family. Many odd trees and animals such as the mouse and monkey, snake, tiger, and so on are associated with one or the other deity of the pantheon, and, as such, are respected and even worshipped. Respect for all varieties of life is an aspect of the same basic theme. The same attitude to nature is reflected in the psychology of Yoga. The typical yogi aspires to live in the deep forests of the Himalayas in harmony with nature. Neither the chilling cold of the mountains nor the roaming beasts of the jungle threaten him. The legendary yogi Cāṅgadeva (of the 13th century) was said to ride a tiger from place to place. What the legend reflects is not so much the taming of the beast but winning him over, which is considered possible because, as the theory goes, man and animal are ultimately manifestations of the same ubiquitous principle. Here again the issue is not the truth of the legend but the attitude it reflects. We can see the contrast between this attitude and that of the behaviorist who aims at controlling animal behavior just as the technologist harnesses the forces of nature.

The difference between the Indian and Western cultures in their typical attitudes toward nature has led to far-reaching consequences with regard to the nature of their psychological theories. The attitudes toward nature influence both the overall direction of psychological inquiry and the implicit view of man. The Man Over Nature attitude leads to a separation of the psychologist from the environment; the psychologist stands apart, over, and above his subject matter; he views the 'problems' as being 'out there' and not within him. Human nature, insofar as it is the subject matter of his inquiry, is part of the world outside him. It is the other people whose behavior interests him, not his own. We shall see later that the focus on "the other" is buttressed by other considerations as well. We must wait until we discuss these other considerations to be able to appreciate the significance of the focus on other people to the exclusion of oneself. Most Indian psychologies singularly lack this "external" orientation that dominates Western perspectives in psychology, notably the behavioristic one. For the Indian psychologist the problems are not the ways of adapting to or conquering the environment. He takes for granted a certain degree of stability in man's relationship with nature in the form of the ecological niche carved out by the agrarian/rural way of life that works in a reasonable harmony with nature. His main concern is to come to terms with himself, to discover the nature within himself and not the outside world; his orientation is primarily "internal," not "external."

Assumptions about Human Nature

Contemporary psychologists generally tend to avoid any discussion of "human nature." Such an attitude is quite understandable as speculation and sweeping generalizations asserting that human nature is such-and-such has led us nowhere in the past. Notwithstanding such hesitations, however, it remains that broad generalizations about human nature often form the very basis on which entire psychological theories are based. The psychologist's refusal to discuss such broad generalizations sometimes means that he has taken a set of certain generalizations as fundamental principles or axiomatic truths whose validity is not questioned. One of the most central and common implicit principles of this nature is the assumption that man seeks pleasure and avoids pain.

The origin in Western thought of the idea that men always seek pleasure and avoid pain is very old. One of its earliest proponents was the Greek philosopher Epicurus (341–270 B.C.). The credit for more systematic formulation of this principle, called psychological hedonism, goes to Jeremy Bentham (1748–1842), who maintained that pain and pleasure are our "sovereign masters" (Bentham, 1789/1948, p. 1). Starting with this assumption, he developed his "hedonistic calculus," aimed at measuring the degree of pleasure and pain. He also tried to establish the basic dimensions or qualities of pleasure and pain, such as intensity, duration, certainty, proximity, and the like. The other qualities of pleasure include fecundity or productiveness, which means that they are likely to be followed by other pleasures, and purity, which refers to the kind of pleasures that are not likely to produce pain as a consequence of their enjoyment.

Gordon W. Allport (1968) has pointed out how Bentham's ideas influenced later thinking in Western philosophy, economics, and, more particularly, psychology. John Stuart Mill (1806–1873) developed the Principle of Utility (which is Bentham's name for the hedonistic doctrine) into the utilitarian principles of ethics (greatest good of the greatest number) and the political philosophy of the individualistic *"laissez-faire"* system. The doctrine of "economic man" (one who is supposed to be guided by the profit motive) obviously involves a hedonistic assumption. Further, Herbert Spencer (1820–1903) linked hedonism with Darwinian evolution. He pointed out that pleasurable activities are largely those that help survival of the individual or the species—eating and sex, for instance—while pain is associated with danger and death.

Freud considered pleasure-seeking the main characteristic of men who are motivated by the instinctual energy called the libido. In his theory this force was symbolized by Eros, the Greek god of love. Toward the end of the 19th century, Thorndike (1898) enunciated the "Law of Effect," which is often considered the basic law of learning. According to this law, the responses that result in pleasure are "stamped in" and those resulting in pain are "stamped out." Half-a-century later, Dollard and Miller (1950, p. 9) found unacceptable Freud's open acceptance of the experience of pleasure as a principle that guides behavior as well as Thorndike's implicit reference to the conscious experience of pleasure and pain. The reason for such a reaction was the taboo on the study of consciousness acquired by American psychology as a result of the failure of the method of introspection in studying the nature of consciousness. (I shall have more to say on this issue in the next chapter.) At any rate, Dollard and Miller clearly stated that in their theory, "The principle of reinforcement has been substituted for Freud's pleasure principle." Modern learning theory, including its Skinnerian formulation, still involves the basic hedonistic principle, although most learning theorists meticulously avoid any reference to the "mentalistic" notions of pleasure and pain. Again, as noted by Allport, the principle of tension reduction, which is central to Lewinian Field Theory and other systems of Western psychology, is also a variation of the same, hedonistic principle.

Man's passion for pleasure and aversion to pain has been recognized as much in the Indian tradition as in the West. Patañjali makes specific reference to these in two of his aphorisms (2.7–8). Tilak (1915/1956, Ch. 5) has asserted that most Indian thinkers have accepted the thesis that human beings always try to maximize pleasure and minimize pain. It appears that the assumption that humans pursue pleasure is a feature common to Western and Indian thought, as is the assumption that the universe is lawful, which we noted earlier.

Considerable attention has been given in the Indian tradition to the analysis of types and qualities of pleasure. The *Bhagavad-Gītā* (18,36–39), for instance, distinguishes between the pleasures that are followed by pain and vice-versa, somewhat like Bentham's distinction between pure and impure pleasures. However, the similarity between the Western and Indian trends nearly ends at this point. The *Gītā* bases its analysis of qualities of pleasure and pain on the Sāṅkhya theory of three guṇas, namely, sattva, rajas, and tamas, which were described earlier. Further, there is a considerable difference between the Western and Indian concepts of happiness, as distinguished from pleasure. We shall discuss this difference in a separate section toward the end of this chapter, which is devoted to ideas about the most desirable states of man.

From a psychological point of view, we need to note an important difference between the Western and Indian psychologies which is related to the common assumption of the pleasure-seeking tendency of human beings. Despite the central place offered to pleasure-seeking and pain-avoidance in the behaviorist and psychoanalytical theories, there is no focus on the human being as an *enjoyer* of pleasure and a *sufferer* from pain. As a matter of fact, the terms enjoyer and sufferer sound artificial and awkward, as they are seldom used in the English language. By contrast, the common Sanskrit word bhoktṛ connotes man as both enjoyer and sufferer. The view of man as the experiencer of pleasure or pain, happiness or misery, health or sickness, of good luck or misfortune, is of *central importance* to the Indian psychologies. The concept of man as "doer," that is, as agent of action, is called kartṛ and is inextricably related to the concept of man as the experiencer of the consequences of his actions, pleasurable or painful. I am not here referring to simple terminological differences but to important differences in the views of man. I realize that the distinction is subtle, and its significance may not be readily understood at this time, nor can it be explained in detail at this point. Hopefully the significance will become apparent as we go along.

The Assumption of Egoism and the Value of Individualism

At this point let me return to the assumption of pleasure-seeking from a slightly different point of view. As pointed out by Allport (1968, p. 15), ". . . hedonism is a doctrine of self-centredness. A person who seeks pleasure and avoids pain is inevitably serving his own affective interest." Thomas Hobbes (1588–1679) recognized the human pursuit of pleasure as the other hedonists did, but he placed even greater emphasis on egoism. He asserted in his celebrated work, *Leviathan:* "So that in the first place, I put for a general inclination for all mankind a perpetual and restlesse desire of Power after power that ceaseth only in Death" (Hobbes, 1651/1962, p. 75). Further, he suggested that the pursuit of power would lead to a perpetual state of warfare, with each man pitted against each other man (his occasional inclination for peace arising only from his fear of death). (See Hobbes, 1651/1962, p. 98.) But since life would be impossible if each individual fought continuously for his selfish goals, men accept a higher power of the state, which Hobbes called the Leviathan.

The assumption of the egoistic nature of human beings is congenial with an individualistic social philosophy. John Stuart Mill (1806–1873) accepted Bentham's assumption that humans pursue pleasure, and went ahead to build a theory of morality that justifies the pursuit of pleasure. However, Mill tempered the individualism of Hobbes by emphasizing that the quantity of pleasure measured by the "greatest good of the greatest number of people" should be the moral goal of society. Yet, individualism was extolled as a virtue, and Mill's essay *On Liberty* (1859/1962) became the manifesto of libertarian political ideology. This ideology implicitly sanctions unmitigated self-indulgence. Such advocacy contradicts the Christian value of self-denial, which has also been a dominant value in the Western world. Indeed, Mill himself has criticized the Calvinist prescription of an ascetic life as "insidious" and even as a "cramped and dwarfed" view of human beings (Mill, 1859/1962, p. 191).

Notwithstanding this contradiction between the individualist philosophy and the Christian ideals, it is a fact that Protestantism paradoxically sanctioned the amassing of wealth (see Bakan, 1966, p. 17). Ascetic denial of present enjoyment was prescribed mainly as a means of assuring possession of worldly goods for future pleasure. According to the widely acclaimed thesis of Max Weber (1904–5/1958), the Puritan principle of asceticism among the Protestant sects formed the very basis for the formation of capital in the free-enterprise economy of the Western world.

We may distinguish between two types of individualism: the first, called descriptive or theoretical individualism, refers to the axiomatic assumption which suggests that men are selfish by nature; and the second, often called prescriptive individualism, refers to an ideology which condones or sanctions egoistic striving. The two types of individualism are conceptually distinguishable, but they are often mixed and intertwined, since they usually supplement and support each other. Nietzsche (1844–1900), for instance, assumed the will to power as a fundamental principle of nature, and also admired "supermen" or strong-willed and powerful people such as Alexander the Great, Napoleon and others. He even advocated rule by such people. There is a third, romantic or mystical type of individualism that should be distinguished from the theoretical individualism and egoistic ideology mentioned above. This type of individualism does not seek power, as does the Nietzschean brand. It essentially asks that the individual be left alone by society to develop and behave the way he pleases. Rousseau (1712–1778) is a well-known advocate of romantic individualism. He believed that the child would develop into a healthy, moral and mature person if simply left alone, since he considered social influence to be mostly negative, malignant, and unnecessary. The existential philosopher and mystic Martin Buber (1947/1965) also considers the social environment of the modern man uncongenial and even oppressive. Like Rousseau, he is disenchanted with the social effects of industrialization and advocates that people be left alone. His style of individualism is particularly concerned with having to face the existential vacuum of the alienated man of modern society.

Western psychology developed under the influence of the individualistic assumptions and values mentioned above. Nietzsche's ideas, for instance, directly influenced the psychoanalyst Alfred Adler. As is well known, Adler disagreed with his teacher and associate, Sigmund Freud, regarding the place of sexual drive in the human make-up. In the introduction to his book entitled *The Neurotic Constitution,* Adler wrote: "This formula: 'I wish to be a complete man' is the guiding fiction in every neurosis. . . . The libido, the sex-impulses and the tendencies to sexual perversions arrange themselves in accordance with this guiding principle, no matter whence they originate. Nietzsche's 'Will to power' and 'Will to seem' embrace many of our views . . . the sensation of pleasure originates in a feeling of power, that of pain in a feeling of feebleness *(Ohnmacht)*" (Adler, 1926/1972, p. ix: It seems to me that emphasis on will to power is quite characteristic of Adler's writings although he seems to have changed in this respect later on). Allport (1968, p. 17) has rightly pointed out that, although most present-day psychologists avoid a unitary conceptualization like Adler's sovereign motive for power, many in fact lay heavy emphasis on the same. Such emphasis is reflected in the importance of self-esteem in their conceptualization.

It makes sense to conclude that a psychology based on the assumption of a basic human drive for power would emphasize self-esteem. As we saw earlier, Hobbes, who conceived of a sovereign motive for power, pictured the society as a battlefield where everybody is fighting against everyone else. To put it mildly, everyone is involved in the game of one-upmanship. Festinger (1954) has proposed a "social comparison theory," starting with the assumption that people continually compare themselves with similar others around them. Feelings of inferiority or superiority are products of such continual comparisons. Carl Rogers (1959) has considered self-esteem the most critical variable determining mental health. Rogers's view is similar to Adler's in considering lack of adequate self-esteem or feelings of inferiority as a main cause of neurosis. The role of the therapist, then, is to help the client reconcile his unsatisfactory self-image with his "ideal" self. As we shall soon see, the view of Indian psychology on this issue is quite different.

It must be admitted that all psychologists who have emphasized the role of self-esteem in their theories of personality do not assume a sovereign motive for power as Hobbes or Nietzsche did. The more commonly accepted concept is that of self-actualization, which is regarded as a master motive (Goldstein, 1939/1963; Maslow, 1970; Rogers, 1959).

Self-actualization as conceptualized by these psychologists does not imply precisely the same kind of ruthless pursuit of narrowly selfish goals at the cost of others as was implied by Hobbes and Nietzsche. Yet, it has usually meant the actualization of one's *potential,* that is, particular *abilities* which are initially latent, but manifest in success or accomplishment in one or another type of worldly pursuit. In Goldstein's view, self-actualization particularly involves overcoming "the disturbance arising from the clash with the world," and includes the "joy of conquest" (Goldstein, 1939/1963, p. 305). Maslow's view of self-actualization, however, is humanistic and existential rather than pragmatic and Draconian. Among the group of people he studied as typically self-actualizing persons was Henry David Thoreau (1817–1862) who did not believe in using power and amassing material possessions. Nonetheless, Thoreau is an exception to Maslow's list, the majority of whom were neither saints nor "drop-outs" from competitive society, but were highly accomplished in art (*e.g.* Beethoven), science (Einstein), or politics (Lincoln, Jefferson). Maslow even claims that most of his self-actualized persons had mystical or spiritual experiences (although not necessarily religious in character). I must hasten to note at this point that the meaning and significance of what Maslow calls mystical and spiritual experience is quite different from the meaning and significance of samādhi and other mystical experiences Patañjali has described. Maslow's view of self-actualization is clearly influenced by the dominant Western (or more typically American) model of individualism.

The nature of egoistic individualism in American psychology is characterized, among other things, by the negative valuation given to those who turn out to be powerless in face of pressure of groups to conform or of the demands from a commanding authority. Asch (1952), for instance, tried to show that yielding to group pressure often leads to distortion in perception. Crutchfield (1955) described the compliant individual as lacking in ego strength and leadership qualities, low in intelligence, and as generally having other undesirable qualities. Milgram's (1963) well-known studies of obedience demonstrated how a person who complies with the apparently legitimate demands of conventional authority may violate important moral norms and lose his personal integrity. (Milgram's subjects did not mind giving high-voltage shocks to the experimenter's accomplice, although they sincerely believed that the latter was in great pain.) The issue is not the theoretical importance or methodological ingenuity of these experiments, which is indeed beyond question. The point is that conformity and obedience are consistently viewed in a negative light, and the value of individualism is implicitly extolled. It is not difficult to find other instances of the high value of egoistic individualism in American psychology (see Hogan, 1975).

The limitations of psychological theories that assume a universal drive for power or attach importance to egoistic striving has been particularly noticed in the field of social psychology. Dennis Krebs (1970) has noted in his review of the literature on altruism that the grand theories of human nature such as psychoanalytic and reinforcement theories, which assume a basically selfish character in man, have been challenged by the recent studies of self-sacrificial behavior. It is beginning to be realized that altruistic behavior is as much a part of human nature as selfish or egoistic behavior. D. T. Campbell (1965) has argued that the "overly individualistic assumption" about human motivation common to modern learning theory, Lewinian topology, cognitive congruity theory, as well as psychoanalysis, is unable to explain the individual willingness to fight and die for his own group. Says Campbell (1965, p. 306): "Altruism and self-seeking can coexist just as do exploratory curiosity and fear of the novel."

Campbell (1965) has considered his paper on altruistic motives as being different form his previous style of thinking in social psychology, which was dominated by Hullian reinforcement theory. In a tone of self-directed protest, he criticizes the individualistic assumption of human motivation as "skin-surface hedonism." Campbell is a late convert to the assumption of coexisting drives of self-seeking and self-surrender, in comparison to others like Angyal (1941), who had earlier proposed the coexistence in human beings of two mutually opposite motivational forces, a self-seeking drive which he called *autonomy* and its opposite, a tendency to surrender willingly to something larger, or a superordinate whole (such as a group), which he called *homonomy*. In the same vein, David Bakan (1966, pp. 14–15) has proposed the coexistence of two opposite "fundamental modalities of existence." The first, called *agency*, manifests itself in "isolation, alienation and aloneness," in the urge to master, as well as in "self-assertion, self-protection, and self-expansion." The second, called *communion*, manifests itself in one's urge to seek union with, or be part of, something larger than the limited field within which the individual tends to isolate himself under the influence of the agency principle.

After this rather long discussion of the individualist orientation common in Western psychology, let me now turn to an examination of how the Indian thinkers have dealt with the same issue.

Patañjali has assumed a basic sense of egoism (asmitā) common among men (2.6). He also recognizes a natural urge for self-preservation (abhiniveśa) among all living creatures (2.9). Since most Indian thinkers accept the principle of transmigration of the soul, it is believed that the craving for preservation of oneself arises from a fear of the death, which ended the individual's previous incarnation. (See Woods, 1914/1972, p. 117.) Also, since the cycle of birth, death, and rebirth is supposed to continue on and on until the individual attains liberation (mokṣa, nirvāṇa), the will to survive is ceaseless, and so is the fear of death. A wise man who understands the principle of rebirth need not be afraid of death since he will be reborn anyway. Yet, says Patañjali, even wise men are not free from the craving for self-preservation, so deep-rooted is the urge for self-preservation. The issue here is not the validity of the doctrine of rebirth. The point is that Indian psychology, too, assumes a basic sense of egoism among men and a universal urge for self-preservation.

It would be useful to compare the Indian and Western views of egoism at this point. It appears that Patañjali's concept of *abhiniveśa* or the drive for self-preservation is somewhat similar to the Darwinian notion of the instinct for survival. The Darwinian as well as Indian types of theories are usually faced with the observation of the coexistence of selfish and self-sacrificial, or dominating and submissive tendencies. Milgram (1974), who adopts a Darwinian perspective, has suggested, for instance, that when two autonomous organisms face each other, one of them must cede control to the other—or else both would tend to control or even annihilate the other. Such struggle for individual survival would ultimately be harmful for the survival of the species as a whole.

To protect the species, nature has built reflexive empathic reactions into the biological make-up of the organism, just as reflexive aggression is built in the interest of the individual member's survival. The Indian thinkers have tried to explain the paradoxical coexistence of self-seeking and altruism in a different manner, as we shall see shortly. The individualistic urge for survival (Patañjali's "abhiniveśa") is a result of the experiencing individual's primordial ignorance of his true nature, which is eternal and not ephemeral as the species–specific existence makes it appear. As such, Patañjali lists egoism (asmitā) as well as abhiniveśa among the various hindrances (kleśa) on the path to the goal of samādhi.

Patañjali's view of egoism is different from the Hobbesian view of egoistic power-seeking. In general, the Indian view recognizes the self-seeking nature of men, but does not emphasize egoism as many Western psychologies do. While there is such a difference at the descriptive level (*i.e.* about what human beings are *believed* to be like), there is also a difference on the prescriptive level. The Hindu culture has generally stressed self-sacrifice rather than self-aggrandizement and self-seeking. (How far people practice such a prescription is not the issue here). The Indian value of self-denial is reflected, for instance, in the common observation that most parents expect their young sons and daughters to place the interests of their parents and families ahead of their own careers, marriages, and so on. A popular Sanskrit verse states the ideal thus:

> An individual may be sacrificed for the sake of a family, a family for a town, and a town for a province. But, for the sake of the Self one may give up the whole world.

In this translation of the traditional verse, I have deliberately spelled the word self with a capital "S" because the verse implies that it is only for the pursuit of self-realization or for the pursuit of one's spiritual development that one can legitimately relinquish all social obligations. This prescription implies a variety of individualism somewhat similar to the mystical individualism of Martin Buber mentioned earlier. It asks that the individual be left alone to deal with his personal existential predicament.

Indian psychology is individualistic in this sense. It focuses almost entirely on individual self-realization. The guiding principle of Indian psychology is to assist an individual in his *own* spiritual advancement. In this respect it contrasts sharply with Max Meyer's (1922) "Psychology of the Other One." As we have noted before, a focus on the "other one" such as Meyer's has influenced behaviorism in such a way that the study of anything subjective, private, related to consciousness, the self, or to one's own personal life, is considered outside of the scope of psychology (see Chapter 1).

The de-emphasis on the assumption of the power-seeking nature of man has implications for therapeutic application of the principles of psychology. Although a clinical psychology based on principles of the Yoga or Vedānta systems has not yet developed into a modern type of professionalism, I have observed that the traditional role of a guru involves a certain type of therapeutic function vis-à-vis the role of śiṣya or disciple. In this type of therapeutic (call them "paratherapeutic" if you prefer) relations, the focus is on a radical transformation of the disciple's "self." Yet, unlike the Rogerian approach, there is little emphasis on self-esteem. Insofar as psychoneurotic problems in relation to lack of adequate self-esteem arise mainly from the social comparison process in the competitive game of one-upmanship, the "client" is directed to consider such comparisons as unnecessary and irrelevant. We shall deal with the Indian view of the transformation of the "self" in the process of self-realization in Chapter 5, and with the role of the guru in assisting in this process in the last chapter.

Assumptions Regarding the Rationality or Irrationality of Man. There are two distinct trends in Western theories of psychology: one assumes that man is basically rational and the other assumes that man is basically irrational. The theories of cognitive dissonance and congruity in social psychology (*e.g.*, Festinger, 1957; Osgood and Tannenbaum, 1955) are typical examples of theories which implicitly assume the rationality of man in contrast to psychoanalytic theory, which assumes that man is driven by pleasure-seeking drives of the id that are basically irrational.

The special taste for reasoning is a part of the classical Greek heritage of the West. During the medieval period, the importance of reason in the Western view of man seemed to decline as churchmen like St. Bernard defended faith against reason during the long, drawn-out controversy over the value of faith *versus* reason (see Jones, 1969, Vol. 2, pp. 196–207). With the Enlightenment of the 18th century, however, the place of reason was restored. Reason began to be regarded not only as more valuable than faith, but also as a natural characteristic of men. Although to various thinkers of 18th-century Europe, "reason" meant anything from common sense to strict logical deduction, most seemed to agree that all men possess an almost equal ability to reason. The Utilitarians like Bentham and Mill coupled reason with hedonism: men were supposed to be able to measure rationally whether the outcome of a certain course of action would lead to a balance of pleasure or pain.

The theories of cognitive dissonance and congruity developed against the background of such rationalistic ideas in the history of Western philosophy. Festinger (1957), for instance, based his theory of cognitive dissonance on the assumption that dissonance arising (at least partly) from *logical inconsistency* is psychologically uncomfortable, and that it motivates a person to reduce the dissonance and achieve consonance. This assumption makes transparent the implicit view of man as a rational being.

Game theory, which entered psychology via economics, is a systematic attempt at theory-building based on the assumptions of rationality and self-seeking in human nature. John von Neumann tried to apply rigorous mathematical methods (Neumann and Morgenstern, 1953) to bargaining behavior as it manifests in parlor games (bridge, poker, chess, and the like) where each player tries to seek advantage over the other. Neumann and Morgenstern started with a basic assumption about human motivation, namely that "the consumer desires to obtain a maximum of utility or satisfaction and the entrepreneur a maximum of profits" (p. 8). They also stated that "The individual who attempts to obtain these respective maxima is also said to act 'rationally'," although they admitted that ". . . . there exists, at present, no satisfactory treatment of the question of rational behavior." Their next main assumption is that a utility is a numerically measurable quantity. Once numbers are assigned to the basic concept of utility or "satisfaction," the way to apply sophisticated mathematical methods becomes wide open. Although the difficulty in assigning particular numerical indices to elusive psychological entities such as satisfaction was realized, it was hoped that the problems in measurement would eventually be solved. It was hoped that, just as initial difficulties in the measurement of temperature were surmounted, and physics no longer needs to depend on the human sensations of warm and cold, psychologists, too, will solve problems of measurement which are typical of their field of study. Here, as in many other instances, the enthusiasm for following the model of the successful natural sciences is obvious.

It should also be obvious that the inspiration of game theory comes directly from Bentham's hedonistic calculus. The model of man as a pleasure-seeking, selfish, and rational being is preserved—and systematically elaborated. The pioneering work of von Neumann has been followed up and the mathematical theory of gaming has been applied to such diverse forms of human behavior as gambling, economic and political bargaining (whether of single individuals in parlor games and in the market place, or of business corporations and oil-cartel nations), the problems of management *versus* labor, and international military strategy (see Shubik, 1964). Indeed game theory has become popular across the world as a framework for interdisciplinary studies of a great variety of social, economic, and military problems. As a well-developed branch of mathematics, game theory offers us an invaluable tool for the analysis of the *logical structure* of problems which arise in connection with the necessity of making decisions. It is particularly useful when the decisions are to be based on available information about the consequences of a variety of possible alternative courses of action. Rapoport (1966) has provided us with an authoritative overview of the essential ideas involved in the game-theory approach. He has quoted the British philosopher, R. B. Braithwaite, who expressed a great hope for the future of game theory: "Perhaps in another three hundred years' time economic, and political, and other branches of moral philosophy will bask in the radiation of one source—the theory of games of strategy—whose prototype was kindled around the poker tables of Princeton." (See Rapoport, p. 188) Despite such a high level of enthusiasm about its promise, several difficulties in this approach are apparent.

It is neither possible nor necessary to attempt a detailed evaluation of game theory. Yet, it would be useful to consider a few points here so as to help us in understanding the implications and consequences of the assumptions on which such theories are based. Game theory has certainly been useful to operators of gambling casinos, where the rules of the game, as well as the payoffs, are clearly specified, and the probabilities of outcomes can be estimated fairly accurately. Any other "real life" applications, such as planning strategy on the battlefield, are beset by formidable difficulties. First, in real life, fewer strategies are available to choose from as compared to alternatives available in parlor games; and the estimation of probabilities of outcomes (such as the number of lives a general may have to sacrifice in the event of possible alternatives of choice in strategy, weather conditions, accuracy of intelligence, and so on) are usually no better than arbitrary hunches. Second, probabilities of outcome are relatively easily estimated when similar past events have been well recorded. In real life the prediction of outcomes is often difficult because sufficient data on similar past events is not available. Thus, it may be difficult to predict the success of a product, of a brand-new technology, or of a young colt running its first race. Third, one must also estimate the strategies or utilities adopted by the counterplayers, which must often be based on blind guesswork.

Granted that some of these difficulties are problems of practical application rather than deficiencies of the model itself, there are other issues related to the model itself and the fundamental assumptions on which the theory is based. Real-life situations are far more complex than even the most sophisticated models. As Rapoport (1966, p. 214) has remarked, "even the most drastic 'stripping down' of a conflict to the simplest conceivable level (for there is no conflict simpler than a 2 × 2 game) reveals a *maze of assumptions* which must be made to get anywhere with the analysis" (emphasis added). Further, the most fundamental difficulty lies in the very definition of rationality. As mentioned earlier, the term "rational," as most game theorists define it, means seeking to maximize one's own expected gain (Rapoport, p. 74). This definition hardly differs from that of selfishness, and it usually implies a narrow form of egoism with little or no reference to an "enlightened" form of self-interest. Also, it usually implies gains in tangible terms, such as money or other goods, that can be counted in numerical terms. The term rationality is stripped of its usual meaning of logical reasoning or consistency. The so-called rationality of human beings is thus reduced to a mere skin-deep hedonism. Even if rationality were to be defined in a broader and more sensible way, it is doubtful whether human behavior can be explained on the basis of rationality alone (see Rapoport, 1966, p. 206).

From the above discussion it should be quite clear that, despite its apparent emphasis or rationality, game theory is mainly an extension of the Benthamian view of man as a self-seeking creature. Here rationality is far from a master motive; reason is a mere tool of the self-seeking drive. The influence of the Benthamian view of human nature is extended well beyond game theory in modern psychology. At least one more example can be cited where the meaning of rationality is extended beyond the pursuit of narrowly selfish gains. Piliavin, Rodin and Piliavin (1969), for instance, have suggested that altruistic behavior (such as that reflected in bystanders' attempting to offer help to a sick or drunk person) can be explained in terms of a cost–reward matrix. Thus, a person will help a needy individual if the rewards associated with helping (praise from the beneficiary or from others such as friends) exceed the costs involved in helping (mainly effort, possible discomfort, or danger involved in reactions from the potential beneficiary, as well as self-blame and censure from others in the event of not helping). It is implicitly assumed that all human beings are continually involved in a "rational" evaluation of the cost–reward matrix in any and all types of occasions. (The Piliavin experiment in fact dealt with the observation of passengers of an urban subway when they were confronted with the "choice" between helping or not helping a drunk or sick-looking passenger. It is assumed that one engages in the exercise of hedonistic calculus even while making split-second judgments between two stops on a subway ride!) It should be clear that in this type of approach, morally disparate reasons for action—ranging from fear of possible physical danger in helping and praise or blame from others on the one hand, to self-blame or satisfaction in doing one's duty on the other—are all measured by the same yardstick of utilitarian advantage. It is explicitly believed that helping behavior does not arise from inherent "altruistic" motivation, but from a "selfish" desire to rid oneself from an unpleasant state such as self-blame.[7] The Piliavin approach is a good example of how the meaning of pleasure and pain are stretched to a point where they lose their significance. Sometimes the axiomatic principles of pleasure-seeking, self-seeking and rationality (as is implicit in the human use of hedonistic calculus) are considered ultimate and inviolable, and, instead of critically examining the basic assumptions, observations that contradict the axiom are twisted to somehow appear consonant with the axioms.

While cognitive psychology and game theory accept different types of rationality in man, there are other theories that assume a basic irrationality of man. Prominent among these is the psychoanalytic theory. One of Freud's basic concepts was the id, the core of the human psyche and a storehouse of all of the instinctual forces of biological origin. The id was said to be guided by feelings of pleasure–unpleasure which had a "despotic force" so strong that no other agency of the psyche could nullify it. Freud maintained that the psychological process of the id (called the primary processes) were not "subject to the critical restrictions of logic" (Freud, 1940/1964, p. 198). Freud tried to show how the wish-fulfilling nature of instinctual forces determines not only the content of fantasy and dreams, but also our cognitive processes such as memory. Both game theory and psychoanalysis consider the supremacy of pleasure-seeking in human nature. But while game theory implicitly assumes that the power of reasoning remains intact while serving the self-seeking interests of the master motive, psychoanalytic theory implies that the "blind" forces of the id nearly always cloud the reasoning process, leading to the distortion of truth. The intellect remains in the service of emotions and may even invent arguments that have a plausible ring of rationality, and thus "rationalize" or justify the basically irrational motives.

Freud was not the first in the Western tradition to recognize the distorting effect of emotions on cognitive processes. In his well-known work *De Anima,* Aristotle remarked: ". . . we are easily deceived respecting the operations of sense-perception when we are excited by emotions . . . and the more deeply one is under the influence of emotion, the less similarity is required to give rise to the illusory impressions."[8] To illustrate his point, Aristotle suggested that given only little resemblance between a familiar and an unfamiliar object, a coward suspects that his enemy is approaching, while a person influenced by an amorous desire thinks his beloved is approaching. More than two thousand years later, experimental psychologists formalized Aristotle's conjecture into a concept called "autism," and experimentally demonstrated that perceiving, learning, remembering, and thinking are influenced by needs, values, and emotions. For instance, in a classic experiment Levine, Chein and Murphy (1942) showed that the number of times experimental subjects associated ambiguous figures with food objects varied systematically with the strength of hunger as measured by the number of hours they had stayed without food. Hungry persons perceive food where there is none; the stronger the pangs of hunger, the greater the chances of perceiving non-food objects as food.

The same psychological principle, namely that emotions often distort cognitive processes, was recognized by Indian thinkers around the time of Aristotle, or perhaps even earlier. The *Bhagavad-Gītā* (2.62–63), for instance, states it in the following manner:

> When a man concentrates on the objects of sense a desire generates toward the same. From desire comes craving and craving begets rage. Confusion follows rage and loss of memory is the consequence. Loss of intellect follows this train, and—a man without intellect is destined to death.

It would be useful to note here that, as pointed out by Tilak (1915/1956) in his translation of the *Gītā,* it is the inability to obtain the desired objects that transforms a craving into anger. A student of modern psychology can quickly note the similarity between this particular point and the well-known "frustration aggression hypothesis." This hypothesis states that it is the blocking of an individual's progress to his goal which leads to frustration, which then leads to aggression (Miller, 1941). Obviously Western and Indian thinkers separated by great distances and long time intervals have independently arrived at strikingly similar observations about human behavior. It certainly remains to the credit of the modern Western psychologists that they worked out in detail the general ideas originally conceived by philosophers of the past. It is questionable, however, whether one can reasonably construe universal principles such as the basic human rationality or irrationality of man by starting with some general observations, and then going on to construct entire models of man based on such principles. While it makes sense to say that the influence of emotions *sometimes* leads to distortion in cognition, it does not follow that human beings are always, or even "basically" irrational in nature. Again, while it seems that some individuals feel discomfort in facing logical contradiction, it does not follow that the need for consistency is a universal motivational force operating with equal strength among all human beings at all times—as the cognitive theorists usually imply. At any rate, theories that place great accent on either rationality or on irrationality could not both be right at the same time.

At this point it would be appropriate to compare the Indian position vis-à-vis the assumption of the rationality or irrationality of man. In contrast with the Western psychologies, which are divided in their emphasis on either rationality or irrationality, the Indian systems do not appear to emphasize either aspect in man. Although the *Gītā* recognizes the distorting effects of emotions as noted earlier, no assumption of basic irrationality of human nature is concluded from such observations. The emotions like lust (kāma) or anger (krodha) are considered manifestation of rajas, one of the three guṇas or qualities of Prakṛti. In man, as in everything else in nature, all three guṇas must be present at all times, although any one of them may dominate at a given time while others recede or lay dormant. Thus, a person may be misled while under the influence of the emotive characteristics of the rajas guṇa, but right knowledge or wisdom will dawn on him as soon as the sattva guṇa becomes dominant. Given this view of continually changing characteristics of men as a result of dominating and receding qualities, it follows that human nature is not considered *either* rational *or* irrational. It is assumed, in other words, that man is capable of being wise (or "rational") although he is occasionally irrational or blindly led by emotions. This is, on the whole, a more balanced view in comparison with those views that stress either rationality or irrationality. There is a major drawback to the theory of guṇas, however. It does not clearly specify the conditions under which one or the other quality would dominate.

The contradictory emphases on rationality *versus* irrationality in the Western theories of psychology parallel the divergent values regarding the place of reason in life in the history of ideas in the West. As noted earlier, rationalists and antirationalists have repeatedly entered into controversies in the history of Western thought. Back in the 4th century (A.D.) the supporters of Christian orthodoxy fought against the rational arguments of the Gnostics, Arians, and other "heretics"; during the medieval period the faith–reason controversy arose over the metaphysical issue of universals; in the 18th century the Romanticists revolted against the philosophies of the Age of Reason; and in the modern period the phenomenologists and intuitionists such as Bergson have strongly opposed such analytical philosophies as positivism. Small wonder, then, that psychologists influenced by the divergent philosophical views have developed models of man that consider man as *either* rational *or* irrational. The history of thought in India, by contrast, has not involved major controversies on the place of reason in life. Likewise, there are no models of man of Indian origin that assume human nature to be either wholly rational or wholly irrational.

Assumptions about the Human Condition

The imperfections of human existence, the widespread experience of misery, ignorance, or anxiety, are recognized equally well perhaps everywhere in the world. If human existence is perceived as nothing less than ideal, then there is no reason why anyone should do anything about it. The need for religion as well as for science arises when the prevalence of human misery and ignorance are recognized. Indian as well as most Western psychologists explicitly or implicitly recognize the unpleasant aspects of the human condition.

Buddha's pessimistic view of the human condition is well known. The burden of Buddhist teaching is that all is suffering. The misery of saṁsāra, or the eternal cycle of birth and death, is considered the most real, and the foremost aim of man is to escape from it. The concept of saṁsāra, which implies the doctrine of rebirth as well as the opinion that the eternal cycle of birth and death is full of misery, is a pan-Indian theme. It is accepted by Hindus as well as Buddhists, with the only exception being the heterodox school of the hedonist, Cārvāka. The Sāṅkhya system very explicitly holds that human experience is sorrowful. In fact, *Sāṅkhya Kārikā,* a basic text of the Sāṅkhya philosophy, begins with the statement that man, oppressed by the experience of suffering, desires a way out of his plight. The author of the *Kārikā* hastens to add, however, that human misery does not exist either in an invariable or an absolute way. There *are* known means to escape from suffering, and that is what the Sāṅkhya system deals with (see Raja, 1963). Patañjali's Yoga system borrows this basic idea from the Sāṅkhya system. In one of the aphorisms (2.15) Patañjali exclaims: "For the discriminating individual all is nothing but pain." He prescribes the various techniques of Yoga which are designed to rid oneself of the experience of misery in life.

Duḥkha is a Sanskrit term usually translated as "pain and misery." What do the Indian thinkers mean when they use such a term? Do they simply mean physical pain, or poverty, privation, drought and destruction, and other such conditions, which we know have plagued the Indian continent from time to time throughout history? Do they imply something else in addition? A careful look at the history of Indian thought reveals that the word duḥkha has a broad connotation involving the various shades of meaning just mentioned, and, in addition, associated with a specific view of the human condition. This view is a common and recurrent theme of the Indian culture. Let me try to explain it.

In one of the older Upaniṣads called the *Maitri Upaniṣad,* there is the tale of a king called Bṛhadratha who abdicated his throne, assigned it to his son, and, having reached a state of indifference to the world (vairāgya), approached a holy man called Śākyāyana. The holy man, an ascetic, offered him a boon, and the old king asked only for the knowledge of the Self (ātman). He did not seek any worldly pleasure, because, he said: "In this body, which is afflicted with desire, anger, covetousness, delusion, fear, despondency, envy, separation from the desirable, union with the undesirable, hunger, thirst, senility, death, disease, sorrow, and the like, what is the good of enjoyment of desires?" (Hume, 1931, p. 413)

In the brief paragraph just quoted we get a glimpse of the traditional Indian view of the human condition. There is great concern about all forms of suffering. However, this concern is associated not simply with a desire for their removal, but also with a lack of attraction for worldly pleasures and a *quest for knowledge.* It is interesting to note that, during the Upaniṣadic period of Indian history, which represents the earliest phase of the philosophic quest in India, the passionate expression of suffering is associated *not* with gloating over doomsday, but with the awakening of the desire for knowledge. It is even more interesting to note the contrast between the Hindu and the Christian traditions. It is well known that in the latter tradition, the desire for knowledge is associated with the downfall of man. As the legend of the *Old Testament* has it, Adam was condemned to a miserable life of hard labor because he dared to eat the fruit of the tree of knowledge.

The tales and conversations that appear in the Upaniṣads have no place in these philosophical treatises like the *Sāṅkhya Kārikā.* The passionate, poetic expressions about the human condition are replaced by very brief analytic statements. Thus, the first kārikā or aphorism simply mentions three types of human suffering. Since the author of the *Kārikā* did not feel the need to describe or even indicate what the three types of suffering were like, it appears that, as early as the second or the third century A.D. when they were probably written, the threefold classification must have been well-known and accepted. The three types of suffering are: (1) ādhibhautika meaning suffering arising from "material" causes outside the individual, such as flood, fire, drought, falling objects, biting insects, attacking enemies, and the like; (2) ādhidaivika meaning suffering with a mysterious origin, such as deities, demons, or ghosts; and (3) adhyātmika, meaning the suffering pertaining to oneself either in physical form, such as pain arising from disease or bodily harm, or in psychological form, such as anxiety, fear, anger, and so on. The tripartite division of suffering is a lasting theme of Indian thought, and there seems to be an overall emphasis on the last-mentioned form of suffering, namely that pertaining to the self. (The reader may remember Tilak's classification of types of knowledge under the same three headings with an emphasis on adhyātmika knowledge, mentioned in the previous chapter.) Also, there is usually a focus on the sufferer (bhoktṛ) and the right orientation he must maintain in facing the experience of pain. The Sāṅkhya theory holds that the self (Puruṣa) is only a passive spectator who feels involved with the events around him only due to the ignorance of his true nature. As such, the individual must isolate or withdraw himself from the world so that in the state of isolation (called Kaivalya) he shall be free from all misery. Patañjali's Yoga elaborates on this theme insofar as his eightfold path specifies the techniques of attaining the state of isolation.

The Upaniṣadic view of the sorrowful nature of human existence and the theory of threefold classification of human misery have persisted throughout the Indian tradition. During the early Ninth century, Śaṅkara (788–820 A.D.), the most influential exponent of the non-dualistic philosophy of Vedānta, restated the same view of human suffering. His views are expressed in one of his poems (popularly called "The Song of Carpaṭapañjarikā") in a much better way than in the terse prose of his intricate logical arguments. It is impossible to convey the beauty of his lyrical style. Yet, let me try to paraphrase and briefly sample the sense of his ideas.

> The body is decrepit, hair turned grey, the mouth is toothless, the old frame needs crutches; yet the desires aren't satiated. Lost in play during childhood, chasing girls in youth, ridden by anxiety during senility—never a free moment to ponder on the beyond. Birth comes after death, to be followed by death, then only to lie again, in the mother's paunch. Save me, O Lord, from this cycle, eternal, formidable, and impassable—without your grace. One more day follows every day, there'll be another night, after tonight and another fortnight after this one. Month after month, year after year, time passes without ceasing of desire. . . . Who am I? Where do I come from? (A. C. Paranjpe, trans.)

In the unbroken tradition of the writings of the saints in almost every language of India, we see a passionate expression of the same type of feelings. During the early part of the 17th century the saint Rāmadās, for instance, wrote (in an octet of verse called *Karuṇāṣṭake*):

> I'd never find happiness in sensual pleasures. Everything is worthless, O Lord, without your grace . . . My mind wanders despite my effort to restrain it. My attachment to the folks is too strong to cut . . . My heart burns in

> billion cycles of life and death. Have pity on me, O Lord! You are the ocean of mercy (A. C. Paranjpe, trans.).

A contemporary of Rāmdās, the Marāṭhī saint-poet Tukārām summed it up in a flat declaration: Upon searching one finds but a grain of happiness, and alas, there's suffering mighty as a mountain.

The Indian obsession with the theme of suffering *(duḥkha)* parallels the Western theme of evil. The Christian philosophers, in particular, were faced with the problem of adequately explaining the origin of evil. Since their monotheist faith conceived God as the omniscient, omnipotent, and all-good creator of the world, God had to be held responsible for everything that existed or happened in the world, the good aspects as well as all the bad ones. If God were indeed all-good, why did he create a world full of suffering, beset by its famines, plagues, and wars? Since He is omniscient, He could not be considered ignorant of the evils that afflict the world. If He were really omnipotent, He could have eradicated all evil. Even if man were held responsible for his misery, at least partly as the result of his own wrongdoing, one may ask: why did the perfect and well-meaning God create such an imperfect and fallible creature as man? The 3rd-century Persian thinker called Mani posed dilemmas of exactly this type and tried to answer them. Following the Zoroastrian model of the eternal principles of good and evil, Mani proposed a kind of metaphysical dualism. He held that God is indeed good, but He is finite, and is limited by the evil power of Satan.

Such a dualistic conception was obviously far from acceptable to orthodox monotheist Christianity. Manicheism, or Mani's philosophy, was considered a wicked "heresy." The violent reaction of Christian orthodoxy succeeded in nearly eradicating the Manichean movement by about the 5th or 6th century. But, as W. T. Jones has suggested in his *History of Western Philosophy,* (Jones, 1969, Vol. 2, p. 68): "The fact is that Manicheism is a tough and recurring view that, refusing to stay defeated, has cropped up again and again in the history of the West."

The history of the Manichean heresy points to some important characteristics of Western thought that are in sharp contrast to the Indian approach to the problem of human suffering. The strong influence of the monotheistic view of the Judeo-Christian tradition had led the problem of suffering and evil to theological battles, in contrast to the Indian tradition, where the problem was considered largely outside the context of theology. Although the tripartite classification of human suffering ascribed part of human misery to dieties and other supernatural forces, attention could not be focused on any single deity among the plethora of deities in the Indian pantheon that could be held responsible for evil and human suffering. In the West, once the issue of human suffering became engulfed in theological squabbles, it seems to have been diverted from the field of psychology, where it should reasonably and legitimately have been discussed. Further, the West has shown greater interest in tracing the origin of suffering to somewhere outside the individual (such as God or nature), than in tracing it to the "inner" or psychological sources. By contrast, again, the Indians focused on the sufferer while, alas, paying little attention to controlling nature to avert several causes of suffering such as flood or drought.

I do not mean to suggest that the West totally neglected the inner sources of suffering, nor that the Indians were totally unconcerned with the control of natural causes of suffering. The question is one of relative emphasis, and the difference between the Indian and Western approaches in their relative emphasis on inner and outer sources is clear beyond doubt. There is another type of difference between them. The Indian view of suffering emphasizes the experience of pain, the ephemeral quality of life, and the insatiability and persistence of desire. By contrast, the Christians have overemphasized the feelings of sin and guilt. The Western man's fear of damnation on account of his violation of God's commandments has no parallel in the Indian continent (except of course among the small number of Christians who have found a home in India since as early as the first century A.D.). The impact of this contrast in cultural themes is certainly reflected in the psychological thought of India and of the West. Indian psychology is mainly guided by the desire to find release from the pervasive suffering in life. In the West, however, there appears no such single dominant theme as is seen in the Indian tradition. In my view, there are three rather distinct trends in Western psychology (which roughly correspond with psychoanalysis, behaviorism, and existential psychology) representing three different implicit views about the human condition.

In his well-known book, *Civilization and Its Discontents,* Freud (1930/1961) has described his pessimistic view of the human condition. He considered three basic sources of unhappiness and suffering: the body, "which is doomed to decay and dissolution and which cannot even do without pain and anxiety as warning signals"; the external world which is full of "merciless forces of destruction"; and our relations to other men (Freud, 1930/1961, p. 77). A reader may be struck by a strange similarity between this analysis and the tripartite classification of suffering in the Indian tradition which we noted earlier. However, unlike the Indians, Freud was not concerned with the insatiable desires of the eternal saṁsāra; his main emphasis was on the pervasive feelings of guilt arising from the pricking conscience. In his view a pervasive sense of guilt is an inevitable result of man's relation to other men. Having witnessed the devastating effects of World War I, Freud was convinced that mankind is driven by an instinct of aggression which is as powerful as the drive for self-preservation. From the beginning of history all civilizations have inevitably been led to devise ways to curb man's warlikeness. If cultures had been unable to have their members internalize the commandment "Love thy neighbor," human beings would have destroyed one another long ago. While the various internalized restrictions of ethical systems have been effective in maintaining some peace among societies, the price men have had to pay for this achievement is very high—in Freud's view, that is. This is because, every now and then, an individual has to forgo one or another pleasure he desires, and as a result he has to carry a sense of guilt whenever he violates any of his culture's commandments. Thus, the human mind becomes an eternal battleground for the conflict between man's desire for pleasure (Eros) and his instinctive desire for destruction (Thanatos). According to Freud, the "fatal inevitability of guilt" has plagued possibly the whole of mankind, making men eternally unhappy.

Freud's view of the human condition as being excessively guilt-laden is a modified version of the Judeo-Christian view of the sinfulness of human beings. While both the Christians and classical psychoanalysts view human beings as guilt-ridden, Freud blamed religion, particularly the Christian faith, for causing this condition. In *The Future of an Illusion* Freud (1927/1961, p. 43) concluded that religion was the "universal obsessional neurosis of humanity," since it created a persistent fear of punishment by God, whom the Christians conceived in the image of a disciplining father. Further, Freud held that psychoanalysis was the science that would help eradicate the evil spell of the illusion called religion.

Although other psychoanalysts have deviated from Freud's rather extreme position, their view of the human condition is largely dominated by Freud's original position. The emphasis on anxiety and, to a varying extent, on guilt is clearly seen in most psychoanalytical writings. The behaviorists' view of the human condition, however, is not so clearly reflected in their writings. Having been inspired by the views of Darwin and Pavlov, the behaviorists have been interested in the study of nonhuman animals. The behaviorists, at least in the initial stages, were mainly interested in observing caged animals. Can we extricate from animal studies the researcher's implicit ideas about the human condition? Can we conclude that, like their experimental animals, the humans, too, were usually supposed to be in a state of hunger and sexual deprivation? The writings of Watson and Hull are indeed of little use in even guessing their view of the human condition. With Skinner, however, we have more hope in this respect. This is true in spite of his attempt to meticulously avoid any reference to feelings such as pleasure or pain (*e.g.* 1974, pp. 47–48). Although such avoidance is characteristic of his writings as a "scientist," it is not typical of his writings as a novelist or a social reformer. Note, for instance, the following statement made by Skinner in his preface to the 1969 edition of his utopian novel *Walden Two:* "Build a way of life in which people live together without *quarelling,* in a social climate of trust rather than *suspicion,* of love rather than *jealousy,* of cooperation rather than *competition*" (Skinner, 1948/1969, p. vii, emphasis added). It should be clear that the emphasized words in the statement reflect Skinner's implicit view of the human condition. If he did not truly believe in the prevalence of such imperfections of the human existence, why would he imagine (and even strive to actually build) a utopian society devoid of such foibles?

Since it is futile to try to extrapolate any further the behaviorist view of the human condition, I shall turn to the position of existential psychologists on this issue. In this matter the existential psychologists such as Binswanger, Boss, Laing, and Rollo May have been considerably influenced by the writings of the existential philosophers. It is my impression that the best expression of the existential position is found in the novels of Sartre and Camus, the popular and prominent men of letters from France, just as the Indian philosophers' views have been better expressed in their poetry.

Antoine Roquentin, the hero of Sartre's (1938/1964) novel *Nausea,* describes his conditions vividly in the form of diaries. Here are a few excerpts:

> Things are bad! Things are very bad: I have it, the Nausea . . . The Nausea is not inside me: I feel it *out there* in the wall, in the suspenders, everywhere around me. It makes itself one with the cafe, I am the one who is within *it* . . . (pp. 18–20).
>
> And it was true, I had always realized it; I hadn't the right to exist. I had appeared by chance, I existed like a stone, a plant or a microbe. My life put out feelers toward small pleasures in every direction. Sometimes it sent out vague signals; at other times I felt nothing more than a harmless buzzing. (p. 84)
>
> I jump up: it would be much better if I could only stop thinking. Thoughts are the dullest things. Duller than flesh. They stretch out and there's no end to them and they leave a funny taste in the mouth . . . It goes, it goes . . . and there's no end to it. It's worse than the rest because I feel responsible and have complicity in it. For example, this sort of painful rumination: *I exist,* I am the one who keeps it up. I. The body lives by itself once it has begun. But thought—*I* am the one who continues it, unrolls it. I exist. How ser-

> pentine is the feeling of existing—I unwind it, slowly . . . If I could keep myself from thinking!
>
> My thought is *me:* that's why I can't stop. I exist because I think . . . and I can't stop myself from thinking. At this very moment—it's frightful—if I exist, it is because I am horrified at existing. *I am the one* who pulls myself from the nothingness to which I aspire: the hatred, the disgust of existing, there are as many ways to *make* myself exist, to thrust myself into existence. Thoughts are born at the back of me, like sudden giddiness, I feel them being born behind my head . . . (Sartre, 1938/1964, pp. 99–100).

The burning passion of Sartre's character reminds us of the intense feelings of the Indian saint-poets, but the nature of their condition is indeed worlds away. Unlike the Indians, there is no lamenting about the insatiable desire, the feeling of being stuck in a rut. Here the overriding theme is futility, absurdity, and the apparently accidental nature of life itself. The hero of Camus' (1946/1967) novel, *The Outsider,* further exemplifies the basic theme of existential philosophy. He attends his own mother's funeral without any feeling of loss or sorrow; he shoots to death a man who was by no means an enemy—and feels no remorse for his action; and goes through a murder trial without any fear of the impending long sentence. Such lack of relevant emotion is not to be ascribed to a schizophrenic or psychopathic character, but to a condition of apathy, utter uninvolvement and fateful "alienation" from oneself. Camus is surely successful in depicting a person who is truly an "outsider" to the entire human civilization. The underlying theme, once again, is the same as Sartre's, namely, absurdity. Camus' essay, *The Myth of Sisyphus,* likens the human condition to the hero of a Greek myth who was condemned by the gods to ceaselessly roll a rock to the top of a mountain, from whence the stone would fall back to the bottom (Camus, 1955/1969).

The existential view of the human condition needs no more explanation than a string of words the reader of existential literature stumbles over every now and then. Here is a partial list of a few popular epithets: absurdity, alienation, despair, estrangement, existential dread, futility, homelessness, meaninglessness, nausea, nihilism, nothingness, rootlessness . . .

Existentialism is a fairly recent movement, which moved to prominence in Europe after World War II and influenced philosophy, literature, and art, as well as psychology. There have been diverse trends within the movement and the above characterization of the existentialist view of the human condition cannot be claimed as representative. In fact, Sartre has been criticized for an excessively morbid characterization of Roquentin's mood. Nevertheless, a high degree of pessimism is a common characteristic of most existentialist thinkers. Freud, too, was pessimistic, but he did not emphasize alienation and meaninglessness as the existentialists do. As noted earlier, Freud's position was attributable directly to the Christian tradition, despite his attack on religion, insofar as he believed in a pervasive guilt among men. The existential position, however, is not so easily relatable to the Western tradition. To some extent, the existential mood is a truly modern phenomenon resulting from certain unique aspects of modern civilization. Despite its novelty, the roots of existentialism run deep into the history of Western thought. It would be useful to briefly account for the place of existentialism in the history of Western thought, as such account will help us understand its view of the human condition and its psychological implications.

The rise of existentialism in the 20th century can be considered a new round of the age-old rivalry of the non-rationalist view against the rationalist position. William Barrett (1958) has suggested (in his book, *Irrational Man*) that existential philosophy is a new version of the irrationalist view of man rooted in the Hebraic or Judeo-Christian tradition, in contrast to the rationalist view rooted in the Hellenic or Greek legacy of the Western civilization. We have noted before that an earlier round of this rivalry took place in the medieval period in the form of the faith–reason controversy. The modern context is, of course, different than the medieval one. The problems of the 20th century were anticipated in the early 19th century by the Danish intellectual, Kierkegaard, followed by Dostoevsky in Russia, and Nietzsche in Germany.

Kierkegaard reacted sharply to the rationalist tradition by refusing to deal with the problem of human existence in its typical detached and impersonal manner. In his view the proposition "I exist" could not be analysed in purely abstract, metaphysical terms as Socrates, or more particularly, Descartes and Kant had done. For him, human existence inevitably involves the agony and torment of having to choose particular actions in concrete situations, as, for instance, breaking an engagement with a particular girl (as, in fact, he had to do with his fiancée, Regine Olsen). No amount of dispassionate rational analysis could satisfactorily deal with the human condition in such situations, nor could the abstract, universal principles be of great help in making actual decisions in one's personal life. Kierkegaard's approach was one of intense personal involvement—an approach that is totally lacking in behaviorist psychology, based as it is on the rationalist as opposed to the nonrationalist tradition. Kierkegaard was concerned with the "Single One," the unique and particular person, and not the abstract and highly generalized image of man. He tried to restore the respectability of the study of the subjective aspects of human beings, as against the objective: The intense feelings of man had no place in abstract logical analysis of general principles. By emphasizing the place of a particular person and his experience, Kierkegaard paved the way for the uninhibited expression of the intimate, and even apparently morbid, feelings characteristic of later existentialist writers.

Kierkegaard's emphasis on the "Single One" makes sense in the context of the urban and early-industrial European society in which he lived. He spoke bitterly of the *"en masse"* happenings in cities which, he thought, were devoid of passion. He was indeed a genius, much ahead of his contemporaries in understanding the nature of "alienation" of man from other men (particularly when he is lost in the crowds of cities). Kierkegaard's analysis of the alienation of modern man is so prophetic and insightful that, in Barrett's words: ". . . even contemporary efforts at journalistic sociology, like Riesman's (1950) *The Lonely Crowd* or Whyte's (1956) *The Organization Man* are still repeating and documenting his insights" (Barrett, 1958, p. 173).

The Age of Reason in the history of Europe nourished the growth of science and technology. This was followed by industrialization. Industries could not grow without capitalism. The combination of industrialization and capitalism led to a new social organization. Marx was quick to see the economic and political implications of capitalism, namely exploitation. Marx was also insightful in identifying the psychological costs of industrialization—the alienation of the worker from the products of his labor, and thus from his own self. Marx's response to industrialization and capitalism was the politics of communism. Marxists, who were deeply involved in politics, seemed to have no time to deal with the psychology of alienation. Besides, Marx adopted a materialist metaphysics which leaves little scope for an introspective analysis of mental states. It was long before Marxism made inroads into Russia that the Russian novelist Dostoevsky reacted against rationalism and technology. He derided rationalism as exhibiting a "2 × 2" type of thinking and mocked technology, calling it a "Crystal Palace." With his subtle observations of the human condition, Dostoevsky became a source of inspiration for the existentialists of the 20th century.

Nietzsche's attack on the rationalist view was aimed at its very fundamental principles. He not only criticized the despiritualizing influence of science and industry but also questioned the basic concepts of cause and effect. He rejected the "psychological lack of freedom" implicit in the determinist view of science. Whether Nietzsche was justified in his criticism of the rationalist view is a separate issue that cannot be discussed within the limitations of this book. However, the psychological implications of the rejection of determinism are relevant here. It is clear that a person who rejects determinism finds it difficult to explain the orderliness of the universe. As such, he must be prepared to consider the world as possibly a chaotic place. Kierkegaard faced a similar dilemma, but found solace in clinging to the conventional Christian world view, which assumes orderliness in the moral sphere. Nietzsche, however, took a dismal view of such a moralistic, religious perspective. He suggested that men invented "bad conscience," *i.e.*, unpleasant, oppressive morals, in an attempt to tame their once powerful instincts while trying to become sociable and pacific creatures. In holding this view, Nietzsche anticipated Freud's (1930/1961) arguments in *Civilization and Its Discontents*. Nietzsche saw the futility of religion in modern society and, as is well known, declared that God is dead.

Nietzsche's world is thus a world of chaos, a Godless world without moral order, with no recourse to rely on nature since nothing like causality works. Moreover, Nietzsche found reason to be misleading and considered all thinking a useless sign of weakness. His view is appropriately described as nihilism. Nietzsche at least left scope for the powerful overman to conquer and rule the jungle whatever way he pleased. However, Sartre's Roquentin was in Nietzsche's chaotic world without the power to subdue the chaos, so he was left in a dangerous and totally meaningless world with no hope anywhere. Sartre's characters represent a pathetic image of modern man's view of the world.

Let me leave the metaphysics and ethics of existentialism to the philosopher at this point and turn to psychology. The first thing to note is that existential psychology arose against the backdrop of the image of the typical human condition described by existential thinkers from Kierkegaard to Sartre. The main thrust of existential psychology is to analyze the nature of such experience; to illustrate and describe how it manifests itself among concrete individuals, such as patients in their clinics; to attempt to explain the conditions and psychological processes that lead to such experience; and then to suggest ways of alleviating such a condition. It appears that the illustrative cases described by existential analysts such as Binswanger (1958 a; 1958 b) depict a somewhat different condition than that described by existential philosophers like Kierkegaard, or the condition of characters in the novels of Sartre and Camus.[9] Nevertheless, the overall emphasis on meaninglessness and desperation dominates existential analysis.

As we have just seen, there are major differences among the various Western and Indian theories about the human condition. Most systems of psychology develop techniques for redress from the undesirable aspects of the human condition. Such techniques may be called "therapeutic" in the broadest sense of the term. Techniques like the psychoanalytic procedure, behavior therapy, Daseinsanalysis of existential psychology, various breathing exercises of the yogi, and the like, belong to the domain of "applied" psychology. The discussion of such techniques has no place in this chapter devoted to basic assumptions and values. We shall examine certain aspects of the applied setting in Chapter 6. At this point, it is necessary to address ourselves to another question. If the psychologist's ideas about the typical human condition mark the starting point of his action enterprise, what is the goal toward which he tries to move? In other words, what is the ideal human condition to which the psychologist's efforts are aimed? The remainder of this chapter will be devoted to an examination of this issue.

The Ideal Human Condition

To a majority of psychologists today, just the mention of an ideal or most desirable human condition is anathema. As was noted in the previous chapter, the "value-free" stance of modern psychology encourages an objective, nonpartisan development of knowledge. The student of psychology is taught to abstain from value judgments and to avoid prescription of any kind. It is suggested that the appropriate way of studying personality is to make it purely descriptive. Yet, value commitments are inevitable by-products of social existence and, as a participant in society, the "objective" psychologist can rarely disassociate himself from his society's cherished values. The apparently objective and descriptive analysis of personality is often a facade which hides implicit values. Gergen (1973, p. 311) has unmasked the psychologists' seemingly dispassionate account of personality by pointing out that most of them "would feel insulted if characterized as low in self-esteem, high in approval-seeking, cognitively undifferentiated, authoritarian, anal–compulsive, field-dependent, or close-minded." Almost any descriptive account of personality involves a hidden message that conveys to us which characteristics of personality are idealized or sought after and which are vilified. A reader can easily decipher the messages unless he has been desensitized to them by the zeitgeist of value-free science.

The behaviorist writings appear to be the most value-free. The emphasis on elegance in methodology, and a focus upon molecular units of behavior (such as conditioning of the eye-blink reflex) enable them to dodge the more significant value-laden issues in the study of behavior. Learning theory, which is the central feature of the behaviorist viewpoint, seems to focus upon the identification and development of the most efficient forms of learning, without regard to the content of what is learned. The behaviorist techniques of programmed learning and behavior modification aim at helping people learn the appropriate behaviors in the most efficient manner. Granted the efficacy of some of these techniques, the important issue is what constitutes the "appropriate" behavior the technologist aims to reinforce. Since it is hard to find any explicit statement of the types of behavior the behavior therapist considers appropriate, we may guess or even try to "impute" notions of propriety that seem to be implicitly held by the behavior therapist. I can suggest two slightly different views as alternative hypotheses in this regard. First, the behavior theorist may consider those types of behavior appropriate (and therefore worth reinforcing) that help adapt the individual to his environment. The value of adaptation follows Darwinian biology. The struggle for survival is built into the natural order, and those behaviors that promote survival value are considered adaptive.

The view of adaptive behavior as appropriate behavior looks quite simple and straightforward on the surface, but its implications are not always clear. To clarify the point, let us take the following instances of adaptive behavior: The polar bear, the fast-mutating genes of viruses, as well as a politician who modifies his ways to the prevailing public mood—all these are examples of successful adaptation to the respective environments. It follows, therefore, that these behavior patterns may be considered "appropriate." Some moralists may call the politician an opportunist, or may point to his "corruption," but those who have committed themselves to value-free science need not be distracted by the moralists' arguments, since they are irrelevant to their views of scientific activity! A second hypothesis regarding the behavior therapist's implicit view of appropriate behavior is that the patterns of behavior that are prescribed by the Government, Church, and other such social institutions are considered appropriate behaviors by the behavior therapist. Conformity with the norms of the establishment often avoids conflicts with the institutional authority and thus improves an individual's chances for survival in society. Reinforcement of behaviors that follow established norms helps the survival of not only the client, but also the therapist, who is usually an employee of the establishment.

One difficulty in trying to explicate the behavior therapists' view of appropriate behavior is that their attention is usually focused on stamping out specific behaviors such as bed-wetting, nail-biting, excessive drinking, and stealing, which are considered obviously and almost universally improper. Focus on such specific behaviors helps avoid the general issue of the propriety of behaviors in the complex and changing situations that arise in daily life. A somewhat less "molecular" perspective is adopted by the social learning theorists who describe the processes of "modeling," or the ways in which an individual, say a member of a delinquent gang, may imitate the elaborate behavior pattern of a model, such as the gang leader. Yet, the social learning theorists usually neglect the problem of how the young person chooses one of the many different models that the society presents before him. Further, any discussion of models, or of issues such as the most desirable model or ideal personality type, is as irrelevant to the social learning theorist as it is to the behavior therapist. Here, once again, Skinner proves to be an exception to the general trend among the behaviorists. As we noted earlier, he refers to peace, love and cooperation as desirable qualities among men in the preface of *Walden Two*. But Skinner aims at a heaven on earth; his utopia describes the ideal condition of the human society as a whole and, as a consequence of his focus on the whole society, we know little about his ideas regarding the desirable aspects of human beings as individual persons.

Freud, however, was reasonably explicit about what, in his opinion, was the best thing human beings could attain. Although his impression about the most prevalent characteristic of the human condition was quite negative, as we noted earlier, he was clear about where to find the highest form of happiness. Thus, he said: ". . . sexual love . . . has given us our most intense experience of an overwhelming sensation of pleasure and has thus furnished us with a pattern for our search for happiness" (Freud, 1930/1961, p. 82). Freud did recognize the pleasure involved in the pursuit of knowledge and in the enjoyment of the great works of art. But such pleasure was only satisfaction through fantasy, a kind of "mild narcosis" which is "not strong enough to make us forget real misery" (p. 81). He thought that the idea of seeking freedom from suffering by "killing off the instincts" was only a false hope.[10] Further, he declared that "the feeling of happiness derived from the satisfaction of a wild instinctual impulse untamed by the ego is incomparably more intense than that derived from sating an instinct that had been tamed" (Freud, 1930/1961, p. 79).[11]

Given this view of the highest happiness attainable by men, the role of the psychoanalyst becomes one of facilitating the patient's pursuit of happiness by relieving him from the burden of guilt feelings generated by the repression or "taming" of his raw instinctual impulses. It is not necessary to repeat the relationship of Freud's views to the "Victorian" morals of his time. It may be noted, however, that, excepting perhaps the old pagan philosophies such as the Epicurean or hedonistic doctrines, the Freudian view of the ideal human condition is not influenced by the religio-philosophical thinking of the Western tradition.

Both the behaviorist and psychoanalytical theories manifest the antireligious and antiphilosophical character of modern Western psychologies. As noted in the previous chapter, this character follows from an historical trend in the process of the development of psychology as a natural science. McClelland's research on the achievement motive is one of the rare exceptions to this general trend: In the extensive work of McClelland and his associates, qualities such as striving for excellence, spirit for enterprise, readiness to wait and forgo immediate reward in lieu of an expected greater reward at a later time, are extolled as desirable characteristics in men (McClelland, 1961; McClelland *et al.*, 1953). The value of achievement as reflected in this type of research is a direct influence of the "Protestant Ethic." According to the Puritan doctrines popular among several Protestant sects, hard work, asceticism (in the sense of frugal living), and striving for success are considered positive values. Self-denial and devotion to duty were looked upon as signs of belonging to God's "Elect"—groups to be saved by His choice. It was believed that God caused His Elect to prosper in worldly life. It has been suggested that such beliefs and values have provided a work ethic and the "spirit of capitalism" manifested in several Western societies. The popularity of McClelland's work in America can be ascribed partly to the fact that it derives support from, and provides support to, the prevalent Puritanism, and partly to the similarly supportive role of the secular capitalist value of acquiring "bigger" and "more" of everything. It is appropriate to say that, by and large, modern Western psychology reflects very little influence of pagan or Judeo-Christian concepts of the *desirable* human condition or ideals and virtues, such as Aristotle's "rational man," the British concept of a gentleman, or the Christian views of salvation and the Lord's Elect. Although existential psychology is an exception to the antiphilosophical trend in modern psychology, it has much to say about the negative aspects of the human condition, and nothing at all on the positive aspects.

Ever since modern psychologists in the West began to turn away from their philosophical and religious roots, their thinking has been influenced by ideas in biology and medicine. Freud, for instance, was himself a medical practitioner, and as such was primarily concerned with helping those who had obvious "problems" or those who were clearly miserable. Freeing such persons from their maladies is certainly a difficult and laudable task. Nevertheless, restoring normalcy among the abnormal is only half of what can be expected of a well-rounded and full-fledged psychology. The other half must concern itself with the striving of the "normal" person to the more desirable state of fulfilment and contentment, or perhaps with his goal of reaching the highest possible state of happiness.

The lack of emphasis on the positive aspects of the human condition was beginning to be recognized in American psychology in the 1950s. Reaction to this newly recognized deficency was expressed in the literature, and some psychologists attempted to provide the badly needed corrective by suggesting positive models. A few of these attempts will be briefly mentioned here.

Marie Jahoda (1953; 1955) was one of the earliest and the most prominent among American psychologists who moved in this direction. She criticized the then-prevalent view of mental health, suggesting that mere absence of mental disease, acting or feeling like the majority of people do, or, in other words, conforming to a statistical norm, or even successful survival in society, may not be the hallmarks of mental health. Mastery rather than mere adaptation to the environment; unity or maintenance of stable internal organization; and ability to perceive oneself and the world realistically were suggested as main indicators of *positive mental health.*

A few years after the publication of Marie Jahoda's papers in the early 1950s, Robert White expressed the same spirit, moving in the positive direction. His work focused more sharply on the concepts of motivation than on those of mental health. He noted that there was among psychologists, a "deepening discontent" with the Freudian emphasis on reduction of anxiety as well as with the Hullian view of motivation, which emphasizes reduction of the instinctual drives for food and sex (White, 1959). Conceiving of motivation merely in terms of tension-reduction through consummatory climax, escape from danger or pain, or simply in terms of replenishing deficiencies in bodily tissues, was considered inadequate in accounting for human or animal behavior. Instead, White emphasized the drive of organisms toward exploring and mastering the environment. He suggested the term "competence" to designate this broadened concept of motivation. In his view, satisfaction among most organisms lies not in the decline of their activity to a point of "bored passivity," but in the feeling of efficacy they derive from actively mastering the environment. This was certainly a move in the "positive" direction, like Jahoda's.

Perhaps the most ardent and relentless critic of the psychoanalyst and behaviorist emphases on the "negative" aspects of human beings was Abraham Maslow. Maslow is the only psychologist who made a deliberate attempt to search for persons who were positively healthy and free from guilt, shame, and anxiety. He has given a descriptive account of the important characteristics of a small group of people who were chosen as typically "self-actualizing." The main criterion for the selection of such persons was that they should be "doing the best that they are capable of doing, reminding us of Nietzsche's exhortation, 'Become what thou art'" (Maslow, 1970, p. 150). This implies that the model of self-actualization emphasizes the actualization of potential capacities in the form of mastering various tasks or becoming successful in the world. It may be noted that here Maslow shares the main characteristic of positive health suggested by Marie Jahoda, namely mastery. We have already noted in our discussion of the assumption of human nature that the Nietzschean emphasis on "will to power," including the concept of self-actualization has influenced Western psychological thought. At this point it is necessary to examine Maslow's view of self-actualizing persons so far as it involves his ideas about the ideal human condition.

Among the important characteristics of self-actualizing persons, Maslow has mentioned spontaneity, simplicity, and naturalness. According to Maslow, self-actualizing persons are generally concerned about one problem or the other, and focus their attention more on the problem itself than on themselves. Their orientation is usually unselfish and impersonal. They manifest a genuine desire to help the human race. They are democratic in the sense that they are friendly with anyone of suitable character regardless of class, education, political belief, race, or color. They appear conventional, insofar as they are tolerant of harmless folkways of the people around them in manner, language, dress, and so on, and accept the local customs. However, their choice of values is entirely autonomous and in no way do they accept blindly what the society in general considers right. By and large, Maslow's self-actualizing persons seemed to transcend the limitations of the particular culture of their society. Their most important characteristic is their attitude of detachment. A self-actualizing person is undisturbed by circumstances that produce turmoil in others. He does not react violently to personal misfortunes as many people do. Maslow has also claimed that "subjective expressions that have been called mystic experience and described so well by William James" were common experiences for most, though not all, of the self-actualizing persons studied by him. He was quick to add, however, that "It is quite important to dissociate this experience from any theological or supernatural reference, even though for thousands of years they have been linked" (Maslow, 1970, p. 164).

Even casual acquaintance with Maslow's description of self-actualizing persons would be enough to make us realize that, although his research began with the intention of studying psychological health, it has gone well past the limitations of the conventional medical model of health. Maslow's self-actualizing persons have much more than Jahoda's positive mental health. In particular, they have many moral qualities such as unselfishness and love for mankind. Moreover, they seem to have certain characteristics such as a sense of fulfilment, contentment, inner peace (emotionally "unruffled"), and intense "mystic" experiences, which are obviously considered desirable. Maslow has labeled this aspect of his concept of self-actualization "gratification health" or "happiness health" (Maslow, 1970, p. 68). This type of interest in "happiness" sharply contrasts with the "skin-deep hedonism" implicit in the behaviorist and psychoanalytical theories of psychology. Because of his defiant resistance to a "value free" science, Maslow's ideas found little acceptance in the academic establishment. Yet, the idea of self-actualization has become popular among many people outside the conventional universities and mental clinics. Many techniques have been devised and applied in a variety of "therapeutic" activities such as T-groups, encounter groups, sensitivity training, and, particularly, "growth groups," which have tried to facilitate self-actualization among their clients.

It is not necessary for our purposes to examine the reliability of Maslow's research techniques, nor the validity of the conclusions of his studies. Nor is it necessary to evaluate the success or failure of techniques designed to attain self-actualization or "personal growth." But it is important to note that in Maslow's writings we find some effort to conceptualize the positive aspects of the human condition; efforts in this direction are few and far between in modern Western psychology.

As the concept of mental health begins to broaden, it brings in ideas like personal growth, fulfilment, and the like, which involve the age-old concern for human happiness. In a short article published in the *Journal of Humanistic Psychology,* Erwin Fellows (1966) surveyed the research on happiness in Western philosophy and psychology. He quoted the following words of Lin Yutang to express his conclusion about the study of happiness in Western philosophy: "The most studiously avoided subject in Western philosophy is that of happiness." As for psychology, he reiterates psychologist H. A. Murray's impression that the neglect by psychologists of the study of happiness is "one of the strangest, least interpretable symptoms of our time."

I tend to agree with Fellows's conclusion about the neglect of the study of happiness in Western psychology, although I do not agree with his conclusion regarding its neglect in Western philosophy. It is not difficult to understand why positive aspects of the human condition are so neglected in modern Western psychology. There are two sides to this issue: first, the concept of "happiness," and second, the moral issue of what human beings ought to be like. Most psychologists, in their enthusiasm for the natural science model, have left both these aspects to the philosophers and theologians. Yet, through their interest in adjustment, mastery of the environment, control of behavior ("control for what?"), or in explicit or implicit utopias, an implicit stand on these issues does creep into psychological theories. By sharp contrast, psychological thought of the Indian tradition has not been in such a plight. Since the Indian psychologists did not have to face the long conflict between science and religion as in the West, they were never pressured to avoid ethical and spiritual issues.

Fellows's criticism of Western philosophy seems to be too harsh to be justifiable. Philosophers in the West *did* try to examine the nature of happiness. Plato, for instance, distinguished between the qualities of pleasure: "necessary" pleasures, which include bringing the body back to equilibrium by, say, eating or drinking, and "harmless" pleasures such as the enjoyment of smells, sounds, and the like. He also distinguished between pleasure and happiness. His concept of happiness included thinking, reasoning, or "intellectual" pleasures, as well as attainment of balance and harmony in life. The discussion of happiness was closely tied to the definition of the "good," and thus the nature of happiness was discussed in debates over ethical issues right from the ancient times. Epicurus (341–306 B.C.) and his followers were particularly involved in the discussion of such issues. It is in the medieval period that theological issues dominated the views of happiness. The secular interests were revitalized during the Age of Reason and the Utilitarians took seriously the issue of defining the nature of happiness. John Stuart Mill, for instance, asserted the superiority of "mental" over bodily pleasures: "It is better to be a human being dissatisfied than a pig satisfied," he said. Then he added that it is "better to be Socrates dissatisfied than a fool satisfied. And if the fool, or the pig, are of a different opinion, it is because they only know their side of the question. The other party to the comparison knows both sides." (See Mill, 1863/1962, p. 260).

B. G. Tilak (1915/1956), while discussing the views of happiness in the Indian and Western philosophies, referred to the above quotation by Mill and suggested that these ideas are in line with the Indian view. Tilak has suggested that, although the desirability of pain-avoidance and the human pursuit of pleasure are almost universally taken for granted, little thought is generally given to finding out what constitutes the highest and most lasting form of pleasure. The Indian philosophers, however, have taken this issue seriously. In fact, the consideration of the highest and most lasting form of happiness is a central issue in Indian philosophy. On the whole, this issue has been more elaborately and extensively treated in Indian philosophy than in Western philosophy. Each school of Indian philosophy has a different concept of the highest form of happiness. It is neither possible nor necessary to discuss at length these various conceptions.[12] It would be useful, however, to identify a few common themes and certain concepts that seem to be more relevant to psychology than ethics.

One of the oldest themes relevant to this endeavor can be traced back to the early period of the Upaniṣads. In the *Kaṭha Upaniṣad* there is an interesting dialogue between Yama, the God of Death, and Naciketas, a young boy who is assigned to the former by the boy's father in a fit of anger. Yama finds this unexpected stranger at his door and finds out that the boy has been waiting for three days during his leave of absence. To make good for his inability to extend hospitality, Yama grants three boons to his young guest. The boy asks first for his return to a forgiving father, then for the knowledge of sacrificial rituals leading to heaven, and thirdly asks for knowledge of what comes after death. Yama grants the first two wishes, but balks at the third, offering instead, cattle, horses and elephants, gold, lovely maidens—a great abode on earth. Naciketas, however, persists in arguing that a man cannot attain true satisfaction with any amount of wealth. (All the worldly things, he had realized, could not be carried along when it is time to meet the God of Death.) Yama is pleased to find that the boy has learned to make the critical distinction between the pleasant (preyas), on the one hand, and the intrinsically desirable and better (śreyas), on the other. The balance of the Upaniṣad is devoted to the explanation of śreyas as being the same as the true realization of the self (ātman). (See R. E. Hume, 1931, pp. 341ff)

That an infinite amount of wealth cannot lead to the highest and lasting forms of happiness is an ancient, pervasive, and lasting theme of the Hindu view of life. The reader may recall that the same theme was reiterated in a conversation between the old king Bṛhadratha and the ascetic Śākyāyana from the *Maitri Upaniṣad,* which was referred to earlier. This theme is most succinctly stated in a single statement in the well-known Manu's book of laws: "Desire is never extinguished by the enjoyment of desired objects; it only grows stronger like a fire (fed) with clarified butter." (*Manusmṛti,* 2.94)[13] The epitome of this view is illustrated in the myth of the king Yayāti, a man who assiduously and enthusiastically pursues every conceivable form of sensual pleasure, and after long years spent in the middle of a large harem in the most affluent palace, fails to find lasting satisfaction.

As a student of psychology familiar with Freud's concept of the Oedipus complex, I am tempted to coin the term "Yayāti Complex" to designate the theme illustrated by the myth of Yayāti. This Yayāti Complex appears truly alien to the Western culture and is, in fact, diametrically opposed to Freud's views of happiness. As mentioned before, Freud thought that the satiation of untamed instinctual desires was what would make one most happy. Further, in Freud's view, Yoga involves "killing off the instincts" in order to defend oneself against the suffering caused by the refusal of the external world to sate our needs.[14] Such a view of Yoga is common in the West. Moreover, the Hindu view that demands extreme asceticism is often considered to be a killjoy attitude to life. This is clearly a mistaken interpretation of the Hindu view of life. It should be noted that the sating of sexual desires (kāma) and the acquisition of wealth (artha) are prescribed, along with the other obligations by the religious way of life (dharma) for every member of the society. Normally, a person is required to fulfill the obligations of dharma, artha, and kāma before being considered eligible to pursue the goal of liberating the Self (mokṣa). By and large, sex is not considered sinful. The *Kāma Sūtra* of Vātsyāyana is one of the world's oldest descriptive ("empirical") studies of sex, and it is by no means considered a clandestine document. The erotic sculptures of the temples of Khajurāho and Konarak illustrate the idealization of sexual pleasure-seeking found in certain sections of the Hindu society. Moreover, some religious sects—such as certain Tāntric cults—prescribe sex as a means of attaining spiritual development. Nevertheless, it would be appropriate to say that the quotation from *Manusmrti* mentioned above represents the most dominant view of happiness, which is deeply rooted in the Hindu culture.

What the myth of Yayāti is intended to convey is that satiation of sensual desires and the accumulation of wealth enabling us to satiate the same is *not enough* if one aims at anything higher than the "ordinary" pleasures. It is not to be interpreted to mean that satiation of sensual desires is useless and that everyone must leave the world and become a hermit. Although several techniques of Yoga are designed for "taming the body," these are recommended only for those who have attained the state of vairāgya, or a feeling that continual pursuit of pleasure, wealth, and power is not enough—after trying one's hand. Yayāti and Bṛhadratha were kings who had acquired a lot of wealth and power and had enjoyed much during their life time. Young Naciketas asked for knowledge of what happens after death only *after* acquiring the knowledge of how to reach heaven, the eternal abode of drinks and damsels. One may conclude that Naciketas was precocious in attaining vairāgya. In this respect he was like the well-known young prince Siddhārtha (who was to become the Buddha).

In defense of the thesis of the insatiability of desires, it is often argued that *if* wealth and power were enough, the innumerable emperors in the history of the world should have been the happiest people on earth. There is a belief popular among many Indians that Alexander the Great felt miserable when he thought that there was no more land left for him to conquer, after he annexed the Indian kingdom of Punjab to his empire. The idea is that there will always be frustration at the top because deprivation is relative. Even modern psychology testifies to this effect in the form of a popular theory called the "theory of relative deprivation." Once a person begins to look for "more and bigger" of everything, there will always be *something* left unconquered and unattained. After all, what happened to the billionaire Howard Hughes? Was he really happy and contented?

Here we have hit the limitations of cultural and moral relativism, as far as psychological theory goes. If I were to pursue the line of argument begun in the previous paragraph, I might sound evangelical. There are moral overtones to these arguments: relevant prescriptions would follow in terms of a program of applied psychology for those who accept a fundamental thesis such as the one of the insatiable nature of desires. The techniques of Yoga are based on such an assumption, just as Freudian therapy is based on the thesis that freedom from anxiety cannot be attained by suppressing one's libidinal desires. For those who accept such themes as part of their cultural heritage, the techniques and their goals are unquestionable. They would be highly questionable, however, for those outside the culture. Here, instead of searching for cultural universals, one may focus on "relationism," Mannheim's formula for the sociology of knowledge. In other words, what cross-cultural psychology can and should do is more than merely point out that psychological knowledge is culturally relative; it should first identify cultural themes that are significant from the point of view of psychology, and then work out the implications of such themes for specific aspects of psychological theories.

A direct implication for the thesis of insatiability of desires is expressed in the following type of questions: If the satiation of the sensual desires is not enough to attain the highest form of happiness, what is required? What is the nature of the highest happiness? How can it be attained?

It is precisely these questions that many Indian thinkers have considered the foremost in importance. Patañjali's Yoga system considers kaivalya (literally, isolation) as the highest and the most desirable state of man. Kaivalya is a complex concept like ānanda, apavarga, hita, kalyāṇa, mokṣa, nirvāṇa, nihśreyasa, śreyas, and other similar ones, that represent the views of various schools of thought about the highest and the most desirable human condition. It would be impossible to convey the meanings of them here; it would take volumes to do so. Also, because most of these concepts are based upon complex theories in ontology and epistemology, they would make little sense without an appreciation of such theories. For instance, the Pūrva Mīmaṁsā school of philosophy emphasizes the release of the individual from the eternal cycle of birth, death, and rebirth as the goal of life. The greatest concern here is the fear of being reborn into another (miserable) form of existence (and this is a common Indian concern). This involves the assumption of existence after death which is shared by many religions including Christianity. It is better to avoid these types of issues as they are likely to be of minimal interest to most contemporary psychologists. Instead, it would be useful to briefly explain those aspects of the Indian concepts of happiness that refer to states of consciousness, the nature of the self, and to the behavioral manifestations of the state of highest happiness.

In the four chapters that follow, I propose to discuss at length some Indian contributions to the understanding of states of consciousness, the nature of the self, and to the problem of changing personality or behavior patterns from a less desirable to a relatively more desirable state of affairs. It is only after such discussion that I expect to make reasonable sense of the Indian view of the ideal human condition. Yet, let me attempt a very brief sketch of the basic ideas. These should provide some basis for comparison with the Western views described earlier, and will also set the tone for the remainder of the book.

The briefest common description of the Indian view of ideal human condition uses the trilogy of terms "sat," "cit" and "ānanda." These are usually translated as Being, Consciousness, and Bliss, respectively. They can be loosely interpreted to convey (1) a state of "being" in an ontological, existential sense (An alternative meaning of sat is truth—satyam); (2) a quality of sentience, or a state of pure consciousness that does not differentiate between the experiencer and the "object" of his awareness; and (3) blissfulness that implies an indescribable and intense type of joyous, beatific, or mystical experience. According to Patañjali, who accepts the dualistic ontology of the Sāṅkhya philosophy, the Puruṣa or Self attains the state of kaivalya or isolation when he detaches himself completely from Prakṛti, which is the principle that constitutes the manifold objects of the material world, including the body. In psychological terms, a person can attain a state of kaivalya by gradually withdrawing from the objects of his senses, by controlling the flow of his thought processes so as to reach complete concentration or one-pointedness. In a series of steps the practice of Yoga is ultimately believed to lead the aspirant to a state called asṁprajñāta (or noncogitive) samādhi, which leads him to the state of kaivalya. The Yogic breathing exercises are aids in the long psychological process of a complete transformation of personality. In place of kaivalya of the dualist Sāṅkhya, the non-dualist Vedānta philosophy speaks of mukti or release from ignorance, and from the ongoing process of action (karma) and its inevitable consequences. According to this view, an individual is released from the miseries that follow from the eternal cycle of karma as soon as he attains knowledge of his real self. It is claimed that the real self (ātman) is Brahman or the ubiquitous single principle of which Being, Consciousness, and Bliss are natural qualities. The natural blissfulness of existence is thus restored when misconceptions of the nature of self are dispelled.

Notwithstanding the differences in terminology used by the dualist and non-dualist philosophers in describing the highest state of human existence, its psychological characteristics are the same. It is only the explanation of this state in ontological terms and of how its knowledge is attained (its epistemology) that are different. The psychological analysis of the underlying process leading to this state is the specialty of Patañjali's Yoga, and the major systems of Indian philosophy seem to accept or adopt it. Thus, Patañjali explains the attainment of "psychic" powers or skills in extrasensory perception, the various forms of samādhi and the like, which signal various landmarks on the pathway to the state of existence, variously termed kaivalya, mukti, nirvāṇa, and so on. This highest state is considered immensely joyous or blissful. It is also considered to be beyond description or ineffable. It is said to be unique and far more intense than, for example, the ordinary experiences of joy acquired by eating, sexual gratification, winning or attaining success in wordly affairs.

We shall return to the detailed examination of the psychology of the "higher" states of consciousness in Chapter 4, which is devoted to two major Indian theories of consciousness. But a few points must be mentioned here relating to the concept of happiness. First, persons who are able to attain the highest state are considered to be extremely rare—maybe one in several million, or perhaps even rarer than that. The journey from the ordinary, normal state to the most superior state is a long one and we can, of course, find many persons who are at various points in between. The tradition has it that there is a possibility of regression along the way; there are innumerable stories about yogis who have fallen from their path by trying to use and demonstrate their extrasensory powers, and have thus been sidetracked on power- or ego-"trips." Second, those who finally attain the state of supreme ecstacy may not retain it over long periods of time. There is even a school of thought which holds that the rare being who reaches such a state does not survive afterwards because, the highest possible state being achieved, there is no purpose for which the processes of life should continue. However, another, more commonly held belief is that such persons do survive, if only for the benefit of mankind. A common term used to refer to such saintly beings is *jīvanmukta,* or the living one who has attained mukti or release from ignorance, the consequences of past action, and from all forms of misery resulting from the past. The *Bhagavad-Gītā,* a compendium of essential contributions of major schools of Indian thought, describes the ideal human condition such persons manifest. In the second chapter (verses 56–72), devoted to the Sāṅkhya-Yoga perspective, there is a description of the *sthitaprajña,* "one whose mind is stable"; the ideal devotee of God is described in the 12th chapter (13–19); and the 14th chapter (22–27) describes the "character of him who is beyond the three guṇas, namely sattva, rajas, tamas." All these descriptions refer to the same state of happiness, indicating that aspirants who properly follow the guidelines set by Jñāna Yoga (or the path of knowledge), Rāja Yoga (which is prescribed by Patañjali), Bhakti Yoga, (the path of devotion), Karma Yoga (the method of detached action) or other established schools of adhyātma, reach, ultimately, the same extremely desirable state of existence. Let me try to present a brief account of the description of the ideal human condition from the *Bhagavad-Gītā.*

The first and foremost characteristic of a sthitaprajña is his deep inner sense of contentment (ātmanyeva ātmanā tuṣṭaḥ) (*Bhagavad-Gītā* 2.55), which arises from the relinquishing of various desires (kāmān)—or of the pursuit of selfish worldly goals such as acquisition of wealth, fame, and so on. Such a person is unruffled by the minor joys and sorrows between which ordinary human beings keep oscillating. He is unaffected by fear, anger, confusion, bewilderment, and other forms of emotional excitement. He does not hanker for any personal gains, nor is he afraid of losing what he has. As such, he cannot be moved by praise, nor can he be pressured by any sort of threats or blame. Having the broadest sympathies, extending to all creatures, he is not exclusively attached to a family, institution, or any other particular group. In this sense, such a person is a man of no fixed abode (aniketa). Welfare of humanity as a whole is his constant concern and, therefore, he need not discriminate between friend and foe. The oft-repeated terms in the *Bhagavad-Gītā* are extreme selflessness and lack of egoism of any sort (nirmamo nirahaṁkāraḥ). A possible misunderstanding is that the relinquishing of all desires would imply that such a person does not even desire to speak to anyone, or even to eat and drink. As long as the body survives one would, of course, continue to feel hunger, thirst, and pain, as well as comfort. Being unaffected by ordinary feelings of joy, sorrow or anger should not be misconstrued as a lack of capacity to experience such feelings, or as the inability to distinguish between pleasing or angering circumstances. The condition of happiness and inner contentment beyond joy and sorrow could only be expressed metaphorically;

the *Bhagavad-Gītā* uses the metaphor of the ocean that keeps its level despite the continuous flow of mighty rivers that empty themselves into it. We are here speaking of a human character of immense depth.

Are we speaking about an ideal which is so high as to stay forever in our imagination and never come true? Not at all. It is firmly believed that such persons as described in the *Bhagavad-Gītā* have in fact existed in flesh and blood. Again, those who had the good fortune of reaching such heights are not just a few prophets of the past, those chosen by God to lead the earthlings. Saint Tukārām (poem no. 2325) remarks in a short poem that mokṣa is not a gift that God could bestow upon anyone hand-picked by Him at His sweet will! Only those who deserve it as a reward for their effort can get it, and no one who deserves it can be denied the same. Moreover, it is believed that there has been an unbroken tradition of persons who attained this very high goal; almost every generation could point to at least a single human being who made it up to there. It is commonly believed, for instance, that in recent times Rāmakṛṣṇa Paramahaṁsa (1836–1886) and Ramana Maharṣi (1879–1950) reached this most coveted state. Their biographies may offer a glimpse of the behavioral characteristics of persons who are considered to be sthitaprajña or a jīvanmukta.

The rarity of persons who reach the highest state is partly explained in terms of the pervasiveness of māyā or "primeval illusion," which is the root cause of the mistaken notions of the self, which, in turn is the cause of misery. Notwithstanding the pervasive nature of māyā, every individual is believed to have the potential for reaching the highest state of happiness. This belief follows from a fundamental assumption of the Vedānta philosophy that every existing soul is ultimately part and parcel of Brahman, the ultimate reality, of which blissfulness is an unmistakable characteristic. The only reason most of us do not experience our existence as blissful is that we are ignorant of the true nature of ourselves. Some day, every one of us may reach the coveted state of self-realization. Indeed, the Indian view offers a great sense of hope, since it is believed that, should one fail to reach the goal before death, the journey can be continued in subsequent incarnations of the soul. Nevertheless, the Indian concept of happiness does not represent an other-worldly goal. Kaivalya or mukti are not restricted to a place called heaven where no one can enter without a death certificate.

It is paradoxical that, despite the promise of emancipation from all narrow social loyalties for those who reach the goal of adhyātma, the primary impulse leading to adhyātma sounds extremely individualistic. After all, the pursuit of kaivalya or mukti aims primarily at the happiness of only those who strive for it; it is not a utopia promising happiness for all, collectively that is, nor is it a panacea for all of the world's ills. But for those interested in psychology, the fact that the goal of Yoga and Vedānta theories is primarily individualistic should not pose a problem. After all, the legitimate focus of psychology is on the individual, is it not?

I have argued that a complete and well-rounded theory of psychology should have a well-defined concept of the ideal human condition which can serve as a goal for its applied branch. I have looked for such concepts in major Indian and Western psychologies, and have tried to explicate them where they seem to be implicit. Given the foregoing account, how do their views of the ideal human condition compare with each other?

A clear difference of views in this respect can be seen between existential psychologies on the one hand, and the Yogic and Vedāntic psychologies on the other. Although all three of these theories hold that the experience of most human beings is usually full of misery, the existentialists seem to believe that there is little hope (if any) for attaining a happy state of existence, while the Yoga and Vedāntic theorists claim that a very high state of happiness is indeed attainable. Freud, too, was pessimistic about the human condition. Although he implied that freedom from anxiety and the attainment of some form of happiness are possible, his view of happiness is almost entirely different from the Yoga and Vedāntic views of happiness. Again, as noted before, the behaviorist view of the ideal human condition is the least explicit of all. If my imputations about their implicit view are correct, then a desirable condition of an individual may be considered to follow simply from his being able to adapt to his environment. Others have considered mastery of the environment an important source of satisfaction.

The value of mastering the environment appears in many forms in Western psychological theories. Mastery of the environment is implicit in Marie Jahoda's view of positive mental health, and in Robert White's concept of competence motivation. Skinner's utopian view involves the theme of mastery of environment in a very different way. Unlike the focus on the individual apparent in Jahoda's and White's views, Skinner's emphasis is not so much on the individual as on the society as a whole. The society as a whole can attain a desirable, utopian state of peace, harmony, and order by altering the entire social environment and by "programming" each individual according to the laws of behavioral analysis.

Although these things have been said before, it seemed necessary to repeat them here in order to make clear to the reader the contrast between these Western and Indian views. The yogi aims at controlling his own states of consciousness in order to attain a happy state, rather than at mastering the "environment." It is true though, that a yogi is said to be able to read other people's thoughts, levitate, become invisible to others, and to acquire other such powers which he can use to control others, and thereby control his "environment" in some way. However, as noted before, Patañjali (3.37) specifically considers such powers *(siddhis)* obstacles to the goal of samādhi. It is, of course, true that many people practice Yoga specifically to attain such powers, and certain later writings on various forms of Yoga seem to be obsessed with the idea of attaining more and more exotic varieties of powers. Such forms of so-called Yoga, and the power-mongering attitude they reflect, have little respectability (if any) from the point of view of established doctrines of the Indian tradition. Neither the validity of the claims to the miraculous power, nor the relative popularity of views that favor or oppose the seeking of such powers, are important for our consideration.

Here it is important to note the way in which cultural values have influenced psychological theories. I have argued that the typical orientation of the Western tradition is Man Over Nature. A favorable view of mastering the environment and the acquisition of powers for this purpose are consonant with this attitude to nature, and are clearly reflected in the psychological theories just mentioned. I have also argued that the typical view of the Indian tradition is Man In Nature and that this attitude does not favor the seeking of power. From the foregoing discussion, it should be clear that these contrasting cultural themes of India and the West have systematically influenced the views of the ideal human condition implicit in the psychological theories of the respective traditions. If my arguments have any force, they illustrate "relationism" in a Mannheimian sense.

Some may point out that there is a similarity between the Maslowian ideal of the self-actualizing person and the Indian ideal of sthitaprajña. I must admit that there are certain similarities between these two models. Both emphasize detached outlooks, and both stress emotional stability and unselfishness. Perhaps these are universal ideals shared by traditions that are disparate in many other ways. Despite these similarities, however, there are certain clear differences between the Maslowian and Indian views. It may be recalled, for instance, that Maslow insisted on the nontheological character of his subjects' mystical experiences, while Indian views expressed in the *Bhagavad-Gītā* and other sources do not share such a definite aversion to a reference to God. It may also be noted that Maslow is, after all, a rebel; he rebelled against the established view of Western psychology as a "science" that is set out to control the forces of nature. He also rebelled against the value-neutral stance of the behavioristic ideas that have dominated Western psychology, and even criticized the antireligious orientation of "scientific" psychology. (See Maslow, 1964/1970) Nonetheless, his view of the self-actualizing person is distinctly secular and achievement-oriented; it stands in contrast to the Indian views of sthitaprajña and jīvanmukta. The Indian psychologies aim at transforming an individual into a jīvanmukta, who is no less than a saint. The Western psychologists seem to have given over the value of saintliness to the Church. If the Church has undertaken to "canonize" those who have displayed saintliness, must the psychologist abrogate his right to acknowledge selflessness, kindness, magnanimity of heart, and other such human qualities? Is saintliness forever polluted by the touch of some religious fanatic? Is it an exclusive product patented by the Church, Inc.? Answers to such questions obviously beg statements of opinion, but, as far as the psychologist is concerned, opinions on such issues are important, insofar as they determine the kind of psychology he will choose.

Notes

1. A rather similar approach to identifying assumptions underlying the "orthodox Western psychology" appears in Charles Tart's book, *Transpersonal Psychologies*. (Tart, 1975) I wish to acknowledge that I have benefitted from Tart's parallel approach. Readers familiar with Tart's essay would note several differences in our treatments of similar issues.
2. Comte labeled this primitive stage "the theological stage." He suggested that every field of inquiry passes inevitably through metaphysical and scientific stages which are successive and superior to previous stages. In the "scientistic" and positivist spirit (which many modern psychologists share), the word metaphysical variously implies speculative, philosophical, non-empirical, intuitive, experiential or mystical ways of knowing. Intuitive and mystical knowledge is considered not simply nonlogical or nonrational but irrational, inferior, or downright wrong. Tilak (1915/1956) has translated the Comtian terms theological, metaphysical and scientific, as ādhidaivika, adhyātmika and ādhibhautika respectively. He has used the word adhyātmika to describe knowledge based on mystical experience of the type a yogi obtains in the state of samādhi, and the word ādhibhautika to characterize the view of natural science. Further, Tilak has strongly argued that these two spheres of knowledge are independent and useful, each in its own right. He is clearly opposed to Comte's view of superiority of natural science. This approach by Tilak represents the spirit of the Indian tradition and contrasts with the dominant Western viewpoint which is well argued by the philosopher Bertrand Russell in his essay called "Mysticism and Logic." (See Russell, 1921, pp. 1–32)
3. For a perspective on Einstein's view of the predictability of events see P. W. Bridgman's essay, "Determinism in Modern Science," originally published in the *British Journal of Philosophy of Science* in 1955, and reproduced by Sidney Hook (1958) in his book, *Determinism and Freedom*.

4. Certainly there is a trend in modern psychology to pay attention to moral issues. Nonetheless, the Humean dichotomy of *is* versus *ought* (i.e., of matters of fact versus those of value) is as deeply rooted in psychology as it is in the Western *zeitgeist*. Thus, most psychologists who study moral reasoning, like the Piagetians, for instance, restrict themselves to the discovery of general laws (e.g., sequential stages in the development of moral reasoning) and avoid the discussion of moral issues as such. As noted in Chapter 2 of this book, Kohlberg (1971), a prominent researcher in the field of moral development, has gone so far as to suggest that he has developed a novel approach, whereby moral issues can be resolved on the basis of factual data, a view which is reflected in the very title of his paper, "From is to aught; How to commit the naturalistic fallacy and get away with it in the study of moral development."
5. The Sāṅkhya philosophy is one of the oldest systems in India. It is traced back to Kapila, who lived around the 7th century B.C. The basic text for Sāṅkhya philosophy is *Sāṅkhya Kārikā* of Īśvarakṛṣṇa (2nd or 3rd century A.D.). Several editions of this Sanskrit text are available; one by Raja (1963) is listed in the Reference section. Brief, authoritative outlines of the basic concepts are available in historical accounts of Indian philosophy by Dasgupta (1922), Hiriyanna (1932) and Radhakrishnan (1929).
6. The continuity of the animate and inanimate, human, and animal world is an old theme of the Indian view of life. Due to the prevalence of this view there was no chance of resistance to Darwinian theory similar to the theological opposition to it in the West.
7. The paradox of treating altruism as simply another (if enlightened) form of self-seeking is not new to Indian psychology. *The Bṛhadāraṇyaka Upaniṣad* (2.4.1–11; 4.5.1–15), for instance, deals with the same paradox in a dialogue between the sage Yājñavalkya and his two wives, Maitreyī and Kātyāyanī (See Hume, 1931, pp. 98–102 and 144–147). Says Yājñavalkya: "Not for the husband is a husband dear, but for the love of the Self (ātman) a husband is dear," and goes on to substitute son, cattle, and the gods. At the end of the series he adds a conclusion that sums it up: "Not for love of all is all dear, but for the love of Self all is dear." The trick in this style of argument is the dual meaning of ātman, which is taken to mean the individual as well as a speck of the ubiquitous principle called Brahman that pervades all beings of the universe. Yājñavalkya thus exhorts his wives to try to understand the true nature of the Self, so that once they understand it to be identical with the Universal Self or the Brahman, their narrow, selfish love for objects will be transformed into a genuine love for humanity, and indeed for all creatures. It should be clear that there is a basic difference between the Upaniṣadic resolution of the paradox for love of others as love of self, and the Piliavin type of resolution of the same paradox. While Piliavin *et al.* try to reduce altruism to Benthamian egoistic striving, the Upaniṣads try to transform the love of self into the realization of the ultimate reality.
8. W. D. Ross (Ed.) *The Works of Aristotle*. Vol. 3, Ch. 2, 460 b, Oxford: Clarendon Press, 1931.
9. The difference in the nature of the human condition as portrayed by the characters of Sartre and Camus is partly due to their fictitious nature, in contrast to the "real-life" cases described by the existential analysts. Also, the cases examined by existential psychiatrists are clearly pathological; they land in the clinic because they are in need of help or outside intervention. It makes sense to assume that the existential philosophers' own personal predicament is reflected in the characters of their creation. But, Sartre and Camus were great intellectuals, creative men with highly sensitive minds, whose depth of experience can hardly be considered parallel with "ordinary"

men. Their condition must be far different from the patients in clinics described by existential psychiatrists. Let us assume that there is a certain patient, a schizophrenic, for instance, who is both overly guilt-ridden and anxiety-prone. A psychoanalytically oriented psychologist would probably consider the patient's guilt his most important symptom, while an existential analyst would probably focus on his chaotic thought pattern. We may note in this connection that Laing's interpretation of schizophrenia typically emphasizes this aspect (Laing, 1960). Such in interpretation is explained simply in terms of the world view of the theorist. On the epistemological level the same can be explained in terms of the influence of the philosophical presuppositions that mold the outcome of an inquiry.

10. In *Civilization and Its Discontents* Freud (1930, p. 79) has expressed his disapproval of efforts to "master the internal sources of our needs." He specifically adds that "The extreme form of this is brought about by killing off the instincts, as is prescribed by the worldly wisdom of the East and practised by Yoga." According to Freud, such taming of the desires implies relinquishing all activities and amounts to sacrificing one's own life. He did not think that it was possible to completely relinquish the very aim of satisfying instinctual desires. This means that one would be always involved in obtaining instinctual gratification and, further, that those who had tried to tame their desires would never get the joy of sating the "wild instinctual impulse" that was considered *the* highest form of happiness. The typical Indian view is certainly different from Freud's. First, the yogi believes that a complete mastery over sexual desires *is* possible; second, successive and successful disappearance of desires does not amount to "sacrificing" one's life; and most of all, as we shall note in the remainder of the chapter, the Indian theories claim that much higher forms of happiness are attainable than the sating of wild instinctual desires. I must therefore conclude that Freud either didn't accept their claims, or that he misunderstood the real nature of Yoga.

11. This view of Freud is often interpreted to mean that he advocated the most uninhibited sating of sexual desires. Many an advocate of "free love" and promiscuity has enlisted Freud on his side, and there is no end to the cheap popularization and vulgarization of his views. Erik Erikson (1968, p. 136) has noted that Freud, when asked what he thought a normal person should be able to do well, simply said, "Lieben und arbeiten" ("to love and to work"). Erikson further explains that "when Freud said 'love', he meant the generosity of intimacy as well as genital love" and that by work he meant general work productiveness without being preoccupied to the extent of losing "his right or capacity to be sexual and a loving being."

12. R. V. De Smet of the De Nobili College of Pune, India, has given a concise account of the views of the major Indian philosophers on the highest form of happiness in his article entitled "Ānanda" in the *Marathi Encyclopaedia of Philosophy* (D. D. Vadekar, Ed., *Marāṭhī Tattvajñāna Mahākośa*, Vol. I, p. 74).

13. These words are quoted from the standard translation of *Manusmṛti* by G. Buhler published in *The Laws of Manu*, Vol. XXV of the "Sacred Books of the East" series under the editorship of F. Max Müller. The original translation, published in 1886 by the Oxford University Press was reprinted in 1964 by Motilal Banarsidass of Varanasi, India.

14. See Note 10, above.

3

CONSCIOUSNESS: SOME WESTERN VIEWS

In the previous chapters we were concerned mainly with extratheoretical factors relating to Indian and Western psychologies; no theoretical issues pertaining to particular topics within the field of psychology were discussed. In this chapter we move on to a direct discussion of divergent points of view on a specific topic, namely, consciousness. This topic has been a matter of concern for Indian as well as Western psychologists. Wilhelm Wundt and William James, founding fathers of modern German and American psychology, respectively, considered consciousness as one of the most important issues of psychology. Wundt developed the method of introspection as a technique for the study of consciousness. Around the turn of the century, German and American psychology journals were flooded with reports of introspective studies. By the second decade of this century, however, the method of introspection was considered a failure and, with the advent of behaviorism, the study of consciousness became a disreputable enterprise. After neglecting it for about half a century, psychologists have recently revived their interest in the study of consciousness. Within the past decade consciousness has emerged as a popular field of investigation in its many-splendored facets called the "altered states" of consciousness.

The Vedānta theorists have elaborately discussed the nature of wakeful, dream, and sleep states. In addition, they have described an uncommon state which they have labelled the "Fourth" state of consciousness. The Yoga system of Patañjali is concerned with the study of the following mental processes: the processes leading to valid cog-

Notes for Chapter 3 are on p. 172.

nition (such as direct perception, logical thinking, and the acceptance of reliable testimony), those leading to erroneous cognition (such as the experience of illusions), as well as mental processes involved in imagining, sleeping, dreaming, and recollecting.[1]

It is hardly surprising that the study of the states of consciousness such as wakeful, sleep, and dream states emerged independently in the Indian and Western traditions in different periods of history. After all, the cycle of wakeful and sleep states is common not only to mankind but even to many animal species. It is but natural that people in any part of the world and of any period of history would be curious about such universal or "panhuman" phenomena. Even members of the so-called "primitive" cultures have developed their own "theories" of dreaming. Anthropologists, particularly those who were enthused by Freud's interesting insights into the nature of dreams, have documented not only the dreams described by members of diverse cultures, but also their views about the meaning, significance, and causes of dreaming. We cannot start to build an "etic" theory of dreaming by comparing all the formal and informal theories implicit in the folklore of the world—although it may be interesting and even worthwhile to do so. We may begin by comparing selected formal theories of consciousness from the Indian and Western traditions and examine how they are related to the thought pattern of the cultures of their origin.

Most modern Western views of consciousness have been influenced, one way or another, by the Cartesian view of the world which divided reality between two ontological categories: the conscious mental substance on the one hand, and the non-conscious material substance on the other. Since Descartes, generations of Western philosophers and psychologists have started their theorizing against the backdrop of the mind-matter dichotomy. Once such a dichotomy is accepted, it becomes necessary somehow to account for the interdependence of the mind and the body since a fundamental disparity between the mental and material substances is taken for granted. The basic dilemma is: how can intangible entities such as thoughts (e.g., an "intention" to move) cause changes in the tangible, physical world (such as moving a leg)? Numerous ways of resolving this dilemma have been suggested. The latest candidate for a proposed resolution of the "mind–body problem" is the identity theory, which proposes that consciousness is identical with the physico-chemical processes of the brain. (Feigl, 1958/1967; Place, 1956) The contemporary philosophers are still debating this issue and no satisfactory resolution of the dilemma is in sight (see O'Connor, 1969). Given the great diversity of opinion on this issue, and the seemingly endless controversy among partisans of particular positions, many psychologists seem to be embarrassed by having to face the mind–body problem. They would rather forget the issue altogether and not have to worry about their own position vis-à-vis the mind-body problem. But the issue is too important to neglect, and the nature of the history of Western psychology is such that, no matter how hard one may try to avoid the issue, nearly every psychologist ends up accepting one or other traditional solution to the mind–body problem as his implicit starting point. The difference in implicitly held views on the mind–body issue is a major factor in accounting for the divergence of approaches to consciousness in Western psychology.

As noted in the previous chapter, the Indian systems of psychology, too, are based on divergent ontological doctrines such as the dualism of Sāṅkhya and the monism of the Vedānta theorists. However, the Indian debate over monism *versus* dualism is quite different from the Western issue of mind–body dualism, particularly in view of its implications for psychological theory. Although we do not have to examine the East–West differences on metaphysical issues as such, we should note that the Indian psychologists have been less concerned with the nature of the relationship between the body and the mind than have the Western psychologists. The major concern for the Indians has been the nature of what are sometimes called the "mystical" states of consciousness—and how to attain them. That the Western psychologists have largely neglected the study of so-called mystical states is well known. Despite such differences, there are some remarkable similarities in some specific points discussed by Indian and Western psychologists. We shall note some such similarities in the following section of this chapter.

William James and his Concept of the "Stream of Consciousness"

James, a pioneer in the study of consciousness among modern Western psychologists, has provided an excellent descriptive account of the subjective or "inner" aspect of life which he called the stream of thought or the stream of consciousness.[2] That "states of mind" succeed one another within a person was considered by James "the fundamental fact." "Now we are seeing, now hearing; now reasoning, now willing; now recollecting, now expecting; now loving, now hating; and in a hundred ways we know our minds to be alternatively engaged." (James, 1890/1950, Vol. 1, p. 230) There is a *constant change* in our consciousness, and this goes on throughout the span of our life. We do find that there are occasional interruptions in our consciousness, as produced by anaesthetics, epilepsy, fainting, and so on. Despite such time gaps, notes James, there is a sensible *continuity* in our "thought" or consciousness.

"When Paul and Peter wake up in the same bed, and recognize that they have been asleep, each one of them mentally reaches back and makes connection with but *one* of the two streams of thought which were broken by the sleeping hours" (James, 1890/1950, Vol. 1, p. 238). Each one of us picks up the thread of his or her *own* string of thoughts. Each person keeps his thoughts to himself. In James's words: "No thought ever comes into direct *sight* of a thought in another personal consciousness than its own. Absolute insulation, irreducible pluralism, is the law" (James, 1890/1950, Vol. 1, p. 226). Within each person, all thoughts throughout the entire "chain" or "train" belong together; they are connected by way of ownership of the same self or the "I." Despite time gaps, consciousness "does not appear to itself chopped up in bits." "It is nothing jointed; it flows." James put it quite aptly: "A 'river' or a 'stream' are the metaphors by which it is most naturally described" (James, 1890/1950, Vol. 1, p. 239).

It is interesting to note that James was neither alone, nor the first one to use this "most natural" metaphor to describe the nature of consciousness. Vyāsa, who lived around 400 A.D., used precisely the same metaphor (cittanadī) to describe the same phenomenon in his commentary on one of the aphorisms of Pantañjali (1.12) According to Vyāsa, the various operations of the mind (vṛttayaḥ) leave certain impressions behind. These impressions are believed to reside within the organism for indefinite periods of time and resurface into consciousness at an appropriate moment of time. These revived processes, again, leave behind impressions (saṁskārāḥ) of their own. This cycle of mental processes, their impressions, and mental processes brought back by these impressions, goes on eternally. This cycle results in the flowing character of conscious experience.[3]

The basic idea is that there is a thread of continuity in the processes of consciousness. The events in the past, present, and future are not random or unconnected, but systematically related. Without the connection of present states with those of the past, how could one pick up the thread of past events in his own life? A variety of psychological concepts such as memory, learning, self, and others have been used to help explain the continuity in the subjective aspect of our lives. That experiences of the past leave behind some kind of "record" which is capable of storage and retrieval (as in the case of memory) is a discovery common to most Indian as well as Western theories. Although it is not possible, at this time, to go into detailed comparison of theories on this issue, it may be pointed out, for example, that in psychoanalytic theory, the "unconscious" is considered to be a storehouse of memories of past events. In learning theory, the consequences of past behavior are said to build up a "repertoire" of responses within the organism. Yogic psychology uses the term *karmāśaya* to express a similar idea.[4] We shall return to this issue at a later point.

At this point, we must note that, besides his emphasis on the continuity aspect of consciousness, William James has rightly emphasized the implicit "I," the owner of the thoughts, as it were, who is present throughout the length of the stream of consciousness. In James's words: "It seems as if the elementary psychic fact were not *thought* or *this thought* or *that thought*, but *my thought*, every thought being *owned* . . . The universal conscious fact is not 'feelings and thoughts exist', but 'I think', and 'I feel'." (James, 1890/1950, Vol. 1, p. 226, emphasis original)[5] It is interesting that Patañjali, too, has considered the I-ness (asmitā) as being a constant concomitant of the mental processes (vṛttayaḥ) that appear in the stream of consciousness. Despite this important similarity between James and Patañjali, however, their positions are considerably different on the issue of the nature of the "I" or the self. This is a complex issue which must be considered at length. We shall return to it in Chapter 5.

James's account of the stream of consciousness introduces us briefly to the phenomenon which constitutes important subject-matter for psychology. The questions which the psychologists try to answer in relation to experiential states and mental processes can be phrased as follows: What is the precise nature of these phenomena? What is the correct manner of investigating such phenomena and how can we make sure that our methods lead to valid knowledge about them? What is the best way of dealing with subjective events in practice? The first of these questions relates to the ontological categories involved in our views of reality; the second refers to the epistemological issues underlying the investigative mode; and the third type of questeion confronts us with the goals of applied psychology. It will be useful to keep these questions in mind while discussing the major Indian and Western views of consciousness.

It is not without hesitation that I am undertaking to outline the major trends of Indian and Western thought on the nature of consciousness. Part of my hesitation arises simply from the fact that the vast literature on this topic is by no means easy to summarize. Anyone who wishes to undertake such a task must select only part of what is available. It is indeed difficult to outline clear and universally acceptable principles on what to choose and what not to. Some arbitrariness is bound to enter into the process of commission and omission. Also, some bias enters in the process of comparing Indian and Western views, because one tends to emphasize those aspects of established viewpoints which are either clearly similar or considerably divergent. Relative emphasis on a point here, and criticism of another point there may initially appear rather arbitrary or even unnecessary, but I hope that such selective emphasis and criticism will make sense after the various views are explained and compared. Other difficulties arise due to the diversity of opinions within any trend or "school" of thought, and the controversial nature of the issues with which we will deal. It is by no means easy to identify the opinion that is most representative of a given trend, and to offer its "correct" interpretation. Obviously, alternative interpretations are possible. The reader is therefore requested to bear with me if he does not agree with some of my points.

Structuralism: The Introspectionist Approach

Every student of modern psychology has heard of the structuralist approach to the study of consciousness pioneered by Wilhelm Wundt. It is also well-known that Wundt devised the method of classical introspection which was practiced by his students Ach, Marbe, and others in Germany, and Titchener in the United States. Books on the history of Western psychology declare that the method of introspection failed to arrive at any reliable and meaningful results and point out the reasons why. Boring's 1953 article on the history of introspection provides an excellent account of the issues involved, and it is unnecessary to deal in detail with the same issue here. There are, however, certain reasons why it will be useful to examine certain selected aspects of introspectionism. First, I think that the impact of the failure of introspectionism on the course of development of modern psychology is greater and deeper than is ordinarily recognized. The deep-rooted reluctance of many modern psychologists to consider the study of private events in the domain of consciousness as a legitimate enterprise for psychology can be understood only in relation to the background of the failure of inrospectionism. Second, certain problems relating to the study of consciousness can be properly explained in light of the difficulties encountered by classical introspection. Third, as we shall note in detail later on in this section, Patañjali had recognized, in a precise manner, the nature of the pitfalls in the method of introspection. A comparative study such as this one must take note of the insightful observations made by Indian thinkers, long before their Western counterparts arrived at the same conclusions.

Wundt's approach to the study of consciousness can be properly understood only in light of the historical background of his day. Wundt's rightful place in the history of Western psychology is that of a pioneer in the application of the empirical approach to the study of psychological phenomena. What he rebelled against was the speculative, armchair, or purely deductive approach, which he derided as "metaphysical." He insisted on the use of observation under controlled conditions, or experimental methodology, which had proved to be highly successful in the natural sciences. While he was definitely opposed to the continuation of psychology as a branch of philosophy, he was also opposed to reducing psychology to physiology. Again, despite his opposition to metaphysical theories, which he considered "intellectualistic" (perhaps meaning unproductive and useless), he explicitly took a particular position on the metaphysical issue of mind versus matter. Wundt explicitly stated that he was a psychophysical parallelist (Wundt, 1897, pp. 317–318).

The Wundtian variety of psychophysical parallelism is a rather complicated doctrine. Wundt rejected the Cartesian view of an unextended, indivisible, thinking substance of which minds were supposed to be made. He thought that "the concept of mind-substance is 'mythological'." Thus, belief in mental monism was out of the question. He also rejected materialism, because, he thought, any attempt to reduce psychology to physiology of the brain would entirely neglect the important task of "the interpretation of psychological experience" (Wundt, 1897, pp. 313–314). If one begins to conceptualize with the Cartesian dualism as his starting point, and rejects monism of either the mental or material variety, one is necessarily left with a dualist position. Surely, Wundt was a dualist. (Anyone who explicitly adopts the position of psychophysical parallelism implicitly admits some kind of duality of mind and matter.) In keeping with his dualistic position Wundt suggested the need for two independent sets of laws: one to account for the mental, subjective phenomena, and another to account for the objective, material phenomena. Despite such a dualistic view of the world, however, Wundt was reluctant to hypothesize two different types of "substances" which constitute the mental and material entities. Wundt not only rejected distinct ontological categories of the mental and material, but also insisted on the unity of experience, which, he thought, provided a common basis for the subjective world of psychology and the objective world of the natural sciences. What, then, is the basis of the Wundtian variety of dualism? The distinct spheres of psychology and natural science emerge from two distinct *points of view* which we can take in dealing with our experience. Focusing on the experiencing subject or *immediate experience* leads to psychology, while focusing on the *objects of experience—mediate experience*—leads to the natural sciences.

The distinction between mediate and immediate standpoints has an epistemological significance. It is based on a distinction between the subject who is the *knower*, on the one hand, and the *objects of knowledge,* on the other. Introspection involves the reflexive mode of knowing in which the knower focuses on himself rather than on the external objects. But then, what is it that he is supposed to "spect" within himself? The answer is "contents" of psychical experience or conscious content such as sensations, images, and so on. Thus, for instance, a person looking at the cup of coffee in front of him could watch closely the *experience* of the sight of the cup: its whiteness, the level of brightness, the smoothness of texture, or the mildly pleasant character of the bittersweet taste of the coffee still lingering on the tip of the tongue. As this simple example indicates, the emphasis here is not on the object-of-sight, such as the cup, but on the sight-of-the-object. Wundt considered the experiences of sight, touch, or sound to be describable in terms of their attributes such as intensity or extensity, and divisible in terms of their basic elements. The aim of Wundtian psychology was first to break down the contents of experience into basic elements, and then to formulate the laws of their combination. This represents an obvious attempt to fashion psychology after the model of chemistry.

It is clear that Wundtian psychology reified mental phenomena, that is, it treated occurrences such as sight of an object as if they were physical objects. Mental occurrences were considered describable in terms such as extensity or intensity, idioms which are ordinarily used in describing physical phenomena. Such usage involves an error, first, in creating two logical categories, mental and physical (which are implicit in his explicit acceptance of psychophysical parallelism), and then expecting that the same language can be used to adequately describe constructs in both categories. This, in Gilbert Ryle's words, involves a "category mistake" (see Ryle, 1949, p. 17ff.). It appears that Wundt had recognized the possibility of an error of this type when he remarked: "Psychical facts are *occurrences,* not objects; they take place, like all occurrences in time and are never the same at a given point of time as they were the preceding moment" (Wundt, 1897, p. 14). Despite the recognition of the transitory nature of sensations, ideas and feelings, however, Wundtian psychology treated them as though they were stable. If they were not considered stable, how would one expect to find elements such as those of chemistry?

Basic to Wundt's approach to consciousness was the crucial distinction between "subjective process" and "objective content" (Wundt, 1897, p. 16). Anyone dealing with consciousness must recognize the processual nature of thinking, seeing, dreaming, imagining, and similar other mental occurrences. It is the movement in time of such processes that gives the "stream" of consciousness its flowing character. Wundt recognized this aspect of consciousness, but he was clearly more interested in content than process. Titchener, a student of Wundt who carried his master's approach to the New World, and clarified, elaborated, and defended it, had more to say about the distinction between process and content. He stressed that "experience is continuous and a function of time: so that a psychology whose elements are sensations . . . is a process psychology . . . " (Titchener, 1909/1967, p. 27). Thoughts and memories appear and disappear constantly, and during their brief appearances, they grow, change, and decay very rapidly. The Indian thinkers clearly recognized this. In the *Gītā* (6.34) Arjuna says: "The mind, O Kṛṣṇa, is very fickle, impetuous, and obstinate. I find it as difficult to control as the wind." The yogi, as well as the introspectionist, must face difficulties in dealing with the rapidity of the conscious processes. Titchener, who made it his life's business to conduct introspectionist studies, borrowed the lucid expression of William James in describing the nature of this difficulty: "The attempt at introspective analysis . . . is in fact like seizing a spinning top to catch its motion, or trying to run up the gas quickly enough to see how the darkness looks" (James, 1890/1950, Vol. 1, p. 244). James apparently gave up trying to stop the top or quickly turning off the gas jet, but Titchener persisted.

One of the various ways in which introspectionists tried to cope with the rapid downpour of contents in the flowing stream of consciousness was to restrict to a short interval the period within which an experimental observation is made. A standard procedure, for instance, was to present the subject with a single word, such as "white," and ask him to respond as quickly as possible with the first word that occurred to him, such as "snow," "black," or whatever. (This procedure was followed by several psychologists of those days because of their interest in "associationism" and because the newly invented Hipp's chronoscope had raised the hope of measuring very short intervals of time.) The experimenter would then ask his subjects to disclose the "contents" of their consciousness during that short interval lasting no more than a fraction of a second. The subject would then describe such things as the visual image of a blank paper, or the elaborate imagery of a soft snowflake touching the fingers on a cold, snowy day on a tree-clad mountain slope, and so on. The subjects were encouraged to describe in great detail the entire imagery which may have flashed through their minds during a very short interval. As noted by Boring (1953), it often took twenty minutes for the subject to describe the conscious contents of a span of a second and a half, and by the time the subject had begun his description, the event to be described was already a thousand seconds old. This description of the method of introspection should help us understand why introspection always results in retrospection. Needless to say, one of the problems of introspection arises from the fact that one has to rely on memories while retrospecting. As is well known, memories are often treacherously unreliable, even over short time intervals.

Since introspection involves observing one's own "inner" experiences, it requires a person to be an observer at the same instant that he is the object of his own observation. Decades before Wundt launched his introspectionist program of research, the French philosopher Auguste Comte had pointed out the virtual impossibility of this task. Comte said:

> It is clear that, by an inevitable necessity, the human mind can observe all phenomena directly, except its own. Otherwise, by whom would the observation be made? . . . The thinker cannot cut himself in two—one of the parts reasoning while the other is looking on. Since in this case the organ observed and the observing organ are identical, how could any observation be made? The principle of this so-called psychological method is therefore entirely worthless. (Comte, 1830/1970, p. 21.)

The issue, once again, is epistemological. It refers to the distinction between the knower and the object of knowledge and to the relationship between them. The Indian philosophers have been considering this issue since before the Greek period. The *Bṛhadāraṇyaka Upaniṣad* (2.4.14), which is one of the older works of Indian philosophy, poses the question as follows: "For where there is duality (dvaita), as it were (iva), there one sees another . . . there one understands another . . . Lo, whereby would one understand the understander?" (See Hume, 1931, pp. 101–102). Patañjali (4.20) had confronted precisely the same problem in his work. He declares: "There cannot be a cognition of both, (the thinker and his thought) at the same time" (ekasamaye ca ubhayānanavadhāraṇam). He goes ahead to point out in the next aphorism that, if one thought were to be made the object of knowledge of another thought (which is what happens when one retrospects), there would be an infinite regress, because one would need an additional thinker to think about his own thought, and so on. Moreover, in the same aphorism (4.21) he points out that, if one thought be considered to be making observations about another thought of the same person, this situation would pose the problem of memories (smṛtisaṁkaraḥ). After carefully reading Patañjali, I am thoroughly convinced that in these two aphorisms (4.20,21) he was cryptically pointing out precisely the same pitfalls that are found in introspection and were noted by Comte and Boring, namely the impossibility of becoming the cognizer and the object of cognition at the same time, and the problem of the unreliability of the memories involved in retrospection. In clearly stating these problems, Patañjali anticipated what Comte and psychologists such as Boring were to conclude almost two thousand years later.

It is conceivable that the questions posed by the Upaniṣhads, as well as the answers suggested by Patañjali, were quite unknown to the Western psychologists of the 19th and 20th centuries. But Comte's work could have been known to Wundt, although I do not know whether Wundt was actually aware of Comte's arguments regarding introspection. William James did know about Comte; in fact, the latter has been extensively quoted by James in his chapter on methods. Since Titchener had obviously read James, he must have been aware of Comte's objections to introspection. Titchener (1909/1967) devoted a whole chapter of his *Lectures* to the issue of subject–object relationship, and even pointed out how Brentano saved himself from the infinite regress of an idea of an idea, and so on (p. 47). Yet, instead of coming to grips with this important epistemological issue, Titchener remarks: "I think, indeed, the less we hear in psychology of subject and object, the better for us and for the science." As for James, he was convinced that Comte was right. The method of introspection, he admitted, is "difficult and fallible." However, he said, the difficulty of introspection is "simply that of the observation of whatever kind" (see James, 1890/1950, Vol. 1, p. 191).

If William James was convinced about the inefficacy of the method of introspection, why did he try to rationalize and justify its use? Part of the reason was that he had a *hope* that, despite the initial lack of agreement among introspectionists, a final consensus might arise sometime in the future. He also thought that the newly developing method of experiment, which asked every moment for introspective data, was trying to eliminate uncertainties in observation "by operating on a large scale and taking statistical means." "This method," he said, "taxes patience to the utmost, and could have hardly arisen in a country whose natives could be *bored*. Such Germans as Weber, Fechner . . . and Wundt obviously cannot . . ." (James, 1890/1950, Vol. 1, p. 192). Moreover, James thought that the status of psychology during the heyday of introspectionism was like the "Chemistry of Lavoisier, or Anatomy before the microscope was used." The last part of this quotation seems to me the most significant of all. From Wundt in Germany to James in the United States, the psychologists in the West were dazzled by the success of the natural sciences, and they thought that the success of psychology was assured, if only we would develop and use laboratory methods like those of the natural sciences. Such an attitude toward the methodology of natural sciences was a part of the Western *zeitgeist* in the days of Wundt and James, and the same attitude prevails among many Western psychologists today. In the case of some psychologists such as Titchener, the zeal for imitating natural sciences went beyond reasonable limits to the extent of becoming blind to the sound arguments of Comte.

Before closing the discussion of introspectionism, it would be useful to briefly note another point. It would appear that, since introspection implies looking "inward," it has a focus on the self. The Titchenerian introspection, however, was devoid of the deeply personal involvement that often leads to self-absorptive introspection. It was *designed* to be impersonal in character; unlike self-absorptive introspection which often occurs when the person is alone, Titchenerian introspection occurred specifically in interpersonal situations. Except in a few cases where the experimenter was also the subject of his experiment, making observations of his own conscious content, the "observer" was a trained subject other than the experimenter, a graduate student working with the experimenter, for instance. After all, Titchenerian introspection was not a spontaneous undertaking such as that of a young person who starts self-examination of his personal life, retrospects, introspects, and then writes a diary. In a typical experiment: the experimenter (*E*) sets up the task and instructs the subject (*S*), explaining the nature of his job. The *S* then introspects while he does a particular task (such as judging which of the two given weights is heavier, completing an incomplete sentence, or a similar task), and reports to the *E* what is going on in his mind. The typical introspectionist experiment thus occurs in a *structured interpersonal situation.* The *S* works toward a goal set by the instructions (which the Germans called *Aufgabe*), which are given by the *E*. Small wonder that the *S*'s report would depend considerably on what he thinks is expected of him. Also, if the experimenters in different laboratories use different types of instructions, it would follow that the *S*'s in different laboratories would respond differently.

The above rationale helps explain why psychologists in different laboratories in Germany and the United States disagreed with one another during the age of systematic experimental introspection. I must admit here that what I have just said is based on insights borrowed from very recent developments in social psychology. There is a growing body of literature on what is called the social psychology of the psychology experiment. Martin Orne (1962) has pointed out that subjects who volunteer for participation in a psychological experiment often go out of the way to fulfill the perceived expectations of the experimenter. Moreover, as Rosenthal (1966) has insightfully shown, the experimenters are often guided by their theoretical biases. Due to their commitment to a set of favorite hypotheses, they may unwittingly offer clues to the subject in such a way that the *S*'s responses help "prove" (rather than test) the

E's preconceived hypothesis. Knowing the pitfalls arising from experimenter bias and from what Orne has called the "demand characteristics of the experiment," many contemporary psychologists are attempting to develop precautionary measures to help avoid such sources of error. The introspectionists of the turn of the century could not benefit from these recent developments in social psychology. Now, with the research of the intervening decades upon us, we can ascertain some of the reasons for the quarreling among the introspectionists and for the unrealiability of their work.

The Psychology without Consciousness: The Behaviorist Approach

The second decade of this century proved to be a major turning point in the study of consciousness in American psychology. The main factor in bringing about major changes in perspective was a bitter controversy among the German and American introspectionists. The controversy was about the nature of the "elements" of consciousness which they had set out to discover. Introspectionists at the Würzberg school claimed that they had discovered a new phenomenon called "imageless thought." This claim was a major blow to Titchener's views, which held that conscious content was always composed of basic elements such as sensations and images. If thoughts were not composed of images, of what were they made? Titchener thought he knew the answer. He insisted that the so-called imageless thoughts were, in part, vague evanescent patterns of sensations and images and, in part, meanings and inferences. Further, he argued that meanings and inferences must be kept out of introspective analysis because psychology must restrict itself purely to the task of description. As pointed out by Boring (1953, p. 174), introspection without inference and meaning becomes "a dull taxonomic account of sensory events, which . . . are peculiarly uninteresting to the American scientific temper." The controversy among introspectionists over the issue of imageless thought proved to be inconclusive and was considered by many to be a futile exercise.

A strong reaction against the inconclusive and seemingly unproductive investigations of the introspectionists was expressed by John B. Watson in an article published in the *Psychological Review* in 1913. He flatly declared that the method of introspection had "failed signally." Since the method of introspection was thus far considered the royal road to the study of consciousness, its apparent failure raised a critical concern regarding the fruitfulness of studying consciousness. There was a second major concern that also raised doubts regarding the meaningfulness of studies of consciousness. This concern arose from a growing tendency among psychologists (especially among those who were studying "animal consciousness") to attribute feelings, hopes, and intentions to rats and dogs. Lloyd Morgan had rightly cautioned against such "anthropomorphism." Watson, who was himself involved in the study of animal consciousness, took Morgan's hint as a pointer to an additional danger-zone in the study of consciousness.

In the light of this historical background, Watson arrived at the following conclusion: "The time seems to have come when psychology must discard all reference to consciousness; when it no longer deludes itself into thinking that it is making mental states the object of observation" (Watson, 1913, p. 163). Stated this way, Watson's proposal for a new program for psychology can be seen to be prompted mainly by methodological considerations. It is true that the particular Titchenerian form of introspection does not provide an adequate method for observing mental states, but to conclude on this basis that the study of consciousness must be eliminated from the field of psychology is to throw the baby out with the bath water. If Watson's message were restricted solely to a slogan for eliminating the study of consciousness, it would have been simply negative in character. His appeal was effective because he made positive suggestions by proposing *what* should be studied instead, and what should be the *purpose* of such a study.

The typical attraction for emulating the natural sciences, a dislike for speculative philosophizing, and a faith in the usefulness of the method of experiment were characteristics of the Western academic *zeitgeist* for a long time. Wundt had shared them as much as Watson had. But, while Wundt had no sympathy for speculative psychology, he at least clarified his view on the body–mind issue. Watson, however, had no patience for philosophy. "Those time-honored relics of philosophical speculation," said Watson, "need trouble the student of behavior as little as they trouble the student of physics. The consideration of the mind–body problem affects neither the type of problem selected nor the solution of the problem." Many Western psychologists seem to hold these views. I submit that, notwithstanding their disclaimers, most psychologists today, like Watson in 1913, implicitly take a position on the philosophical issue of the mind–body relationship that *does* affect the type of problem selected *and* the nature of the solution selected. Watson, for instance, implicitly accepted a material monist view of the world. He declared mental states to be a non-issue by fiat; chose to study behavior (meaning, primarily, or perhaps even exclusively, the movement of limbs in three-dimensional space) as the only subject matter in psychology fit for scientific investigation; accepted formulations of problems purely in physicochemical terms; and, finally, sought to solve human problems by manipulating the physical environment. In short, Watson's behaviorist program involves a philosophical doctrine that provides an *a priori* basis for its conceptual framework. In trying to emulate the natural sciences, behaviorism follows a particular investigative and applicational mode. All these aspects of the behaviorist formula have their own deeper implications and limitations, which need to be critically examined.

Some two decades after the publication in 1913 of Watson's behaviorist "manifesto," the philosopher Rudolph Carnap (1932–33/1959) provided arguments in defence of a materialist or "physicalist" view of the world and also proposed an epistemological justification for the investigative formula proposed by Watson. Carnap, who was a member of a group of logical positivists popularly called the "Vienna Circle," suggested that all propositions in psychology describe physical occurrences. He considered the language of physics to be the universal intersubjective language and thought of all sciences, including psychology, as branches of physics. The logical positivists considered public verifiability of propositions as the only criterion of their validity. All unverifiable statements were, therefore, considered meaningless. Hempel (1935/1949), for instance, argued that a statement such as "I have a toothache" is meaningful only to the extent to which specific bodily conditions such as a decayed tooth, changes in blood pressure, slowing of bodily processes, or other concomitant conditions of the body can be publicly observed.

The positivist demand for public verifiability implies that agreement is the criterion of truth. Since headaches, dreams, wishes, or such other mental events cannot be observed by anyone other than their "owner," all such phenomena are considered to be outside the scope of meaningful inquiry. Although Watson did not forward such explicit arguments, in effect he implied them when he suggested that we cannot study consciousness because mental states are not objects suitable for observation. Today it may be difficult to find many psychologists who explicitly base their approach on principles of logical positivism. Skinner (1974), for instance, says in *About Behaviorism* (p. 16) that he does not insist on truth by agreement. He does not deny the possibility of self-observation, nor its usefulness, nor does he deny that the so-called mental events such as dreams and fantasies do, in fact, occur. Notwithstanding these concessions, however, Skinner meticulously avoids verbal reports which ordinarily provide data for the study of consciousness. This is typical of an approach to psychological issues prevalent in the contemporary world, which considers consciousness essentially a non-issue. I choose to call this approach "a psychology without consciousness." I conceive of this approach as an ideal-type, a typical pattern of thought which is relatively internally consistent. It involves a distinctive mode of investigation and application of its principles to the solution of practical problems. Although Skinner's radical behaviorism seems to closely approximate this ideal type, I do not intend to attach this label to any particular theory. Whether or not Hullian or other brands of behaviorism closely approximate this ideal type is not the issue here. The purpose is to try to understand basic issues in the study of consciousness, while trying to identify and discuss certain typical approaches prevalent in contemporary Western psychology.

For advocates of a psychology without consciousness, the primary consideration for bypassing the domain of consciousness is methodology. Skinner, for instance, complains about "the limitations and inaccuracies of self-descriptive repertoires" (see Skinner, 1964, pp. 93–94). Surely there are many problems in the use of self-reports as data for psychological studies. So long as I am unable to see the world through someone else's eyes, or experience another person's toothache myself, there is no simple solution to the "other minds" problem. I would agree with Skinner when he points out that "We cannot avoid the responsibility of showing how a private event can ever come to be described by the individual or, in the same sense, be known to him" (Skinner, 1953, p. 280). How is a person able to identify a particular kind of experience as pain? How does he learn to label a certain variety of sensation yellow, red, and so on?

Here again we may agree with Skinner who points out that a child learns to name colors correctly because the verbal community in which he is raised "reinforces" him when he describes snow or milk as being white and refuses to reinforce him if he refers to such objects as blue. The child begins to distinguish between various shades of pain: the feeling of discomfort during indigestion, mild pain when he gets bruised, or the shooting pain which accompanies a decayed tooth. In other words, we learn to identify the nuances of a great variety of complex internal states during the process of socialization, just as we acquire a set of symbols to refer to publicly observable objects in the world. We must also recognize, as Skinner clearly points out, that learning about inner states is possible under conditions in which the verbal community has access to public information (Skinner, 1964, p. 91). Thus, for instance, it is possible for me to tell my child that the pain he suffered when he fell onto a carpet from the sofa cannot be as intense as the pain he might experience with a broken bone that can be seen on an X-ray screen. Our ability to discriminate finely among inner as well as outer stimuli is a product of the socialization process.

A group of people who consensually associate certain symbols with respective types of stimuli, or, in other words, a verbal community, is an essential prerequisite for the cultivation of knowledge in any field. Communication of knowledge in *any* branch of science requires a complex set of symbols, as well as specialized discriminative capacities among members of a scientific community. Some people think that in natural sciences, where verification of propositions often depends upon making simple sensory discriminations such as reading the pointer on a dial, complex discriminative capacities may not be required. "But," as noted by Sigmund Koch, "the pointer is hooked up, both materially and inferentially, to a complex system of events, and the physicist must be attuned to relationships of great subtlety in that system . . . " (Koch, 1964, p. 28). The field of psychology is no exception to this general requirement—namely, that practitioners of any specialty must have a set of complex discriminative abilities relevant to their field of study. Moreover, the field of psychology makes another special demand on its practitioners. They are required to discriminate among not only objective stimuli accessible to public observation (like the physicists' pointer-readings), but also among subjective events such as the various shades of pain.

Let us take a simple example. The psychologist asks his subject: "How are you feeling now?" The subject says: "I feel depressed." The verification of such statements requires, first of all, that both the investigator and the subject understand each other and that both refer to the same type of experience to which the word "depressed" refers. Second, we must make sure that the subject is not malingering. A simple reason why verbal reports are notoriously unreliable is that man has the cherished privilege of believing one thing and saying another. This poses a major difficulty particularly in social psychology where emotionally loaded and socially relevant topics (such as sex, prejudice, or morals) are investigated. Many subjects tend to give socially desirable responses rather than reveal their privately held beliefs. The main problem in the use of verbal reports of issues relating to the private world, however, is not the inadequacy of language, but the lack of trustfulness on the part of the subject and trustworthiness on the part of the investigator.

Boring (1953, p. 181) has pointed out that the introspectionists invariably trusted their subjects. Well, they had to, because in their investigative strategy the role of the subject was to be an *observer* of his own experiences. In accepting this role he had to take the *responsibility* for accurately disclosing what was held in the privacy of his consciousness. Boring has made insightful comments on how the behaviorists transformed the investigative mode. "Behaviourism," he says, "shifts the locus of scientific responsibility from the observering subject to the experimenter who becomes the observer *of* the subject. In this way it is possible to bring to psychological observation irresponsible and untrained subjects—animals, children, the feebleminded, the mentally ill, and also the untrained normal human adult" (Boring, 1953, pp. 184–185). There is no objection to the study of "irresponsible" and untrained subjects. It is also granted that the psychologist does not, and need not, always require his subjects to make observations about their private worlds. The problem is that many behaviorists have adopted an investigative mode where the experimenter is always the *knower* and the *sole knower*, while the subject is a mere *object of his knowledge*. This epistemic formula has deeper implications than are apparent at first glance.

Implicit in this approach is the assumption that whatever is inside the subject's private world is a mystery and must forever continue to be a mystery. This assumption contributes to what David Bakan (1965) has called the "mystery complex" of contemporary psychology. The Skinnerian approach to psychology has been rightly labelled the black-box model. The experimenter does not ask his subjects any questions. He does not have to communicate with the subjects, whether they are animals, children, or responsible adults. Communication, like trust, is a mutual affair. Certainly the behaviorists communicate with other experimenters, but the subjects are treated as if they must always remain outside the community of the psychologists. The experimenter's relationship with the subject is a one-way affair. He manipulates the subject's environment and observes the latter's behavior. As experimenter he is uninterested in the subject's opinions, values, and attitudes toward himself or the experiment. Many experimenters also take it for granted that knowing the purpose of the experiment is none of the subject's business.

It is clear that a psychology without consciousness ignores the feelings, values, and intentions of the subject, but what about those of the experimenter himself? At least with respect to his own private world, the experimenter does not have to face the barrier of Privileged Access. However, many psychologists choose to ignore events in their own conscious domain as well. There are two possible reasons for the psychologist to ignore his own feelings and values. First, the impersonal stance of the objectivist, analytical tradition common among many behaviorists leads them to avoid issues relating to personal involvement and values in the name of value-free science. Second, psychologists, such as Skinner, have deliberately chosen to confine themselves to what the early behaviorist, Max Meyer, called the "psychology of the other one" in order to completely bypass feelings and states of mind. The reader may remember that, as noted in Chapter 1, the main reason for Max Meyer to focus on "the other one" was to leave the issue of the self or the soul to the theologians. Given the background of the conflict between science and religion, it makes sense for a psychologist like Meyer to stake out his own territory away from the influence of the theologian. In contrast to Meyer, Skinner was instrumental in strengthening the behaviorist focus on "the other one" for entirely different reasons. For Skinner, anything that is concerned with consciousness is anathema. Since the concepts of self and consciousness are inextricably related to each other, self becomes irrelevant as a topic of study for a psychology without consciousness—and so does the self in the sense of personal involvement.

A materialist conception of the world is clearly consistent with a psychology without consciousness. As noted before, material monism is implicit in Watson's formulation of behaviorism. It may be pointed out that the same is true about Skinner's formulations. Note, for instance, that the James–Lange theory of emotion is perhaps the only idea that Skinner borrows from William James. The Jamesian view that emotions can be equated with bodily states (being angry means nothing but faster heartbeat and the behavior of striking) is certainly consistent with Skinner's view of man—no matter how inconsistent it is with the importance of consciousness in James's own view of man. To the behaviorists, man is nothing more than his body. This view is so common among contemporary psychologists that many psychologists would tend to say: "If man is not simply his body, what else is he?" The meaning and significance of this question can be understood only in the context of the mind–body problem, a hotly debated topic in the history of Western thought since the time of Descartes. What a modern psychologist implies by posing such a question is that there is no ghost in the machine; mind or consciousness are meaningless issues in the study of man.

Machines, in Descartes' days, used to mimic the motions of the human body, but those machines were pretty crude when compared with modern robots that can carry out scientific experiments on the Moon and Mars. Descartes considered the ability to think as an exclusive property of human beings. Today's computers have a capacity to "think." With the increasing complexity and versatility of the new "machines," the gap between a man and a robot is rapidly decreasing in many different ways. Today the model of man-as-machine is not an abstract hypothesis as it was in the days of La Mettrie (1709–1751). Many contemporary philosophers have argued that the mind–body problem is a pseudo-issue. It is suggested that, since we do not need the concept of consciousness to understand the nature of machines, robots or androids, it is equally unnecessary in the understanding of man.

Space does not permit me to examine the mind–body issue in light of modern "androidology." (For a brief review of various positions on this issue, see Hook, 1960). What is particularly relevant for our purpose is not the relative merits of the arguments supporting or refuting the view that man and machine are similar, but the implications for the practice of psychology that follow from the idea that human beings are no different from automatons. The first implication, once again, is that it is considered legitimate to avoid the study of the subjective aspect of human life. If one wants to avoid the problems of consciousness, one can do so without having to provide any reasons for it. It is useless to cite the anthropomorphic tendency among some animal psychologists to justify avoiding the study of consciousness. And to point to the possibility that some machines may think, choose, or "will" like humans do is equally useless as a justification for adopting a psychology without consciousness. It may even be possible to design computers that can lie or cheat. Such an accomplishment of technology may rob the human race of its uniqueness of possession of this cherished talent. But the fact that some men (or machines) lie does not constitute an adequate justification for throwing away trustworthy reports of private events.

Important implications for applied psychology follow from the adoption of a psychology without consciousness—especially because it implies a purely materialist view of man. The psychologist who adopts such a viewpoint may assume that his subject matter is not different from the objects studied by the natural scientists. Thus, human beings may be considered passive and as open to control as rocks, plants, or other material objects. A psychologist who considers feelings, intentions, and other such mental phenomena inappropriate as subject matter of study is also likely to think of sympathy or empathy for his subject as being inappropriate. Such a stance makes it easy to sidestep the intricate moral issues concerning the relationship between the psychologist and his subject.

The goal of prediction and control of behavior is consistent with the approach typical of a psychology without consciousness. As noted before, the implicit epistemology of this model considers the observing and observed entities (knower and the known) as being separate; the experimenter is the observer *of* the subject's behavior. At the applicational level, too, the two are separated; the experimenter is the controller and the subject is a mere object under his control. The technology for controlling the behavior of the "other one" is quite consistent with a psychology without consciousness.

David Bakan's analysis of the mystery–mastery complex of contemporary psychology is most directly applicable to a psychology without consciousness (Bakan, 1965). The characterization of man as an empty, black box devoid of consciousness lends itself to the desire for controlling men with the use of psychological technology. Finally, it may be suggested that the mastery complex of psychology thrives in a culture which emphasizes mastering of the world through science and technology.

Psychology of the Unconscious: The Freudian Approach

Unlike both structuralism and behaviorism, which developed in an academic setting, Freud's approach to consciousness developed within a clinical context. Although the scope of Freud's work extended far beyond therapeutic work within the clinic, the immediate goal of relieving the patient from his agony has gone a long way in shaping the psychoanalytic approach. At any rate, it would be useful to first examine the origins of psychoanalytic theory in the clinical setting and then see what perspective it can offer on the problem of consciousness.

Early in his career Freud learned from Charcot to use hypnosis in removing "hysterical" symptoms such as functional paralysis and amnesia. Once, while experimenting with the use of hypnosis and similar techniques in therapy, Freud and his colleague Breuer hit upon the device of allowing the patient to talk about anything that came to his mind. They observed that, if a patient is allowed to talk while he lets his thoughts wander, he sometimes recalls the circumstances under which his troubles first began. Further, if he is encouraged to pursue even the weakest links in the train of his thought, he often stumbles over memories of past events and begins to understand how and why he began to feel or behave the way he does. Once the reasons for the origin of the trouble are understood, the awkward neurotic symptoms (such as the washing of hands 100 times a day) begin to disappear. Freud systematically followed the lead provided by these (somewhat accidental) discoveries and developed a therapeutic technique, which is called the "talking out" method or the method of free association. It is a mark of genius that Freud was able to develop not only a therapeutic technique, but also an elaborate theoretical framework for psychology, starting from the relatively simple idea that talking out one's troubles helps relieve anxiety.

Even the briefest description of the method of free association would indicate that what Freud was dealing with is the most basic process of consciousness, namely the usual, day-to-day phenomenon whereby one idea leads to another, and still another, and still another, and so on, in a continuous chain. It is essentially the same phenomenon both William James and Vyāsa described metaphorically as a "stream" of consciousness. Freud's technique of free association can be appropriately described by slightly extending the metaphor of the stream: it involves *facilitating* the "flow" of thoughts. Thus, the patient is encouraged to follow the weakest of links between one idea and the next, even when the connection between them appears quite silly. The therapist does everything to minimize possible obstruction of the free flow of the stream of thoughts. For instance, the patient is asked to lie on a couch and physically relax, so his stiff posture does not distract him from whatever he may be thinking about. The therapist avoids interruptions, keeping silent most of the time while the patient keeps thinking aloud. The legendary analyst does not even face the patient, lest his expressions provide distractions. Under such facilitating conditions, the patient's thoughts flow in an uninhibited manner. We may extend the metaphor a bit further to say that, during free association, the flow of thoughts acquires full force; like a torrent, it washes out obstructions which heretofore prevented certain memories and thoughts from seeking expression in the person's conscious awareness.

Freud's ideas are indeed suitable for an extensive use of metaphor. The stream of thoughts seems to emerge from somewhere—perhaps like a spring from a vast underground storehouse. Memories of past events appear to emerge from somewhere at the back of the head—as if old, no-longer-used articles were pulled out from a dark attic where they lay for years and years. Freud had an unusual knack for transforming such metaphors into theoretical constructs. The vast storehouse, the place from whence thoughts emerge or the place where the memories are stored, was called the unconscious. The unconscious is the territory of the *id*, the core of our psyche, which essentially contains "everything that is inherited." (Here inheritance implies all the drives of biological origin.) The most important characteristic of our drives is to seek pleasure. Freud thought of our pleasure-seeking impulses as being essentially "blind"—with respect to the physical or social consequences of their expression, that is. Since it is dangerous for the individual to try to fulfil any and all of his wishes, like his desire for making love with his neighbor's wife, for instance, the psyche needs an agency to protect itself from such sources of danger. Freud considered the ego to be such a protective agency.

The dangers involved in an uninhibited fulfilment of our blind impulses are not restricted to the dangers from the external world. The desire to make love to a neighbor's wife, for instance, may conflict with our own sense of propriety which we may have internalized during the process of socialization. Freud conceived of the internalized social norms (exhortations like "thou shalt . . . " or "thou shalt not . . . ") to form an agency within the psyche, which he called the superego. The human psyche is thus composed of the id, the ego, and the superego. This triumverate of concepts constitutes the basic cornerstone of the Freudian model. As we shall see in a moment, these concepts help explain the key features of the psychoanalytic view of states of consciousness.

The most distinctive characteristic of the Freudian approach to consciousness is its extraordinary emphasis on the unconscious. The unconscious constitutes the most extensive region of the psyche. The conscious zone is but a small portion of the entire psyche—like the tip of an iceberg. During wakeful periods, the ego and the superego work together harmoniously to safeguard the frontiers of consciousness by resisting the expression of the unruly, lawless, and undesirable wishes into the conscious region. Since the ego is, after all, an offshoot of the original and basic id, it occasionally breaks off its relations with the world by withdrawing itself from the senses. This allows the id to return to its earliest, intrauterine state, which is sleep. Thus, during sleep the id is mostly free from the constraints imposed by the repressive forces of the ego and the superego. The freedom of the id from the repressive forces of the superego is particularly evidenced in dream states by the fact that childhood events which may not ordinarily be recalled are brought back into the preconscious zone of dreams. It is also evidenced by the fact that occasionally one sees oneself doing things in dreams that one is prevented from doing while awake, such as walking naked on the street. All these interesting ideas from Freud's elaborate model have become matters of common knowledge, thanks to the innumerable popularizers of psychoanalysis.

Freud must be given all the credit for the construction of an elaborate and internally consistent conceptual model that tries to account for the major states of consciousness: wakeful, sleep, and dream. His approach to consciousness is complex and original; it is not easy to place it neatly in the context of traditional philosophical issues like the mind–body problem. Freud's nonconformity with any established line of thought in the Western philosophy can by no means be considered to be the result of naïveté. In the opening paragraph of his *Outline of Psychoanalysis* Freud says: "We know two things concerning what we call psyche or mental life: firstly, its bodily organ and scene of action, the brain (or nervous system), and secondly, our acts of consciousness, which are immediate data . . . " (Freud, 1940/1964, p. 144). He suggests this as a *basic assumption*. He agrees that the discussion of this assumption lies within the sphere of philosophy, but supports it because its justification "lies in its results." What Freud has implied by the two "things" mentioned in the above quotation is obviously the Cartesian duality of the body and mind. "Everything that lies between these two terminal points," said Freud, "is unknown to us and, so far as we are aware, there is no direct relation between them" (Freud, 1940/1964, p. 144). Having said this, Freud leaves the issue right there; he had hardly any interest in discussing in detail the nature of the relationship between the body and the mind. From the abovementioned quotations, it would appear that Freud believed in some kind of non-interactive dualism. However, it is clear that Freud was not a psychophysical parallelist as was Wundt. The concept of energy is central to the Freudian model. It is possible that Freud thought psychic energy was the same as physical energy, given that Freud's teacher Brücke was a colleague of von Helmholtz, a physicist who enunciated the law of conservation of energy. But then Freud would seem to be a physicalist. But this does not stand to reason either, because the concept of consciousness is so important in his theories. Perhaps we need not try hard to assign Freud to a particular position on the mind–body problem.

At any rate, it seems to me that the conceptual distinction between the *processes* of consciousness as opposed to the *contents* of consciousness is of great importance in understanding the Freudian model. It may be suggested, for instance, that the method of free association deals basically with the processes of consciousness, namely thinking, remembering, imagining, daydreaming, and the like. The psychoanalytic technique can be said to involve a deliberate attempt to *control* such processes, insofar as the therapist tries to induce an uninhibited and free transition from one idea, thought, or memory to another. The patient's words can be said to describe the contents of his consciousness. They constitute the primary *data* which become available for the analyst (and the patient) to interpret. The method of free association thus serves as an investigative technique. It also serves as a technique of therapy. It will be useful to briefly examine both aspects of this method.

The "talking out" method often brings about an immediate sense of relief. When a person confides in a close friend that he may have committed a criminal act, perhaps by unwittingly pulling a trigger, for instance, he unburdens himself of a feeling of guilt. The same kind of cathartic effect may be obtained in a religious confession or during a session with an analyst. But the psychoanalytic therapy is obviously much more than that. The psychoanalyst aims at bringing out sources of anxiety that may have been forgotten, having been unconsciously *repressed*. Some relief from anxiety is obtained during the course of psychoanalytic therapy due to the release of psychic tensions arising from the repression of unpleasant memories and desires. However, an easy and uninhibited flow of the stream of consciousness, such as the one attained during a psychoanalytic session, does not provide an adequate cure by itself. A critical element of therapy involves an *understanding* of the nature of symptoms. It is easy to see that the element of understanding relates to the content rather than the process aspect of consciousness.

Understanding, as an element of psychoanalytic therapy, is not simply the discovery of the connection between the nature of symptoms, such as the frequent washing of hands and the circumstances under which such symptoms of obsession arose, from the sight of blood in an attempted abortion, for example. Understanding, in the sense of discovering the *real meaning* hidden behind the apparent or *manifest contents* of consciousness, is a critical aspect of the psychoanalytic therapy. An example from one of Freud's famous case studies may help clarify the distinction between the real meanings versus the manifest contents of consciousness. One of Freud's patients, a little boy named Hans, had acquired an intense, irrational fear, or phobia, of horses. The boy used to be afraid not only of the sight of actual horses on the street, but also of the horses in his imagination. According to Freud's persuasive arguments, the little boy was not really afraid of the horses, but, rather, his own father for whom he had acquired a feeling of hatred (for threatening to deprive him of his mother's love). But, since the little boy also loved and admired his father, suggests Freud, Hans *projected* his fear onto the horses (which wore blinkers that looked like his father's glasses). There are innumerable examples in Freud's voluminous writings of such symbolic interpretations of the contents of consciousness. The particular importance and appeal of Freud's approach lies in his demonstration that arriving at such understanding of symbolic meaning has practical benefits. Hans, for instance, was rid of his phobia (fear of horses) when he was told what the horses really stood for. (See Freud, 1909/1962.)

Freud's theory of neurosis, as well as the efficacy of the therapeutic technique, have been criticized from various angles. (For an interesting review of criticisms of the case of little Hans see Brown, 1965, Ch. 8.) It is beyond the scope of this book to evaluate the merits of psychoanalytic therapy. It is important for us to note that an important aspect of Freud's approach to consciousness involves the symbolic interpretation of the contents of consciousness. Although space does not permit me to forward arguments to substantiate my views, to me it makes a good deal of sense to try to discover the symbolic meanings of the contents of consciousness because I am convinced that we sometimes do not really mean what we say or think. Whether psychoanalysts often carry their enthusiasm for symbolism too far and whether dreams involve pervasive sexual symbolism are controversial details which are beyond the scope of the present work.

At this point, it would be useful to compare the psychoanalytic view of processes and contents of consciousness with that of Titchenerian structuralism. Titchener, it may be recalled, emphasized contents to the neglect of the processual aspect of consciousness. Titchener also insisted on leaving the meanings of conscious content out of the introspective analyses. The difference between the Freudian approach and the above-mentioned aspects of the structuralist approach is too obvious to need comment. There are some other differences which may not be so obvious. Like structuralism, psychoanalysis, too, involves "introspection." But the introspection (as well as retrospection) involved in psychoanalysis is vastly different from the Titchenerian variety introspection. While the Titchenerian introspection is deliberately impersonal, psychoanalytic introspection is deeply personal. Further, while lapses in memory are detrimental to the success of Titchenerian introspection (or rather, retrospection), Freud often made deft use of forgetting by trying to identify the wishes and desires that may have led to forgetting.

There are some other important points of contrast between the structuralist and psychoanalytical approaches. These pertain to the interpersonal context in which the structuralist and psychoanalytic forms of introspection occur. Although introspection (or retrospection) can occur only within the private world of a single individual, both the structuralist and the psychoanalytical investigations occur most often in the interpersonal situation of the laboratory or the clinic. As noted before, the structuralist investigators were inevitably required to trust their subjects. They accepted the subject's word for what he "saw" in his own mind. In psychoanalysis, too, it is implicitly assumed that there is a trusting relationship between the subject and the analyst. Psychoanalysis is primarily a therapeutic relationship where the patient voluntarily approaches an analyst of his choice. It is largely inconceivable that he would choose a doctor who is not trustworthy. The psychoanalyst working in the medical setting is bound by the same medical ethic (as the Hippocratic oath, for instance) which has been part of the established custom of most modern societies. The patient can expect the same rules to apply whether he goes to a general practitioner, to a physiotherapist, or to a specialist in psychotherapy. In other words, a patient who consults a psychoanalyst normally assumes that the therapist is a trustworthy member of the medical profession. Moreover, should the patient feel any time during the course of therapy that his analyst's motives or competence are suspect, the patient is free to immediately terminate their relationship. Further, as long as their relationship continues, the patient does not *have* to accept the analyst's interpretations. The analyst, too, knows that his interpretations of the patient's conscious content are not going to bring about a cure unless the latter finds them meaningful and acceptable.

Freud recognized the deeply personal nature of the interaction of therapist and client which makes both of them potentially vulnerable to the protective, overprotective, possessive, or destructive impulses from the other side of the relationship. It is important in a professional relationship to avoid personal entanglement, for the simple reason that the therapist or the client may become the target of the other's love, sexual desire, or aggression. The need for objectivity also demands that personal involvement be kept out of the professional relationship. Moreover, a therapist can hardly afford to become emotionally involved with his numerous patients.

Freud's explicit view of the nature of the relationship between the analyst and his client was "candor on one side and strict discretion on the other" (Freud, 1940/1964, p. 174). Despite such an unwritten pact between the two, information about the patient's private world does not necessarily keep flowing without problems. At an early stage in the process of the development of his techniques, Freud realized that the patient often develops feelings of admiration and love, as well as those of resentment and hatred, toward the analyst. This, he thought, was a *transference* of the patient's feelings toward his own parents onto a substitute target, namely the analyst. With a unique type of shrewdness, Freud turned this obstacle to the advantage for both the analyst and the patient by viewing the patient's attitudes toward the doctor as an additional source of data. Since he believed that an individual's character owes a great deal to the way in which he deals with his ambivalent feelings about his own parents, the projection of his feelings onto the therapist could be taken as a clue to the patient's character.

The purpose of discussing in this book the concept of transference is, once again, not to evaluate psychoanalysis as a therapeutic technique. Nor do I intend to contest the thesis of universality of ambivalent feelings towards one's parents. The point is that Freud's postulation of the theme of transference illustrates his recognition of the dynamic nature of the relationship between the therapist and the patient or, for that matter, between the psychologist and his subject. To have recognized this aspect of the applicational and investigative modes of psychology remains to the credit side of the psychoanalytic approach. In this respect, Freud's insight stands in contrast with the structuralist as well as behaviorist models which have largely neglected this aspect.

Before closing our account of the psychoanalytic approach, it would be useful to note one more point. This pertains to the training of an entrant into the profession of psychoanalysis. From the beginning of the psychoanalytic movement, psychoanalysts have made it a practice to require a trainee to undergo an analysis of his own psyche before he undertakes to analyze others. It makes sense that a person who has undergone an examination of his own conscious mind may be sensitized to recognize similar problems in his patient. Finally, a doctor may not ask the patient to undergo any kind of self-examination which he has not himself dared to undergo.

The reader may not at this time appreciate the importance of the various points that are being raised about a particular theory. It is hoped that the significance of certain aspects of each theory may become clearer when it is shown how they contrast with a theory discussed at a later time. Moreover, it is expected that the meaning and significance of various aspects of the Indian theories could be understood and appreciated by comparing them with the various aspects of the Western approaches being mentioned here one by one.

The Psychophysiological Approach: Relationship between Mind and Brain

The heart was once believed to be the seat of the mind. Descartes thought that the seat of interaction between the soul and the body was the pineal gland, which is located deep inside the skull. In modern times, it is widely believed that mental events are a function of the brain. Consonant with this belief, some of the contemporary attempts in understanding the nature of consciousness are focused upon the study of the structure and function of the brain. These attempts have been aided by great advances in the knowledge of the neuroanatomy of the brain and by sophisticated equipment that allows us to monitor the electrical activity of a live brain. Highly specialized techniques have been developed to help locate even minute parts of particular neural cells in the brain, to electrochemically stimulate specific neural cells by inserting electrodes deep inside the brain, and to monitor their electrical activity.

Brain research lies on those frontiers of psychology where issues in psychology overlap with issues in anatomy, physiology, neurology, pharmacology, biology, and medicine. The rapid developments in these related fields during the past several years have had a continual impact on psychology. This has resulted in the emergence and growth of such "hybrid" specialities as psychophysiology, neuropsychology, and psychobiology. A great portion of the literature in these special areas of study relates to highly technical matters that are far-removed from the typical psychological issues relating to the nature of consciousness. Nevertheless, issues such as the relation of consciousness to the human brain, or of the implications of a "biology without consciousness," appear even in the middle of writings focused on technical matters (e.g., Eccles, 1953; Efron, 1967; Kety, 1960).

The mind–body problem is clearly a matter of concern for researchers in the fields such as psychophysiology, neuropsychology, and psychobiology. Prominent researchers in the field like Sir John Eccles, Karl Pribram, R. W. Sperry, and W. R. Uttal, have written extensively on this problem. In recent years, philosophers and brain researchers have exchanged views and findings in at least two conferences (Karczmar and Eccles, 1972; Globus, Maxwell and Savodnik, 1976). The close collaboration between Sir John Eccles, a brain researcher, and Sir Karl Popper, a philosopher, has resulted in a major book called *The Self and its Brain* (1977). There is a great diversity of opinion among brain researchers on the mind–body relationship. Eccles, for instance, joins Popper in adopting an interactionist position, while Uttal (1978) advocates the "psychoneural identity theory." In contrast to both these positions, Sperry (1976) has proposed an "emergentist" theory which suggests that mental events are "functional derivatives" emerging from the physicochemical events in the brain. He does not equate brain events completely with mental events and thus rejects the "psychoneural identity theory"; he does not imply epiphenomenalism insofar as he grants causal potency to mental events; and he categorically rejects the conventional form of interactionist dualism. Indeed it is difficult to place Sperry's position among conventional, well-known resolutions of the mind–body problem.

Given such diversity of opinion, it is impossible to identify a particular position on the mind–body problem as being the representative position of the psychophysiological approach. Nevertheless, there are indications that the psychoneural identity theory is perhaps the most popular one among researchers in this field. Karl Pribram (1971, p. 377) has noted, for instance, that many researchers influenced by the Anglo-American tradition tend to adopt the view that mental events are identical to brain events. Psychophysiologists often borrow the psychoneural identity thesis from contemporary philosophers. Various formulations of the identity thesis are obviously popular among contemporary Western philosophers (e.g., Armstrong, 1968; Feigl, 1958/1967; Place, 1956; and Smart, 1962). However, there is usually a difference between the philosophers' and psychologists' view of the identity thesis. For instance, Uttal (1973, p. 623), a psychobiologist, explicitly states that he takes the identity thesis as an *axiom*, but the philosopher U. T. Place (1956) proposes the thesis "consciousness is a process in the brain" as a *hypothesis*. There is an obvious difference between the adoption of a proposition as an axiom, that is, as an established truth, and as a hypothesis. The philosopher Feigl (1958/1967, p. 9) says the following words of caution: "I am inclined to believe strongly in the fruitfulness of the physicalistic research program . . . for biology and psychology. But *qua* analytic philosopher my intellectual conscience demands that I do not prejudge the issue of reducibility (explainability) in an *a priori* manner."

Few psychophysiologists are as explicit as Uttal in stating that they take the identity thesis as an axiom. Yet, this thesis seems to have been *implicitly* adopted by a majority of psychobiologists as an *a priori* truth. They hope to "explain" the nature of mental events by trying to "reduce" them to the concomitant brain events. There are important implications of this approach which need to be explained here. First, granted that the psychophysiologist cannot work in a conceptual vacuum, it does not make sense to adopt a controversial proposition such as the psychoneural identity thesis as an established truth. By adopting it as an axiom, the psychophysiologist forecloses the issue, rules out alternative hypotheses by fiat, and is likely to be so biased as to neglect the evidence that goes against his favorite position. We shall note some instances of bias arising from the identity thesis later on in this section. A second problem relating to the psychoneural identity thesis arises from an attempt to explain the nature of mental events by "reducing" them to concomitant brain events. To be able to understand the nature of this problem it is necessary to understand what is generally meant by "reductionism."

Reductionism usually refers to a program of explaining causal relationships and order in hierarchically ordered "levels" of organization. Here, as in "General System Theory" which offers a popular cross-disciplinary conceptual framework, phenomena in mental, biological, and physical domains are seen as being arranged in a sequence of "levels." Placed at the top of the hierarchy are events in the mental domain, such as thoughts, values, and intentions; then comes the organismic level of the whole body which functions as a "system"; then we have the level of system of biological cells, such as neural cells which work as systems in themselves; then we find the large molecules such as the DNA and RNA; next comes the level of atoms which work like systems in their own right; and finally, the subatomic level at the bottom. According to the reductionist point of view, it is assumed that events in a lower level "cause" changes at a higher level, but a reverse order of causation or "downward causation" is denied. Thus, a psychophysiologist, who explicitly or implicitly adopts a reductionist viewpoint, assumes that mental events are an end product of a causal chain which begins at the subatomic level.

Seen this way, thoughts and other events in the domain of consciousness are viewed as being causally impotent and ineffectual. Although their occurrence is not denied, thoughts are mere "epiphenomena." When a psychophysiologist adopts a reductionist approach, he expects to "reduce" mental events to the corresponding physicochemical events in the brain so that they are ultimately explained in terms of the laws of physics. According to Uttal (1978, pp. 81–82), the metaphysical position assumed by many contemporary psychobiologists is reductionistic, mechanistic, physicalistic, and monistic. If this is correct, how is this approach different from Rudolph Carnap's physicalism adopted by many behaviorists?

As an answer to this question I may suggest that, unlike the behaviorists, the psychophysiologists do not consider consciousness to be a non-issue. Rather, in sharp contrast to "a psychology without consciousness" described before, the researchers in the field of psychophysiology or psychobiology consider dreams, sensory experience, perception and cognition, and other such phenomena as the very subject matter for study. Although many psychophysiologists accept the psychoneural identity thesis, and thus reject mind and matter as two separate ontological categories, they implicitly grant two distinct ways of knowing. Thus, one and the same "psychoneural event" is subjectively experienced and is describable in a phenomenological language; and it is also objectively observed and describable in terms of the language of physics. We may say that, in a sense, a psychophysiological explanation involves an attempt to translate a phenomenological description of mental events into the language of physics.

To illustrate the typical psychophysiological approach to the study of consciousness, reference may be made to the pioneering work of Aserinsky and Kleitman (1953). In the early 1950s, they made an interesting observation in their laboratory—namely that the recordings of electrical potentials in the eye muscles of their subjects showed periodic variations during sleep. They thought that the eye movements might be occurring while the subject was "seeing" various objects in his dream. To test the hypothesis, they awakened their subjects when the instruments indicated rapid eye movements (REMs). Surprisingly, about 80–85% of the subjects whose recordings showed REMs combined with low voltage electrical waves on the electroencephalograph (which is a characteristic of what is called Stage 1 sleep) reported that they were actually dreaming at the time they were awakened. This experimental finding has been considered a major breakthrough in the methodology in the study of mental events because it provides an objectively observable signal indicating the occurrence of a private event.

During the subsequent years, more interesting observations were made. Dement and Kleitman (1957) noted that the estimated length of the dreaming period correlates with the length of the period over which REMs are recorded immediately prior to awakening. They also found that the direction of the REMs corresponds with the direction of the movement of objects seen to be moving according to the dream report. For instance, the instruments recorded vertical eye movements in the case of a subject who saw a man climbing stairs in his dream. Berger and Oswald (1962) observed that the density of REM records is high when the subject recalls having seen a high amount of physical activity in his dream. Such early studies seemed to indicate that the subjective reports of dreams corresponded closely with the objective measures of the concomitant bodily states. Over the years, electrophysiological studies of sleep and dreams have developed into an active field of research in many laboratories across the world. Within a period of just over a decade after his famous discovery, Kleitman (1963) reported over 4,000 publications in the field, and many more have been published during the intervening years. It is impossible to survey and summarize them here. Nevertheless, it seems reasonable to conclude that the early leads in an effort to establish a correspondence between dream content and objective indices of physical events (such as the direction of motion of objects reported in dreams and the direction of eye movements recorded on instruments) have not taken the researchers very far. No one-to-one relationship between specific aspects of the dream experience, on the one hand, and any electrophysiological indices, on the other hand, has been established.

The psychophysiological studies of sensory experience have a longer history than the studies of dreaming. At about the middle of the past century, Johannes Müller tried to show that whether we hear a sound or see a light depends on *which* neurons are excited. Around the same time, Fechner's studies in psychophysics tried to establish a relationship between the experience of loudness or brightness of a stimulus and its physical properties. Contemporary psychophysiology of sensory experience tries to understand how the sense organs transform the energy impinging on them into appropriate electrochemical signals and transmit them to specific areas of the brain which contain specialized neural cells capable of "decoding" the signals. It is believed that the nature of sensory experience depends on the location of the neural cells excited, their number and pattern, as well as the strength and frequency of their excitation. The thrust of the psychophysiological studies lies in trying to decipher the "code" involved in translating the information received by the sense organs and in "interpreting" the signals which are transmitted to the brain. Notwithstanding the great advances in the physiology of the sense organs, there seems to be little success yet in deciphering the neural code. In a book devoted to the theories of sensory coding Uttal (1973, p. 631) concludes: "It is clear that there is no satisfying general explanation of the relationship between the structure of our brains and the process of our minds."

It is necessary to recognize the immense complexities involved in the task of deciphering the "neural code" or of understanding the "language of the brain." The central nervous system of human bodies contains billions of neural cells which are interconnected to form a very complex network. Although specific areas of the brain are known to be specialized in particular functions, such as vision or the coordination of muscles in the hand and so on, the brain seems to work *as a whole*. Parts that are not ordinarily specialized in a particular function are able to acquire that function as indicated by the fact that functions normally carried by damaged tissues are taken over or "recovered" by other parts of the brain. Although each neuron may play a specific and unique role in mental functions—for example, the storage and retrieval of memories of particular events—there are too many mental events and too many brain cells to try to establish one-to-one connections. Moreover, since neurons are interconnected by criss-crossing fibers, subjective experiences may depend on an organization of the activity of aggregates of neurons.

E. Roy John (1967, p. 420), a noted electrophysiologist, expresses this view in the following words: "Subjective experience cannot be attributed to the activity of particular cells whose function is to mediate the content of consciousness, but must be a property of organized aggregates themselves." Following this line of thought, electrophysiologists like John, Sutton, Walter, and others have tried to relate subjective events like perceptual or cognitive tasks to patterns of electrical activity of large aggregates of neurons. A typical experimental procedure following this approach involves giving the subject a perceptual or cognitive task (such as judging the size or shape of stimulus figures, reading meaningful or meaningless words and so on), and recording the electrical potentials evoked by various areas of the brain while performing such tasks. Consistently recurring *wave shapes* of such "evoked potentials" are then identified and are taken as being indicative of the *temporal pattern* of the average activity of an ensemble of neural cells involved in the subjective experience associated with the cognitive tasks. In his selective survey of such experiments, E. Roy John (1967, pp. 403 ff.) notes that distinctive wave shapes have been found to be associated with the experience of expected versus unexpected events, meaningful *versus* meaningless stimuli, and erroneous *versus* correct judgments. The identification of distinctive, recurrent wave shapes is not as easy a task as it would seem to be at the outset. Despite this methodological difficulty, many experiments are being conducted and promising results obtained. However, no electrophysiologists seem to claim that the correspondence between mental events and evoked potentials is established, either over a broad range of events, or at a high level of certainty.

Perhaps the most popular and widely publicized theme of contemporary psychophysiology is the "alpha experience"—a pleasant state of relaxation—which is said to arise when the brain produces "alpha waves," steady rhythmic electrical activity within the range of about 8 to 13 cycles per second (usually recorded from the occipital region of the brain). This experience or "alpha state" has been associated with meditation, since high amplitude alpha waves have been found to occur in the EEG recordings of Zen masters, yogis supposed to have been in samādhi states, and of students of Yoga (Wallace, 1970; Anand, Chhina, and Singh, 1961; and Kasamatsu and Hirai, 1972). This finding has attracted the attention of many people who desire to attain a pleasant and relaxed state of mind and of those who value the positive outcomes of Zen, Yoga, and other forms of meditation. A method of attaining an alpha state was developed by Joe Kamiya (1972) who demonstrated that it is possible to voluntarily enhance the production of alpha waves by simply providing a person with a signal as soon as his brain begins to emit such waves. This method uses an electronic instrument which is designed to "screen" the electrical activity of the brain and sound a buzzer or light a bulb as soon as the waves within a designated range of frequency occur in its input. This technique of controlling the electrical activity of the brain is called "biofeedback," since it is based on the feedback of information about a rhythmical biological function of the body. It is not yet clear what psychological strategies and physiological mechanisms are involved in the voluntary control of bodily functions which are ordinarily controlled "automatically" by the autonomic nervous system. But it is clear that most individuals are capable of voluntarily enhancing their alpha output, although some are more capable than others.

It is common knowledge that the popular use of biofeedback training for the purpose of experiencing the alpha state reached faddish proportions in the United States in the 1970s. It is unnecessary to comment on the lucrative commercialization of alpha conditioning involving the use of cheap electronic gadgets and promises of assorted benefits that were supposed to follow from the alpha experience—relaxation, improved speed in reading, powers of extrasensory perception, growth of human potentials, enlightening samādhi or instant nirvāṇa. This is also not the place to examine therapeutic uses of the biofeedback technique which may indeed be effective in the treatment of certain psychosomatic disorders. It must be noted, however, that the popularity of the alpha experience depends on (a) the desirable qualities attributed to the alpha experience, and (b) the assumption that the alpha experience always accompanies the production of alpha waves. It will be useful for us to examine the validity of the claims regarding the qualities of the alpha experience, as well as the assumption about the co-occurrence of the alpha experience and the so-called alpha state. To this point, I shall briefly summarize some relevant research findings regarding the alpha experience and then turn to the issue of validation of statements regarding private events like the alpha experience, which is an issue of broader significance.

Early studies of Yogic and Zen meditation (Anand, Chhina and Singh, 1961; Bagchi and Wenger, 1957/1971; and Kasamatsu and Hirai, 1972) indicated the presence of alpha waves in the EEG recordings during meditation. None of these papers speak of a specific type of experience designated as "alpha state" or "alpha experience." While Anand *et al.* (1961) claim that all of their subjects had obtained a samādhi state, they do not say what *type* of a samādhi experience was involved (a Yogic account of several "levels" or types of samādhi experience will be discussed in the next chapter). They make a general statement that yogis practicing Rāja Yoga remain in a state of "ecstasy" (mahānand) during samādhi, but provide no verbal descriptions given by their subjects. Bagchi and Wenger (1957/1971) did ask their subjects to provide verbal reports, but such reports are not discussed in their oft-quoted paper. They clearly state that "none of the subjects claimed they reached this (samādhi) state during the experiments." Thus, there is no reason to believe that these experiments with yogis refer to the same type of experience.

In contrast to these Indian studies, the Kasamatsu and Hirai (1972) study of Japanese Zen meditation deals with the degree of EEG changes in various *stages* of Zen meditation. The "stages" were identified in two distinct ways: first, in terms of years spent by the subjects in Zen training—less than 5 years, between 6 to 20 years, and from 20 to 40 years, and second, in terms of "the disciples' mental states, which were evaluated by a Zen master." We are not told what criteria are used by the masters in rating the "proficiency" of their disciples, nor how anyone could ascertain someone else's private experience. The Japanese data indicate that "the degrees of EEG changes during Zen meditation are parallel with the disciple's proficiency in Zen training," but increased alpha amplitude is not claimed to be a characteristic of high proficiency in meditation. Although a general pattern or a series of changes involving an initial increase and a latter *decrease* of alpha frequency is observed as being typical, Kasamatsu and Hirai (1972) note that "this series of changes cannot always be observed in all Zen subjects." Their report does not include verbal descriptions of subjects' experiences during the experiment. However, it is claimed that "Zen meditation is purely a subjective experience completed by a concentration which holds the inner mind calm, pure and serene." Finally, "the *authors* call this state of mind the relaxed awakening with steady responsiveness" (emphasis added).

It should be clear from the brief accounts of selected psychophysiological studies of meditative states that they do not claim to be dealing with one specific type of experience; they do not provide detailed accounts of how the subjects feel during the period of EEG recordings; and all of them do not report a uniform, one-to-one relationship between the occurrence of alpha waves and something called the "alpha state." With these observations in mind, we may now turn to certain trends in relation to the North American studies relating to the alpha experience. It is neither possible nor necessary to survey the vast number of studies reported in this field. Certain trends in this literature may be noted insofar as they throw light on certain aspects of the psychophysiological approach to the study of consciousness.

Except for certain studies focusing on "Transcendental Meditation" (e.g., Wallace, 1970), a majority of North American studies relating to the alpha experience have been done outside the context of meditation. Both inside and outside of the context of meditation, pleasantness and relaxation have been qualities most commonly ascribed to the alpha experience. In Joe Kamiya's (1972, p. 526) most well-known paper describing the production of alpha with the help of biofeedback training, for instance, the subjects emitting high alpha waves were said to experience a state of pleasant relaxation. Subsequent studies have characterized the alpha experience in the following manner: pleasant feeling states (Brown, 1970); pleasant feeling, well-being, pleasure, tranquility, relaxation (Brown, 1971); relaxation, letting go, floating, feeling of pleasure, security, sensual warmth (Nowlis and Kamiya, 1970). It is needless to quote more studies to indicate the trend. Such descriptions of the alpha state are based upon subjects' verbal reports. Kamiya, a pioneer and leader in the biofeedback movement, *infers* that the alpha state must be *desirable* on the basis of his observation that subjects who were trained to enhance as well as suppress their alpha tended to stay in a high alpha state when no specific instructions were given to either increase or decrease their alpha output. He *alluded* to more desirable qualities of the alpha state by mentioning that ". . . I have a list a mile long from various people who call me . . . to ask if they can come over and serve as subjects" (Kamiya, 1972, p. 527).

In much of the literature published in the initial years of the biofeedback movement it was implicitly taken for granted that a subject experienced what was called the "alpha state" whenever his brain began or increased its output of alpha waves. Over the years, however, the invariable association between the alpha experience or the alpha state has been questioned. Walsh (1974) for instance, hypothesized that the subjects in many of the experiments on the "alpha state" may have reported having pleasant experiences because they were somehow led to expect such experiences during the experiment. To test the hypothesis, he conducted an experiment in which subjects were told that they will be given feedback training, but half of them were given correct feedback with increased alpha and the rest were given *false feedback.* Besides, half the subjects in each of these two conditions were given suggestions that they can expect to have a pleasant experience as in Zen meditative states called satori, but the other half were not given such suggestions. The results showed that, for "alpha experience" to occur, both the alpha activity as well as an "alpha set," i.e. *expectations* for the possibility of such an experience were necessary; neither the alpha activity nor the alpha set alone is sufficient. On the basis of such results, Walsh ascribes the observations about the pleasantness of the alpha state reported by researchers like Kamiya to the "demand characteristics" of their experiments, that is, to the biasing effect of expectations aroused by tacit or inadvertent suggestions provided by the experimental setting. More recently Plotkin (1976) has published a report of his experiments along with a survey of the extensive literature on alpha feedback. Space does not permit me to summarize his work or other similar reports. Suffice it to say that the new research findings indicate that enhanced levels of alpha activity are not invariably accompanied by the "alpha experience." In fact, it has been noted that in some subjects enhanced alpha activity is associated with *unpleasant* feelings such as intense anger, fear, frustration, or sadness (Plotkin, 1976, p. 85).

In summary, research on the alpha state indicates, as does psychophysiological research regarding sensory, perceptual and dream experience, that it is hard to find significant and reliable evidence on the co-occurrence of mental events and specific electrophysiological conditions of the brain. It is hoped, of course, that further research may bring forth more conclusive and significant observations in this regard. Psychophysiological research is bound to continue as long as such hope exists. This is fine as far as it goes. But what can we learn from contemporary research about the strengths and weaknesses of the psychophysiological approach to the study of consciousness? What can we say about its basic assumptions, epistemic principles and applicational strategies?

As far as the basic assumptions are concerned, it is necessary to say that the implicit acceptance of the psychoneural identity thesis as an axiom must be viewed with caution. Such acceptance is likely to bias a researcher, as the literature on alpha experience has shown. Instead of asking an open question, "Are there any states of consciousness associated with a particular condition of the brain?" one tends to view initially observed associations between mental and brain states as being necessary and invariable—and inadvertently contributes to the biasing "demand characteristics" of the experiment.

Regarding the epistemic principles involved in a psychophysiological approach, it is necessary to note that the issue of validation is not as often nor as clearly discussed in the literature as are the positions on the mind–body problem. One of the rare papers devoted to the examination of this issue is a paper titled "Electrophysiological Studies of Dreaming as the Prototype of a New Strategy in the Study of Consciousness" by Stoyva and Kamiya (1968). In this paper heralding a "new" strategy, the authors advocated "construct validation" of the "hypothetical construct" of dreaming by "converging operations," that is, by corroborating verbal reports with objectively verifiable indicators of concomitant neural activity. They admit that the "ultimate criterion of dreaming is the verbal report of the subject." They also suggest that the beginning of the acceptance of verbal reports as evidence is "something of a landmark in the troubled history of the introspective method and its place in psychology." They specifically note that verbal report is a "more neutral term than is introspection, and is less encumbered by the theoretical baggage of bygone controversies." Indeed it is important to recognize the deeply apologetic acceptance of verbal reports reflected in the words of Stoyva and Kamiya against the historical background of the bitter controversies over the structuralist use of introspection, and the triumph of Watsonian objectivism and behaviorism. It took well over half a century before many North American psychologists began to even grudgingly accept verbal reports and legitimize the study of private events. Although the 1970s have witnessed an increasing acceptance in North America of psychophysiological and cognitive approaches that deal with private events, the "objective" data are largely preferred over "subjective" reports. It is paradoxical, again, that, notwithstanding the overall preference for objective data, verbal reports are beginning to be accepted in an *uncritical* manner. The simultaneous preference for objective data and an uncritical acceptance of verbal reports is illustrated in numerous psychophysiological studies of the "alpha experience."

To be able to examine this issue more closely, it is necessary to recognize, once again, that psychophysiological studies must be based on two sets of data, subjective and objective. If the psychophysiological approach is to be a reasonable way of studying events in the domain of consciousness, it must ask subjects to disclose to the experimenter what was experienced privately during the period of the recording of brain events. Subjective data must depend on such disclosure, even if it is communicated to the experimenter by a nonverbal act such as pressing a button. As noted by the philosopher Baier (1962), as far as the validity of data concerning private events is concerned, ". . . the person whose private state it is has the final epistemological authority, for it does not make sense to say 'I have a pain unless I am mistaken'." Once we ask a person to be a subject in a psychophysiological or other type of investigation concerning mental events, we must be prepared to take his word for what he says he experienced. Problems often arise because untrained persons are allowed to be subjects in an experiment, persons who are too willing to please the experimenter by helping him in "proving" his hypothesis.

Here we may turn to Indian psychologists who have specified the conditions under which verbal testimony may be considered acceptable. Vācaspati Miśra identifies in his commentary of one of Patañjali's aphorisms (1–7) the following as characteristics of persons whose verbal testimony (āgama) may be acceptable: understanding of the relevant principles (tattvadarśana), "compassionateness" (kāruṇya), and expertise in the use of the relevant instruments (karaṇapāṭava). What this means as applied to studies of mental events can be explained as follows. First, to qualify as an appropriate subject, a person must understand the relevant concepts or principles such as "alpha experience," " nagging pain," or whatever, so that he can understand *what type* of private events are being studied, and use appropriate terms to describe them. Second, his motives in participating in the study must be beyond suspicion and his attitudes (e.g., "compassionateness" or a genuine desire to help the experimenter in his search for the truth of the matter) must be clearly known. Thus, we would not admit anyone who would try to please the experimenter, or be swayed by the "demand characteristics" of the investigation. Third, only a person who knows how to use the relevant "instruments" such as appropriate discriminative abilities, can participate in a study. Thus, we cannot use a color-blind person in a study of visual sensation, a child who has yet to learn to distinguish between dreaming, fantasy, and reality in a study on dreaming, and so on. To state it briefly, we must be able to trust the subject's ability to discriminate among the nuances of experience under study, to use appropriate terms to describe them, and to speak his mind without fear or favor. It may not be easy to judge the trustworthiness of a subject, but it is inappropriate to use just any available subject for experiments, as is often done in contemporary laboratories. It is important to remember that the introspectionists of Würzberg and Cornell understood some of these problems and hence insisted on the use of highly trained subjects. Many contemporary psychophysiologists have returned to introspection (by way of accepting verbal report), but have been unable to insist on tions in selecting their subjects.

Before closing our account of the psychophysiological approach I must note the applicational strategies associated with it. Reference has already been made to biofeedback technique, which is being used not only to enhance alpha output and receive the attendant benefits, but also to control mind and body in various ways. It would be better to neglect the "commercial" exploitation and unjustifiable promises which have sometimes been associated with the biofeedback movement and focus on its distinctive and positive aspects. It is important to note that biofeedback is a method of *autogenic* training. It helps a person control *his own* mind and body. In this respect, it contrasts sharply with the behavior modification approach which usually emphasizes control of environmental conditions (rather than that of mental events and autonomic functions) and focuses on management of change by the therapist rather than by client's initiative. It may well be that biofeedback methods will not be able to help a person attain the satori or samādhi states described by Zen and Yoga traditions. Nevertheless, the popularity of biofeedback in North America indicates a turn toward autogenic rather than external control, which is characteristic of the Eastern approaches.

To some extent, the biofeedback approach implies the idea "mind over body" in that attempt is made to induce pleasurable states with nonphysical means. A different type of application of the knowledge of the structure and function of the brain involves the direct manipulation of the brain through surgical, electrical, or chemical means. In simple terms, it can be called the "physical control of the mind." The basic idea is, of course, very old. For ages people have sought relief from suffering and enhancement of pleasure through such physical means as exercise or physical relaxation. Drugs have been used since the ancient times as anaesthetics and also as means of inducing ecstasy and euphoria. The legendary *soma*, an elixir of the ancient Hindus, has recently been popularly known in the West, thanks to Aldous Huxley, who tried to revive the legend. LSD, the modern elixir or "mind-expanding" drug, is said to produce an instant ecstasy, barring, of course, some "bad trips." All these can be considered examples of "physical" control of the mind. Although the historic roots of physical control of the mind are very old, modern forms of this ancient art are based upon fairly recent advances in electrophysiology, psychopharmacology, and psychosurgery. Brain researchers have recently shown that it is possible to electrically stimulate particular areas of the brain of a monkey and make it behave aggressively toward another monkey. They can even stop a charging bull by sending signals into its brain through a distant radio. Surgical removal of parts of the brain is known to be therapeutically effective for some human patients. With the help of electrodes implanted in the human skull, doctors have been able to allay excessive anxiety reactions in patients and even to induce pleasurable, orgastic, or euphoric experiences.

Jose M. R. Delgado, a well-known physiologist and author of *Physical Control of the Mind* (1969), has summarized the results of numerous experiments of the type mentioned above. He puts the central point in a nutshell: "Physical damage, the loss of a beloved child, or apocalyptic disaster cannot make us suffer if some of our cerebral structures have been blocked by anesthesia. Pleasure is not in the skin being caressed, or in a full stomach, but somewhere in the cranial vault" (Delgado, 1969, p. 117). It follows from this view that, in order to avoid pain or seek pleasure, what we really need to do is to know the appropriate locations in the brain associated with the desired pleasure or unwanted pain, and to activate those centers with the help of appropriate physicochemical means. It is also implicit in this view that states of consciousness can be completely controlled by physicochemical means, because, after all, the mind is but a physical entity. Without going into a discussion of the validity of the materialist view of the mind, it may be suggested that, to the extent that pleasure and pain can be controlled through physical means, advances in science and technology will make more and more power available for such control. Obviously, there are ethical issues associated with the use of such technology. A razor can be used for healing as well as killing. The Hippocratic oath guides the doctor to use his skills in beneficial rather than harmful ways, and we may hope that the spirit of the medical ethic may successfully extend to psychophysiology as well. This, of course, is only a hope. It is only as strong (or weak) as the hope that nuclear technology will eventually be used for constructive rather than destructive purposes.

The Phenomenological and Existential Approaches

An account of the Western views of consciousness would certainly be incomplete without a discussion of the phenomenological and existential approaches. Most of the approaches discussed so far follow the natural science model. Two of these approaches, namely psychophysiology and the "psychology without consciousness," have favored the object side of the subject–object dichotomy, and have found support from the analytical and positivist schools of Western philosophy. By contrast, the existential and phenomenological approaches in psychology have favored the subject side of the subject–object dichotomy. They have derived inspiration from philosophers like Kierkegaard and Husserl who tried to provide an alternative to the positivistic and analytical philosophies. Husserl, in particular, was negatively disposed toward the natural science approach to problems of life. As a result, his view of consciousness differs radically from the approaches discussed before insofar as they are based on the natural science model.

Although, as systems of philosophy, phenomenology and existentialism have distinct characteristics, they are mutually supportive and overlapping in many respects. Together these two schools of modern Western philosophy have influenced a broad range of ideas in modern Western psychology and psychiatry, although such influence is felt more on the European continent than the North American. Although phenomenological psychology is recognized as a major alternative to behaviorism in the United States (Wann, 1964), the impact of phenomenology is far greater than is often realized. The various cognitive viewpoints in American psychology, as well as Gestalt theory, consider it important to account for the subject's view of the world, and, to that extent, adopt a phenomenological perspective. To understand the nature and scope of existential and phenomenological viewpoints, and to be able to appreciate their distinctive approaches to consciousness, it will be useful to trace the historical development of the key concepts of the major thinkers of this tradition.

We must begin the account of modern phenomenology with the German philosopher Franz Brentano (1838–1917). As in the case of many other Western philosophers, Brentano's starting point for his thoughts on consciousness was Cartesian mind–body dualism. In trying to explain the distinctive features of mental phenomena in contrast to physical entities, Brentano introduced the concept of *intentionality*. By this he meant the characteristic of having a reference to, or being *directed* toward, something. Brentano argued that all processes of consciousness always involve a reference to some object. Thus, we always think *about* an object or an idea, believe *in* a statement, desire *for* an object, and so on. The intended objects do not have to exist. We may think, for instance, about a *sasquatch* or a snowman, or hope to ride imaginary spaceships. Nevertheless, we cannot believe, think, imagine, wish, or intend without referring to an *intended object,* whether real or imaginary. Brentano maintained that physical phenomena do not involve a reference to an object like mental phenomena do. It follows, then, that consciousness is always consciousness *of* something.

The next important landmark in the development of phenomenological thought is the work of Edmund Husserl (1859–1938), who was directly influenced by Brentano's ideas about the nature of consciousness. Husserl, too, was concerned with the Cartesian mind–body dualism. However, Husserl's criticism of Descartes is unique insofar as it is rooted in his deeply personal approach to philosophy. As noted by Herbert Spiegelberg (1965, Vol. 1, pp. 81–82) in his account of the history of the phenomenological movement, Husserl once wrote in his diary how tormented he felt about the lack of clarity in his own ideas. He said that life was unbearable to him because of this inability to achieve clarity in his own ideas. The word "apodictic," meaning absolute certainty, appears quite frequently in his writing. Early in his career Husserl began to adopt an attitude of universal doubt, discard every dubitable presupposition, and launched an ambitious plan to build a new system of philosophy based on absolutely indubitable propositions. Like Descartes, who had started a similar project, he found an absolutely indubitable starting point of all inquiry, namely the dictum "I think, therefore I am." Although Husserl revered Descartes for having identified the most indubitable truth, he was greatly dissatisfied with the Cartesian philosophy, which he thought had adopted many scholastic dogmas without proper scrutiny. In *Cartesian Meditations* Husserl (1933/1977) outlines his program for the reformulation of philosophy starting from the abovementioned Cartesian dictum.

Husserl's intensely personal approach to life and philosophy stands out as rather unique against the background of the impersonal, purely analytic approach to philosophy that has dominated the Western tradition since the Greek period. In being so personally involved and in objecting to the many adverse effects of the adoption of a natural science to the problems of human life, Husserl was like Kierkegaard. He strongly objected to the objective view of the human spirit—although he did not take to religious faith to solve his spiritual problems as Kierkegaard did.

It is impossible to understand and appreciate Husserl's ideas without reference to his strong and persistent opposition to "naturalism," that is, the attitude reflected in natural science that considers man a mere object in the spatiotemporal world. Certainly, Husserl was opposed to the natural science viewpoint, but his attack on science was not of the popular romantic variety. Husserl was opposed to science neither because of his religious beliefs nor from fear of mad scientists misusing their scientific knowledge—as the Romanticists were. He could very well understand the increasing popularity of science as a consequence of its ability to provide useful technology. In fact, Husserl appreciated the spirit of science insofar as it reflected a serious pursuit of knowledge, and even aspired to turn philosophy into a "rigorous science" as opposed to loose speculation. We must note that he was careful in directing his attack against "naturalism," not against "natural science." Clearly, Husserl was critical of certain *aspects* of the scientific approach, and certain *attitudes* associated with a world view which starts with the objective view of the world and extends it to all human concerns. It will be useful to identify the aspects of science related attitudes which Husserl was opposed to insofar as they have influenced the phenomenological approach to consciousness.

Husserl was well aware of the views of Mannheim, Scheler and other sociologists of knowledge who had pointed out the cultural relativity of scientific knowledge. (We have noted some of their ideas in Chapter 1.) In fact, Scheler and Husserl not only knew each other well, but have been considered co-founders of the phenomenological movement. Like the sociologists of knowledge, Husserl saw the enterprise of science itself as a sociocultural phenomenon influenced by the values of the scientist and his society. Moreover, he was particularly concerned about the inability and unwillingness of science to view the scientist himself—his values, the meaning of his life for him, and the place of science in the scientist's personal, subjective life. Husserl thought that the cool, dispassionate analysis of "facts" of the objective world may give us ways of controlling nature, but it tells us nothing about the purposes for which knowledge of nature should be used. He was well aware of the advances in physics in the study of space and time, but he thought the complex formulas and mathematical equations of physics help us little in understanding the subjective perceptions of space and time which guide the course of our lives. It is in this sense that he remarked "Einstein does nothing to reformulate the space and time in which our actual life takes place." (See Husserl, 1936/1965, p. 186.) Husserl traced the roots of European science to ancient Greece, particularly to the materialistic and deterministic views of Democritus. It is particularly the materialistic view of man as implied in and promoted by natural science which he was particularly opposed to. Thus, he said, "To speak of the spirit as reality . . . presumably a real . . . annex to bodies and having its spatiotemporal being within nature, is an absurdity." (See Husserl, 1936/1965, 184–185.) Husserl took such implications of the "naturalist" attitudes as being the cause of the "Crisis of European Man." Given the fact that he wrote about the European Crisis in 1935, when the Nazis had been in power for two years, it is easy to see how serious and far-reaching the consequences of naturalism were in his opinion.

At any rate, being critical of a naturalistic or materialistic view of man was an important aspect of Husserl's views of consciousness. Viewed against the mind–matter dualism, which was deeply entrenched in the world view of Europe of his time, Husserl's call for a study of consciousness could be easily construed as acceptance of an idealist or mental monist position. Husserl was aware of not only the possibility of such an interpretation of his views, but also of a possible lapse into solipsism. So he made it specifically clear (in Husserl, 1913/1962, Section 32) that he did *not* deny this world as the sophists did, or doubt its existence as the skeptics did. He further clarified (in Husserl, 1913/1962, Section 55) that he did not follow Berkeleyan idealism. It seems that Husserl tried to steer clear of the mind–body problem by avoiding its discussion, and it does not matter whether he avoided the issue for lack of interest, or merely as a strategy. It is important to note that his justification for turning to the inner world of experience was based not so much on ontological grounds as on epistemological. Thus, he opens his well-known book, *Ideas: General Introduction to Pure Phenomenology*, with the statement, "Natural knowledge begins with experience and remains with experience." (Husserl, 1913/1962)

For Husserl the domain of experience in general, and the region of "pure consciousness" in particular, was the "wonder of all wonders." He designed a special method for exploring this wondrous region and referred to it variously as "bracketing," "phenomenal reduction," "epoché," and so on. Before describing this method, I must note the various phenomena within this domain which he recognized along with the terms he borrowed or coined to describe them.

As noted, Husserl followed Brentano in recognizing the intentional nature of consciousness; he recognized that feeling, willing, judging, behaving, and other such "acts" of consciousness were always *directed* toward their "objects." The word "object" as used here does not mean a physical "thing" in a spatiotemporal world, but anything—a thought, outcome, result, memory, imaginary entity like a centaur, or whatever—toward which the thinking, hoping, expecting, remembering, or imagining is directed (the subject–object dichotomy is implied here). It is also implied that the ego or the "I" is the subject whose "acts" appear in experience. Husserl distinguished between "acts" and "contents" of consciousness in much the same way as was common in his days. Thus, he placed thinking, remembering, imagining, and other such "processual" aspects of experience in one category called "acts" of consciousness or Cartesian "cogitations." These were recognized as being "countless *fluctuations*," and were distinguished from sensory "contents," meaning experiences such as color, touch, sound and the like. He called them "hyletic" data (after Greek word *"hyle,"* meaning matter), since they provide the "material" which could be arranged into various forms or shapes. According to Husserl (1913/1962, Section 85), "Sensory data offer themselves as material for intentional informings or bestowals of meaning."

Husserl was strongly opposed to a mechanical analysis of conscious content which was attempted by the Wundtian introspectionists in the German universities of his time. To him such analysis was a typical instance of a "natural attitude" which adopted the natural science model and tried to break down human experience into meaningless "elements." His phenomenological approach to consciousness attempted to understand and describe *how* the sensory data are organized so as to *bestow meanings* to their configurations. This approach stands in sharp contrast with Titchener's introspection, which deliberately avoided meanings. I am not sure whether Husserl was aware of Titchener's work in the United States. However, he was well acquainted with William James's view of consciousness. (See Spiegelberg, 1965, Vol. 1, pp. 111–117 for James's influence on Husserl.) Husserl adopted James's view of the stream of consciousness and, like James, focused on the problem of Pure Ego or the selfsame "I" which underlies the stream of consciousness. I shall postpone the discussion of Husserl's view of the Ego to a separate chapter on that topic (Chapter 5) and return now to his views of the method of "bracketing."

"Bracketing" is primarily a device for exploring the whole region of consciousness, but, as we shall see in the following discussion, its significance is far greater than mere methodological tool. It *begins* as a methodological device, then tries to gradually shift one's attention to various aspects of consciousness, and aims at ultimately bringing about a complete "personal transformation." It is assumed that at the beginning of this journey one recognizes that one holds a natural attitude, that is, that the objective world is given, that it is "always there for us," and that one is an object within it. Husserl's method demands at the outset that the belief in the reality of the object world "out there" be temporarily suspended, or held in abeyance, so as to be able to focus one's attention on the "inner" world of consciousness. The whole spatiotemporal world is thus "bracketed" or "put in parenthesis" by adopting a pervasive and universal (if only temporary) *doubt* about its very existence. As long as one engages in the examination of the domain of consciousness one *abstains* from making *any* judgment about the nature of everything that belongs to the fact-world. This stance is called the phenomenological *epoché,* after the Greek word "epoché," meaning abstaining from judgment. This is not as simple as it may sound because by this method Husserl expects to "disconnect" oneself from the standards, findings, conclusions and values of *all* natural and social sciences which deal with the world of facts and try to interpret them. This does not mean that one necessarily *rejects* the validity of the findings of various sciences while adopting the method of bracketing, but it means that one rejects any and every presupposition or axiom about the nature of the world. Needless to say, Husserl demands a great deal from anyone who wishes to adopt his approach to consciousness, since it is not easy to rid oneself of all presuppositions.

Aside from the difficulties in ridding oneself of all presuppositions, the task of Husserlian phenomenological analysis appears to be a special type of introspection. Once the attention is "withdrawn" from the world "out there," Husserl wants us to attend to the sensory data and see that they form various shapes and configurations in the "flow" of consciousness. These data are presented in our experience in a continuous variation of patterns—as in the case of a table viewed from different angles, for instance. Husserlian analysis is geared to examine *how* the ever-changing patterns of sensory data are united in apperception so as to "constitute" the meaning of an object for us. This type of approach is sometimes called *constitutive phenomenology*. The immediate goal of such analysis is to help us identify the "essence" of the objects thus perceived. The word "essence" as used by Husserl simply means "that which accounts for the unity and sameness of the object as 'meant' or intended in consciousness." Clarification of such intentional meanings free from externally imposed presuppositions is expected to provide a pure or "eidetic" account of the world as intended. The Husserlian approach points out that, in the ultimate analysis, all views of the world—including the most sophisticated "scientific" accounts of the world—as similarly *constituted* in the intentional mode of consciousness.

In his well-known book, *Ideas,* Husserl (1913/1962, Section 33) suggested that his method of "bracketing" was to be split into several steps of gradual "reduction." (It is necessary to note that the word reduction should not mislead us. It has nothing to do with the behavioristic reduction of the complex into simple, smaller units, or of mental events into material events. In fact, the Husserlian "reduction" takes us from the empirical level of consciousness to successively deeper levels of consciousness.) Unfortunately, *Ideas* gives us only a sketchy account of just two levels of phenomenological reduction. As his students and sympathetic interpreters (such as Fink, 1933/1970; and Lauer, 1958/1965) have painfully noted, Husserl never gave a complete account of all the steps. Lauer (1958/1965, pp. 46–64) has reconstructed an account of six levels of phenomenological reduction, but space does not permit me to examine them even briefly. Having noted its initial step (suspending judgment about the natural world) and its thrust on accounting for the "constitutive" function, it is enough to note here that Husserl expected his method to finally lead to the region of "pure consciousness."

What is the nature of "pure consciousness" to which the Husserlian reduction is supposed to lead? In a discussion of the "region of pure consciousness" Husserl (1913/1962, Section 53) notes the following: "If the experience in question—the feeling of joy in the example selected—loses this intentional form (and it might quite conceivably do so), it suffers a change . . . but only one which simplifies it *into pure consciousness,* so that it loses all its meaning as a natural event." This description is interesting and important for various reasons. First, it suggests that pure consciousness is not intentional, that is, directed to an object. This position is particularly intriguing because Husserl often indicated that consciousness is *always* consciousness *of* something. Second, if indeed pure consciousness is not intentional, does it not contain an "act" constituting a meaning by way of a configuration of "content," as is supposed to be the case with "ordinary" consciousness at all times? Although I do not see any explicit answer to this question, there seems to be a hint in his writing that his method of bracketing may involve not only an analysis of the constitutive or "meaning bestowing" function of consciousness, by way of description of its contents, but also a possibility (if not a deliberate attempt) to *control* the acts of consciousness. It is important to note in this regard the following words of Husserl (Husserl, 1913/1962, Section 31): "On a closer view, moreover, the 'bracketing' image is . . . better suited to the sphere of the object, just as the expression 'to put out of action' better suits the sphere of the Act of Consciousness." The metaphor "put out of action" conveys the idea that the Husserlian method involves some kind of control of the flow of consciousness which halts the fluctuating "acts" of consciousness such as thinking, imagining, remembering and the like. As we shall see in the next chapter, the Yogic approach to consciousness explicitly describes a state of consciousness beyond intentionality and even suggests specific ways of attaining it by *deliberately* controlling the "acts" of consciousness.

In his statements from *Ideas* quoted above, Husserl (1913/1962, Section 53) suggests that a person "might quite conceivably" lose the intentional character of consciousness. This means that here, the experience of "absolute consciousness" or experience beyond intentionality is a mere *possibility*. In the subsequent section, however, Husserl (1913/1962, Section 54) has suggested that the "absolute experience" is not a "metaphysical construction," but, with an appropriate shifting of the standpoint, it is "indubitably manifest in all its absoluteness and immediately given in intuition." Can such statements relating to "absolute experience" or "pure consciousness" be validated? If so, how? We find a suggested answer to these questions in the response to Husserl's critics given by his trusted student, Eugen Fink (1933/1970, pp. 104–116). He suggests that to be able to acquire the knowledge attainable with the use of phenomenological method it is necessary to *actually perform* the reduction as suggested by Husserl. He notes that all talk of knowledge which is different from everyday knowing (including such as the knowledge of physics) "presupposes *actually having been involved with it*." He goes ahead to say that this is particularly true about the modes of knowing and experiencing involved in phenomenological reduction since its methods require the suspension of the natural attitude and take us to an unfamiliar domain.

We may now ask: Where does the phenomenological method lead us? Do the types of knowledge and experience attainable through Husserlian methods lead to any useful application? Husserl's own writings give us little about the eidetic knowledge promised by his methods. In fact, his works give very few examples of "eidetic reduction" and they tell us little if anything new. As far as the constitutive phenomenology is concerned, it seems fair to say that although Husserl's writings give us few examples of useful application of his method of reduction, his forceful writings have proved greatly influential in promoting the study of the subjective aspect of life. First, they helped in the recognition of the domain of consciousness as a legitimate subject matter for study. Second, under Husserl's influence, numerous psychologists undertook studies of consciousness which did not mimic natural sciences like the structuralists did. There are many examples of constitutive phenomenological analysis which provide descriptive accounts of sensory and perceptual experiences and of intentional acts of consciousness. It is neither possible nor necessary to review such studies. There is an interesting observation about the nature and outcome of phenomenological reduction of "epoché" which needs to be mentioned here insofar as it has implications for potential application.

> Perhaps it will become apparent that the total phenomenological attitude and the corresponding *epoché* is called upon to bring about a complete per-

> sonal transformation *(Wandlung)* which might be compared to a religious conversion, but which even beyond it has the significance of the greatest existential conversion that is expected of mankind. (*Husserliana VI,* p. 140, as quoted by Spiegelberg, 1965, Vol. 1, p. 136)

It would appear from the above remark that Husserl's method has something very valuable to offer by way of its application. But, as indicated by Spiegelberg (1975, p. 68) in his more recent book *Doing Phenomenology,* there seems to be nothing more than a mere hint about valuable "existential" benefits that may follow from Husserl's approach to consciousness. It would therefore be proper to terminate our discussion of Husserl's reductive phenomenology and turn to other general trends in the fields of phenomenology and existential psychology.

Martin Heidegger, a junior contemporary and onetime associate of Husserl, is one of the most influential thinkers in the phenomenological and existential movements. His influence is deep and widespread ranging from the existential philosophy of Jean-Paul Sartre, theologians Paul Tillich and Rudolf Bultmann, and psychologists and psychoanalysts such as Ludwig Binswanger and Medard Boss. *Being and Time,* Heidegger's magnum opus, is a widely-known and influential work (Heidegger, 1927/1962). Filled with brilliant insights and new concepts, this book proved to be enigmatic due to the novelty of its concepts, new terms coined to express them, and its unique style. It is not necessary to either outline his philosophy fully or to account for its wide influence, since we are concerned only with the implication of his ideas insofar as they have contributed a distinct approach to the study of consciousness.

Heidegger was dissatisfied with philosophies of the past, and, like some of the geniuses of the history of Western philosophy such as Descartes, Kant, and even Husserl, he had set out to undertake a fundamental revision of philosophy. His main complaint against past philosophies was that none of them had really tried to understand and explain the problem of *human existence.* I must hasten to add that the significance of this complaint makes sense only when we understand what he means by human existence. He coined the term "Dasein" to describe a human being who is seen as an entity that understands itself, is concerned about its Being, conceives of alternative possibilities of its existence, and has the ability to choose to be itself or not itself. While explaining such aspects of his views of a human being, Heidegger adds that "only the particular Dasein decides its existence, whether it does so by taking hold or by neglecting" (Heidegger, 1927/1962, p. 33). His emphasis on the *particular*—as opposed to the general and the universal—colors his entire perspective on man. The first and simple implication of such emphasis is that a human being is not to be seen as just one of the innumerable objects of the world. This stance can be easily seen as being similar to Husserl's objection to naturalism. Certainly Heidegger shared with Husserl a disapproval of the "naturalist" view of man. But Heidegger surpassed Husserl in his criticism of naturalism by striking at the very root of naturalism—by questioning the Cartesian dualism which opens the way for a materialist view of man and the world.

Heidegger objects to the Cartesian definitions of the mind as a thinking substance and matter as extended substance by raising doubts about the notion of substance. (See Heidegger, 1927/1962, Section 19). In effect, he rejects mind and matter as ontological categories. Moreover, he strikes at a still deeper level of the issue when he questions the conventional meaning of ontology as it has been understood and practiced in the West. For Heidegger ontology as a science of Being seems to make little sense when Being is understood in terms of some abstract and impersonal, objective notion of reality. He insists on the *actuality* of human existence which must be understood in terms of the average "everydayness" of experience; we have no right to define it in terms of "dogmatic constructions." Thus, he not only rejects the notion of man as mind-plus-body, but objects to the consideration of thinking as the *essence* of mind, just as he opposes the view of the mind as a thinking substance. In a sentence (which has often been quoted as being a typical representation of his "existential" viewpoint) Heidegger says "The 'essence' of Dasein lies in its existence" (Heidegger, 1927/1962, Section 9.) The consideration of existence is more important to him that that of essence. It is in this sense that he complained that the "am" part of the Cartesian dictum "I think, therefore I am" has been neglected. What this means is that the importance given to the consideration of the "I" or ego and his cogitations or acts of consciousness has diverted our attention from the problems of human *existence*—which include the human problems of considering future possibilities and of choosing among them.

It follows from what has just been said that, in Heidegger's view, the nature of consciousness is not an important issue. Nevertheless, his position requires a close examination of the subjective aspect of life. Although this may seem paradoxical, it follows from Heidegger's view that each human being is a *particular* Dasein or an individual who has his own sphere of what he considers "mine." This individual Dasein is not to be seen as an object within the spatiotemporal world. Rather, the region of space which is within the reach of the individual, as well as those objects which are "on hand" to be used as utensils or instruments, are to be seen as parts of the Dasein. Seen this way, Heidegger's view of space is similar to Husserl's view of subjective as opposed to objective space. Each individual Dasein is "thrown" into a particular kind of situation and feels concerned about things as "one" who is constantly concerned about keeping a proper distance from others. It follows, then, that the only way to understand the nature of human existence is to view the individual Dasein from *its* vantage point.

Against this background, it is easy to describe Heidegger's strategy for understanding the nature of human existence. It requires us to see the individual's view of himself and the world from his own vantage point. It is implied that each individual "constructs" his view of the world. This is similar to Husserl's constitutive phenomenology which emphasizes the meaning-bestowing function of consciousness. However, Heidegger recommends neither a simple description of an individual's perspective of the world, nor a step-by-step reduction as in Husserlian bracketing. Instead, Heidegger recommends an *interpretation* of the individual's meanings since he believes that the real meanings are "hidden" rather than directly perceived. He sees the task of interpreting the meaning in individual Dasein as being similar to the task of interpreting the correct meanings hidden behind the scriptural texts. Since "hermeneutics" was the name given to the principles for interpreting texts such as the Bible, Heidegger's way of "doing" phenomenology is called *hermeneutic phenomenology*.

Psychologists like Paul Ricoeur (1974) have followed the footsteps of Heidegger in explaining how the hermeneutical method can be applied to the study of not only psychology but all human sciences by considering human action as a "text." Ludwig Binswanger (1958a; 1958b; 1963) has explained how the hermeneutic method can be applied to understand and interpret the private world of psychotic patients. He has given detailed accounts of how his patients' dreams and fantasies could be explained with the help of interpretative techniques typical of his "Daseinsanalysis." Space does not permit me to sample his approach, but it may simply be suggested that Binswanger's method is quite similar to that of the Freudian method of dream analysis—except that there is no emphasis on sexual symbolism as in the case of psychoanalysis, and that Binswanger's analysis follows Heidegger's, rather than the Freudian view of the human condition. (We have noted the difference between the psychoanalytic and existential views of the human condition in Chapter 2.) The similarity between Binswanger's hermeneutics and psychoanalytical interpretation is accounted for only partly by the fact that Binswanger was trained in Freudian psychoanalysis before turning to Heidegger's philosophy. It is accounted for partly by the basic similarity in their approach: both attempt to uncover meanings hidden behind the "contents" of consciousness as they appear in free association, fantasies and dreams. Spiegelberg (1965, pp. 324–325) who has noted this similarity, has remarked that "It is almost suprising that they [*i.e.*, techniques of hermeneutic phenomenology] are not compared and contrasted with the techniques of psychoanalysis in its attempt to uncover the unconscious."

It is difficult to identify specific techniques of hermeneutic phenomenology. Only a few psychologists—such as Paul Ricoeur (1973)—speak explicitly of the hermeneutic method. However, there are several phenomenologically oriented psychologists who have developed their own methods for trying to understand a person's view of the world and interpret it for him. For example, George Kelly (1955), who is considered a phenomenological psychologist, has developed a technique called the "Role Construct Repertory Test," or simply the "Rep Test" to help a therapist in discovering the patient's view of the world. In this test the patient is asked to compare significant persons in his life (such as mother, favorite teacher, the most threatening person he has ever met, and so on) on numerous criteria or personality characteristics. In the process of making such comparisons the patient reveals his view of the world. Kelly analyzes the information generated with the help of the test, using statistical methods (such as factor analysis) to uncover the "basic constructs" or underlying themes used by the patient to interpret the world. If it is found, for instance, that the patient dislikes anyone who is even slightly critical, let alone potentially threatening, the therapist has found a clue that helps interpret the patient's anxiety and anger.

Kelly's method of exploring and interpreting is much different from Binswanger's in that he does not seem to use any structural methods amenable to statistical treatment as Kelly does. In fact Medard Boss, Carl Rogers, Rollo May, and several others are called existential or phenomenological psychologists, but their methods of study are as varied as their therapeutic techniques. Nevertheless, they can be said to share the basic rationale of the phenomenological approach.

The basic rationale of the phenomenological approach may be explained simply in the following manner: We start with a proposition that an individual reacts to the world as he perceives it. Thus, if we would like to understand why a person behaved the way he did, we must find out how he perceives the world around him from his own vantage point. The fact that some people keep a social distance from members of certain groups such as Jews or blacks, for instance, can be properly understood as a consequence of their view of such groups as cunning, mercenary, dirty, or dangerous (Allport, 1958, pp. 210–211). It follows from this rationale that a social psychologist interested in the study of prejudice or intergroup relations should systematically explore the attitudes, opinions, and values—phenomena belonging to the domain of conscious content. It may be noted incidentally that Allport, who often explained and justified the phenomenological approach in the fields of personality and social psychology, derived his inspiration from the philosophy of Wilhelm Dilthey, a German contemporary of Brentano, who had influenced Husserl and Heidegger.

It would be reasonable to say that the scope of psychology extends to any study that undertakes to explore the beliefs, opinions, values, attitudes, intentions, or feelings with an underlying assumption that such exploration will help explain why a person behaves the way he does. The specific manifestation of this approach may vary from one branch of psychology to another. However, this general rationale is implicit in all kinds of social psychological investigations of attitudes and opinions, in various types of cognitive psychology including Piagetian psychology which insists that the child understands the world in a different way in comparison to the adult, in Gestalt psychology, in various studies of perception, in the personality theories of Allport and Carl Rogers—and the list can be extended on and on. It is not necessary for us to survey the entire science of psychology searching for applications of phenomenology, which are myriad. The interested reader may consult the systematic survey of phenomenological viewpoints in psychology published by Spiegelberg (1972). It would be enough for us to point out some important features of the investigative and applicational mode of phenomenology as it relates to consciousness in particular.

The investigative mode of phenomenology rests on the task of acquiring information about the private domain of consciousness. As such, it must face all the problems related to the "privileged access" of this domain which we have discussed before. Thus, the requirement of a common language of communication between the psychologist and the subject, and the need for a trustful relationship between the two must be satisfied as prerequisites for a sound phenomenological investigation. The problem of the "demand characteristics" of an investigation, which was also considered before, is equally relevant. These aspects of the investigations of the conscious domain assume particularly major proportions in social psychology where the topics of investigation (such as attitudes and opinions relating to politics, sex, or morals) are emotionally loaded. In clinical psychology, however, the application of hermeneutic (*i.e.* interpretative) phenomenology brings in a somewhat different problem. This problem pertains to the issue of what constitutes "meaning" of conscious contents, and how one ascertains them. The problem of meaning is a complex one. It brings psychology face to face with semantics and the philosophy of language. The hermeneutic phenomenology of Heidegger has begun to make forays into this relatively uncharted sphere of human insight. It is hard to say whether adequate progress has been made in this direction.

The applicational mode of phenomenological or existential approaches appears to me to be somewhat like this: The patient seeks the analyst's help. The first step for the therapist is to establish rapport with the patient. Using his well-developed skills in interpersonal communication, the analyst then induces his client to disclose his view of himself and the world around him. He may ask the patient to describe his dreams, fantasies, and so on. The therapist then interprets these "data" using certain implicit or explicit "hermeneutic" principles which suggest their "true" meaning. The patient may either accept or reject these interpretations. The acceptable interpretations often provide the patient with an insight into the nature of his condition, which, in turn, leads to a removal of his symptoms and to an alleviation of his agony.

In general, such an approach seems largely restricted to an interpretation of the conscious contents of wakeful and dream states. There is little interest in other states of consciousness, such as sleep, hypnosis, or "mystical" states. Also, by and large, the phenomenological approach focuses heavily on the interpretation of the "meanings" associated with the contents of consciousness. As noted before, Husserl seems to have tried to "put out of action" the acts or processes of consciousness with the help of his methods of bracketing and phenomenological reduction. He has suggested that the method of reduction can lead the experience of "pure consciousness" and has hinted at the attainment of a "complete personal transformation" of great (but unspecified) significance. Other than this rather exceptional case, most phenomenological writings seem to focus on the contents of consciousness, to the relative neglect of the processual aspect of consciousness. At least, as far as the applicational aspect of the phenomenological approach is concerned, nobody seems to have dealt systematically with the possibility of deliberately controlling the processes of consciousness for the purpose of improving the human condition. When I say this, I am comparing the phenomenological approach with that of Yoga. Yoga, as we shall see in the next chapter, aims specifically at controlling the processes of consciousness and almost completely neglects the interpretative analysis of the content of consciousness, which is used quite effectively by phenomenologically oriented social and clinical psychologists.

It appears that Jean Paul Sartre (1943/1966), the originator of existential psychoanalysis (see his *Being and Nothingness*, Part IV, Chapter 2) was interested in dealing with the processes of consciousness which

William James has called the stream of thought. The reader may recall, for instance, an excerpt from Sartre's novel, *Nausea,* which was quoted before (in Chapter 2). It should be clear that what Sartre was concerned with in the situation described in those paragraphs is the continuous flow of thoughts which continue to be born somewhere "at the back" of the person. Sartre feels absolutely certain about the fact of human existence, the same way as Descartes and Husserl did. However, the existential dilemma for Sartre's hero arises from the situation where he cannot do anything with the downpour of his stream of thoughts. Since he cannot stop them, he keeps flowing with them, feeling helplessly at the mercy of the tyranny of this current. Moreover, the agony, a nauseating mood, seems to result from the idea that he is himself responsible for landing where his thoughts take him. He wishes he could stop the flow of ideas or control the stream of his consciousness, but to no avail. Sartre's novel seems to reflect the general inability of existential psychoanalysts to develop an effective technique of dealing with or controlling the stream of consciousness.

This should be the right point to turn to the Indian views of consciousness, because, as we shall see in the next chapter, the Indian thinkers were equally intensely involved with the predicament of having to deal with one's own runaway thoughts. Their reaction to this situation, however, was quite different from that of Sartre. This is because, unlike Sartre, they arrived at the conclusion that one can effectively deal with the processes of consciousness. Moreover, they claimed that the techniques of Yoga can not only enable us to control the stream of consciousness, but to attain states of human existence which have intrinsically desirable qualities.

Notes

1. Patañjali's key term "citta vṛtti" can be reasonably translated as a mental process. One of his aphorisms (1.6) lists five categories or mental processes: pramāṇa, viparyaya, vikalpa, nidrā, and smṛti. These are technical terms defined in separate aphorisms (from 1.7 through 1.11). Since it is difficult to find exact English equivalents for these terms, I have tried to give their nearest approximations. The Vedāntists generally consider suṣupti and svapna, sleep and dreams, respectively, as distinct states of consciousness. Patañjali's use of the term nidrā includes both sleeping and dreaming. Śaṅkara's commentary on Patañjali's aphorism 1.10 points out that the juxtaposition of svapna and nidrā in the latter's aphorism No. 1.38 (svapnanidrājñānālaṁbanam vā) shows that the term nidrā connotes both sleeping and dreaming (see Śaṅkara, a, 1.10).
2. William James's *Principles of Psychology* (1890/1950) contained a chapter called "The Stream of Thought." In a brief edition of this popular book published a few years later, James chose the title "Stream of Consciousness" for an abridged version of the

same chapter. Since the word *thought* is used to refer to a wide range of cognitive processes, the term *stream of thought* is considered synonymous with the stream of consciousness.

3. The words used by Vyāsa in his commentary on Patañjali's aphorism No. 1.5 to describe the cyclical nature of mental processes are as follows: evam vṛttisaṁskāra-cakram aniśam āvartate.
4. Dasgupta (1924/1974, p. 103) has translated the word āśaya as "a vehicle." He provides a definition of āśaya as follows; "āśerate sāṁsārikāḥ puruṣā asminniti āśayaḥ. That in which some thing lives is its vehicle." The metaphor of a vehicle implies continuity and movement through time. The word āśaya can be alternatively interpreted to mean a storehouse as in jalāśaya which means "a lake." Such interpretation would indicate the *storage* of impressions of past experiences, and their retrieval, an essential aspect of the stream of consciousness.
5. Once again, it is important to remember that James's term "thought" connotes a broad range of phenomena. See Note 2 above.

4

CONSCIOUSNESS: TWO INDIAN VIEWS

We have already become familiar with Indian concepts since references to a few Indian ideas relating to consciousness were made in the previous chapter. In this chapter, I propose to discuss two Indian perspectives on consciousness, namely those of the Yoga and Vedānta systems. These two perspectives are not to be considered representative of the full range of Indian perspectives, since the Indian tradition has produced a broad range of divergent theories. Yoga and Vedānta are but two of the six major schools of Brahmanical philosophy. In addition to these schools, there are equally complex and well-developed systems of Buddhists and Jains, along with those of several Tantric cults. The choice of Yoga and Vedānta for discussion here is based on the following considerations: first, the Yoga of Patañjali emphasizes psychological issues so much that it may be considered more a psychological theory than a system of philosophy. Patañjali's aphorisms, as we shall see in this chapter, have given not only a broad set of concepts, but also a well-developed set of techniques for systematic control of the processes of consciousness. Many of these techniques are part of a common tradition from which most schools of Brahmanic, Buddhist, as well as Jain philosophy and religion have drawn heavily. To speak of Yoga, therefore, is to speak of certain common aspects of a broad range of Indian perspectives that are otherwise fairly divergent. Second, the choice of the Advāita (non-dualist) Vedānta perspective is based on the opinion that the monistic doctrine of this school, particularly as propounded by Śaṅkara (788–822 A.D.), is perhaps the most dominant and popular school of Indian philosophy.

Notes for Chapter 4 are on p. 228.

Besides these considerations, the choice of these perspectives is based on the fact that they emphasize the "superior" states of consciousness, which are generally neglected by Western psychologists. It makes sense to include cases of contrast in a comparative study such as this one.

The Yoga of Patañjali

The cryptic style of the Yoga aphorisms makes it essential for the students of Yoga to rely on old, well-known commentaries that have explained the meaning and significance of the original compact text, a text that involves fewer than 200 one- or two-line aphorisms. The most important and well-known of all commentaries is that of Vyāsa (about 4th to 5th century A.D.). (We have already come across Vyāsa's use of the metaphor of the stream in the last chapter.) Next in order of importance are the commentaries of Vācaspati Miśra and Vijñāna Bhikṣu. A less well-known, but very useful commentary is one that is claimed to have been written by Śaṅkara, the Advaita Vedāntic philosopher just mentioned. There are several lesser works on Patañjali, such as those of Bhoja, Nāgeśa, and Baladeva. We need not be concerned with these for our purposes.[1] It is important to remember, once again, that unlike most Western theories, the Indian approaches to consciousness have developed in the context of adhyātma or spiritual life. Although in the *Yoga-Sūtra* Patañjali was not primarily concerned with problems of medicine, he has nevertheless shown that Yoga is analogous to medicine. Vyāsa (2.15) has clarified the analogy between Yoga and medicine as follows: The misery involved in the unending cycle of birth, death, and rebirth is considered similar to a disease. (As already noted in Chapter 2, Patañjali sees the human condition as being full of misery.) Patañjali's theory suggests that the root cause of this disease is the identification of the real Self or the Knower with the objects of his knowledge. (We shall shortly examine this statement.) Patañjali believes that the Self can be restored to a state of health by acquiring knowledge of its real nature. But even the very sketchy account of the medical analogy used by the exponents of Yoga is enough to suggest that Yoga did not emerge from the type of clinical situation from which the Freudian model emerged. In Yoga we are not talking about a therapeutic program aimed simply at helping a patient who is suffering from physical or neurotic symptoms, but a spiritual quest for the *ultimate* release from miseries of life. As in the case of any other theory, we must take into account not only the particular setting within which the theory developed, but also the world view within which its concepts are defined.

Basic Concepts of Yoga

The psychology of Yoga is based upon the dualistic metaphysics of the Sāṅkhya system, which suggests, as we have noted in Chapter 2, two ontological categories or basic principles of reality: the Prakṛti, which underlies the material world, and Puruṣa, which manifests itself in the form of innumerable "souls" residing in all kinds of living creatures. The continual modifications in the world of Prakṛti are governed by the regulative principle of karma. Every living being is associated with a Puruṣa. The Puruṣa is metaphorically described as an immutable "light" (sadāprakāśasvarūpa) because it accounts for the "illuminating" character of consciousness. In Yoga, as in Sāṅkhya, the essential (and perhaps the only) characteristic of Puruṣa is an absolute, pure sentience (cit) or simply the capacity to become aware and to experience. When the term Puruṣa is used with reference to human beings, it is often considered synonymous with the real Self. The Puruṣa never participates in any activity or change. All activity lies within the domain of the material world. Although Puruṣa and Prakṛti are essentially separate principles, they have become entangled with one another due to primeval ignorance (avidyā). There is no explanation of the cause of this ignorance. It is considered beginningless—although it can be ended by realizing the true nature of the Self. The first product of the contact of Puruṣa with Prakṛti is called Mahat or Buddhi in Sāṅkhya, and the same is generally called citta in Yoga (see Vācaspati Miśra, 1.1.[2] See also Radhakrishnan, 1929, Vol. 2, p. 345). This union is the original cause (kāraṇacitta) from which originate the individual phenomenal selves (as distinguished from the unattached real Selves or Puruṣas), which become involved in a perpetual journey from one life cycle to the next.

The citta, as a cause, is all-pervading—like the skies. The effect of this cause manifests itself in the form of separate phenomenal selves associated with each individual Puruṣa. This kāryacitta or citta-as-effect (normally referred to only as citta, rather than kāryacitta) always exists in the form of its states, which are called vṛttis.

The preceding paragraphs sketch the philosophical background of Yoga psychology. We are not concerned here with the cosmological principles of the Sāṅkhya philosophy, so we shall leave the Sāṅkhya account of the evolution and dissolution of the world of Prakṛti—their doctrine of the reincarnation of the souls—and other such issues to the philosopher, and start with citta and its vṛttis or activities which are key concepts of the Yoga psychology. Citta stands for all that is psychological in man. It is primarily the seat of all experiences and the repository of their residual effects. It includes the living principle within human beings.

It also refers to the totality of the senses, the ego, and the intellect. The term citta may, therefore, be translated generally as the mind.

Since the Puruṣa is a totally passive entity, its "association" with a citta provides the latter with nothing except the *capacity* to become aware or illuminated, that is, to be able to experience pleasure or pain, and to acquire knowledge as one does from being a mere witness or passive spectator. There is only a reflection, as it were, of the pure sentience of Puruṣa in the citta. What remains in the citta in the absence of this reflection is only material Prakṛti. Vyāsa (1.2), therefore, considers citta to be a part of the world of Prakṛti. Like everything else in the domain of Prakṛti, the citta involves the three basic qualities (guṇas): sattva or luminosity, rajas or activity, and tamas or heaviness and inertia. (The reader may recall that the nature of the guṇas was described briefly in Chapter 2.) Due to the constant interplay of these qualities, the citta is involved in incessant modifications. These modifications, called vṛttis, are classified by Patañjali into five major categories.

The *first* category of vṛttis is called *pramāṇa*. The word pramā means valid cognition, and pramāṇa is a means of acquiring valid cognition. Patañjali (1.7) lists direct perception or pratyakṣa, inference or anumāna, and verbal testimony from a trustworthy person or āgama[3] as categories of the means of obtaining valid knowledge. These categories refer to epistemic principles for validation of statements commonly discussed in most philosophical systems of India. Patañjali's reference to these principles seems to imply that the Yoga system accepts these as epistemic criteria. It is important to remember, however, that here Patañjali is mainly concerned with the description of the various psychic events or processes of consciousness. We must therefore consider the pramāṇas primarily *cognitive processes* leading to valid cognition. Such emphasis becomes quite clear when we note that the *second* category of vṛttis listed by Patañjali: *viparyaya* (1.8) is defined as the types of cognitive processes that lead to erroneous cognition. Vyāsa gives perception of two moons as an example of viparyaya. What Vyāsa means, I think, is the situation created by pressing one eyeball with a finger while looking at the moon so that two non-superimposed images give rise to the illusion of two moons. What is referred to here, obviously, is a set of cognitive processes that are involved in perceptual illusions.

The *third* category of vṛttis, called *vikalpa,* refers to imagination or fantasy. The term is defined in terms of entities that have no counterparts in the objective world. Vijñāna Bhikṣu gives a typical Indian example of this category, namely, the horns of a rabbit. Western examples might be centaurs, unicorns, or other products of fantasy. The connotation of this term is not restricted to engaging in pure fantasy; it also includes ideation, conjecturing, supposing, or hypothesizing. Thus, the making of hypothetical "constructs" is part of this category of vṛttis. Obviously, the entities to which such constructs refer are not purely imaginary like the horns of a rabbit.

The *fourth* category is *nidrā* or sleep. This is considered a special kind of modification of the citta because, unlike in other states, during sleeping there seems to be an absence of direct, cognitive experience. Yet, one must be having some kind of experience during sleep since, upon awakening, one often says: "I had a good night's sleep," or "I didn't sleep well," and so on. The *fifth* and final category of vṛttis is *smṛti* or "recollection," which is simply defined as the "not dropping off" of what is once experienced.[4]

The vṛttis thus include a broad variety of mental processes including perceiving, thinking, imagining, sleeping, and recollecting. Clearly what Yoga is concerned with is mental processes or the processes of consciousness. Patañjali (1.2) defines Yoga as the control or restraint (nirodha) of the processes of consciousness. Upon attainment of a complete restraint of these processes, the Self is said to be restored to its original state, devoid of all experience of the misery that usually accompanies the common mental states listed above. To put it simply, an ideal human condition, free from all miseries, is said to be attained through the control of mental processes. This, of course, is what is claimed by the yogis; we shall examine the theoretical basis of this claim. On the practical side, Yoga offers a systematic method of attaining mastery over one's mental processes. I shall briefly outline the basic steps in the practice of Yoga in subsequent sections of this chapter. Before describing these theoretical and practical aspects of Yoga, I have to first explain some other related concepts.

Vyāsa describes several "stages" or conditions of citta, characterizing the way in which the mind predominantly functions during a given period of time, and then explains how far these conditions are suitable (or unsuitable) for the practice of Yoga. These are: (1) wandering (kṣipta), (2) stupefied (mūḍha), (3) occasionally steady (vikṣipta), (4) one-pointed (ekāgra), and (5) restrained (niruddha). Of these five planes, the first one refers to a restless condition, wherein a person follows his momentary predilection in thought and action while engaging himself actively in any business of life. The second plane refers to a relatively lethargic condition, as in a state of drowsiness or sleep. Here the mind is not active, but slowing down. A person in this condition is clearly far from having his mind under control. Both these conditions are considered unsuitable for Yoga. The third plane refers to the condition of an occasionally steady but easily distracted mind. As an example of this occasionally-steady state we may think of a person who is involved in his or her day-to-day activities and absorbed in whatever task happens to be on hand at that time, but is relatively easily distracted by anything else that also demands attention—such as a tap on the door. Even this condition is considered unsuitable for Yoga. The fourth condition is described as one-pointed, which means that a person in this condition is so deeply involved in something that he cannot easily be distracted. The mental and physical activities are completely harnessed to accomplish whatever task is undertaken. Any and every desire or action-tendency that might interfere with the focused attention is kept under control. Such a condition is considered desirable for the practice of Yoga. The technique of Yoga is designed to facilitate the attainment of a condition of complete restraint of all mental activities. This is the hallmark of the fifth plane mentioned above.

The first three planes of the mind, namely the wandering, stupefied, and occasionally-steady states, are sometimes collectively referred to as the vyutthāna condition (Bhoja, 1969 ed., 3.9). Vyutthāna is defined as the condition of being aroused and activated in various forms so that the contents of the mind are shaped by whatever is being attended to (Śaṅkara, a, 3.9).[5] Such activities of the mind as perceiving, thinking, imagining, remembering, and the like are directed toward something. As can be easily seen, the struggle for survival demands that human beings, like all other organisms, attend to whatever conditions may demand their attention. A state of arousal is a necessary condition for survival. But even when we are not involved in an active struggle with the environment, the mind continues to be active and directed to one thing or another. Thus, in moments of rest we may remember past events and daydream about future ones. Even during sleep one "wanders around" as one dreams. The normal states of arousal and activity are contrasted with those states in which all activity is restrained. A person with a restrained mind is said to be in a state of samādhi which literally means a condition of being "held in place" or "put together."

Restraint is obviously the most crucial aspect of Yoga. Patañjali *defines* Yoga as the restraint of the processes of consciousness.[6] Clearly, it is the activity of the mind that is to be restrained. There is a clear emphasis on the processual, dynamic aspect of consciousness in the Yogic approach. Indeed it is possible to characterize vṛttis as both processes such as recollecting or sleeping on the one hand, and also as products of these processes (for instance, memories) or as states associated with them (such as sleep and the like) on the other hand. Nevertheless, it is the former characterization which is more appropriate for Yoga. The Yogic emphasis on the processual aspect of consciousness is similar to Brentano's emphasis on acts or functions of the mind, in contrast to Wundt's and Titchener's emphases on mental content. As we shall see later in this chapter, the Vedānta approach stands in contrast to Yoga in this respect insofar as Vedānta considers sleep and dreams to be states rather than processes of consciousness. Since the relative emphasis on dynamic *versus* static aspects of consciousness accounts for some important differences among various theories, it will be useful to examine the Yogic approach in this respect.

The term vṛtti is derived from the root vṛt which means "to turn." The usual meanings of the word vṛtti include "mode of conduct," "course of action," and "activities," especially such activities as are involved in making a living. Vijñāna Bhikṣu (1971 ed., 1.5) defines vṛttis specifically as activities (vyāpārāḥ) and suggests that they are the business of the citta, just as worshipping God is the business of the priest. Dasgupta (1924, pp. 48–49) explains the Yogic view of the activities of the citta as follows: "A particular content of thought is illuminated and then passed over. The ideas arise, are illuminated, and pass away . . . Thought as such is always moving."

What Dasgupta is trying to explain is the evanescent character of the contents of consciousness. What is implicit here is clearly the same as the distinction between the processes and the contents of consciousness. We have noted in the previous chapter that one of the basic difficulties in the use of the Titchenerian method of introspection is the evanescent, fleeting nature of the contents of consciousness. We also noted earlier that Patañjali (4.20) had clearly pointed out that it is impossible to acquire knowledge of consciousness by using the method of introspection. In the Yogic approach, one is not supposed to observe and describe the contents of consciousness, such as the sight of colors or sound of musical notes (as the structuralists tried to do). One is supposed to deliberately alter one's thought processes so as to speed up or slow down the flow of passing contents. Before describing the Yogic techniques of attaining such control over the stream of consciousness, it is necessary to account for a few more concepts that are central to the Yogic theory of consciousness.

Dasgupta (1924, p. 102) has noted that vṛttis are thought of as being mānasa karma, that is, "mental work" or mental activity. It is common in the Indian tradition to think of karma or activity in three aspects, namely the motor or bodily aspect (kāyika), the verbal aspect (vācika), and the mental aspect (mānasa). This view implies that the mental and the physical aspects of man are not dichotomized; they are placed on the same continuum. This is different from some Western theories that draw a sharp line between the mind and the body, thought and action.

Similarly, no sharp line is drawn in Indian philosophy between the experiential aspect of the thinking process and spoken words or "verbal behavior." In this respect the Yogic view appears to be similar to that of Skinner when he speaks of "verbal behavior" and "perceptual behavior" as being on a par with the bodily aspects of behavior. The apparent similarity, however, should not mislead us. It should be clear that Skinner puts the perceptual, verbal, and bodily aspects together because of his implicit material monism, while in Yoga the mental, verbal, and bodily aspects are brought together by the broad, encompassing concept of karma.

As noted in Chapter 2, karma or action is a central concept in Indian thought. It is often associated with (although it does not necessarily imply the acceptance of) the Law of Karma, which states that all actions are part of a cosmic system, where every action is part of the lawful sequence of cause and effect. All vṛttis or activities of the mind are caused and, in turn, lead to effects of their own. All vṛttis leave behind their residual effects (called "saṁskāra"s), which can potentially reappear in a form resembling the form of the original experiences (svavyañjakāñjana). As noted in Chapter 3, Vyāsa accounts for the flowing character of the stream of consciousness in terms of the eternal cycle of experiences, their residual effects, the re-emergence of vṛttis as consequences of the residual potencies, and so on.

The residual effects, saṁskāras, are like memories insofar as they imply storage and retrieval of impressions left behind by experiences or behaviors. Patañjali (4.9) explicitly considers saṁskāras to be very similar to memories. The two terms, saṁskāra and smṛti (memories), are not exactly synonymous, however, since the former is a broader and more inclusive concept. Vyāsa (1978 ed., 4.9) notes in his commentary, for instance, that saṁskāras can also be considered as desires (vāsanā). Whatever is carried forward by an individual with him as a consequence of an experience (such as the taste of honey) includes not only a cognitive/informational component (such as the faint "image" of the sweet taste I can reproduce in my mind), but also a motivational component (such as a desire to obtain honey again).

Dasgupta (1922, Vol. 1, p. 263) has explained a subtle difference in the usage of the term saṁskāra and vāsanā as follows:

> The meaning of saṁskāra in Hindu philosophy is . . . the impressions . . . of the objects experienced. All our experiences whether cognitive, emotional or conative exist in sub-conscious states and may under suitable conditions be reproduced as memory (smṛti). The word vāsanā . . . refers to the tendencies of the past lives, most of which lie dormant in the mind. But saṁskāras are

the sub-conscious states which are being constantly generated by experience. Vāsanās are innate saṁskāras not acquired in this life.

The residual effects of all mental and physical activity are considered to be cumulative. The traces left behind by all experience are accumulated and carried forward from one life cycle to the next in the unending cycle of birth and death. The citta, which is both the seat of all experiences as well as the repository of their effects, carries within it all the residual potencies. The totality of the effects of past experiences and behavior is called karmāśaya. The concept of karmāśaya, in turn, is intricately connected with the Yogic theory of the "ripening" or "fructification" of karmas (karmavipāka). This theory assumes that the residual effects of past karma are stored in the citta—like seeds that germinate and come to fruition under appropriate conditions. The ripening of karmic residues is manifest in the following three forms: species (jāti), span of life (āyuṣ), and experience, that is, enjoyment or suffering (bhoga). What this means is that, at the time of termination of a life cycle, during the onward journey of a soul or puruṣa, whether the soul will be reborn as a member of an animal (tiryak) or human species will depend on what kind of unfructified karmic residues have been accumulated by that time (see Vyāsa, 4.8). The same will determine how long that cycle will last under normal conditions—barring cases of accidental death. Finally, enjoyment will result as a fruit of meritorious actions of the past and the individual will suffer as a result of demerit.[7]

Let us now return to the Yogic concept of vṛttis. One important aspect of the vṛttis or processes of consciousness is the suffering (kleśa) which is often their unmistakable characteristic. According to Patañjali (2.3–5) the root cause of all suffering, the major affliction, is "misconception" (avidyā), whereby one mistakes the non-self for the self, the impermanent for the permanent, bad for good, and misery for happiness. This theory of the origin of misery assumes that sensual enjoyment does not lead to lasting, pure, unmixed happiness. It is therefore considered imprudent or unwise to relentlessly pursue transitory sources of worldly enjoyment such as wealth and power as if they were permanent. The identification of the self with one's body is considered another aspect of the basic confusion between the permanent and the impermanent. (We shall examine the concept of self in detail in the next chapter.) This basic misconception breeds the following specific afflictions or sources of suffering: egoism (asmitā), seeking (rāga, as in pleasure-seeking), avoidance (dveṣa, such as avoidance of pain), and love of life or "will to live" (abhiniveśa).

Once again we are in a territory common to the psychologies of both India and the West. As noted in Chapter 2, pleasure-seeking and pain-avoidance are almost universally considered unmistakable characteristics of human nature. Struggle for survival is considered the very basic characteristic of all organisms, and one which the Western theories (particularly those influenced by Darwin) have taken for granted. While both Yogic and Western approaches like psychoanalysis and behaviorism take these tendencies for granted, they differ radically in terms of how they deal with them. The behaviorists, for instance, assume that organisms tend to seek certain stimuli and avoid others, although the Skinnerians meticulously avoid any reference to pleasure or pain, which are experiential or subjective aspects of life. Having taken the positive tendencies (seeking, approaching) and the negative ones (avoiding) for granted, behaviorists try to develop ways of manipulating the conditions around organisms so as to control their behavior. Psychoanalysis, on its part, focuses on the pleasure-seeking tendencies of the psyche and has developed techniques for minimizing anxieties and other negative aspects of the human condition and maximizing the satisfaction of libidinal desires. Yoga, by contrast, aims at controlling one's own processes of consciousness (rather than controlling the behavior of others), minimizing the force of pleasure-seeking drives, and maximizing spiritual satisfaction (rather than sensual gratification).

The Practical Aspects of Yoga: The Eight "Limbs"

Given the conceptual framework of the processes of consciousness, the law of storage and retrieval of their impressions, and a view of the origins of miseries associated with those processes, we can now proceed with a brief account of the techniques of their systematic control. Here we deal with the practical aspect of Yoga (kriyāyoga). The goals for the practice of these techniques are clearly set out. The first goal is the attenuation of miseries; the second, the attainment of samādhi or trance states (Patañjali, 2.2). The practical aspect of Yoga is divided into eight parts or "limbs" that can be listed under the following labels: restraints, observances, postures, breathing exercises, the withdrawal of senses from their objects, concentration, contemplation, and trance (Patañjali, 2.29). Let us consider these eight aspects of Yoga practice one by one.

1. Restraints (yama). This aspect involves a set of prescriptions that require an initiate to abstain from the following: inflicting injuries, falsehood, theft, incontinence or lust, and avarice. In no way are these restrictions to be considered lightly or to be narrowly conceived. The principle of non-injury (ahiṁsā), for instance is conceived broadly as avoiding malice toward all living creatures at all times. This restraint is a categorical imperative that holds true irrespective of variations in place, time, or circumstance (Patañjali, 2.31). As Radhakrishnan (1929, Vol. 2, p. 353) points out, the rule against killing is not to be relaxed even against the infidels, enemies of the country, renegades of religion or the blasphemers of the Brahmins.

2. Observances (niyama). This aspect recommends the cultivation of the following virtues: cleanliness, contentment, ascetic self-control, study, and devotion to God. Vyāsa (2.32) explains these in some detail. Cleanliness involves bodily hygiene as well as the cleansing of the mind of evil thoughts. Contentment is defined as the absence of desire for more possessions than one has already acquired. Ascetic self-control requires the imposition of strict limitations on eating, drinking, sitting, speaking, and other such behavior, so as to attain and test one's determination and endurance. Study is specifically explained as study of the means of attaining self-realization or spiritual liberation. Devotion to God, as interpreted by Vyāsa, involves relinquishment of the fruits of all actions to God. This means that one has to become dispassionate about obtaining even the legitimate rewards for one's own work. It must be added here that the Yogic concept of God is not the same as the concept of the Creator God, who has the power to do and undo anything, or to bless anyone with His grace. God is defined simply as a special type of Puruṣa or Self that is untouched by any accumulated residues of past karmas that perpetuate misery (Patañjali 1.24). Yoga, after all, is a system closely related to the atheist theory of the Sāṅkhyas. The Yogic conception of God is perhaps as "secular" as one can get!

I must pause here for a critical look at these aspects of Yoga from the viewpoint of secular science. The above description of Yoga would be enough to induce many students of modern psychology to categorize Yoga as a moralistic religion that should not even pretend to be a science. Such a reaction would be further confirmed if I were to add that Patañjali recommends that, whenever an aspirant begins to feel tempted by bad ideas, he should counter them with opposite thoughts. This strategy is no different, one may say, from the Church fathers' exhortation: exercise your "will-power" against the thoughts of sin. Freud, as we know very well, characterized this conflict within the psyche as the struggle of the natural instincts against the socially imposed rules of morality. It was Freud's view, again, that ascribed the discontents of our civilization to the repressive rules of the "thou shalt" and "thou shalt not" variety.

Here I must point out, once again, that the psychology of Yoga cannot be evaluated according to the standards of Western psychology, which are the products of the bitter struggle of science against religion.

Moreover, the concept of God in Yoga is vastly different from the view of God that stifled the growth of inquisitive minds in the history of Western civilization. In fact, it is possible to argue that, as far as the Yogic view is concerned, it is the psychological theory (which accounts for the nature of experience) that has influenced the concept of God rather than the reverse. This should be clear if we note that, as indicated above, God in Yoga is someone who does not carry the burden of repeating some responses and avoiding others under the influence of the eternal drive to seek pleasure and avoid pain. God is not a master, but just another soul that is exempt from the game of reward and punishment we all seem to have imposed on ourselves. Further, the virtues are to be acquired not to please God, but to attain release from perpetual misery. God in Yoga seems to be a means to attain self-realization. According to Vijñāna Bhikṣu (2.45), the dedication of one's powers to God is to be viewed primarily in terms of its being instrumental in attaining samādhi.[8] As we shall soon see, an image of God is used as a means, as a convenient object upon which to concentrate. As Geraldine Coster (1934, pp. 82–83) put it: "Here again we have a reversal of values between east and west. The western mystic sets high value on one-pointedness because it leads the soul to God; the eastern yogi sets high value on the conception of God because it leads to one-pointedness."

I am not sure I can go further than this, because to extend this discussion would be to examine the various Eastern and Western conceptions of God, and to generate more controversy than conciliation. Let me, therefore, turn to another possible criticism of the restraints and observances prescribed by Yoga.

First, a philosophy of life that asks us to be satisfied with what we have would appear to be an insipid formula for a man of the world. It seems like the defeatist outlook of a man who is afraid of facing the challenges of life. Second, the proscriptions of Yoga seem to be extremely demanding. If people were to stop killing, hating, telling lies, and be temperate, what more could anyone ask of them? Moreover, practitioners of Yoga are supposed to be self-controlled and contented. If only a sizable minority of the population were to practice just the first two aspects of Yoga, a utopian society would be around the corner. Isn't Yoga asking for much more than most idealists ask? An apologist of Yoga may respond to such criticisms somewhat as follows: Yoga makes a fundamental assumption that lasting happiness cannot be attained through the acquisition of more and more wealth and power. Therefore, it is not recommended for those who enjoy the unending struggle for one-upmanship. This does not, of course, mean that the Yogic techniques are designed for the social recluse or the hermit, nor does it foster defeatism and dropping out of society. On the contrary, it dares you to undertake the task of putting the inner, psychological world in order, which is not necessarily easier than conquering the "outer" world. Certainly the Yoga system sets forth a stringent and demanding ethical code. But this demand is based neither on the fear of damnation nor on the promise of utopia. It is based on a promise that something more satisfying than worldly success, and something even more worthwhile than following an ethical code, is indeed attainable. Yoga is meant for those who wish to pursue such other-than-worldly (and I do not mean other-worldly) goals and also believe in the credibility of this promise.

3. *Posture (āsana).* Patañjali (2.46) mentions stability (sthira) and comfort (sukha) as the criteria for the right posture. He does not mention the names of any particular postures. Vyāsa, however, mentions some half-dozen postures, starting with the well-known "lotus posture" (padmāsana), and Vācaspati Miśra describes them briefly. Vyāsa also points out that, according to Patañjali (2.47), comfort and stability are secured only when effort involved in attaining a posture is slackened, or when the mind is made to rest on the infinite. Stability of the posture ensures sustained effort without changing one's bodily position every now and then. Likewise, if one sits in an odd posture in which some muscles are pulled, causing discomfort, it will cause distraction. It is, therefore, clearly advisable to sit in a comfortable position. It is implied here that any posture suitable to one's style and constitution may be chosen, as long as it provides stability and comfort. It is also implied that the body must remain at ease while the person remains alert. The strategy here is somewhat similar to that of conventional psychoanalytic therapy, where the patient is asked to recline comfortably on a sofa so that he will not be distracted while engaging in free association.

4. *Breathing Exercises (prāṇāyāma).* Patañjali explains the nature and significance of breathing exercises in four aphorisms (2.49–52), and the commentators have fairly long accounts of them. These exercises involve the systematic regulation of inhalation, exhalation, and the holding of breath. The exercises become increasingly complex and subtle as variations are introduced, in terms of whether the flow of breath is arrested after inspiration, after expiration, or both, and in terms of the duration and frequency of control.

What does one attain with the help of the breathing exercises? According to Vyāsa (2.52), "the karma capable of covering the discriminative thinking dwindles away" as a result of practicing breath control. (See Woods, 1914, p. 196) It is not easy to say exactly what this means, but an attempt may be made to paraphrase the commentators. Breathing exercises have the capacity to dampen one's infatuation with one's ability to think, which sometimes overcomes us during moments of intellectual insight. To me, what this means, in simpler words, is that breathing exercises make us less enthusiastic than usual about continuing to think in a syllogistic fashion. Since a syllogistic or problem-solving type of thinking often leads to moments of illuminating insight, one may tend to pursue such thinking more and more ardently. The purpose of Yoga, however, is to retard and ultimately to stop the stream of thoughts. It follows, therefore, that Yoga prescribes such practices as are believed to dampen one's enthusiasm to continue thinking. Here it is reasonable to ask: Why would breathing exercises have the kind of effect Patañjali and his commentators have suggested? This is an interesting question, but I do not even have a good guess to offer, let alone a satisfactory answer.

5. Withdrawing of the Senses from Their Objects (pratyāhāra). Withdrawal of the senses means simply that a person does not allow his eyes to wander around looking for things, nor his ears to pick up sounds from the environment, and so on. The activity of the senses in locating, recognizing, and interpreting stimuli is thus restrained. The extroverted or outward-bound direction of the senses is changed and turned "inward."

The five aspects of Yogic practices described so far are considered "external" or peripheral aspects of Yoga relative to the next three, which form the inner core. Before starting our account of the final steps, it would be useful to review the previous steps.

A person who is serious about pursuing Yoga has, first of all, disciplined his general conduct of life. The common ethical rules against stealing, against injury, and the like are followed. Besides its intrinsic value, there is a simple practical benefit that follows from moral conduct. It sets the person free from feelings of nagging guilt that may interfere with his attempt to concentrate on Yogic practices. Lust is brought reasonably under control, so there is no strong urge arousing the body and mind to seek a mate. There is a reasonable level of contentment, so there is no fear of falling prices on the stock market, no lure to bargains, nor concern about a competitor clinching a deal. Obviously, we are not talking about a guilt-ridden person ready for a confession, or a tense, anxiety-ridden "neurotic" seeking relief from the stresses arising from a competitive life.

Here we may note that Patañjali (1.30) has listed the following as obstacles or hindrances which distract a person from the path of Yoga: disease, languor, indecision, carelessness, sloth, sensuality, and instability. One who suffers from such "problems" or "symptoms" is not considered entirely suitable for the practice of Yoga. Nevertheless, it may be true that persons experiencing some of the types of problems mentioned above benefit from the practice of appropriate postures and breathing exercises. Thus, selected Yogic practices may be prescribed for sick persons or mental patients, just as exercises are. In fact, recent research indicates that certain Yogic postures and other practices can be effectively used in treating various types of pathology. How can we reconcile the apparent contradiction between Patañjali's caution just mentioned and therapeutic benefits of certain Yogic practices?

What Patañjali means, perhaps, is that the *higher* reaches of Yoga are not meant for those who are physically or mentally sick. At least it makes sense to say that, before one can undertake the "core" practices of Yoga, one must be not only free from any signs of neurosis (let alone the more serious forms of pathology), but have the autonomy and self-control characteristic of "positive mental health." It will be clear after we take a look at the core practices (antaraṅga) of Yoga (to be outlined in the following paragraphs) that they are designed as a means of attaining superior states of the human condition, much beyond the "normal" range of mental health. To say the least, it is doubtful whether the core practices could be recommended for the type of persons who ought to be the patients of a modern clinical psychologist.

6. Concentration (dhāraṇā). This is literally defined as the "binding" of the processes of consciousness ("citta vṛtti"s) to a particular place (Patañjali 3.1). What this means is that the adept now begins to control his thought processes. The first step in this direction is to focus attention on a particular place such as the tip of his nose, or his navel, or on a desired object in front of him, such as an idol of a favored deity. Thus, a person, while sitting in a stable and comfortable posture, stops looking at the hangings on the wall or objects on the floor, and so on, and thereby avoids drifting from one chain of ideas associated with the first object to another string of ideas associated with the second object, and so on.

It is easy to see that this strategy contrasts sharply with that of psychoanalytic free association described before (in Chapter 3). In psychoanalysis, the patient is encouraged to follow each and every link between ideas, which may be connected with one another in endless chains. The ideas must keep coming, no matter how diverse and apparently unrelated they may be. Not so in Yoga. While psychoanalytic free-association facilitates the flow of ideas in the stream of consciousness, Yoga tries to retard the flow. There is another important difference between the psychoanalytic and Yogic approaches to consciousness. Interpretation of the hidden meanings underlying the "contents" of consciousness is of great importance for psychoanalysis. By contrast, Yoga neglects the "meaning" of the contents as well as their descriptive characteristics (such as quality or intensity of colors, sounds, and the like, which the structuralists were exploring).

The reader may also note that, in its endeavor to control the flow of ideas, the Yogic approach to consciousness sharply contrasts with that of Sartre. It may be recalled that, as noted in Chapter 2, Sartre has depicted the hero of his novel *Nausea* as hopelessly unable to control the incessant flow of his ideas. The Yogi's response to the problem is obviously very different from Sartre's. One can only speculate about the reasons for the difference in response to a common problem. It is possible that innumerable persons around the world and throughout the history of mankind have tried to control their runaway streams of consciousness and failed. Sartre's hero is just an example of a rather common experience of failure. It appears that some individuals in the early history of the civilization who had some success in dealing with their streams of consciousness taught the method to the next generation. Over the centuries, in a cultural milieu that valued success in such tasks, a systematic technique of autogenic control such as that of Yoga developed. Sartre's hero simply illustrates the case of modern individuals who remain unaware of a cultural legacy specifying the steps to be taken for effectively controlling one's stream of consciousness.

7. Contemplation (dhyāna). The next step involves an attempt to hold onto thoughts, ideas, or an image (pratyaya) of whatever object one has chosen to concentrate his attention upon. Thus, the stream of consciousness flows with homogenous rather than heterogenous content: it steadily carries forward ideas closely related to just one object, or perhaps just one image of that object.[9]

8. Samādhi. The term samādhi has often been translated as "trance." But this is inaccurate, and it is difficult to find an accurate English equivalent. The term samādhi refers to a complex concept requiring an elaborate discussion. We may begin such a discussion by pointing out that a person involved in a process of steady contemplation attains the state of samādhi when the contemplation transforms itself almost completely into the shape of its object and the contemplation loses itself, as it were, (svarūpeṇa śūnyamiva) in the process. It is necessary to add here that, at this initial stage, the yogi attains only a primary or "lower" level of samādhi, As we shall see in the later sections of this chapter, the Yoga theory distinguishes among several levels of samādhi. At this point in our discussion it may simply be noted that samādhi is a complex concept descriptive of a set of several "altered" states of consciousness. This concept is perhaps the most crucial aspect of the Yogic theory of consciousness. We must consider a few other related ideas before we examine it in detail.

The last three of the eight limbs or aids of Yoga mentioned above, namely, concentration, contemplation, and samādhi, are collectively called restraint (saṁyama). It should be clear that these three must occur one after another in the particular sequence in which they are mentioned. It would be absurd, for instance, to say that one attains steady contemplation before retarding a rapidly moving train of his thoughts. A stepwise progression is an important characteristic of the later "limbs" of Yoga, starting with the withdrawal of the senses: first is concentration, then contemplation, and finally the various samādhi states, which we shall soon describe. This sequential characteristic of the stages of the yogi's progress has important epistemological implications, which will be considered in some detail in later sections of this chapter.

Here we must examine an important by-product of the yogi's ability to exercise restraint on his thought processes by way of withdrawal, concentration, and contemplation. Patañjali claims that, by exercising such restraint on various objects, the yogi can acquire several types of powers. A major portion of the third chapter of Patañjali's book is concerned with the description of various powers (siddhis or vibhūtis). The following is a partial list of powers which a yogi can attain: the knowledge of past and future; the knowledge of previous incarnations of the soul; the power to read minds or have knowledge of other minds; the power to become invisible; the power to become as strong as an elephant; the knowledge of the structure of the body; knowledge of the structure of galaxies and of their motion; freedom from hunger and thirst; the power to enter someone else's body; and the power of levitation.

This list is not supposed to refer to the tricks of a skilled magician. The yogis are believed to be able to acquire genuine power, not merely an ability to create illusions. As pointed out by Radhakrishnan (1929, Vol. 2, p. 367), the Yoga system does not consider the supernormal powers of a yogi to be miraculous interferences with the laws of nature. After all, it is a cardinal assumption of Yoga that the Law of Karma reigns supreme. The world, according to Yoga, is as orderly as it is for modern science. What appears to be a contravention of the laws of the physical world as we know it is considered to be in conformity with the principles of some other parts of the cosmic order. If the Yogi's supernormal powers are based upon certain laws of the cosmic system so far unknown to modern science, then the principles regulating the underlying phenomena must be open to systematic inquiry. I think, at any rate, that the Yogic claims regarding the possession of special powers should be open to critical inquiry in order to determine whether they exist. Moreover, the claims are not the core of Yoga. Yoga could be a more-or-less complete system even without them.

This topic of miraculous powers brings us to one of the most sensitive zones of the world view of modern science. Any reference to extrasensory perception, mindreading, psychokinesis, and other such so-called "paranormal" phenomena usually arouses feelings of suspicion and distrust in the community of modern psychologists. Many of them, being suspicious about the claims of special powers, insist that any such claims must be examined with the most critical eyes and rigorous methods of inquiry. Such insistence is quite reasonable in the case of the charlatan who wishes to pass off his magic tricks for supernatural powers. The usefulness of the double-blind technique in experiments in extrasensory perception, the need for statistics to ascertain that the alleged phenomenon is not simply a product of chance variation, and such other sophisticated applications of common sense are obviously useful and needed in this field of inquiry.

While there is clearly a need for a critical approach and for meticulous methods to safeguard against plain gullibility, there is also a need to guard against the supposedly openminded investigator who is secretly committed to a scientistic world view. Such an investigator may try hard to disprove any claims to supernormal powers. Tart (1975, p. 119) has pointed out how a certain author, who reviewed experimental evidence about extrasensory perception for *Science* magazine, concluded that the data must be erroneous or fraudulent because he *knew* that the alleged phenomena are impossible.

The community of modern psychologists seems to be polarized between believers and non-believers in paranormal phenomena. Such polarization must be attributed to a clash of world views, which, in turn, can be at least partly traced to the troubled history of Western science. Here, once again, it would be useful to adopt the detached perspective recommended by the sociologists of knowledge. At this point, let us stop being concerned with problems of the present zeitgeist and return to Patañjali's view of the superior powers attainable through the practice of yoga.

As mentioned before, Patañjali (3.37) considers the superior powers obstacles in the yogi's progress towards the higher goal of samādhi. In his commentary, Vyāsa (3.50) has illustrated the Yogic view with the help of a vivid narrative of a story. In this story, a yogi is offered a flying chariot, a life of strength, comfort, and plenty, as well as willing and attractive nymphs by "those in high places." The reluctant yogi is persuaded to accept the offer as legitimate reward for his devotion, hardships, and endurance. Vyāsa's advice to a yogi under the pressure of such enticing lures is that he remind himself of the "terrible fire" of the unending cycle of birth, death, and rebirth. It is important that the yogi not allow the light of Yoga to be extinguished by the gusty winds of desire. The moral of the story is clear. The value of inner contentment and enlightenment offered by samādhi is considered to be much greater than the pleasures offered by wealth and power. The story also conveys to us the strong fears Indians have had of the miseries of the cycle of birth and death. This fearful concern for the miseries of life seems to have been as strong in the Indian tradition as the fear of sin and damnation has been to the followers of the Judeo-Christian tradition in the West.

We should now terminate our side trip into the land of "magical" powers and return to the eighth and final "limb" of Yoga, namely samādhi. As noted, the word samādhi refers to a set of "altered" states of consciousness. This set is arranged in a hierarchical sequence of levels, since the mastery of the previous step is considered essential for advancing to the next level. Yogis who have scaled this ladder have described the crucial characteristics of each level. For the sake of convenience in understanding the nature of these levels, the series has been sliced in different ways, and various terms have been suggested to designate the subsets of the series created by such conceptual slicing. One way of dividing the total set involves a division of the samādhi states into two major categories. The first category is called saṁprajñāta samādhi because it lies within the range of the cognitive aspect of consciousness. The second category, of states which lie beyond the range of the cognitive aspect of consciousness, is called asaṁprajñāta samādhi. We shall start our account of the samādhi states by describing how various levels of saṁprajñāta samādhi emerge as the yogi attains a gradual but complete transformation of the cognitive aspect of consciousness.

We may recall that, by way of preparation, the yogi chooses to concentrate his attention on a particular object. He avoids drifting from one chain of ideas associated with a certain object to another chain associated with another object, and so on. Suppose the yogi has chosen to think of a cow he saw standing in a pasture across the yard.[10] Now let us assume that the yogi has been able to continue to think about the cow only, without switching from his present train of thought to other trains of thought related to his house, his clothes, coming events, or any other thing. Thus, he may remember when he bought the cow, from whom, how much milk it fetches, and so on. When he is successful in avoiding thoughts about any other object over a reasonably long period of time, he tries to hold on to a single thought, maybe just "This is a cow." It is clear that the yogi's stream of consciousness is gradually undergoing a change. The process of emergence and disappearance of ideas is retarded. Fewer ideas now pass through the mind than during an equal period of the ordinary wakeful state. This condition may be described by a metaphor: the stream of consciousness is no longer cascading, like the waters of a rapid, stumbling over new objects every now and then. Like a mountain river reaching the plains, the turbulence in its flow is reduced. Gradually even the ripples get smaller and fewer and the stream renders itself more and more "transparent."

Patañjali (1.41) uses the metaphor of a transparent crystal to describe the state of a yogi who has restrained the stream of his consciousness. The mind becomes as clear as a high-quality crystal that accurately reflects whatever object upon which it may rest. Because the wandering thoughts no longer interfere with the yogi's sustained attention, the yogi's cognitive apparatus functions more and more effectively. Having attained such transparency of mind, the yogi's further progress depends upon focusing his attention first on gross then on finer aspects of the object of his cognition (grāhya). He then shifts his attention to the means of cognitions, the senses (grahaṇa), and finally turns his attention inward so as to focus on "himself," that is, upon the Self as Knower (grahītṛ). The successive levels of samādhi emerge as the yogi becomes successful in withdrawing his attention from the object through the senses to the very basis of his ability to know and to experience, namely the Self.

The Various Levels of Samādhi

Before we begin to consider the various levels of samādhi, it will be useful to schematically represent the stepwise progression in the form of a chart. Figure 1 designates the various levels by their Sanskrit names and provides a very brief characterization of each.

1. Savitarka samādhi. (Patañjali, 1.42) The yogi attains a primary level of samādhi when he is successful in holding onto a particular idea in a steadfast manner over a reasonably long period of time. It is called savitarka, meaning "with conjecture and reasoning," since the yogi's state of consciousness at this stage is believed to be characterized by such aspects of cognition. This state is not considerably different from the ordinary wakeful state, as far as the cognitive aspect of consciousness is concerned. Let us assume once again that the yogi has now rested his mind on a single thought such as "This is a cow" in a sustained manner. In this condition the yogi may subvocally say the word cow, while, at the same time, he is actually viewing a particular cow. We may appreciate that the word *cow* is not simply a sound but also a concept

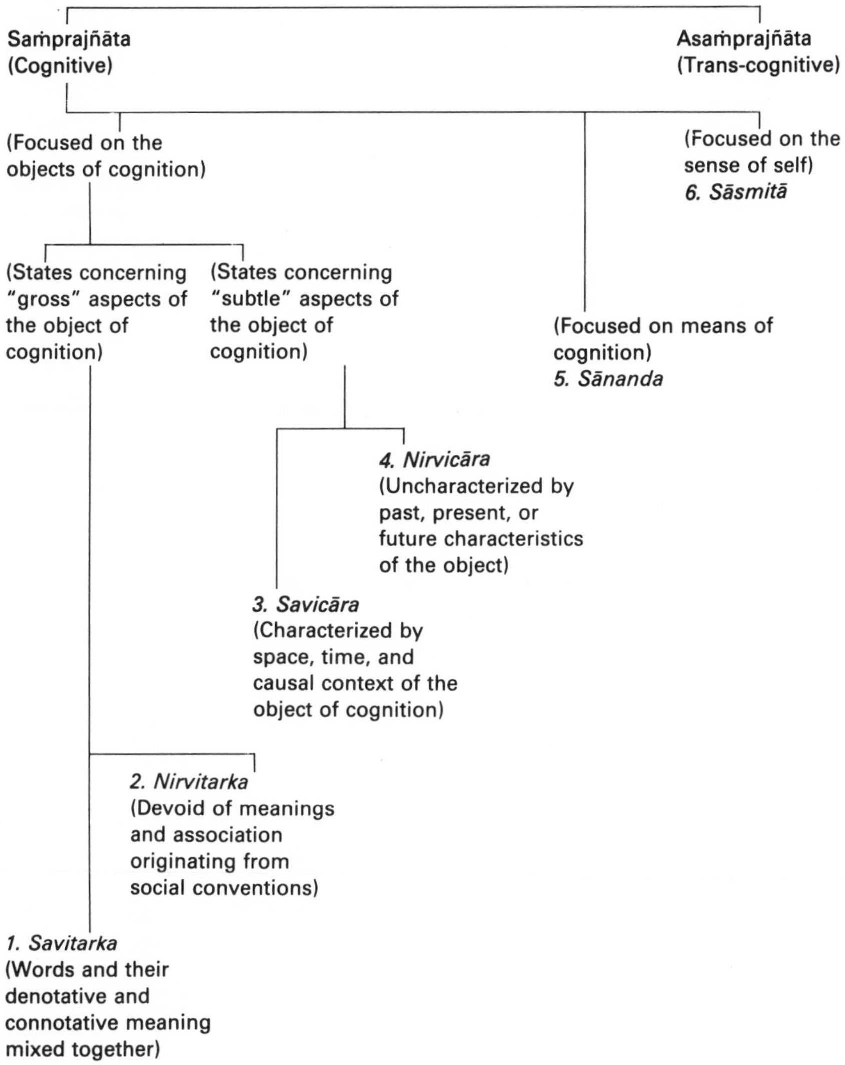

Figure 1. *Levels of the samādhi state.*

impregnated with the meaning the word connotes. A single act of cognition involved in recognizing a common object like a cow may involve the visual image of a cow and a certain configuration of sound that constitutes the word *cow*. Further, it would also involve the connotative meaning of the word *cow* as a particular species of animal, a source of milk, an object of one's possession, or whatever other ideas the person may associate with the object as a result of his previous experience. A single act of cognition is thus a complex phenomenon in itself. As can be easily seen, this view of cognition is not very different from the contemporary view.

The Yoga theorists have emphasized a particular aspect of the complexity of the cognitive act, namely the fact that the word, the concept, and the object the word denotes all appear to be indiscriminately fused in our ordinary states of consciousness. They have pointed out that the word, the concept, and the object are in fact very different types of entities. Thus, words like "cow" are composed of particular consonants and vowels and are configurations of sound. The object, the cow itself, is a material object with a particular form and is composed of parts like the dewlap, tail, legs, hooves, horns, and so on. The concept of a cow, by contrast, is an abstract incorporeal entity which has the property of "illuminating" the mind. Cognition thus involves an act of bringing together—superimposing or fusing—such diverse types of entities.

2. Nirvitarka samādhi. (Patañjali, 1.43) It is obvious that it is through socialization that we are able to associate objects with appropriate words and their connotative meanings. Without socialization, we would not be able to cognize objects in the manner in which we become accustomed to cognizing them. This is because, first of all, object–word associations are a matter of social convention (saṁketa). Second, because no society could afford to designate every single object around it by a separate verbal symbol (since there are too many objects in the world) words like "cow" are selected to designate all the objects in a class of objects. Modern psychology tells us how even primitive organisms are capable of adapting to their complex environments by learning to generalize responses to common categories of stimuli. The Yoga theorists point out that the use of common labels to designate classes of objects involves not only generalization but abstraction. Thus, words representing classes of objects become associated with a conglomeration of ideas derived from the processes of abstraction and inference and turn them into concepts. Moreover, we usually tend to include in a concept attributes inferred not only from our personal experiences, but also those we learn through other people. Whenever we encounter any specific object, its sight invokes the memories of whatever has been learned about the class to which that object belongs. Nirvitarka samādhi is attained when the yogi dispels from his mind all such memories. In this condition, the yogi is said to acquire a superior form of direct perception (para pratyakṣa. Vyāsa, 1.43).

Once again, the theory of cognition implicit in this account of Nirvitarka samādhi is generally consistent with the views prevalent in contemporary psychology. In their textbook of psychology, Woodworth and Schlosberg (1954, p. 609) note, for instance, that "behavior governed by concepts requires that the same response shall be made to objects of the same class." They have described the early experiments by Long on concept-formation in children and Heidbreder's classic experiments on concept-formation in adults. These experiments have analyzed the processes of learning whereby children and adults begin to identify characteristics common to classes of objects—such as geometric shapes or complex designs—and begin to associate common nonverbal or verbal responses to objects in each class. Social psychologists have pointed out how individuals develop generic concepts through personal experience and through hearsay and social learning. To illustrate the point, let us take the hypothetical example of a young teacher moving into a racially mixed neighborhood. Having never previously come across or heard of the Mexican community called Chicanos, she may begin to recognize children who have a certain type of accent and certain types of surnames as generally having certain problems in learning. She may begin to form an image of such children as generally less intelligent than others on the basis of her own experience and, through genuine concern for them, she may begin to give special attention to them. Gradually, she may learn that these children belong to a particular ethnic group called Chicanos. She may also learn from other teachers their opinions about Chicano children. More information about this community may be obtained from the media, history books, novels, and so on. Her "image" of Chicanos, thus formed, is likely to be invoked every time she encounters any particular member of this community.

As can easily be seen, once a generalized image of a class of people is formed, it is likely to create problems regarding the perception of a particular member of that class. Social psychologists have shown how ethnic stereotypes based on generalization often *distort* social perception. Thus, the teacher in our hypothetical example may prejudge a new Chicano boy in her class as being average in intelligence while this particular boy may in fact be very bright. Upon discovering the boy's brightness, the teacher may overestimate his intellectual capacity, as she may continue to view him in contrast with the average Chicano boys she has met before. Such errors in judgment may be avoided if a person avoids viewing each individual in light of previously formed generalized images.

When the psychology of Yoga suggests that the yogi can shed all verbal conventions acquired through social learning, it implies that he can dispel the stereotypical images that lead to erroneous judgments such as the one described above. It also implies that, when a yogi reaches the Nirvitarka stage of samādhi, he dispels from his mind all forms of social learning, irrespective of the harmful or beneficial character of such learning. There are several aspects of connotation of ordinary concepts which result from particular social conventions, and these are implicit in the usage of the concept only in those societies where those conventions prevail. Thus, for an orthodox Hindu the cow is a sacred animal, while for a farmer on the American prairie the cow may just be an animal to be fattened before being sent to the butcher. The moon may be a complex symbol of love and beauty to a romantic poet, while it may be just another planet in the solar system for an astronomer. None of these connotations of the respective concepts are inevitable or essential in the cognition of the cow or moon as objects *per se*. Yet, for persons with specific social backgrounds, these particular meanings may be natural aspects of their comprehension of the respective objects. While the examples of specifically social components given above may be relatively clear and obvious, there are many subtle aspects of our day-to-day cognition that are similarly—but not so obviously—socially determined. Insofar as Yoga implies the expulsion (from consciousness) of all memories based on the conventional use of words, it means the unlearning of *all* socially learned verbal conventions.

Insofar as the unlearning of verbal conventions is considered to be a step toward the attainment of superior forms of cognition, the Yoga theory is critical of the social influence on knowledge. In this respect, the Yogic approach is somewhat similar to that of sociology of knowledge which also points to the limitations of knowledge originating from social influence. Although both the yogis and the sociologists of knowledge strive to transcend the socially imposed limitations of knowledge, their ultimate goals as well as their strategies are vastly different. The sociologists of knowledge, as noted before, are concerned with the identification and removal of specific limitations to the pursuit of knowledge arising from cultural background, ideological framework, and the social position of the seekers of knowledge. The yogis are not concerned with such specific sources of the limitations on knowledge, nor are they concerned with knowledge in the form of a discipline pursued by a community of specialists. In sharp contrast to most scientific endeavours, which seek to arrive at a set of general principles applicable to a set of phenomena, the technique of Yoga aims to focus exclusively on a particular object at a time so as to be able to ultimately transform the cognitive process itself. The Yoga system claims that, by ridding himself of the socially learned component of knowledge, the yogi is able to acquire a superior form of cognition of whatever object he chooses to concentrate upon. The knowledge of past and future events, knowledge of other minds, and other such forms of "extrasensory" knowledge are attained through deliberate and systematic modification of the ordinary mode of cognition. It is important to note, however, that the attainment of such extraordinary forms of knowledge is a mere by-product, rather than the goal of Yogic practices. The goal of Yoga is to ultimately transcend all forms of cognition, ordinary as well as extraordinary.

Now let us grant for the time being that the yogi in the Nirvitarka stage of samādhi dispels the conventional aspects of meanings attached to the object of cognition which prevail in his society. In what way does this step transform the yogi's comprehension of the object he may have chosen to meditate upon? An answer to this question is not found in Patañjali's cryptic aphorism relating to this issue (1.43), but the discussion of it in the major commentaries provides some help. The thrust of the arguments is that the yogi, having shed the peripheral connotations attached to the objects, is now able to focus upon the most essential properties of the thing. In other words, the yogi ignores the peripheral or incidental properties of the object and is now able to comprehend the thing-in-itself.

This point can be explained with the help of the illustrations used by the various commentators of Patañjali. First, Vyāsa makes the distinction between the part and the whole, suggesting that the essential property of an object lies in a particular configuration of its parts which unite them into a whole, and not in the parts taken separately. Vācaspati Miśra (1.43) illustrates this point with the example of a clay pot, the essence of which lies in its wholeness, making it useful as a container for water, honey, and other fluids. If the pot were struck by a hammer, you might still have all the pieces and particles of clay which together made the pot, but they no longer constitute the pot as a receptacle. Thus, although the pot is in some respects the same as the clay particles that make it, it is not identical to the particles as such. Śaṅkara (a, 1.43) gives a similar example. If someone lops the ears or cuts the tail off a cow, it remains the same cow belonging to the same owner; the "cowness" of the cow lies in the organic unity of her limbs, and not in the limbs themselves.

The issue here is the same as the one John Locke and other Western philosophers discussed in relation to the self-sameness and identity of an object. Locke (1823/1963, Vol. 2, p. 49) made the same point when he argued that a colt, sometimes lean and sometimes fat, remains the same horse. An acorn, grown into a huge oak tree, then cut down, remains the same tree, because the treeness of an oak lies in its organic unity. A rock, however, does not remain the same rock after being broken into pieces, since, according to Locke, the essence of a material thing like a rock lies in the material substance and not its unity. Locke had accepted Descartes' position that extension is a property of material substance which, if changed, alters the thing itself. The Yoga theorists argued along exactly similar lines when they distinguished between substance (vastu) and the thing-in-itself (dharmin)—along with its attributes—on the one hand, and their qualities (dharma—which are at least theoretically separable from it), and states (avasthā) on the other hand. The issue underlying these distinctions is philosophical; it is primarily concerned with the metaphysical issue of an essence, a Kantian *noumenon,* or the reality underlying the appearances of things. It is not possible to compare the Indian and Western thoughts on this philosophical issue within the limited scope of this work. It is enough to note at this point that, according to Yoga theory, the yogi in the Nirvitarka samādhi state comprehends nothing but the most essential characteristics of the object of his concentration.

Having thus envisioned the essential characteristics of the object of his concentration, in the Nirvitarka stage of samādhi, the yogi moves from the relatively gross to increasingly finer and more subtle aspects of the object. To be able to understand what the Yoga theorists mean by the fine aspects of an object, I must explain their theory of the nature of physical objects. We must be very careful in our examination of the Yogic views in this regard, because the Old-World view is quite different from the modern, scientific world view many of us may consider necessarily superior.

The Yoga theorists believed (like many of us believe today) that physical objects are composed of small, unitary particles, or atoms, of certain basic elements. Their view of basic elements, however, was more like the view of the ancient Greeks than that of contemporary chemistry. The basic elements were considered to be five in number, namely, earth, water, fire, air, and space (ākāśa). All physical objects were believed to be composed of atoms of four of these elements, except ākāśa. The subtle aspect of each element was called tanmātra, literally meaning "merely that." Each tanmātra thus represents the element itself or its "substance." The tanmātra for the earth element was believed to be odorific or olfactory in nature, and tanmātras corresponding to water, fire, air, and space were considered to be in the nature of taste, color (or form, rūpa), touch, and sound, respectively.

Today this view of material objects would seem primitive and outmoded in light of the knowledge of modern physics and chemistry. Let us grant that the Yoga theorists lacked adequate knowledge of the nature of the physical world which we can now derive easily and confidently from the contemporary natural sciences. But the lack of sophistication of the Yogic approach in this regard need not be considered a great drawback as far as its theory of consciousness is concerned. Whatever the nature of the basic elements of matter, and whether they be five, ninety-two, or whatever in number, it remains true today (as it was in ancient times) that our knowledge of the physical world ultimately depends on our five sense organs. In all likelihood, the basic characteristics of the human psychic equipment have remained relatively unchanged for millennia, although the physical aids like the telescope, radio, the electron microscope have vastly extended the reach of our eyes and ears. It must be remembered here, once again, that Yoga focuses on the nature of cognition with an intention to go beyond the cognitive aspect of consciousness. What is crucial in understanding the Yogic approach is the point that the yogi operating at the Savicāra samādhi level focuses on the five aspects of the objects. It should now be clear that by five aspects of the object they mean the olfactory, gustatory, visual, tactile, and auditory sensations that enable us to know that object. Whether or not there are separate basic elements of matter corresponding to the five sense modalities is not a critical issue here. That sensory experience is the root of all knowledge is an empiricist principle prevalent in the West, especially since the British philosopher Locke stressed it in the 17th century. The same principle can be said to be implicit in Yoga. We have already seen that, in the initial stages of samādhi, the yogi has expelled from his mind all the peripheral thoughts associated with an object, and even the connotative meanings associated with the social usage of the words. The thrust of the Yogic technique is to successively rid oneself of all peripheral and incidental associations, then focus only on the essential features of the object, and further narrow one's attention to the basic sensory elements, on which rest the knowledge of any object.

3. *Savicāra samādhi.* (Patañjali, 1.44). According to Vyāsa, Savicāra samādhi arises when the yogi concentrates on the subtle aspects of the object that manifest themselves (abhivyakta) in a single act of cognition (ekabuddhi). It is implied here that, unlike in the previous stages of samādhi, the yogi's attention is not focused on the inessential, or even the most essential, aspects of the object as a whole. Vyāsa (1.44) suggests that, in this state, the cognition of the object is characterized by the space, time and cause.[11] I think that here the reference to space and time suggest that, notwithstanding the lack of focus on the object as whole,

the object is still "contextualized" in space and time. What this means is that the object is viewed in the context of its environs—perhaps in the sense that the object stands out in the yogi's perceptual field, just as objects do in the "ordinary" mode of perception. Although, as indicated by Vyāsa, the yogi focuses upon only those characteristics of the object that are perceived (nirgrāhya) at the time of his attention, the yogi may be aware of the temporal context in which color, odor, and other characteristics of the object appeared in the single initial act of cognition. It is not difficult to make sense of Vyāsa's reference to space and time in his laconic account of Savicāra samādhi in this manner. However, it is not so easy to understand the meaning and significance of his reference to cause. Here we must turn to Vācaspati for help.

According to Vācaspati Miśra (1.44), the reference to cause in this context implies the elemental tanmātras that constitute the object. As indicated above, according to the Yogic view of the world, particular things in the world are formed as a result of a combination in various proportions of the five basic elemental atoms or tanmātras. The tanmātras constitute, and thereby "cause" the object's existence. This notion of cause is clearly similar to Aristotle's notion of material cause. At any rate, are we supposed to understand that Vyāsa's reference to cause implies that the yogi in the Savicāra samādhi state is interested in the comprehension of causality? Obviously not, because the goal of Yoga is not to seek causal explanations; at least that is not the purpose of trying to attain the samādhi states. Given that the major purpose of the Yogic exercises is to help alter one's states of consciousness, the reference to cause in this context must be understood in terms of its psychological significance. The psychological significance of a reference to tanmātras as cause in this context follows from the *sensory experience* to which they are supposed to lead. What this means is that, at this stage of his progress, the yogi focuses on the sensory attributes on which his cognition of the object is based. It may be, that an understanding of the Yogic theory of tanmātric causation helps a yogi in switching his attention from the gross to the fine aspects of the object. The validity or nonvalidity of the theory would not matter as long as one begins to shift one's attention from the object "out there" to its representation in sensory experience, since such a shift is the key to the yogi's progression to the next stage.

4. *Nirvicāra samādhi.* (Patañjali, 1.44). According to Vyāsa (1.44), this state is attained when the yogi's cognition is no longer characterized by the past, present, or future characteristics which did, do, or will particularize the object of his cognition. Here the yogi's cognition is

dissociated completely from the spatiotemporal context within which the object of his cognition is located. The cognition in this state (samādhi prajñā) is characterized or "colored" (uparañjayati) by the tanmātras alone. Vyāsa adds that the cognition at this stage is completely identified with the object so that it "loses itself," so to speak, in the process. What this seems to mean is that, in the Nivicāra samādhi state, the yogi's attention is withdrawn from the object "out there"; he is fully absorbed into the *experience of the object*.

The attainment of Nirvicāra samādhi is an important landmark in the yogi's progress, as important benefits are said to follow when he becomes an expert in attaining this state (and perhaps in maintaining it). According to Patañjali (1.47), the first outcome of such expertise is the experience of an inner bliss (adhyātmaprasādaḥ). Vyāsa describes a person who has this stage of progress in the following manner: "One who attains this state sheds all misery (aśocyaḥ) . . . He stands atop a high cliff, looking down on ordinary, miserable mortals standing on the ground below." A second outcome of a yogi's expertise in attaining the Nirvicāra samādhi is the attainment of a "truth-bearing insight" (ṛtaṁbharā prajñā. Patañjali, 1.48). Before going on to a discussion of the next level of samādhi, it would be useful to take a brief look back at Husserl's reductive phenomenology, to compare it with Yoga. Some similarities between the Husserlian and Yogic approaches to consciousness may be noted. Both of them: involve a withdrawal of attention from the external world and a focusing on the inner world of consciousness; advocate the abandoning of all socially learned conventions relating to the knowledge of objects; involve the comprehension of the "essence" of the object of cognition at one or another stage of one's progress toward superior knowledge; claim to be able to attain superior forms of knowledge; have developed techniques for the controlling one's thought processes; and, finally, both of them indicate that the practice of suggested techniques brings about a valuable transformation in the individual's life. There are, of course, differences in the Yogic and phenomenological approaches. For instance, a yogi starts with the aim of an ultimate release from the miseries of life and acquires a superior form of knowledge as an unintended "by-product," so to speak. In contrast, Husserl's reductive phenomenology aims at the attainment of "apodictic" knowledge, but leads to some valuable, but unspecified "spiritual" benefits which do not seem to be clearly intended from the beginning. It would be no great surprise to find many differences between approaches to consciousness that originated from highly contrasting sociohistoric backgrounds. What comes as a surprise, indeed, is that there are such close similarities, in spite of the contrasting backgrounds. At any rate, it would be appropriate to postpone further cross-cultural comparison until the last chapter, and return now to the higher levels of samādhi described in Yoga.

5. Sānanda samādhi. (Patañjali, 1.17). To recapitulate, four levels of samādhi were described so far: Savitarka, Nirvitarka, Savicāra, and Nirvicāra. These four levels are referred to collectively as the sabīja, that is, "seeded" type of samādhi states, because they are based upon external, perceptible objects. The next, higher level of samādhi emerges when the yogi shifts his attention from an object of his cognition (grāhya) to the means of his cognition, his senses (grahaṇa). This step involves a crucial aspect of Yogic strategy, in that the yogi withdraws his attention not only from the external world, but also from any intended object. What occupies the yogi's mind in this condition is only a sensory experience or mere "conscious content." It is important to note that this is different from experience in the previous, Nirvicāra samādhi state, in that it is no longer an experience of an object. Perhaps it would make sense to interpret this in terms of Husserlian concepts. While in our ordinary mode of consciousness the sensory contents (Husserl's "hyletic data") are "constituted" or organized so as to form the impression of an object or the perception of a meaningful whole, the yogi in this state may be said to "unconstitute" or "deconstruct" the cognitive experience.

We may note that the meaning of the term sānanda is "with bliss." Why would the experience that focuses on the "means of cognition" be blissful? According to Vācaspati Miśra (1978 ed., 1.17), the sense organs originated for the purpose of "illuminating" the ego who is the knower. Focusing on the means of cognition (sensory experience?) results in the predominance of sattva guṇa, of which illumination is an inherant characteristic. Since pleasure is another natural characteristic of sattva guṇa, a yogi in this state experiences bliss. I would leave it to the reader to judge the reasonableness of Vācaspati's reasoning and move on to a brief account of the next level of samādhi.[12]

6. Sāsmitā samādhi. (Vācaspati Miśra, 1.17) This stage of samādhi emerges when the yogi continues to further withdraw his attention so it shifts from the senses or sensory content and rests on his sense of self or egoism (asmitā). This state is the last stage of a set of trance states collectively referred to as saṁprajñāta or cognitive trance states. In each of the states described so far, there is an implicit duality between the cognizer and the object of his cognition. In the Sāsmitā samādhi, too, such duality is implied: the cognizer or self as subject is aware of self-as-object. In other words, Sāsmitā samādhi can be considered a special variety of a self-conscious state in which one is not conscious of anything but oneself.

7. *Asaṁprajñāta samādhi.* This state is devoid of all objects of cognition. The experiencing subject is completely withdrawn into himself so that he is no longer conscious of any thing. This condition emerges when all varieties of the processes of consciousness, citta vṛttis like observing, thinking, imagining, dreaming, remembering, and others, are completely restrained. There is no direct sensation, since the mind is withdrawn from external objects, and even the process of emergence and disappearance of images is so constrained that this process comes almost completely to a halt. Śaṅkara (a, 1.18) describes this condition with the help of a beautiful metaphor: the contents of consciousness (pratyaya) begin to fade like the dwindling flames of a fire that is gradually running out of fuel.

Only vivid metaphors may help us in comprehending the concept of Asaṁprajñāta samādhi—and that may only be partial help—because this condition is not only out-of-the-ordinary, but it is also beyond the reach of the discursive mode of thought. Besides metaphors, another sensible way to describe the state of Asaṁprajñāta samādhi is perhaps to place it in the context of Brentano's concepts of acts or processes of consciousness and intentionality. It may be clear from the above description that this state arises when the mind ceases to engage in the various processes or acts of consciousness. As noted before (in Chapter 3), Brentano, as well as his followers like Sartre, assumed that consciousness must always be a consciousness of something. The psychology of Yoga asserts that we are indeed capable of attaining a state of mind that is beyond cognition, where one is no longer conscious of something. This condition or "state" arises when consciousness ceases to be processual, when one is no longer engaged in thinking, wishing, desiring, or otherwise "intending" actual or imaginary "objects."

What Happens after Attaining Samādhi States?

An account of Yoga will be incomplete if we say nothing about what happens after the yogi attains any of the states of samādhi. I have not come across any statements in the major Yogic texts as to how long the states of samādhi last. Convention has it that such states are as short-lived as they are rare. A yogi may remain in samādhi for a few minutes, maybe hours, and, rarely, for a day or so. Only exceptional and legendary figures like Rāmakṛṣṇa Paramahaṁsa were said to be able to pass into a samādhi state at will and stay in it for indefinite periods of time. After being in samādhi for some time, a yogi returns to the ordinary or phenomenal state of consciousness (vyutthāna). As noted by Radhakrishnan (1929, Vol. 2, p. 362), the state of samādhi may soon be broken "by the calls of life."

Benefits from the difficult ascent up the steep ladder of the samādhi states begin to occur during their short-lived experience. Mention has already been made of the following types of gains that accrue during various stages of samādhi: a superior form of direct perception, an essence-envisioning perspective on objects, a truth-bearing insight, an experience of bliss, and so on. It would appear that all these gains may vanish as soon as the yogi returns to the ordinary modes of consciousness. Are there, or are there not, any lasting benefits from the experience of the samādhi states?

The answer to this question is yes, there are important benefits that follow the experience of samādhi and they continue to accumulate throughout the life of a yogi. Although a regression is not inconceivable, a gradual transformation of the entire pattern of life may follow from the experience of samādhi, particularly after the attainment of the Nirvicāra stage. It is difficult to list all the consequences that follow from the experience of the samādhi states, and even more difficult to specify which benefit follows from each level of samādhi. It is possible that, since there are great differences in the characteristics of the various levels of samādhi, what follows from the attainment of one level may be different than what follows from another. Nevertheless, it makes sense to suggest that a yogi who has once experienced a samādhi state begins to release himself gradually from the suffering associated with the ordinary course of life. The psychology of Yoga offers a rationale that explains the process of this release. To understand and appreciate this rationale, we must return to the Yogic principles regarding the cause of suffering, and the mechanisms that tend to perpetuate it through the cycle of birth and rebirth. It may be remembered that, according to Yoga, the root causes of suffering in human life are the "afflictions" associated with the ordinary mode of consciousness. The afflictions are: ignorance about the true nature of the self, egoism, tendency to seek pleasure, tendency to avoid pain, and the "lust" for life (abhiniveśa). It is due to these afflictions that ordinary experiences and behaviors leave their traces in such a way that the individual is impelled to seek those objects that led to pleasurable experiences in the past and to avoid those that were painful. Since the new experiences resulting from contacts with objects in the world leave a new set of traces, the cycle of karma and karmic residues perpetuates. We have noted this before. What the Yoga theory adds at this point is the observation that the samādhi experience, in contrast to the ordinary experiences, tends to impede rather than perpetuate the cycle of karma, its residual effects, and new karma (Patañjali, 1.50).[13]

The Yoga theory admits that the samādhi experiences, too, leave behind their own characteristic residues. But these residues do not impel a person to seek various objects of desire. We may note that the yogi approaches the object of concentration chosen for the yogic exercises in a way that is quite different from the way we usually approach objects of desire, such as tasty food or a prized object. The yogi does not choose to concentrate his attention intensively on a particular object in order to derive an ordinary type of pleasure from his contact with the object. Certainly, he may experience a state of bliss upon reaching the state of Nirvicāra samādhi. But such experience of bliss is not dependent upon the nature of that object. The yogi may use any type of object to concentrate upon. The experience of bliss has nothing to do with the nature of the object of concentration, since it is derived from "inside," as it were, as a result of the transformation of the processes of his consciousness. The traces left behind by the blissful samādhi experience do prompt the yogi to seek more experiences of the same type. Yet, the yogi does not seek the joy of samādhi with a sense of egoism, a lust for life, or a desire for ordinary pleasures dependent on the objects of desire. The experience of bliss is untouched by the afflictions associated with ordinary experiences (which were mentioned before), and, as a result, the traces left behind by these extraordinary experiences do not breed egoism, pleasure-seeking and other such common tendencies.

The yogi may be said to be "reinforced" by the positive character of samādhi experiences, and he seeks more and more of them. As the traces left behind by the initial samādhi experience resurface in the yogi's stream of consciousness, the traces of ordinary experiences of the past are automatically blocked during that period. As residual effects of samādhi experiences accumulate, they strengthen the tendency to seek the inner bliss, and prevent more and more of the tendencies to seek ordinary pleasures from emerging into the stream of consciousness. The result is thus a "positive cycle" leading to a gradual purification of the steam of consciousness, characterized by increased desirelessness and a decreased sense of frustrations and misery. Over a period of time, therefore, the yogi is able to eradicate the stranglehold of the burden of past karma and attains an absolute release from the miseries of life.

The Validation of the Knowledge of the Samādhi States

The discovery of trans-cognitive states of consciousness is the most distinctive achievement of Indian psychology. The Yoga school of psychology is the most specialized of all Hindu schools in providing details about the specific steps one undergoes during the process of transforming the ordinary states of consciousness into a trans-cognitive state. With respect to the Yogic account of the samādhi states an important question arises: how could one ascertain the nature of these states? How could we evaluate the claims of the validity of the statements concerning such states?

This is an important and complex issue, but it may not be possible to answer it adequately at this stage. Instead of examining all its ramifications here, it would be more useful to restrict ourselves to those aspects of the issue to which Patañjali and his commentators have specifically addressed themselves. In this section, therefore, we shall examine some relevant statements from the Yogic texts. We shall return to some related aspects of the issue of validity in the next section of this chapter, since the Vedāntic scholars have more to say about it.

We have already noted that the progress of the yogi through the later "limbs" of Yoga is believed to follow a necessarily step-wise sequence of stages. Patañjali (3.6) mentions that concentration, contemplation, and trance are steps or planes (bhūmayaḥ), implying that they are arranged in a hierarchical sequence. Vyāsa (3.6) explains that no one can arrive at any particular plane without conquering the immediately preceding level. One cannot reach a higher stage by skipping intervening steps. Vācaspati Miśra (3.6) adds that the mastery of the previous step in Yoga is the cause (hetu) of being inclined to seek the knowledge of the next step and also a prerequisite for mastering the next step.[14] As to which is the next immediate plane that must follow a certain plane, no teacher can tell; the practice of Yoga itself can be the only spiritual guide. Vyāsa (3.6) explains the basic principle of the knowledge of the higher states of consciousness when he asserts that only Yoga is the means of the knowledge of Yoga.[15]

The Yogic notion that development proceeds in a sequence of hierarchically ordered stages, and the idea that mastery of a certain way of comprehension is a necessary condition for the attainment of a superior quality of understanding, are similar to Piaget's views of cognitive development. Piaget emphasizes the quality or style of knowing as opposed to the specific content or the quantity of what is learned. Thus, according to Piaget, the child does not simply possess less information about the world than an adult, but the child understands some of the same bits of information in a qualitatively different manner. The child may repeat after his parents the words uttered by them, but the words may mean to him something quite different from their meaning to the adult. A child's uttering the same words as uttered by the adults may not be a guarantee of the correct comprehension of them by the child. Likewise, a repetition of the Yogic propositions about the nature of samādhi states is no guarantee of the adequate understanding the nature of samādhi states. The true knowledge of samādhi states lies in actually experiencing them, not in their verbal description.

Notwithstanding the similarity between the Yogic and Piagetian views about the step-wise progress in the development of knowledge, there is a fundamental difference between them in their descriptions and explanations of the nature of cognitive development. The purpose of Yoga is not simply to offer a description and explanation of the stages of cognitive development. It aims at developing techniques that will help transcend the most superior form of cognition so as to be able to attain superior states of consciousness.

Since the various types of samādhi states are purely a matter of experience, to be able to know them one must *have* them. Anyone who wishes to attain the state of samādhi may attain it by repeating the steps specified by Yoga. As noted, it is claimed by the yogis that, upon exercising a progressive restraint on one's thought processes, one will eventually be led through a specific set of experiences in a step-wise sequence. Such a claim is based on the assumption that, if a certain set of conditions (such as the retardation of the flight of ideas and so on) is created, certain experiences will follow as an inevitable outcome. The Yogic statements about the occurrence of samādhi states are like scientific propositions in that they are "if so, then so" statements specifying the conditions necessary to produce specific outcomes. To verify the validity of the statements, then, all one has to do is to recreate the conditions required to produce the desired outcomes.

The propositions of Yoga are as open to verification as those of natural sciences—although they are not "publicly" verifiable in the exact sense in which the propositions of natural science are supposed to be. (We shall have more to say about public verification toward the end of this section.) All of the basic assumptions and the important propositions of Yoga are clearly and openly stated, and the techniques involved in obtaining the results are described in detail. There are no copyrights preventing the publication of Yogic texts, and nobody holds patents for the exclusive use of its techniques. Just as anyone who repeats the operational steps involved in a scientific experiment is "guaranteed" to get the results described in the standard literature, anyone who wishes to follow the guidelines set by Yoga may be assured of finding what the yogis claim to have discovered. It is my impression, at any rate, that such an assurance *is* implicit in the theory of Yoga.

The statements of Yoga can be said to be "publicly verifiable" in the sense that any interested person has open access to the means of verifying them. (In fact the means of their verification—which primarily involve one's own thought processes—are more easily accessible than the specialized, sophisticated, and often costly instruments required in the verification of many scientific experiments.) If, however, by public verification one means the validation of statements by intersubjective agreement, then, because the statements about samādhi states are not open to intersubjective verification, they will not be publicly verifiable. The nature of samādhi can be only "privately" verified because, like the experience of pain, samādhi belongs to an essentially private domain inaccessible to anyone else. Those committed to the epistemic criterion of the intersubjective verification of truth must refrain from the study of all varieties of private experience, whether they be as commonplace and humdrum as dreams and toothaches, or as uncommon and exotic as the so-called "mystic" experiences. It is possible—and perhaps necessary—to examine the epistemological principles involved in the verification of knowledge pertaining to such superior states of consciousness as samādhi. I shall return to this issue after examining the views of the Vedāntist Śaṅkara who has much to contribute to it.

The Non-Dualist Vedānta of Śaṅkara

Basic Concepts of Advaita (Non-Dualist) Vedānta

Vedānta is perhaps the most popular and dominant of all the schools of Indian thought. The word Vedānta literally means the end of the Vedas which are the most ancient scriptural texts of the Hindus. Such nomenclature follows from the idea that this school of philosophy represents the highest culmination of the philosophic thought of the Vedic sages. Many of the Vedāntic concepts are expressed succinctly in the philosophical discourses called the *Upaniṣads.* The Upaniṣads form the basic authoritative source of Vedāntic doctrines. In a later period, these doctrines were summarized by Bādarāyaṇa in the form of a set of aphorisms. A third important source of Vedānta philosophy is the *Bhagavad-Gītā,* which appears in the form of Lord Kṛṣṇa's exhortations to the heroic warrior Arjuna in the epic *Mahābhārata.* During the early 9th century, Śaṅkara (788–820 A.D.) wrote definitive commentaries on all these sources of Vedāntic thought. He established his particular non-dualistic interpretation of the Vedānta philosophy by trenchantly refuting rival schools of thought prevalent in his day.

Śaṅkara's writings are voluminous. His philosophical thoughts manifest profound insight, subtle logic, and remorseless dialectic. He was far from a disinterested intellectual playing a mere game of logic; he was a man of great compassion and rich, emotional temperament. He was also a poet with a great mastery of the Sanskrit language, which is illustrated by the beautiful verses credited to him. Apart from difficult, technical treatises like his commentary on Bādarāyaṇa's Vedānta aphorisms, Śaṅkara wrote a few lucid and concise treatises like the *Upadeśa-sāhasrī,* which provide a simple introduction to his philosophy. The tradition left behind by Śaṅkara has produced several competent intellectuals like Vidyāraṇya, Sureśvara, Vimuktātmā, Vācaspati Miśra, Dharmarājādhvarīndra and others who added several clearly written texts that explain various aspects of the rich traditional sources of the Vedāntic thought. It is necessary to be extremely selective with regard to the choice of sources, since our purpose is to extract only those ideas that represent the Advita or non-dualist Vedāntic view of consciousness. It is necessary to mention that we are only concerned with the non-dualistic form of Vedānta and not with its alternative interpretations such as the qualified non-dualism of Rāmānuja, the dualism of Madhva, and so on.

The most fundamental doctrine of Vedānta is the thesis that there is a single principle which underlies the infinite variety of forms that manifest themselves in the universe. This principle, called Brahman, is said to be ubiquitous, formless, without any qualities, and essentially indescribable. The Vedic sages speculated about the nature of Brahman. In one of the most beautiful, poetic hymns of the Vedas called the Nāsadīya Sūkta, it was suggested that at the beginning of existence, there may have been neither Being nor Nothingness, neither death nor immortality, neither days nor nights—in other words, no dualities or distinctions which enable us to tell one object from another. Why the original, single entity manifests itself in multifarious forms may remain forever a mystery. The Upaniṣadic philosophers asserted the fundamental unity of reality. In response to any question of the type "Is the nature of Brahman such-and-such?," a Vedāntist will always give one and the same answer: "Not so" (neti). Yet, for the sake of simplicity, the nature of the Brahman has been described in rather approximate terms with a trilogy of terms: Being (sat), Consciousness (cit), and Bliss (ānanda).

We came across this trilogy in Chapter 3 where the terms were considered as being descriptive of the ideal human condition. The commonness of the prominent features of reality and the ideal human condition will begin to make sense if we understand that, since whatever there is, is one and the same thing everywhere in the universe, the essential features of reality, as well as those of human nature, must be ultimately the same. From the point of view of the non-dualist Vedānta, Ātman or the Self is identical with Brahman, the cosmic principle. It is claimed that one realizes the identity of the individual Self with that of the Brahman or Universal Self (paramātman) in a superior state of consciousness called Nirvikalpa Samādhi.

Nirvikalpa samādhi is said to be a Vedāntic term describing the same type of experience as designated by the term Asaṁprajñāta samādhi by the Yogis.[16] Both schools consider such experience as the most desirable one. It is also considered the source of the highest form of knowledge. The main difference between the Vedānta and Yoga philosophies is in their ontological and cosmological doctrines. While Yoga assumes two distinct fundamental principles of reality, namely Puruṣa and Prakṛti, Vedānta postulates a single one. They also differ radically in their accounts of how the cosmos evolved from the basic principle(s). Despite their opposition in such fundamentals, there are important similarities between them, especially in their psychological perspectives. These will begin to appear as we go along.

Having assumed a single, indescribable principle of reality, the Vedāntic philosophers were faced with the difficult task of accounting for the infinitely varied forms of objects in the world. To reconcile the unity of Brahman with the multiplicity of objects of the world, Śaṅkara suggested that the numerous, relatively impermanent objects in the universe are but illusory transformations (vivarta) of the same eternal, basically undifferentiated, and formless Brahman. The world as we see it is thus considered to be a Grand Illusion or Māyā. Śaṅkara's doctrine of the illusory nature of the world is a controversial issue in Indian philosophy. The notion that the whole universe is something like a mirage or a dream is not easily understandable, and, to some people, simply unacceptable. Yet, it can hardly be dismissed as idle talk or a mere *imbroglio*. It is a complex theory and has been very carefully worked out by one of the greatest intellectuals the world has ever produced. At any rate, this is not the place to defend, refute, or even to examine in detail, the Vedāntic doctrine of Māyā. It would be useful to point out, however, that the world is believed to be a mere illusion *only when seen from the vantage point of the superior state of consciousness* experienced in the "altered" state of consciousness called the Nirvikalpa samādhi. The world of plurality, or the phenomenal world (vyāvahārika sattā), is considered perfectly real from the standpoint of the ordinary cognitive states. It is a "lesser" reality, so to speak, only when compared with the "higher order" (pāramārthika sattā).

Śaṅkara's epistemology follows a two-leveled approach. Knowledge is believed to be of two distinct kinds. The first type, called parā vidyā, is obtained in the experience (anubhava) of the identity of the Ātman with the Brahman in the state of Nirvikalpa samādhi. This is the highest form of knowledge. It transcends the limitations of knowledge obtained through any other means. In fact, at this highest level, the word *knowledge* is hardly applicable, because here one transcends the knower–known distinction which is necessarily implied in the ordinary concept of knowledge. While it is considered the ultimate form of "knowledge," its scope is restricted to the domain of the absolute. The second type of knowledge, called aparā vidyā, refers to the knowledge of the phenomenal world. In this domain, we deal with the world extended in space and time (deśa, kāla), and governed by the principle of causality (nimitta). Here it is perfectly legitimate to try to uncover causal relationships with the help of direct, sensory observation, and by drawing legitimate inferences based on the rules of logic. Scientific knowledge, thus, would be considered the penultimate type of knowledge (aparā vidyā). Although the phenomenal world of Māyā turns out to be unreal in an ultimate sense, it has an objective force. Once the Vedāntin leaves the plane of Brahman, or the absolute, he accepts the world as being real and regular in much the same way as the materialist does. In fact, the Vedāntic view of Māyā is almost identical to that of Prakṛti, the Sāṅkhya-Yoga conception of the material world. The *Śvetāśvatara Upaniṣad* (4.10) declares that Māyā is the same as Prakṛti (see Hume, 1931, p. 404), and Śaṅkara supports this view. (Śaṅkara, b, 1.4.3).

The view of Māyā as Prakṛti brings Vedānta very close to the Yogic view of the world in many ways. First of all, the world of Māyā is governed by the Law of Karma which accounts for its regularities. Second, the continual changes in the world are ascribed to the interplay of the three "strands" or guṇas, namely sattva, rajas, and tamas (which we have described before). Third, the Yogic conception of the five basic elements—earth, air, water, fire, and space (ākāśa)—is used in Vedānta as well. This similarity holds, irrespective of the differences between Vedānta and Sāṅkhya-Yoga in their cosmological accounts of how the elements evolved from Māyā or Prakṛti. Finally, the acceptance of the Law of Karma brings into the Vedānta system a series of concepts relating to the nature of the individual such as the unending cycle of birth and death, the theory of the accumulation of the residual effects of experience and behavior (saṁskāra and karmāśaya), the concepts of vāsanā (drives) and smṛti (memory), and so on. Such overlap between the Vedānta and Yoga viewpoints accounts for the similarity in their perspectives regarding the psychological make-up of the individuals.

The Vedāntic term jīva, which literally means "life" or a "living being," is the closest equivalent to the modern concept of an individual organism. In some respects, it is similar to the psychological concept of personality. The core of the jīva is the Ātman or the Self which, as noted, is essentially identical to the Brahman. The place of Ātman in the Vedāntic view of the individual is roughly equivalent to that of the Puruṣa in Yoga. However, one aspect of the difference between the two concepts must be clarified at this point. As noted before, the Puruṣa of Yoga is a principle fundamentally different from that of the material Prakṛti. There are innumerable individual Puruṣas, each being an independent unit like a Leibnitzian monad. The Ātman of Vedānta, by contrast, is simply a reflection of the single, ubiquitous Brahman, and as such, it is no different from the qualityless (nirguṇa) Brahman. Although the Ātman, like the Brahman itself, is not finite, it becomes associated with a finite jīva as a result of avidyā, meaning non-knowledge, nescience, or simply put, ignorance. Avidyā is primordial ignorance; it is as old as Māyā. Under the influence of avidyā, a portion of the infinite Brahman distinguishes itself from the rest of the world, and sets itself apart as an experiencing subject. The "I", or the experiencing subject, identifies himself with his means of relating to the world. These means include the senses, the entire cognitive apparatus, and the body. Such identification of the "I" with the body is the very basis of human individuality.

Since the Ātman is the same as Brahman, he is all-pervading and beyond description. The individual jīva derives its ability to "experience" from the quality of sentience (cit) inherent in the Ātman. Being part of the Brahman, the Ātman is blissful inside and out. He does not need to seek enjoyment through contact with worldly objects. Yet, because of ignorance, he becomes completely identified with the finite jīva. The Ātman conceives of himself as the self or the agent of various activities, and seeks to enjoy the fruits of his action. The activity and enjoyment of the self is made possible by the adjuncts of the jīva, namely the psychic apparatus, the sense organs, the motor organs, and the body.

In this brief account of Vedāntic concepts I have tried to explain the Vedāntist view of the world and of the place of the individual in it. A few more Vedāntic ideas regarding the individual and the nature of the human psychic apparatus should be explained here, since they are crucial in understanding the Vedānta theory of the nature of consciousness. Important in this respect is Śaṅkara's distinction between the gross body (sthūla śarīra) and the subtle body (sūkṣma śarīra). The latter includes the five sense organs, the five motor organs, and an "inner instrument" (antaḥkaraṇa). The inner instrument, in turn, is said to be composed of the following four components:

1. The mind (manas), which manifests itself in the form of the processes of doubting and decision making, and in the processes of analysis and synthesis of ideas, or in other words, the processes of cognitive differentiation and integration.[17]

2. The intellect (buddhi), which is involved in determining a course of action (niścayātmikā), willing, and the like.
3. The ego (ahaṁkāra) as manifest in self-awareness and also in self-seeking, conceit, and so on.
4. The psyche (citta), which is involved in remembering or in the storage of the traces left behind by past actions and experiences. (See Śaṅkara, c, 90–96; Sadānanda, 13.)

It should be clear from the above that the Vedāntic concept of the inner instrument refers to a kind of an inner "agency." Some contemporary psychologists have an aversive reaction to such concepts, since they tend to remind us of a homunculus, or a "ghost in the machine." No matter whether one conceives of an inner agency, or postulates concepts like cognitive differentiation, memory, and so on, it seems inevitable that any psychological theory must take into account all the psychic functions included in the Vedāntic account of the psychic apparatus.

The concept of citta as a seat of memories or a storehouse of the effects of past karma (karmāśaya) is an important common aspect of the Yoga and Vedānta views of the individual. As noted before, the Yoga theory also considers citta a seat of experience. The mental processes such as thinking, imagining, sleeping, remembering, and others are considered various forms of activity (vṛtti) of the citta. Vedānta uses the concept of vṛtti in much the same way as Yoga and ascribes it to the manas rather than the citta. In his commentary on the Vedānta aphorisms, Śaṅkara (b, 2.4.12) specifically mentions that what he means by the term vṛtti is the same as what Patañjali means by the term, and adds the following note: "If the opponent's view does not contradict one's fundamental principles, it may be adopted as one's own." I do not know whether the Vedāntists have "borrowed" the concept of vṛtti from Yoga and "adapted" it to suit their purpose. At any rate, the notion of vṛtti is much less emphasized in Vedānta than in Yoga. While the Yogic view of consciousness emphasizes its processual aspect (vṛtti), Vedānta follows the Upaniṣads in the conceptualization of consciousness primarily in terms of its states. The following are the four states of consciousness according to Vedānta: wakefulness (jāgṛti), dream (svapna), deep sleep (suṣupti) and the "Fourth" state (turīya). The word turīya literally means "the fourth" and is commonly used by Vedāntists to refer to the trance state of Nirvikalpa Samādhi. In the wakeful state, the gross as well as the subtle aspects of the body remain active. The jīva is continually involved in the enjoyment of the objects of pleasure such as flowers, soothing ointments, a mating partner, and so on (Śaṅkara, c, 90–91).

The orientation of consciousness during the wakeful state is primarily extraspective or "outward bound" (bahiḥprajña) since it is directed toward external objects for the sake of enjoyment (Sadānanda, 1929, 17). The Vedānta theorists do not have much more to say about the wakeful state than the few characteristics just mentioned. Perhaps they consider the nature of wakeful state to be too well-known to need an elaborate description and analysis.

The dream state is believed to be an intermediary state between wakefulness and deep sleep, somewhat like a "twilight zone" between daylight and the darkness at night. Here the gross body as well as the senses are at rest; the connection of the jīva with the external world is cut off, but the subtle body is still active. The intellect (buddhi) assumes the role of the experiencer and the doer, and "creates" various objects such as chariots, houses, and so on, for its own experience of enjoyment or suffering. The Ātman remains inactive during dream states, as he does in all other states. The individual "sees" in darkness, as it were, and this is made possible by the self-luminous character of the Ātman (svayaṁjyotiḥ) (Śaṅkara, c, 211). In his commentary on the Vedānta aphorisms, Śaṅkara (b, 3.2.1–7) discusses the nature of dreams at some length. He recognizes that things seen in dreams are like those seen in the waking state and attributes this similarity to the impressions and desires (vāsanā) formed as a result of experiences during the wakeful state. In recognizing the role of desires, Śaṅkara (b, 3.2.4–6) adopts a view similar to that of Freudian theory, which stresses the wish-fulfilling character of dreams. He rejects the view that the soul leaves the body and roams around while dreaming. So far as the Ātman is concerned, he argues, there is no difference between the inside and the outside of the body because in its essence the Ātman is all-pervading. Besides, it is the jīva and not the Ātman that carries the desires as part of the chain of behaviors–traces–desires, leading to new behaviors and so on. Finally, he argues that perceptions in dreams of staying in, moving out, and the like, are to be admitted as illusions.

Śaṅkara (b, 3.2.4) mentions scriptural references to dreams as signs of good or bad omens. For instance, the sight of the dreamer riding an elephant is said to be indicative of future prosperity, and the sign of a person with black teeth indicative of an imminent death. Śaṅkara is willing to grant such symbolic significance to dreams, and even accepts their prognostic value. What Śaṅkara emphasizes most of all, however, is the illusory nature of dreams. He notes, for instance, that a dreamer may see chariots racing when there are no chariots around, no animals to be yoked to them, nor any roads on which to drive them. The dreamer may have neither the materials nor the skills to make a chariot, but he seems nevertheless to be able to create such objects. What may make him the accidental cause of the creation of various objects in his dreams may simply be emotions such as happiness or fear which the dream objects may arouse in him. There are, of course, several clear indications of the illusory nature of dreams. Thus, one dreams of years passing while being asleep only for a short period, or one may report viewing spectacular events while the eyes are actually closed. Moreover, what is seen as a chariot at one moment may turn into a man the next moment, and further into a tree a moment later.

All these arguments about the dream world being illusory are simple and straightforward. Is there any reason to belabor something that is so obvious? Yes, indeed, there is a reason Śaṅkara has stressed this issue. What he is trying to do with the help of these arguments is to drive home the point that the principle of non-contradiction is an important device to distinguish the real from the apparent and illusory. What is seen in dreams is often contradicted not only by the evidence presented by our experience during wakefulness, but also by the fact that events in dreams are often quite absurd. What is important here is not simply the logic of non-contradiction, but that the experiences in one state of consciousness are closer to reality than those in another state of consciousness. Vedānta theorists extend this line of argument to stress that the experience in the superior state of consciousness (in the Nirvikalpa type of Samādhi) takes us one step closer to reality. While dreaming, a person often assumes that what is happening is real, but realizes that it is unreal only after awakening. Likewise, one who attains the Fourth State of Consciousness realizes that the world as he saw it during the wakeful state is also relatively unreal or illusory. We do not need any persuasion to convince us of the unreality of dreams and the relative superiority of wakeful experience because the dream and wakeful states are commonly experienced. The difference between the two is quite clear to everyone who dreams. The nature of reality experienced in the superior states of consciousness is not so clear, however, since the superior states of consciousness are not commonly experienced. Moreover, since the samādhi states cannot be induced by one person in another (as hypnosis can), their nature must be explained with the help of analogy, metaphor, or through spontaneous poetic expression. It makes sense to refer to poetic expressions describing such extraordinary experiences, because they convey the flavor of their qualities better than the analytical statements and terse philosophical arguments in pedantic philosophical works.

Upaniṣadic Accounts of the Fourth State of Consciousness

The Upaniṣads contain several spontaneous expressions describing the nature of the experience of superior states of consciousness. The *Taittirīya Upaniṣad,* for instance, has several references to the experience of the Fourth State. In an oft-quoted verse (2.4) the sage exclaims:

From where the words retreat with the mind,
having failed to reach.
He, who attains that bliss need be afraid of none.

In the next section of the same upaniṣad (Taittirīya 2.5.1), the author first mentions his discovery that his inner self is full of bliss. Then he immediately adds what he spontaneously realizes:

Pleasure (priya) is its head
Delight (moda), the right side
Great delight (pramoda), the left side
Bliss (ānanda), the body
Brahma the lower part.
(R. E. Hume's translation)

What this poem indicates is the idea that the Fourth State of consciousness is so intense, so profound, and so fulfilling, that it seems to fill the entire space. This experience is described metaphorically by suggesting that wherever one would look, to the right or left, to the front or the back, there seemed to be only joy. As the sage moved from one side to another, the intensity of the joy seemed to increase. He was like a tiny speck in the middle of an ocean of happiness.

There are sections of the *Bṛhadāraṇyaka Upaniṣad* in which the sage Yajñavalkya explains to his wife Maitreyī the nature of the Self as realized in the Fourth State of consciousness. The sage points out that, unlike the wakeful state, where one sees an object placed in front of one's face, or smells something sniffed by the nose, or speaks to someone who happens to be around, a person in deep sleep does not see anything, smell anything, or speak to anybody. The acts of seeing or smelling and the like necessarily imply a relationship between a seer on the one hand and an object of sight on the other hand. Even a person engaged in a soliloquy may be speaking to someone else—maybe an absentee or imaginary person, or even his own "other" half. Such a "seer–seen" or "self–other" relationship is absent during deep sleep. It is also absent in the Fourth State of consciousness. Says Yājñavalkya:

For where there is a duality, as it were,
there one sees another;

> there one smells another; there one tastes another;
> there one hears another; there one thinks of another;
> there one touches another; there one understands another.
> But where everything has become just one's own self,
> then whereby and whom would one see . . . smell . . .
> Lo whereby would one understand the understander?
> (*Bṛhadāraṇyaka Upaniṣad*, 4.5.15; also 2.4.14. R. E. Hume, trans.)

Where the Knower himself becomes the object of his knowledge, there is no "other" to know, to see, or to speak to. In this condition, the duality of the subject and the object disappears. Here the process of knowing cannot continue in its ordinary form. Yet, the "knower" does not cease to exist. What, then, happens to the knower? Here is an answer suggested by the *Bṛhadāraṇyaka Upaniṣad* (4.3.30):

> An ocean, a seer alone without duality, becomes he whose world is Brahma, O King!"—thus Yājñavalkya instructed him. "This is a man's highest path. This is his highest achievement. This is his highest world. This is his highest bliss (R. E. Hume, trans.).

Once again, the answer is metaphorical. The seer or the knower, without having any specific object of his sight or knowledge, is like a vast ocean inside and out. What is to be seen (outside), and the one who is doing the seeing (inside), are identical. Like a drop of water surrounded by infinite drops of water, one is entirely indistinguishable from any other.

As can be easily seen, the metaphorical expression of the Upaniṣad is the same as that of the Asaṁprajñāta samādhi of Yoga where the limitations of ordinary cognitive states are transcended. In Yoga the seer is called the Puruṣa, and the non-cognitive samādhi is described as a state of isolation (kaivalya) of the sentient principle of Puruṣa from the material principle of Prakṛti. The Vedāntic interpretation of the same state emphasizes the "transcendence of the triplicity of knower, knowledge, and the known." I am inclined to think that the phenomenon described under different names is the same psychological condition. To put it in terms of the closest available Western concepts, the Fourth State of Consciousness is a type of experience in which one transcends intentionality (or directedness to an "outside" object), an unmistakable feature of the ordinary states of consciousness.

Another matter of distinction between the Yogic and Upaniṣadic accounts of the highest state of samādhi may be noted here. The Vedāntists follow the Upaniṣads in emphasizing the blissfulness of this experience. In the excerpt from the *Bṛhadāraṇyaka Upaniṣad* quoted above, the condition where one transcends the duality of the knower and the known is described as the highest bliss or as the highest achievement. The superlative used to qualify the degree of blissfulness may not really be adequate to convey the profoundness and magnanimity of what it is trying to describe. So the Upaniṣad once again takes recourse to the following metaphorical expression.

> If one is fortunate among men and wealthy, lord over others, best provided with all human enjoyments—that is the highest bliss of men. Now a hundredfold the bliss of men is one bliss of those who have won the fathers' world. Now a hundredfold the bliss of those who have won the fathers' world is one bliss in the Gandharva-world. A hundredfold the bliss in the Gandharva-world is one bliss of the gods who gain their divinity by meritorious works. A hundredfold the bliss of the gods by works is one bliss of the gods by birth and of him who is learned in the Vedas, who is without crookedness, and who is free from desire . . .
>
> (*Bṛhadāraṇyaka Upaniṣad,* 4.3.30. R. E. Hume, trans.)

The first thing to note here is that the bliss is explicitly considered superior to all the enjoyment that can be acquired through wealth and power. It is interesting to note that in this story a powerful king is seeking wisdom from a penniless hermit. It may well be that the story in the Upaniṣad is mere fiction and no real king was involved. Nevertheless, the story teller wants us to believe that the sage's advice is good enough for a real king. At any rate, the Upaniṣad is making a point with the help of a metaphor. The metaphor involves a graded series of heavenly creatures (Gandharvas), like angels, demi-gods, the gods, and so on. The quality of bliss at each subsequent level is a hundred times higher than the level below it. This ordering continues through six successive steps (meaning a value of 10^{12}) before arriving at a description of the level of bliss attained by the realization that the individual self is identical with the ubiquitous Brahman.

This Upaniṣadic way of accounting for the intensity of the blissfulness of the superior state of consciousness is perhaps the most ancient psychometric device. It is somewhat like a modern test for the measurement of "job satisfaction" or "quality of life," where the intervals are logarithmic rather than linear or "equal appearing." A psychometric scale, whether ancient or modern, is basically a metaphorical device used to make tangible what is intrinsically intangible. Keeping aside for a moment the technical issue of the reliability and validity of this ancient "scale," the underlying issue should now be clear. In brief, the Vedānta view follows the Upaniṣads in assigning an extremely high affective value to the experience of the Fourth State of consciousness.

What Happens after the Experience of the Fourth State of Consciousness?

Once a person reaches this Fourth State of Consciousness, what happens next? Like most samādhi states it does not last long. (We have already noted that the Fourth State is not different from the Asaṁprajñāta samādhi of Yoga.) Speaking in terms of the states of consciousness, the cycle of wakefulness and sleep (occasionally interrupted by dreams) is resumed after the termination of the samādhi state. But once the state of Nirvikalpa samādhi is attained, one does not remain the same person after its termination. A moment of realization of the ultimate truth, namely that the individual at the core is the same as the ubiquitous Brahman, is enough to completely transform the life of the individual. In Vedānta it is claimed that the knower of Brahman *becomes* Brahman.[18] What this means is not easy to explain. To put it simply, after attaining the experience of Nirvikalpa samādhi, the individual no longer identifies himself with various "narrow" definitions of the self which he may have acquired since childhood. He no longer pursues narrowly selfish goals and hence does not experience either elation due to success in attaining them, or despair due to failure. As a result, he neither feels vainglorious when praised, nor humiliated when criticized. The self-realized individual does not identify himself with any particular group, and hence stands above pride and prejudice. In brief, such a person becomes saintly in his attitude and behavior, manifesting the ideal human condition called sthitaprajña (characterized by equanimity, tranquility, etc.) as described in Chapter 2. We shall postpone further discussion of the transformation of the pattern of life resulting from the experience of Nirvikalpa samādhi until the next chapter.

The Means of Attaining Superior States of Being

So much for the Vedāntic view of the nature of the states of consciousness. Obviously, the Fourth State of Consciousness is considered extremely desirable. Clearly it is believed to be a means for the attainment of eternal liberation from the miseries of an endless series of life cycles. For those who share this view of its desirability, the next most relevant question is, how does one attain the Fourth State of Consciousness? First of all, the experience of the Fourth State is not considered to be an event over which one accidently stumbles. It is not like a revelation from God granted to someone who is favored by Him. As the 17th-century poet Tukārām (1973), who clearly follows the unbroken Vedāntic tradition, put it in one of his poems (No. 2325): "Liberation is not a gift that God bestows on someone of His choice; it is a condition attainable by anyone who has strong enough determination to acquire it." Śaṅkara (b, 3.4.37) has clearly suggested that the highest knowledge attainable through the experience of the Fourth State of Consciousness is not exclusive; it is accessible to anyone irrespective of his station in life or caste. What are the steps to be taken by those who aspire to this exalted state? Vedāntists suggest the following four basic means for its attainment:

1. The first means involves the correct discrimination between the everlasting and the impermanent. The Brahman is to be recognized as the only permanent form of existence; the phenomenal world is impermanent. This would imply that one must learn to identify oneself as the everlasting Ātman and not identify oneself with the body which is impermanent. It would also mean that one begins to realize that there is some lasting form of happiness different from the worldly gains of wealth and power, which are as transient as the pleasures that they can bring. Striving for the more permanent is a necessary precondition for the journey to liberation. We may note incidentally that here we are not talking about delayed gratification, such as opting for a box of candy later in exchange for a single candy now, or saving now so as to benefit from returns from capital investment in the future. (The concept of delayed gratification is familiar to most contemporary psychologists, as it has been borrowed from the Puritan sects of Protestantism and adapted to contemporary theory and methodology.) Delayed gratification brings more rewards of the same type, even if it would tend to bring them on a relatively permanent basis. Vedānta, by contrast, implies a different type of gratification when it refers to lasting forms of happiness.
2. The second means involves maintaining an attitude of detachment. More specifically, it means that one refrains from hankering for enjoyments expected either in this world or in the existence after death. It should be possible to maintain an attitude of detachment when most forms of enjoyment are recognized to be temporary at best.

3. Acquisition of the following six virtues is the third means:
   a. controlling the mind so as to rest it steadily on one's objective (śama),
   b. withdrawing the senses from the objects of their pleasure (dama),
   c. preventing the mind from modifying itself as it becomes modified when controlled by the external objects (uparati),
   d. enduring hardships and pain without lamenting or becoming anxious (titikṣā),
   e. adopting an attitude of conviction that the theory explained by the scriptures and the directions provided by the teacher (guru) are the correct means for the knowledge of Reality (śraddhā), and
   f. the firm resting of the mind on the formless Brahman without indulging the mind (samādhāna).
4. The fourth means is the cultivation of an intense desire for liberation from the bonds created by egoism and ignorance. (See Śaṅkara, c, 18–28).

Besides the four categories of the means to liberation (sādhana catuṣṭaya), the Vedāntists suggest a general strategy for the attainment of the ideal human condition. Foremost in this respect is the pursuit of inquiry regarding the nature of the self (ātmavicāra). (We shall examine the nature and significance of the inquiry regarding the self in the next chapter.) To this end, the Vedāntists recommend a systematic study of the doctrines of Vedānta as explained in various texts such as the Upaniṣads. An aspirant is advised to approach a qualified teacher (guru) who has learned the principles properly and has also attained self-realization in his own right. Carefully "listening" (śravaṇa) to the non-dualist conclusions of Vedānta philosophy is the first important step in the threefold strategy prescribed for all aspirants. A second step involves repeatedly and deeply contemplating (manana) what is thus learned. In the third step (called nididhyāsana), the aspirant becomes persistently involved in contemplating the non-dual principle of Brahman in such a way that no other thought enters his mind. Having attained this stage, the aspirant is ready to enter the state of samādhi (see Sadānanda, 30).

As can be easily seen, there are many similarities between the Yogic and Vedāntic approaches to the attainment of samādhi. The resemblance between the means and strategies for the attainment of an ideal human condition recommended by both should be particularly clear. Thus, both Yoga and Vedānta recommend refraining from the pursuit of worldly pleasures and from the accumulation of their means (vairāgya, aparigraha), cultivation of the attitude of detachment, studying the doctrines of one's chosen discipline (svādhyāya, śravaṇa), withdrawing the senses from the objects of their pleasure (pratyāhāra, dama), and ascetic self-control (tapa, titikṣā). Radhakrishnan (1929, Vol. 2, p. 616, fn 2) has pointed out that the Vedāntic strategy of studying the principles of Vedānta and their contemplation (śravaṇa and manana) correspond to the Yogic concentration (dhāraṇā) and the steps leading to it, and that the Vedāntic description of persistent contemplation of the non-dual principle (nididhyāsana) is a close equivalent of the Yogic description of an unswerving contemplation (dhyāna). Moreover, the well-known Vedāntist Sadānanda (30) recommends the adoption of a full-scale Yogic approach including all the eight "limbs" of Yoga as described by Patañjali (except that he advises concentration on the non-dual principle of Vedānta rather than any object of the yogi's choice as recommended by Patañjali).[19] Nṛsiṁhasarasvatī, who has written a commentary on Sadānanda's *Vedāntasāra,* has even recommended specific postures described in Haṭha Yoga as appropriate methods in the attainment of Nirvikalpa samādhi.[20]

A comparison between the Yoga and Vedānta theories is bound to indicate several such points of similarity between them. It is necessary to point out, however, that such similarities should not lead us to minimize their differences. The differences between the ontological and cosmological doctrines of Yoga and Vedānta are fundamental and irreconcilable. Notwithstanding the similarities between their views of the ideal human condition, the Yogic ideal of the isolation of the Puruṣa from Prakṛti (kaivalya) is said to be different from the Vedāntic ideal of self-realization, in that the former is said to emphasize the release from misery while the latter emphasizes the attainment of an infinite bliss as well as the adoption of attitudes and behaviors characteristic of a "sthitaprajña." Although some authors assert that the experience called Asaṁprajñāta Samādhi by yogis is no different from what the Vedāntists call Nirvikalpa samādhi, I have met followers of Vedānta who dismiss the Yogic experience as a mere trance state of little value. How does one evaluate such conflicting views? Here, as before, the only sure way of finding out whether the experiences described by one theory are the same as (or different from) those described by another theory is to follow the prescriptions of both these schools and then decide on the basis of one's own experience. If one is unprepared to retrace the steps described by those systems, one must settle the matter with the help of trustworthy persons who claim to have completed both courses. As to where and how to find such persons, I do not know.

Now, from the viewpoint of contemporary Western psychology and psychotherapy, one might have the same reservations regarding the acceptance of the Vedānta approach as regarding the acceptance of the Yogic approach. Vedānta, like Yoga, expects its followers to observe ascetic self-restraint; recommends "faith" in its conventional doctrines; and also expects the followers to take what they get without becoming anxious or feeling miserable. For a secularized modern psychologist, Vedānta (like Yoga) may be more of a religion than a science. Whether or not to admit ascetic self-denial of any brand—Protestant, Yoga, Vedānta, or some other—into psychology is an ideological choice that every psychologist has to make on his own.

The foregoing account of Vedānta would indicate that the theoretical aspect of Vedāntic psychology is specialized in explaining the nature of the states of consciousness with a particular emphasis on the Fourth State of Consciousness. It is but natural that its applied aspect specializes in helping in the attainment of the Fourth State and the ideal human condition to which it leads. It follows, then, that the psychology of Vedānta will have a special appeal for those who share the ideals of Vedānta. Here one may ask: is there anything in the Vedāntic approach that deals with the kind of concerns that are common among psychologists today? Is there anything in Vedānta, for instance, that can shed light on the problem of anxiety? In response to this question I would say that, although the Vedāntists are concerned with the problem of misery in life, there is little explanation in the formal writings of Vedānta on the nature of anxiety (as understood and defined by most schools of contemporary psychology) and on how to deal with it.

It is indeed tempting to ask: "What techniques of psychotherapy can be derived from the principles and techniques of Vedānta as explained in its basic writings?" At this time, at least, I cannot find anything in Vedāntic literature that can readily help us enrich the tool-chest of a modern psychotherapist. The primary goal of Vedānta, namely self-realization, is more akin to the concern of attaining "positive mental health" or a higher sense of fulfillment in life, than to the restoration of an average level of health among those who are clearly in a "pathological" condition. Although it is difficult to find descriptions in the formal writings of Vedānta of techniques suitable for the practice of clinical psychology, it is my impression that sophisticated techniques of counseling based on the principles of Vedānta have already been developed. They are used by holy persons or "gurus." In fact, there is a category of persons in India who are involved in a conventional variety of counseling that does not fit into the Western models of clinical psychology, psychiatry, or even priesthood ("father confessor"). Their approach is often based on the principles of Vedānta. It is quite plausible that we can learn much about the conventional techniques of counseling rooted in the Indian culture and philosophy if we observe such persons at work. We shall examine the possible rationale for a counseling strategy based on the principles of Vedānta in the next chapter. Also, in the final chapter, I shall try to explain the typical conventional role of such "counsellors" in the Indian socio-cultural setting.

The Validation of the Knowledge of the Fourth State of Consciousness

Before closing this chapter, I must respond to an important question. How does Vedānta propose to validate the knowledge relating to the Fourth State of Consciousness? More specifically, how does one evaluate the claims to the attainment of an unusual and highly fulfilling psychological condition like Nirvikalpa samādhi? The answers to these questions are to be found in Śaṅkara's elaborate epistemology.

Śaṅkara has critically considered the conventional sources of knowledge including direct perception (pratyakṣa), reasoning (tarka), and scriptural testimony (śruti). It would be useful to clarify first of all his view of scriptural testimony. He insisted that scriptures (such as the sayings of the Upaniṣadic sages) are to be considered sources of valid knowledge only in those areas where direct observation is not possible. As noted before, the realization of the Brahman is possible only in a special, superior state of consciousness which is beyond the range of ordinary cognitive states. One may, therefore, turn to the scriptures while trying to understand the nature of the Brahman. Śaṅkara flatly declared, however, that "even a hundred scriptures stating that fire is cold cannot be considered valid." (Śaṅkara, d, 18.66). If the scriptures seem to say something that is contrary to what is directly observed, one must assume that the scriptures mean something else, and look for alternative interpretations of the texts. Also, he did not feel obliged to accept scriptures as authority when separate statements in the texts, or inferences following from them, conflicted with one another.

Generations of philosophers have quarreled over the relative superiority of either experience or reason as criteria for truth. The perennial controversy between empiricists and rationalists illustrates this rivalry. It should be clear that experience alone is not adequate in leading us to truth, because experiential evidence is often conflicting. It is therefore inevitable that we seek the help of reason in order to choose between contradictory claims to truth. Then again, reason, without the help of observation, leads to idle speculation. Śaṅkara considered both experience and reason useful as long as they do not lead to contradictory conclusions. He proposed the principle of non-contradiction (abādha) as a guiding principle in the pursuit of truth. It is true however, that Śaṅkara is critical of reason; he has proposed complex and sophisticated arguments to show the inadequacy of logic in comprehending the unobservable realm. By and large, he favors experience over any other source of knowledge, and, to that extent, he may be said to be an empiricist. It must be added however, that Śaṅkara's view of experience as a means to truth is broader than the view of experience which prevails among the Western empiricists. While most Western empiricists consider direct observation during the wakeful state of consciousness to be the sole criterion for truth, Śaṅkara adds to it the evidence offered by the Fourth State of Consciousness as a source of valid knowledge. His view of experience (anubhava) as a source of knowledge is thus broader than the range of experience involved in direct observation (pratyakṣa). To use Tart's expression, the Western view in this respect is state-specific (i.e. restricted to the wakeful state of consciousness), while Śaṅkara's is not so restricted.

We may pause here for a moment and recall Bertrand Russell's dichotomy with logic on one side and mysticism on the other, which was referred to in Chapter 1. Russell provides a good example of how the insights derived from superior states of consciousness are often associated with irrationality, the contemplativeness of a lazy man, religious faith, and even narrow-minded dogmatism. Mysticism is a word often used to encompass everything including intuitive insights, nondiscursive thought, idle contemplation, secret doctrines, "religious experience," and other such epithets which have somewhat negative overtones. The foregoing account of Yoga and Vedānta perspectives on superior states of consciousness should help clarify some of the misconceptions associated with the notions of such states.

Before closing this chapter, one possible criticism of the Yoga and Vedānta claims regarding the nature of the superior states of consciousness needs to be considered. It may be argued that the alleged superior comprehension of reality and the highly satisfying quality of the superior states of consciousness may be evident only to those who have experienced such states. Yoga and Vedānta offer no evidence to those who have never had such experiences. There seems to be no way of testing whether anyone who claims to have experienced the superior states of consciousness has, in fact, experienced them.

An apologist of Yoga and Vedānta would respond to such criticisms in the following way: yes, indeed, there is no way of verifying whether anyone has special experiences of the type of the Fourth State of Consciousness. But this is not a special case; it is like the everyday situation where statements like "I have a headache" must be evaluated solely on the basis of the trustworthiness of the person making such statements. Baier's observation (mentioned in Chapter 3) that the final epistemic authority in the case of such statements lies with their assertor is relevant here. Whether or not one would accept such statements as true depends largely on one's own estimation of the credibility of the assertor.

The issue of credibility of the claims of Yoga and Vedānta thus becomes critical. An opinion regarding this issue prevalent in India is that the authors of the Yoga and Vedānta texts were saintly persons. Their motives were entirely beyond suspicion. Further, the Indian tradition has offered in every generation at least some proponents of the age-old views, proponents who are enlightened sages and have nothing to gain by misleading people. The tradition in fact offers a clue to the correct evaluation of the credibility of persons who claim wisdom based on the experience of the Fourth State of Consciousness. The clue is based on a principle mentioned before, namely, that one who knows Brahman *becomes* Brahman. In other words, a person who has experienced the Fourth State manifests in his behavior the characteristics of a sthitaprajña—the ideal human condition described in Chapter 2. To judge the credibility of claims pertaining to the Fourth State of Consciousness on the basis of the behavioral manifestations of the ideal conditions is both logical (since it follows logically from the principle just mentioned) and utilitarian (since the value of the Fourth State lies in the practical realization of an ideal).

Notes

1. Two English translations of Patañjali's aphorisms along with the commentaries of Vyāsa and Vācaspati Miśra are available. The first one, by Rāma Prasāda, was originally published in 1912 as Vol.IV of the "Sacred Books of the Hindus" series by S. C. Vasu for the Panini Office, Bahadurganj, India. A reprint was published in 1974 by AMS Press, New York 10003. The second, by J. H. Woods, was published in 1914 as Vol.17 of the Harvard Oriental Series. This has been reprinted in 1972 by Motilal Banarsidass of Delhi. Woods's translation is meticulously done, but the philological style is quite cumbersome and the language archaic in comparison to the language of contemporary psychology. S. N. Dasgupta's short volume, *Yoga as Philosophy and Religion,* is a useful guide to Patañjali's concepts. This work has been reprinted, in 1973, by Motilal Banarsidass of Delhi.
2. cittaśabdena buddhimupalakṣyati. Vācaspati Miśra, 1.1.
3. śraddheyārtho vaktā: see Vyāsa, 1.7.
4. Patañjali's five categories of vṛttis seem to cover almost the entire range of the various processes of consciousness, with the notable exception of dreaming. I have found only one reference to dreams in Patañjali (1.38). In his commentary, Śaṅkara (a, 1.10) suggests that Patañjali does not include dream as a sub-category of sleep because his reference to "dream" and "sleep" are juxtaposed in aphorism No. 1.38 (svap-

nanidrājñānālaṁbanam vā), which implies a distinction between the two. He also points out that since dreams obviously involve such content as color, sound, and so on, they do not fit Patañjali's definition of sleep, which is said to be cittavṛtti devoid of pratyaya or "contents" of consciousness.

5. vyutthānam vividhamutthānam calanam pratyayākāreṇa cittasya. (Śaṅkara's commentary, a, 3.9.)
6. yogaścittavṛttinirodhaḥ (Patañjali, 1.2.)
7. The Yogic theory of karma, which connects enjoyment and suffering to meritorious and nonmeritorious actions, follows from the view that the concept of karma assumes orderliness in both the moral and amoral spheres at the same time. This view is too divergent from the perspective of modern science. While there is no point in trying to reconcile the Indian and Western views in this respect, I should mention that there are, in fact, many striking similarities between some of the Yogic concepts just described and certain Western concepts. Note, for instance, that the concept of vāsanā is, remarkably similar to the notions of "instinct" or "drive." Note also that the concept of karmāśaya is remarkably similar to the Freudian concept of the id which represents the sum total of instinctual tendencies acquired prior to the beginning of the life cycle. The concept of karmāśaya is also similar to the Skinnerian concept of the "repertoire" of responses that is "the product of the biological reinforcers to which the species has been made sensitive through natural selection." (Skinner, 1974, p. 176).
8. īśvarapraṇidhānasyaiva tu mukhyataḥ samādhisādhakatvam sūtritam. (Vijñāna Bhikṣu, 2.45.)
9. tulyapratyayānām pravāha ekākāraḥ pratyayasaṁtānaḥ pratyayāntareṇa vijātīyena anākīrṇaḥ. tad dhyānam. (Śaṅkara, a, 3.2.)
10. The choice of a cow for an example is not mine; it comes from the commentators of Patañjali.
11. deśakālanimittānubhavāvacchinneṣu yā samāpattiḥ sā savicāretyucyate. (Vyāsa, 1.44.)
12. It may be noted that, in the case of the first four stages of samādhi which focus on the object, the first two, which emphasize the gross aspects, are paired together under the labels Savitarka and Nirvitarka; the next two, which relate to the five subtle aspects or tanmātras, are also paired as Savicāra and Nirvicāra. The following two, namely the sānanda and sāsmitā levels, which focus on the means of knowledge and on the knower, respectively, do not appear in such paired forms according to Vyāsa and Vācaspati Miśra. Vijñāna Bhikṣu, however, suggests that there is a Nirānanda type of samādhi that follows the Sānanda level, and that a Nirasmitā type follows the Sāsmitā stage of samādhi. There are many other minor commentators of Patañjali who have proposed varying accounts of the samādhi states. A detailed comparison of these divergent accounts is given by Vimalā Karṇāṭak in her doctoral dissertation, published by the Benaras Hindu University Press in 1974. This work is in Hindi.
13. tajjaḥ saṁskāro anyasaṁskārapratibandhī. Patañjali 1.50.
14. jitaḥ pūrvo yoga uttarasya yogasya jñānapravṛttyadhigama hetuḥ (Vācaspati Miśra, 3.6.)
15. yogo yogena jñātavyo yogo yogāt pravartate. (Vyāsa, 3.6.)
16. In his commentary on Sadānanda's Vedāntasāra, Rāmatīrtha has made it clear that, according to the established tradition, the terms Nirvikalpa(ka) and Savikalpa(ka) samādhi, used by the Vedāntins, are descriptive of the same conditions, which the yogis call the Asaṁprajñāta and Saṁprajñāta samādhi, respectively. See Colonel G. A. Jacob's edition, published in Bombay by Pandurang Javaji in 1925, p. 129.

17. The common definition of the manas is "that which is involved in decision-making (saṁkalpa) and doubting (vikalpa)." In their translation of Vidyāraṇya's *Jīvanmukti-viveka*, S. S. Sastri and T. R. S. Ayyangar define the mind as "the instrument with which various kinds of analytic and synthetic processes are brought about." "Analytical and synthetical activity" seems to be a correct translation of saṁkalpa and vikalpa. Vikalpa means "to think as separate," or to differentiate, and saṁkalpa means "to think of things together" or to synthesize.
18. brahmavid brahmaiva bhavati. (*Muṇḍaka Upaniṣad*, 3.2.9.)
19. I am indebted to Swāmi Dayānanda Saraswati for explaining to me this aspect of the difference between the Yogic and Vedāntic approaches to samādhi. I wish to thank him also for pointing out the importance of śravaṇa, manana and nididhyāsana, aspects of the Vedāntic approach I had failed to include in an initial draft of this chapter.
20. See Colonel G. A. Jacob's edition of *Vedāntasāra (op.) cit.*, p. 49.

5

SELF AND IDENTITY

The nature of the self has been a topic of concern in both Indian and Western traditions. "Know thyself" has been an important exhortation for men in the West for ages. The nature of the Self (the Ātman) was one of the central topics of the philosophy of the early Upaniṣads, and has remained important throughout the history of Indian thought. The roots of the philosophical and psychological views of the self may be traced to religious and spiritual concerns in both India and the West. In the Western tradition, for instance, the Judeo-Christian concept of the soul was an ancestor of the contemporary formulations of the self. Descartes, we may recall, conceived of the self as a thinking substance. Being a devout Christian, it seemed inevitable to him to conceive of the soul as immortal because unless the soul continued to exist till the Day of Judgment, God would not be able to pay every man his dues. In the Indian tradition, the immortality of the Ātman seems to have been a corollary to the Law of Karma (at least in some, if not all varieties of its fomulation) in that the assumption of the moral nature of the cosmos does not seem to be justified without also assuming that all of us would be born again to enjoy the fruits of good deeds that are not reaped by the time death comes.

The eschatological concerns about the future of the soul after the death of the body have long disappeared from the philosophical and psychological theories of the West. It would appear that the modern followers of the Yoga and Vedānta traditions are still not averse to believing in the survival of the Puruṣa or the Ātman across life cycles. Yet, they are guided by some of the same concerns about life on earth which prompt the Western theorists to postulate the self. First, a common

Notes for Chapter 5 are on p. 273.

concern is to discover a principle around which human experience would seem to be organized. A second concern is to change the course of life to a more desirable direction. Concepts like self-actualization, self-realization, or knowledge-of-the-self (ātma jñāna) reflect the latter concern. Our discussion of the Indian and Western conceptions of the self and identity will be centered around these common concerns.

The literature on the self is vast. Gordon and Gergen (1968), who reviewed the literature on this topic published in the English language, estimated that there were over 2,000 publications in psychology and sociology. Much has been added since this count was made. Some prominent landmarks and trends can be recognized in this literature. In a chapter of his *Principles* devoted to the discussion of the nature of the self, William James (1890/1950) gave an extensive account of the major contributions to the concept of self and personal identity in the history of Western thought. His writings have become a source of inspiration for such prominent philosophers and psychologists as Husserl and Erikson. Charles Horton Cooley (1902/1964) and George Herbert Mead (1934) pioneered the sociological formulations of the self. Those who follow their lead have formed a thriving school of contemporary sociology which is usually referred to by the name of symbolic interactionism. The ego, which is usually considered equivalent to the self, is a central concept of Freud's psychoanalytic theory. Hartmann, Kris, and Loewestein were amongst the followers of Freud who disliked the emphasis on conflict (against the id and reality) in which the Freudian ego was perennially involved. They therefore conceived of an "autonomous ego" which became the key concept in what came to be called "psychoanalytic ego psychology." Among the more recent psychologists, Carl Rogers has formulated a popular theory and a technique of psychotherapy that has the self as its very central concept.

These formulations of the concept of self are quite different from one another. The diversity among them is nearly as overwhelming as the extensiveness of the literature on it. Gordon W. Allport (1943) once identified the following different (if not unrelated) meanings attached to the term ego and its equivalents: the ego as knower, as object of knowledge, as primitive selfishness, as dominance-drive, as passive organization of mental processes, as a "fighter for ends," as a behavioral system, and as a subjective organization of culture.

Distinctions such as the knower and the known, and concepts similar to primitive selfishness appear in Indian thinking about the self as they do in the Western theories. If we add the many Western theories of the self to the array of Indian perspectives, the range of diversity in the formulations of self and related concepts becomes even greater. It is neither possible nor necessary to try to bring order to this apparent chaos. The purpose here, as elsewhere in this work, is to try to strike common ground between the Indian and Western trends of thought by identifying some common issues, to note some points of similarity and contrast, and then to seek for possible avenues for integration on a common ground.

Personality, Self, Identity

The term personality, like the terms self and ego, has acquired rather diverse meanings. By and large, it is a broad concept that refers to various aspects of the experiences and behaviors of an individual. Implicit in the very concept of personality is the idea that the experiences and behaviors of a person are not a hodge-podge of unrelated events; they form a universe of systematically related phenomena. Thus, the behavior of a person in one situation relates systematically to behavior in other situations in such a way that we expect to find consistent patterns. The descriptions of persons by trait names such as extrovert, aggressive, dominant, and so on, often make sense because persons seem to behave in a reasonably consistent manner. Similarly, the experiences of events in childhood are believed to be systematically related to behavior in adulthood. We therefore expect that the life history of a person may be understood as a meaningful whole rather than an accidental succession of unrelated events. The concept of personality, then, implies that the entire life history of a person (in which all the events relating to him are recorded) can be considered as a unit. Although few personality theories explicitly state such an assumption, the very fact that they choose behaviors of individuals as the subject matter of their study indicates that they consider it an internally connected domain and not a motley collection of unrelated events.

Concepts like the ego and the self are often designed to represent an organizing principle that structures personality. In psychoanalysis, for instance, the ego is an agency of the psyche that balances the frequently conflicting forces of the id and the superego. The relative strength of the ego vis-à-vis the forces of the id and the superego, therefore, determines the structure of personality. Similarly, some social psychologists consider the self to be an organization of roles—meaning that the structure of personality is determined by the relative importance attached by an individual to family, occupation, citizenship, and other roles. It is inevitable that the concept of self reflects those characteristics of human nature the theorist considers particularly important. Thus, anthropologists who view man as primarily a product of culture define the self as a subjective organization of culture, while many social psychologists conceive of the self as an organization of attitudes.

Notwithstanding the proliferation of theories of the self and their uneven popularity among Western psychologists today, there are many contemporary psychologists who are extremely critical of all types of formulations of the concept of the self. Behavioristically inclined psychologists, for instance, often consider concepts like the self and ego to be useless. Such a negative reaction is not based simply on an aversion to the theological roots of the soul (which is the ancestor of the concept of the self). The rejection of self as a useful concept is often based on the close association between the concepts of consciousness and self that arose in Descartes' time. The self, like the soul or the mind, has often signified something other than the body. Those who are committed openly or secretly to a materialist view of the world have no use for a "mentalistic" concept like the self. The self has been looked upon as a "ghost in the machine," or as a homunculus, a tiny man-in-the-chest who moves strings to make the limbs move. Such a tiny man, of course, would be nothing but a phantasm; even as an idea designed to explain the self-motivated character of human beings, it would be useless since this homunculus would need a second homunculus to make the first one work, and so on, *ad infinitum*. The redundancy of the idea of self as homunculus is too obvious to need further comment.

Against this background, it is small wonder that the concept of self has been neglected, particularly by those who follow the behaviorist approach to psychology. Such neglect has resulted in a major blind spot in the behaviorist view of man. Skinner (1953, p. 284) recognized this deficiency when he said, "We may quarrel with any analysis which appeals to a self or a personality as an inner determiner of action, but the facts which have been represented with such devices cannot be ignored." Among the facts which, he thinks, cannot be ignored, he mentions the unity of personality and a "coherent response system." Skinner's comment supports the view expressed before, namely that responses of human beings are "coherent," that is, systematically related to one another. It also recognizes that the purpose of the concept of self is to represent or signify the internal organization and unity of personality.

It is common to associate (or even to equate) the concept of the self with an image of oneself, or some kind of symbolic representation of oneself one carries in one's "head." Thus, if a person pictures himself as a tall, handsome, bright, and kind man who loves his family and country, as a competent engineer who is proud of himself, as an inventor of devices, and so on and so forth, such an "image" may be construed as his "self-concept." To equate the self with a self-image is to restrict its scope to the "cognitive" aspects of personality. No matter how common such restrictive views of the self are, it must be noted that some important formulations of the concept of the self are not so restrictive. William James (1890/1950, Vol. 1, pp. 292 ff) for instance, proposed the following as "constituents" of the self: 1. the Material Self that includes the body, the clothes, and all the material possessions of a person, 2. the Social Self, which includes the various roles he plays in the society, as well as the recognition he receives from those who know him, 3. the Spiritual Self, meaning a person's "psychic faculties and dispositions," as well as his "moral sensibility and his conscience," and 4. the Pure Ego, which refers to the Self as Knower. It should be clear that these components of the self represent different facets of personality.

James did not simply enumerate the constituents of the self, but arranged them in a particular order. Thus, he conceived of the bodily self with its primitive selfishness and sensuality at the base, placed the material self on top of it, and suggested that the spiritual self stands at the apex of the hierarchically arranged selves. Although he admitted that different individuals may not rank the importance of the various constituents of the self in the same order, James thought that there was a "tolerably unanimous opinion" about their relative value. What such conceptualization implies is that personality is assumed to be a multifaceted entity in which the various facets are systematically related to one another. The self is construed as a principle that permeates all the facets of personality, uniting them into an organized whole.

Turning now to the Indian side, we may note that the Vedānta system has developed a set of concepts which roughly parallel the view of personality mentioned above. The Vedāntist concept of jīva is similar to the contemporary concept of personality. The jīva represents everything concerning an individual, including all his experiences and actions throughout his life cycle. The jīva is viewed as a multi-layered entity in which five layers are encased in one another like the concentric sheaths of an onion. The outermost shell refers to the body. It is called the sheath made of food (annamaya kośa) since it may perish for want of nourishment. The next layer inside is named prāṇa which literally means "the breath of life." The concept of prāṇa includes inhaling, exhaling, yawning, and similar bodily processes. This second layer, therefore, refers to the physiological processes that organize the bodily functions. The third, manomaya kośa, involves the sense organs and the "mind" that coordinates their functions. This is considered to be the seat of egoistic striving (ahaṁkāra). It manifests itself in the form of the experience of the "me" and in the involvements with whatever objects that are considered "mine." The fourth sheath, called vijñānamaya kośa, constitutes the intellect and can therefore be said to represent the cognitive aspects of the self, such as self-image or self-representation. The fifth sheath, which is the innermost core of the jīva, is called the ānandamaya kośa. This is the seat of the experience of bliss.

The similarity between William James's view of the hierarchically ordered constituents of the self and the Vedāntic view of concentrically arranged sheaths of the jīva should be clear. Both theorists use the metaphor of systematically arranged layers to represent meaningfully related aspects of personality. They include material as well as nonmaterial aspects of personality in their conceptualization. They also view an element of self-seeking or egoism at the core of personality. Beyond these common modes of conceptualization, however, there is a point of sharp contrast between them. Although the word ātman literally means the self, the concept of Ātman is reserved by Śaṅkara to signify the "real" self which is believed to be different from all the aspects of the jīva. It is of course recognized in Vedānta that the ordinary usage of the terms "I" and "me" refers to one's body, possessions, intimate feelings aroused by them, and other such things that belong to the jīva. However, such usage of the word "self" is considered to be misleading and erroneous, since it does not usually represent the "real" self. In fact Śaṅkara insists that the five sheaths must be considered as non-self, and argues that the Ātman or real self which represents the permanent, unchanging basis of life is mistakenly identified with the impermanent jīva as a result of primeval ignorance (avidyā). This sharp contrast between James's view of the self and Śaṅkara's view of the Ātman is based on divergent opinions on the issue of what accounts for the selfsameness in man. The issue of selfsameness is a crucial issue which needs to be briefly explained here.

It is a matter of universal experience that all of us keep changing in various aspects of our personality throughout our lives, and still maintain the feeling that "I am the same as I was yesterday" and so on. I am no longer a little baby as I once was, nor am I a robust and idealistic youth any more. Over the decades may body has changed in size and shape, and I do not now think of myself the same way as I did last year or the year before. Yet, people recognize me as the same person through the years, and I continue to have a sense of selfsameness. To say that a person (or anything, for that matter) has changed, and has yet remained the same is a *paradox*. It clearly involves the admission that two contradictory statements are true at the same time, since change is the very opposite of sameness. In the Western tradition this paradox has been called the *paradox of identity* and generations of philosophers have tried to resolve it. In the Indian tradition the same problem has appeared in a slightly different form. The Vedāntists, for instance, refer to the same issue when they speak of making a wise discrimination between the permanent and the impermanent (nitya–anitya viveka). The basic issue of sameness *versus* change in personality is surely a common issue considered by Indian and Western psychologists alike.

In order to resolve the paradox of identity we need to be able to reconcile the contradiction between sameness and change. This is like solving a *puzzle*. For example, we should be able to explain what it means when we make the following kinds of statements: that the contents of a glass container are the same although we first saw a piece of ice, then drops of water, or some vapor in a container; that the tree you see in the yard is the same as the sapling I had planted decades ago; that an old man is the same person as the young man he once was. In each case we must be able to say *what* has remained the same. In the first example given above the explanation is simple. We can say that water remains the same despite change in form in the sense that the concept of water refers to the chemical properties of a certain substance, and not to its physical properties, which are secondary. It is also easy to demonstrate that something trapped inside a glass container can be made to appear a solid piece, transparent drops of liquid, or a formless cloud by simply heating or cooling it. At any rate, as far as this example goes, we can say that when we speak of water, we imply that its chemical properties are *essential,* while physical properties are unessential or incidental. With respect to the sameness of a tree, however, the problem of resolving the paradox of identity becomes more difficult; and it becomes much more difficult with personal identity.

Part of the difficulty in understanding the nature of personal identity arises from the enormous complexity of the concept of personality. As noted, personality is considered a multifaceted or multilayered entity, and the views of what constitutes personality differ according to the theorists' views of human nature. We have also noted that the concept of self is designed to represent the organized nature of personality, whereby the various facets of personality are seen as being connected systematically into an organized whole. But the various aspects of the self (such as the material self, the social self, and others described by William James, for instance) are seen as changing from time to time. Therefore, it becomes necessary to account for the continuity and unity of the various "selves." The concept of personal identity is a metatheoretical concept; it implies a Self of selves, as it were, that helps explain the unity, continuity, and selfsameness in man. At this metatheoretical level the issue of personal identity is primarily a philosophical issue. This issue has been discussed by many Indian and Western philosophers, and we shall examine some prominent contributions to this field of study.

Unlike the problem of identity of objects like trees, animals, or stars, the problem of personal identity is not simply a puzzle. It has a distinct psychological aspect. This psychological aspect refers to the experience of continued existence over a period of time, and a sense of having been one and the same person despite diversity in conceptions of oneself and continual changes in them. Erik Erikson has noted that the sense of identity, that is, the sense of continuity and selfsameness, is normally a preconscious rather than conscious experience. Most of us seem to take the diversity in our self-definitions from one situation to another, and the changes in them, in stride, just as we adapt to the changing situations in life. However, under certain circumstances which require a person to face major changes from inside and outside (such as during adolescence, when the society expects a person to change from a child to adult and the body undergoes the radical changes of puberty), the task of gaining and maintaining a sense of selfsameness may not be easy. Erikson has shown with the help of many case studies that the normally unconscious striving for continuity and selfsameness can manifest itself in some youths in the form of conscious yearning for a sense of identity. Erikson's theory of identity formation offers an elaborate description and an insightful analysis of the emotional problems associated with the task of gaining and maintaining a sense of sameness and continuity. He is perhaps the only one among the prominent psychologists today who has addressed himself seriously to the problem of identity. It would therefore be useful to first discuss the psychological aspects of the problem of identity in light of Erik Erikson's theory of identity formation. We shall then turn to the philosophical aspect of the problem in a separate section.

Erik Erikson's Theory of Identity Formation

According to Erikson, "man is, at one and the same time, part of the somatic order of things, as well as a personal and social one" (1968, p. 289). It follows from this view that we must understand the nature of man on three distinct levels: as an organism, in terms of principles of biology; as a social being in terms of sociological principles; and as an organization of experience and behavior as described by theories of personality. From the study of biology we understand that human development is guided by the principle of epigenesis, whereby the body grows according to a ground plan built into the genetic code. The human embryo grows through a successive differentiation of tissues and organs. The pattern of the human life cycle is similarly guided by biological principles so that teething, development of speech, puberty, menopause in the female, decline of sensory capacities in old age, and other such events occur in a sequence. In an analogy of the sequential nature of the biological aspect of maturation, Erikson has proposed that human development proceeds in a series of sequentially ordered stages. Focusing on the psychosocial aspects of personality he suggests that, during the course of development, sensory, motor, and cognitive capacities mature in such a way that individuals become aware of, and are "driven toward," a widening social radius. A second principle guiding the growth of personality arises from the fact that societies tend to develop customs whereby a growing individual is expected to interact with a widening social radius in a sequence that roughly matches the growth pattern of capacities and urges. Experience and behavior of persons, then, is guided by an interaction of biological and social forces.

Erikson proposes eight stages of human development spanning the whole life cycle from birth to old age. It is not necessary for our purposes to examine all the stages in detail. We shall only summarize those aspects that are concerned with the self, with a focus on change and selfsameness.

The social world of a newborn infant is centered around the mother or a mother surrogate on whom the baby must depend for nourishment and support. Having started with a part–whole relationship with the mother prior to birth, the child must gradually become aware of himself as a distinct person. Erikson suggests that in the first stage of development (within the first year or so) the child not only becomes aware of himself as a distinct person, but also begins to develop a mutual, trustful relationship with the mothering individual. The second stage, corresponding to late infancy, is characterized by the development of sensory and motor capacities. The developing capacities enable the child to crawl, stand up, walk, and run. The developing muscles also enable the child to exert voluntary control over the eliminative functions. Parents and others expect the child to be toilet-trained about the same time as its musculature acquires the necessary capacity for voluntary control. Erikson thinks that this period is crucial for the development in the child of a "sense of autonomy" which manifests itself in the child's beginning to "stand on one's own feet" and to resist control by others.

In the third, preschool stage, the child develops cognitive capacities. The child begins to understand words, construct sentences, and to use verbal skills in imagining things. This is a universal age for play and fantasy. The social world of the child widens beyond the family to include playmates. The developing cognitive capacities enable the child to meaningfully recognize various occupational activities of men and women in his vicinity, particularly the routine activities of uniformed persons such as the mailman, nurse, policeman, and so on. Further, the child imitates the activities involved in occupational roles by playing fireman, bus driver and so on in make-believe and play. The child now wants to play doctor or pilot, and wishes to become a teacher, farmer, or the like on becoming an adult. Such anticipation of occupational roles indicates an important step in the development of the self-image which is already developing by the age of four or five. This is the beginning of the child's growing conviction that "I am what I can imagine I will be" (Erikson, 1968, p. 122). Another very important aspect is the development of the ego-ideal. As suggested by Freud, the young boy, awed by the father's power, takes him as an ideal and begins to adopt father's values as his own. This is viewed as the root of the ego-ideal. The disciplining authority of the father, however, often produces as much resentment and hatred as love. The child must learn to resolve the conflicting aspects of his feelings for the father. From the child's own way of resolving this "Oedipus complex" its conscience is formed. Erikson has adopted this Freudian model of the development of character. How far this aspect of the model is cross-culturally applicable is an open question (as noted in Chapter 1). What seems beyond doubt, however, is the observation that the roots of ego-ideal must be traced to early childhood.

During middle childhood or "school age" most societies expect the child to learn the rudiments of technology. While the literate societies make arrangements to teach the child the three R's, preliterate societies usually teach the child some basic skills required for hunting, fishing, farming, or other such means of earning a livelihood. According to Erikson, the child must learn to do various tasks *with* other children and begin to do them *well.* Individual differences begin to appear in the process of learning and the child begins to win recognition for good performance. Depending on the child's relative level of success in learning the expected tasks, the child may develop either an overall "sense of industry" or a "sense of inferiority." The roots of self-esteem can thus be traced back to at least the period of middle childhood, if not earlier.

Adolescence refers to a period of life that marks the transition from childhood to what we call adulthood. This is a period of complex and relatively rapid changes in a number of aspects of personality. It is necessary to examine the nature of personality development during this period rather closely because it is crucial in terms of defining oneself in the social context. It is also important because the maintenance of a sense of inner continuity and sameness becomes difficult for those adolescents who must cope with too many changes in too short a period.

From a biological point of view, childhood ends with the advent of puberty. According to a biological timetable set by the epigenetic principle, a series of biochemical changes are set into the body leading to a spurt in the growth and to the development of secondary sexual characteristics such as pubic and axial hair. The development of the ability to procreate is a clear instance of biologically induced discontinuity in the development of the individual. Coping with the relatively abrupt changes in the body and the newly emerging sexual drive is a difficult task for many adolescents. Social customs sometimes add considerably to the discontinuities of adolescent development. From a sociocultural viewpoint, adolescence involves not only the pubertal transformation of an asexual child to a sexually mature "adult," but also the transition from being an economically dependent and socially non-responsible member of the society to a self-supporting and responsible one. As Ruth Benedict (1938) pointed out decades ago, such transition is fairly continuous in some societies and relatively abrupt in others. The transition can be quite abrupt, for instance, in the case of a girl who is required by society to inhibit her mature sexual urges before marriage but is expected to unlearn all such learned inhibitions suddenly on the wedding night. Among other instances of "discontinuity in cultural conditioning" we may include those young persons who are economically and socially dependent on their parents up to the age of 18 and are suddenly required to start working as full members of the labor force at nineteen with all the responsibilities and privileges of an adult. Such sudden transitions make it difficult for the growing person to reconcile what he or she had been in the past with what he or she is about to become.

The transition from childhood to adulthood is complex irrespective of its relative continuity or discontinuity. Adolescents are faced with an array of "developmental tasks" such as coping with the bodily changes that occur in puberty; the management of increasingly strong sexual urges in conformity with (or in opposition to) the established moral code; choice of, and training in, and occupation one hopes will lead to a promising career; "moving out" of the sphere of parental protection and dominance; finding a partner for life and preparing to raise children of one's own; locating oneself on the social map by finding one's "roots" and sharing a common destiny with a community; and adopting a "view of life" (whether in the form of an implicit or explicit ideology or religion) within which to make sense of one's life. Not all of these tasks are equally important or equally difficult for everyone. There are great variations in the levels of difficulty and degrees of importance attached to the tasks of adolescence from society to society and from one person to another. For instance, the task of choosing an occupation used to be much simpler in the traditional form of Indian society, where the technology offered only a small range of occupations centered around agriculture, and most individuals were assigned by birth to occupations associated with the parents' caste group. By contrast, technologically advanced societies today offer a relatively free choice over a very broad range of occupations. In the latter type of society, occupational choice is more difficult than in the former. Similarly, rapidly changing societies make conventional role models and ideals obsolete fairly quickly and make adolescent development more difficult than in stable societies. Irrespective of such differences across societies, there are individual differences within any given society in the ways of coping with the tasks of adolescent development.

The central task of adolescence is, to use Erikson's phrase, the evolving of a configuration of consistent roles. A configuration of consistent roles may not evolve easily for various reasons. Some individuals find it difficult to choose a way of making a livelihood which is at once challenging and yet within reach, meaningful in terms of values and yet available, providing for adventure and yet not too risky. Landing on the right combination is not always easy. Others may find a way of life satisfactory for one's own needs and values, but this may be unacceptable to a lover, parent, or friend. Some young persons must abandon self images and ideals acquired in childhood as being incompatible with the prospects and possibilities of an anticipated future. Still others are faced with the task of fitting themselves into a culture very different from the one in which they were raised as children. At any rate, those who are unable to settle on a worthwhile and feasible configuration of roles feel confused about the direction of their lives.

Erikson has described a broad range of "symptoms" which are indicative of role confusion among young men and women of late adolescent or early adult stage. The typical symptoms of role confusion are repeated introspection and daydreaming, brooding about the past and the future, inability to concentrate on work, inability to derive satisfaction from work—sometimes despite high levels of success—feeling occasionally worthless and sometimes quite capable and ambitious, inability to start and/or finish routine tasks on time, and, in some cases, a breakdown in the sense of inner sameness and continuity. Although it is quite common to find young persons who experience a few of the symptoms over a brief period of time, it is uncommon to find persons suffering from several such symptoms over a long period of time. Although cases of severe problems in identity formation are relatively rare, a few of such cases have been recorded (see Paranjpe, 1975), and their condition has been called *identity crisis*. Erikson has suggested that the apparently pathological condition called identity crisis is not an affliction (or a "disease"), but a "normative crisis." A normative crisis, like teething or the first menses, is a critical condition conducive to growth, however traumatic it may seem while the individual is suffering through it. Unlike pathological conditions causing a waste of energies, a normative crisis brings sizeable gains in terms of the development of personality.

Fortunately, not every growing person has to face growth pangs leading to such "symptoms," and very few experience difficulties leading to problems major enough to be called a "crisis." Further, even those who seem to experience agonizing confusion over a protracted period of time seem to discover adequate inner resources and/or social supports to sail through the situation and come out with a gain in the form of a sense of identity. Erik Erikson (1956, p. 74) says the following about a developing sense of identity. "An increasing sense of identity . . . is experienced preconsciously as a psycho-social well-being." Its most obvious concomitants are a feeling of "being at home in one's body," a sense of "knowing where one is going," and "an inner assuredness of anticipated recognition from those who count."

It is important to note that a sense of identity is experienced preconsciously. It is not too common for people to ask themselves explicitly the question "Who am I?" Even the odd one who does ask the question "Who am I?" very explicitly is more likely to mean it in a fairly practical rather than a deeply philosophical sense. Thus, upon finding a suitable occupation with a promising career, or a group of friends with whom to share problems and dreams of life, or a leader who gives definite and practical advice on the best course of action for the moment, the young person may say with confidence "I am so and so" and get involved in whatever such a person is supposed to be doing. Once a reasonably satisfying self-definition and a feasible way of life is attained, the young person may not again raise the question "who am I?"—at least not in the way in which it was asked during a typical adolescent stage of confusion.

When we say that a person has acquired a sense of identity it does not mean that he has accepted a certain self-image once and for all. Not even the most crucial self-definitions need be fixed and unchanging to ensure a sense of selfsameness over a long period of time. A sense of identity involves an overall sense of direction, or perhaps a sense of purpose that brings confidence in facing the challenges of life. Erikson puts it very aptly:

> Such a sense of identity is never gained nor maintained once and for all. Like a good conscience, it is constantly lost and regained, although more lasting and more economical methods of maintenance and restoration are evolved and fortified in late adolescence. (Erikson, 1956, p. 74)

What this means perhaps is that, by the time late adolescence arrives, most young persons are able to identify their typical strengths and resources in coping with the challenges of change and growth. They have perhaps tested their strengths in their experiments with life so far so as to feel that, as in the past, a consistent selfhood can be maintained into the future.

Erikson has pointed out that the time for a test of the strength of an individual's sense of identity arrives in early adulthood, in close interpersonal encounters in love and work. He notes that truly mutual personal intimacy in such close relationships as marriage and friendship is possible only after a reasonable sense of identity has been established. Only one who has "found himself" can enter into a deeply personal relationship without fear of being "lost" in the intimate bond. Those who cannot maintain the proper distance between self and others are likely to feel a loss of their independent existence. Also, they may face the danger of isolation due to fear of encroachment by others. While the primary concern of young adulthood is said to be the establishing of identity in bonds of mutual intimacy, the major concern of middle adulthood lies in establishing and guiding the next generation. This concern, technically called generativity, goes far beyond the biological purpose of protection of the young for the survival of the species. It may include, among other things, a striving to contribute to the cultural legacy and to pass on to the younger generation whatever one thinks is worth preserving. One's identity is expressed at this stage in terms of those things within oneself which one would like to see preserved even after one's death in the lives of the younger generation. Finally, in the last stage of the life cycle one may look back, as well as wonder what lies beyond death. Erikson suggests that man, as a psychosocial creature, may experience a renewed identity crisis that might be stated in the words "I am what survives of me" (1968, p. 141).

Having covered the whole range of the life cycle, we now complete our brief and selective account of the Eriksonian perspective on the formation of psychosocial identity. Many questions arise in relation to such a theory. How adequate is the theory as a faithful account of human nature? Does it attach rather diverse meanings to the term identity? How can the theory be tested? Is it cross-culturally applicable? More relevant questions of this nature can be raised, but I shall not try to answer them here since I have discussed these types of issues elsewhere (Paranjpe, 1975). Instead, I shall make a few observations and comments relevant to our purpose.

Erikson's theory of identity offers a descriptive and analytical framework suitable for the study of the entire course of life. It points out how common major concerns of individuals manifest themselves as the pattern of life unfolds from infancy to old age. It leads us to postulate the existence of a central organizing principle of personality that permeates all aspects of personality and unites them into a single whole. In this respect it is somewhat like William James's view of the self. Psychosocial identity as viewed by Erikson goes beyond self-image, self-esteem, ego ideal, roles, and other such aspects of the self, pointing to whatever it is that integrates them all. In particular, Erikson clearly points out that there is a genetic (that is, developmental) continuity of self-representation, and ascribes it to an inner agency, which he calls the ego. Thus, Erikson's theory is concerned with the unity, continuity, and selfsameness of personaltiy. On the basis of his clinical experience and insight he describes the emotional problems that arise when rapid changes and diverse social demands threaten the sense of inner sameness and continuity. But such a theory does not answer an important question: what is it that accounts for the unity, selfsameness, and continuity in personality? This is a philosophical rather than a psychological issue which has been discussed in the Western as well as the Indian philosophical traditions. It would be appropriate to turn to this issue at this point.

What Accounts for the Unity, Continuity, and Sameness in Man?

Body as the Basis of Selfsameness

Common sense attributes the sameness of a person to the continued existence of his body. An important source of my awareness of my continued existence is the continual feedback of kinesthetic and other sensations provided by the body. Undoubtedly the body is an important factor in a person's awareness of his continued existence. Yet, the physical body in itself does not account for the selfsameness of a person. Although we normally refer to a particular physical body when we speak of a person, we do not refer to exactly the same particles of matter when we say that this young man is the same individual I saw as an infant twenty years ago. The body not only grows in size by assimilating food, but the metabolic processes continually replace the material particles that constitute it.

As noted in the previous chapter, we do not speak of persons, animals, or trees remaining the same in the same way in which a piece of rock is said to remain the same. Locke (1823/1963, Vol. 2, p. 50) suggested that the selfsameness of a tree does not lie in the material particles that compose its trunk, bark, and leaves; it is accounted for by the "continuity of insensibly succeeding parts united to the living body of the plant." The treeness of a tree lies in the organic unity of its parts, and in the continuity of its vegetative functions, such as distribution of nutrients from the roots to the leaves, and so on. Locke thus pointed out that the identity or selfsameness of any entity must be associated with the *essential* aspects (*e.g.*, organic unity of parts) rather than *incidental* aspects (particular particles that compose the parts) of that entity. He also pointed out that the issue of selfsameness is intricately connected with those of unity and continuity.

In his *Treatise of Human Nature* (1886/1964, Vol. 1, p. 538), David Hume used a slightly different metaphor to stress the importance of continuity. He pointed out that even a material object like a ship can be said to have remained the same even if all of its parts have been replaced one by one. If I go on replacing parts of my bicycle one-by-one, including the hub, the frame, and every other part, until no single original part is left behind, I can still say that it is the same bicycle. What has remained the same throughout the period is its usefulness toward the same purpose—"for riding upon." The analogy of replacing parts as applied to the human body need not sound very odd in modern times, since transplants of hair, skin, bones, kidneys, and even hearts have become routine operations. We had little difficulty in accepting the proposition that Dr. Christian Barnard's Caucasian patient had remained the same person despite having a Black man's heart ticking in his body. Little wonder, then, that we call it the same body when its material constituents are gradually replaced several times over the life cycle; we can continue using the body for the same old purposes (whatever they may be), despite changes in its phycial composition.

With the rapid advance of the technology for transplanting organs of the human body, even brain transplants are quite likely to be accomplished in the near future. Assuming that the brain is the seat of memories, it is quite likely that Mr. A's body fitted with Mr. B's brain will wake up with B's memories. A strange scenario may be expected to follow. A's body may now recognize Mrs. B as his wife. He may even try to convince her that he is in fact her husband by disclosing the most intimate secrets which she shared only with her husband. Assuming that Mr. B's body is pronounced dead and duly buried, Mr. B's insurer may refuse to settle Mrs. B's claim, arguing that the insured person is in fact alive in the body of Mr. A. We may leave the more dramatic aspects of such a scenario to science fiction and return to the problem of identity.

It is important to recognize that the term identity has two slightly different, but related meanings: (1) the quality or condition of being the same in substance, composition, nature, properties, or particular qualities under consideration; absolute or essential sameness; (2) the condition or fact that a person or thing is itself and not something else (*The Oxford English Dictionary*). The dilemma with regard to insurance involves the problem of identity in the latter, rather than the former sense. The crucial problem in the situation requires the claimant to demonstrate that the dead body is in fact the person insured, and is not somebody else. This aspect of the problem is particularly relevant to the practical social issue of privileges and responsibilities. Thus, when a person wishes to cash a traveler's cheque, he must establish that he is the same person as the one named on the cheque. The prosecution must establish that the accused person is the same individual seen committing the alleged crime by the witness. What is primarily involved here is the identification of persons to ensure that the right privileges are associated with the right persons, and that only persons involved in wrongdoing suffer the consequences. It is in this sense that Locke said that "person" is a *forensic* term. With regard to the former meaning of the term "identity" mentioned above (namely identity as essential sameness), Locke proposed that the essence of a person lies in his memories. He gave the hypothetical example of a prince who once woke up in the body of a cobbler and *vice-versa*. The hypothetical example of switching brains in a transplant operation makes the same point Locke was trying to make with the example of the prince and the cobbler, namely, that memories are more crucial to a person than the physical characteristics or composition of his body. To say the least, man is not simply a body but something more.

The Unity and Sameness of Social Selves

Normally we assume that there is one person associated with each human body. Locke (1823/1963, Vol. 2, p. 59) questioned this assumption and entertained the possibility of finding two distinct persons associated with one and the same body. As noted, Locke was well aware of the vegetative functions that bring about the organic unity of a plant or an animal body. He did not seem to think, however, that the organic unity of the human body would guarantee the unity of personality. His doubts are perhaps well founded; it looks as though his thinking was in the right direction.

R. L. Stevenson (1922) gave an excellent fictional example of two persons in one body in his well-known novel, *The Strange Case of Dr. Jekyll and Mr. Hyde.* But the phenomenon of "split personality" is not purely a product of the creative imaginations of authors like Stevenson, nor of mere speculation by philosophers like Locke. Psychologists have recorded lving examples of multiple personalities (*e.g.*, Lipton, 1943; Prince, 1905; Thigpen and Cleckley, 1954). There seems to be no particular reason to believe that the dissociation of personality at the psychological level, as seen in the cases of multiple personality, from a lack of integration of bodily functions. Integration of personality at the psychosocial level has perhaps little to do with the organic integration at the bodily level (although it is possible to hypothesize that dissociation of personality results from a kind of brain dysfunction). Fortunately, organs like the heart, the lung, and the kidneys carry on their specialized functions without splitting the individual. Even the bilateral hemispheres of the brain, presumably capable of functioning independently of one another, do not compete to split the personality into two.[1] The various "social selves," however, often conflict with one another so as to threaten the unity of personality.

Simultaneous role demands are a common source of intra-personal conflict. The need to attend to a family obligation such as looking after a sick child during office hours is a simple example of an occasional role conflict; high involvement in community activities at the cost of family life is a common example of a persistent source of conflict. There are numerous ways of resolving such conflicts, such as postponing some obligations, taking a leave from work, ordering priorities in consultation with concerned others, and so on. Under persistent cross-pressures some persons compartmentalize life and begin to act like different people in different situations. For example, a person may be an assertive and aggressive army general while at work, and a meek, "henpecked" husband at home; another person may be a pious churchgoer on weekends and an unscrupulous businessman on weekdays. It is also possible to find some whose personalities are "split" as a consequence of divided loyalties. A bigamist, or a double agent would be examples of people who may land in deep trouble or be deeply tormented as a result of conflicting interests. All these are examples of extreme situations leading to major problems. There are innumerable cases, however, where the unity of personality is threatened to some degree as a result of role conflicts. The very nature of social existence requires us to adopt multiple roles, and these different roles require us to develop distinct patterns of behavior suitable to each one of them. Internal consistency and unity of personality is, therefore, bound to be a matter of degree rather than an all-or-nothing phenomenon.

We need to consider the social aspect of personality in some more detail in order to understand and appreciate its significance for an individual's sense of selfsameness and continuity. An individual's deep emotional involvement with others and his identification with the shared goals and ideals of his groups is a bond that unites him with the community to which he belongs. From a social viewpoint a person is the same as the statuses and roles with which he chooses to identify himself. On the one hand, the groups owe their very existence to the identification of individuals with shared values and goals, and, on the other hand, the individual derives from the groups indispensable support for his sense of sameness and continuity. Take, for instance, two friends who meet each other after a gap of a couple of decades. Both of them must have changed in their physical appearance, in terms of social status, self-image and in many other respects. Yet, they may recognize each other and continue to share warm, friendly relations that bolster their sense of belonging to a clique of lifelong friends. Larger groups and communities such as religious or national groups also offer an individual valuable sources of support for the individual's sense of identity. They may offer him a set of ideals that make his life meaningful; accomplishments of the great men of the group may give him something to feel proud of; their glorious tradition may give him a sense of continuity between the events in his life history and those in the history of the community; and the hope for a utopian future may give him a sense of security. Lack of such support would result in a painful sense of isolation, loneliness, uprootedness, alienation, or *anomie*.

Notwithstanding the many claims that the contemporary period of history is an era of alienation of man from his fellow man, it is clear that the vast majority of mankind feels strongly identified with smaller or larger sections of the society. We have noted earlier Erik Erikson's observation that the growing individual is driven toward, and comes to an effective encounter with, a widening social radius. Over the years an individual begins to be aware of, and to identify himself with his family, kin, neighborhood, region, class, race, nation and humanity. For a great many people, the family is the closest ingroup, demanding a great investment of time and energy and commanding a high degree of loyalty. During the process of development of his personality every individual acquires his own pattern of identification with groups. While some individuals identify most closely with the family alone, others may consider an allegiance to either religion, race, nation, or class as the most important thing in their lives. Although concentric loyalties rarely clash, occasions arise when a larger group demands sacrificial loyalty at the cost of allegiance to a smaller group, for example an appeal to join the army in a national crisis at a time when an expectant wife demands close attention, or an appeal to guard regional interests at the risk of national unity. If faced with such conflicts, some individuals may tend to be parochial, while others may opt for a more inclusive view. It should be clear that, by-and-large, there has been a predominance of parochial loyalties throughout the history of the world. If this were not so, the universal brotherhood of mankind would not be a utopian vision, but a reality.

During the socialization process an individual begins to identify categories of people—those who belong to certain region(s), religion(s), class(es) and so on—as *his* kind of people. He develops varying degrees of positive affect toward those who belong to these categories. Very often, as an individual's affinity for his ingroup is either high or low irrespective of the level of his acquaintance with, or knowledge about them. The groups with which a person identifies himself define the "boundaries" of his social self, as it were. Beyond these boundaries are the categories of people about whom the person may be affectively neutral or negative. The sociologist Sumner (1906/1960) observed that there is a common tendency among people to love and be loyal to one's "ingroups" and feel inimical toward "outgroups." (The Vedāntic philosopher Vidyāraṇya made the same observation back in the 14th century.)[2] Sumner called this tendency "ethnocentrism" and modern social scientists have studied it extensively (Adorno *et al.*, 1950; LeVine and Campbell, 1972). An ethnocentric person tends to define himself as the enemy of such and such, as anti-this race, or a crusader against that religion. Strange as it may seem, the persistently negative attitudes of an ethnocentric person have a functional value in maintaining the structure of his personality. Thus, an ethnocentric person may derive a sense of sameness and continuity from this persistent hatred of outgroups in much the same way as another person who loves his own group (without hating aliens) may derive a sense of continuity from being attached to his group.

For some persons love for the ingroup and hatred for the outgroups become far more than just the basis for their sense of sameness and continuity; allegiance and loyalty to the group become the highest values in their lives. Such persons are often willing to sacrifice their lives for their country, race, or religion. The history of civilization is full of examples of fanatical leaders who teach their followers that they are God's chosen people, destined to rule the world, and lead them into holy wars to annihilate the aliens. Such examples represent a sinister and unfortunate aspect of man's social existence. Although identification with groups is mostly inevitable, usually necessary, and sometimes even ennobling, it is true that, for a majority of people, group-belonging is a force that binds the self to a narrow sphere. The boundaries of ingroups cannot be easily extended; persons who truly belong to the whole of humanity are extremely rare.

Whatever be the boundaries of the ingroups and outgroups by which one chooses to define his own view of the world, such boundaries cannot be defined and retained once and for all. In the realm of interpersonal relationships, friendships sometimes turn sour and former enemies sometimes become valuable allies. Similarly, an individual's orientation toward groups may change drastically. For various reasons a favored ingroup may turn into a hated enemy block, as has happened with some ex-Communists who have undergone an ideological conversion and become crusaders against communism. Moreover, it is not impossible to find persons who get fed up with the entire society, "drop out" of the world into an isolated corner (like some of the Indian "saṁnyāsin"s), and live the life of a recluse without necessarily losing a sense of unity and continuity as an individual human being. It is obvious from such examples that, notwithstanding the important role played by group "belongingness" in the maintenance of a sense of selfsameness and continuity among many individuals, solidarity with a group (or a set of ingroups) is neither the only nor an indispensable basis for personal identity. It is necessary to conclude therefore, that there is something at the basis of the selfsameness and continuity of an individual which lies beyond the social aspect of his personality.

Some Cognitive Aspects of the Self: Self Image and Self-Definition

If we ask people to write some twenty different answers to the question "Who am I?" it is common to get the following type of responses:[3]

> I am a Canadian of Italian origin. I am an ambitious young man in my early twenties. I am no longer as dreamy and timid as I once used to be. I am madly in love with a girl whom I hope to marry. After becoming established as a lawyer, I would like to get involved in politics and try to preserve the unity of Canada as a nation. I am a pro-socialist intending to fight against liberal and *laissez-faire* policies of other parties in the coming election. I am a moral conservative strongly opposed to those who demand permissive laws allowing easy abortion . . .

Such a description gives us a good idea of the kind of self-image the young man carries in his "head." It refers to abandoned images of himself (dreamy, timid) and to his anticipated selves (husband, established lawyer). It also provides an example of how an individual defines himself by taking a stand on social, economic, and moral issues like the unity of a nation, rightist or leftist economic policies, the liberalizing of abortion, and so on. Some social psychologists define the self as a set of attitudes. It makes sense to do so given the background of the young man described above. His attitudes are based upon his understanding of his personal characteristics and on his beliefs about the nature of social issues (the cognitive component of attitudes). They reflect his likes and dislikes and also tell us about his preferred course of action (affective and behavioral components of attitudes). Such a set of attitudes provides a relatively internally-consistent framework for his actions and thus partially accounts for the unity of his personality. But his self image, along with his self-defining attitudes must obviously be subject to change from time to time. Although attitudes and beliefs are relatively persistent, they are not fixed or unchanging.

Given the changing nature of social issues and the revisable nature of attitudes and opinions, we can in no way think of the selfsameness of a person in terms of the content of his attitudes. It is sometimes suggested that the structure of attitudes, or the style of a person in dealing with attitude change (rigid, flexible, pragmatic, gullible, and so on) may be more persistent than particular attitudes as such. It is perhaps true that individuals can be identified by unique stylistic features of their thinking and behavior. But it is difficult and perhaps impossible to find specific stylistic features that remain unchanged throughout the life cycle—like the unique pattern of one's finger print, that remains the same through the entire span of life. Also, stylistic features of personality are not as easily defined or clearly identifiable as finger prints are. Although "traits" of personality or other stylistic features of personality indicate some underlying basis for the sameness and continuity of personality, they hardly account for personal identity.

To sum up the discussion of the previous pages, it may be concluded that all the aspects of personality considered so far, namely the body, social selves, and cognitive elements such as self images and attitudes, are involved in continual change. After closely examining the various "selves" William James arrived at the following conclusion: "Thus the identity found by the *I* in its *me* is only a loosely construed thing, an identity 'on the whole', just like that which any outside observer might find in the same assemblage of facts" (James, 1890/1950, Vol. 1, p. 372). The Vedāntists follow a similar logic in implicitly accepting the unity of a person as jīva, but not beyond. We may recall that the five sheaths of the jīva which closely correspond with different aspects of the self mentioned above are considered in Vedānta to be impermanent or continually changing. Since it is impossible to identify a basis for the sameness and continuity of personality in the physical, social, and cognitive aspects, Vedāntist as well as some Western thinkers have tried to locate a basis for personal identity outside the range of the physical, social and cognitive aspects of personality. Erikson, for instance, suggests that "there is more to man's core than identity, . . . there is in fact in each individual an 'I', an observing center of awareness which can transcend and must survive the psychosocial identity . . ." (Erikson, 1968, p. 135).

While we all have at our very cores a center of awareness, it is too close for us to understand and appreciate its nature and significance. It is not easy to clarify the concept of the center of awareness. So let me borrow once again a few lines from Erikson, who has put it very aptly.

> What the "I" reflects on when it sees or contemplates the body, the personality, and the roles to which it is attached for life—not knowing where it was before or will be after—are the various selves which make up our composite Self. There are constant and often shocklike transitions between these selves: consider the nude body self in the dark or suddenly exposed in the light; consider the clothed self among friends or in the company of higher-ups or lower-downs; consider the just awakened drowsy self or the one stepping refreshed out of the surf or the one overcome by retching and fainting; the body self in sexual excitement or in a rage; the competent self and the impotent one; the one on horseback, the one in the dentist's chair, and the one chained and tortured—by men who also say "I." (Erikson, 1968, p. 217)

Although all of us go through such shocklike transitions, there is a continuity in our experience. The "I," as the very seat of all experiences, appears to remain the same throughout the span of our lives. The obvious thrust of these observations is that the basis for selfsameness of the "I" must be located not in the objectively observable and tangible aspects of personality, but in the subjective aspect of life. This issue has been examined by several Indian and Western thinkers. Let us now turn to a brief account of some of their views.

The Unity and Continuity of the Stream of Consciousness: Self as Knower

In Chapter 3 we acquainted ourselves with William James's concept of the stream of consciousness and its Indian equivalent, namely Vyāsa's view of the cittanadī. We may recall that these concepts refer to the continuous succession of mental events or processes of consciousness such as seeing and hearing, remembering and anticipating, wishing and deciding, loving and hating, doubting and reasoning, and all other similar activities of the mind. William James proposed the word Thought (with a capital "T") as a generic term representing a mental event of any of these types. The Yogic term vṛtti is almost an exact equivalent of this concept. As noted by James, each Thought, or each "pulse of cognitive consciousness" dies away quickly to be followed by another, and yet another, and so on. Despite the eternal flux of changing Thoughts, the innumerable and diverse thoughts seem to be "owned" by one and the same Thinker. Yoga, as we have seen, similarly conceives of a Seer (draṣṭṛ) who is considered to be a selfsame "owner" (prabhu) of the citta-vṛttis. A common problem for the Indian and Western thinkers has been: how to explain the unity underlying the diversity of Thoughts, and the selfsameness and continuity of a Thinker who is embroiled in incessant change.

In his classic chapter on the self, William James identified the following three theories as the important historical attempts (among a multitude of others) to explain the unity, selfsameness, and continuity of the Thinker or the Self as Knower: (1) the spiritualist theory of philosophers like Descartes, which considers the self as a substance, (2) the associationist theory of Hume and others, which assigns the unity of the stream of thoughts to the principles of association of ideas, and (3) the transcendentalist theory of Kant. We shall briefly examine these three Western theories with reference to related ideas from Yoga and Vedānta, and then consider James's own conclusions in light of the Indian perspectives on the same issue.

Self as Substance

The concept of substance has acquired different meanings and implications in the history of Western thought. To Aristotle a substance was something real as opposed to something which was mere appearance. It has also meant the essence of a thing as opposed to its inessential characteristics. For Descartes, a substance meant a ground or a substrate in which properties could inhere. He considered the soul to be a substance of which thinking was a natural property. The soul, as the substrate of thoughts, was considered to be a fixed or unchanging base which allows various thoughts to come and go just as the "substance" which we call water remains the same despite the differences in its properties in its gaseous, liquid, and solid forms. For Descartes, there were other considerations that led to the assumption of a permanent soul. Unless the soul was considered immortal, there would be no basis for God to give every man his due on the Day of Judgment.

No contemporary psychologists are likely to be favorably disposed to such notions as immortality, or a "thinking substance" in which thoughts "inhere." The common criticisms of a concept like "thinking substance" are well-known. First, it is simply a verbal device that explains away the selfsameness of a Thinker by imagining a hypothetical entity, and by giving it a label. Also, as pointed out by James (1890/1950, Vol. 1, p. 347), those who postulate a spiritual substance "do not deduce any of the properties of the mental life from otherwise known properties of the soul." Moreover, thinking is considered a process associated with the working of a brain rather than a product emanating from a thinking substance. In fact all these criticisms of the spiritualist theories are well-known and widely accepted. Why, then, was it necessary to mention such an obsolete theory here?

The reason for mentioning it is simple. As in the case of the concept of the soul, the concepts of Puruṣa and Ātman have philosophical and "religious" backgrounds and have been closely associated with the idea of immortality. Moreover, as in the West, the notion of immortality in India arose at least partly from the hope of establishing a just system of rewards and punishments. So the Indian concepts, too, are likely to be viewed as vulnerable to the same kinds of criticism that are leveled against the Western concept of a spiritual substance. I must point out, though, that neither the Yogic Puruṣa nor the Ātman of Vedānta are conceived of as thinking substances. The Yoga theory does make a distinction between properties (dharma) and their substrate (dharmin) in a way similar to Descartes. Yet, this Yogic distinction applies to material objects in the world of Prakṛti and not to the nonmaterial domain of the Puruṣas. Thoughts in the Jamesian sense, that is, the vṛttis, are thought to be activities of the citta in Yoga and of the "inner instrument" (antaḥkaraṇa) in Vedānta. If, as James thought (and as most modern psychologists tend to believe), thinking is made possible by the activity of the brain, the Vedāntic view of thoughts as activities of the inner instrument is much closer to the modern perspective than the Cartesian view of the soul. According to Descartes, the soul was a nonmaterial substance in which thoughts seem to mysteriously appear and disappear. By contrast, the inner instrument of Vedānta is considered inert (jaḍa) or material rather than nonmaterial, just as the Yogic citta is considered part of the material domain, Prakṛti. Also, thoughts are implicitly believed to appear and disappear as dictated by the Law of Karma, and not in a mysterious and unpredictable fashion.

I must add that the concepts of Puruṣa and Ātman are not mere labels or fictions of imagination with no verifiable properties. The nature of Ātman, as noted, is considered blissful, and it is claimed that its blissfulness can actually be experienced in the Fourth State of consciousness. The Vedānta theory derives properties of mental life from the stated properties of the Ātman. Thus, it is said that those who experience the Self as Ātman in the Fourth State of consciousness manifest the highest degree of desirelessness and equanimity of temperament. This proposition is verifiable in two ways. First, as was seen before, specified steps are to be taken to attain such an experience. Second, examples of living persons who have realized the Self have been recorded over the centuries. Thus, although the terms Puruṣa and Ātman are sometimes translated as "soul," they are different in their theoretical status and are not subject to the same type of criticisms as the concept of the soul. We shall consider the Yogic and Vedāntic concepts in some detail towards the end of this chapter.

In the Indian tradition the theological and moral considerations did not hamper speculative philosophy as they did in the West. As noted before, speculative philosophy in the West began to blossom without the burden of the theological constraints after the end of the "dark age." It would be useful to examine some important ideas relating to personal identity expressed by Locke who began the escape from the grip of theological assumptions. Locke shifted his attention from the Cartesian view of the soul as an immortal substance and speculated on what may be considered the most essential aspect of man. As we have already noted, he thought of memories as the essence of individuality and gave the hypothetical example of the prince waking up as a cobbler to illustrate his point. Locke's point is well taken. Memories must be considered as indispensable aid for the continuity of experience as a person. The importance of memories is best illustrated by a pathological condition called the *amnesic fugue* in which an individual forgets his name, his place of residence, his occupation, relatives, and so on, and lands in a hospital or a police station where someone else must find out who he is. What is lost in such conditions is not memory of words and skills learned in the past, and so on, but the memory of all the interpersonal associations that bind one to a social niche. Such cases involve a selective loss of memory and illustrate the role of memories in personal identity. The maintenance of a sense of selfsameness is impossible without the help of memories of the past.

Studies of amnesic fugue (*e.g.*, Abeles and Schilder, 1935) indicate that the loss of personal identity is usually temporary. It lasts no more than a few months in the most severe cases. A plausible explanation of such a condition is that it is a functional disorder that allows a person to temporarily retreat from the pressing emotional problems of life. The relative rarity of amnesic fugue states and their short-lived nature indicate the overall reliability of the human capacity to retain memories and thus maintain continuity in the images of the self. In pointing out the role of memories in personal identity, William James (1890/1950, Vol. 1, p. 372) remarked, "However different the man may be from the youth, both look back on the same childhood, and call it their own." The continuity in the images of the self is made possible by stored memories of the past just as the stream of consciousness derives its continuity from memories. The role of memories in the continuity of personality is accepted without doubt by most Indian as well as Western thinkers. But, we may ask, do memories account for the unity and selfsameness of personality? Do they represent the "essence" of man? It is difficult to say whether memories constitute the essence of man, but it is clear that they do *not* constitute an unchanging element of personality and thus do not form a firm basis for its selfsameness. Taken together, memories form something like a storehouse that is continually "filled" with new impressions and is continually "depleted" as some of the past events are forgotten. One still remembers the abandoned convictions and self-images of the past which are no longer associated with the present "I." While the memories provide a link between the past, present, and future images of the self, the process of remembering cannot account for either their integration or unity.

Humean Associationism: Unity versus Diversity

David Hume followed the footsteps of Locke in emphasizing the role of continuity in understanding the identity of objects. Thus, a ship can be said to remain the same (as a means to ferry you across the river) although its boards may be replaced piece by piece over the years. While the analogy of changing parts of a ship would make sense when we think of the changing composition of the physical body, would the same analogy be applicable in considering the selfsameness of a person as seen from a subjective viewpoint? In resolving this issue Hume adopted his typical empiricist viewpoint, that is, he tried to seek an answer based strictly on experience. Upon examining his own experience he arrived at the following conclusion:

> For my part, when I enter most intimately into what I call *myself* I always stumble on some particular perception or other, of heat or cold, light or shade, love or hatred, pain or pleasure. I never can catch *myself* at any time without a perception, and never can observe anything but the percep-

> tion . . . I may venture to affirm of the rest of mankind, that they . . . are nothing but a bundle or collection of different perceptions, which succeed each other with an inconceivable rapidity, and are in a perpetual flux and movement. (Hume, 1886/1964, Vol. 1, p. 534)

These oft-quoted words constitute an important part of the original statement of Hume's famous "bundle theory" of the mind. If one takes the cognitive states of consciousness as the only source of valid knowledge, one is bound to think of the mind as something that is identified with a different idea or a perception (*e.g.*, James's "Thought" or pulse of cognitive consciousness) at each moment in time. Yet, the diverse ideas that follow one another in succession cannot be considered a chaotic hodge podge. There must be something, after all, that ties the different perceptions or ideas (however loosely) into a bundle. Not just any idea can follow another idea, there must be some system whereby every idea that appears in the stream of consciousness is meaningfully related to the preceding and following ideas. By way of a solution to this problem Hume suggested the laws of association of ideas according to which ideas which were originally connected by similarity (snow and paper, both white), contiguity (flower and butterfly), or in succession (rock throwing and glass breaking) tend to follow one another in the stream of consciousness. The laws of association are considered to be the only bond that joins together the diverse ideas which pass through the stream of consciousness.

The associationist glue provides but a weak bond for the unification of the thoughts in our minds. Although the associationist principles help explain some clustering of ideas, they are hardly adequate for providing a reasonable account of the unity of personality. James rightly criticized the Humean view of the self as "nothing but Diversity, diversity abstract and absolute" (1890/1950, Vol. 1, p. 352). As a matter of fact, Hume himself was far from satisfied with his own solution to the problem of unity and selfsameness of personality. In the appendix to his *Treatise of Human Nature* Hume wrote, "But upon a more strict review of the section concerning *personal identity* I find myself involv'd in such a labyrinth, that, I must confess, I neither know how to correct my former opinions, nor how to render them consistent." (Hume, 1886/1965, Vol. 1, p. 558).

The legacy of Hume still looms large on the scene of contemporary psychology. Many contemporary psychologists who consider themselves empiricists are heirs to the Humean tradition. The empiricist viewpoint today is characterized not only by the Humean insistence that direct observation is the only source of valid knowledge, but also by the Humean scepticism about the problem of unity of personality, and by his "bundle" theory of the mind. Most behaviorists, for instance, follow

Hume in viewing man as simply a series of diverse responses emitted according to the laws of learning (which are a modified version of Hume's laws of association). A number of contemporary psychologists keep away from the Humean labyrinth by entirely avoiding the issue of the unity and selfsameness of personality. But avoiding a problem does not take us closer to its solution.

Kant's Idea of the Transcendental Ego

When Humean empiricism culminated into hopeless scepticism, Kant tried to remedy the situation. While he agreed with the empiricist thesis that all knowledge orginates in experience, he did not accept Hume's view of the mind as a blank slate on which ideas are inscribed by the senses. He conceived of a more active role of the mind in the form of some kind of organizing activity that would pattern the chaotic sensory input so as to make some sense of it. It does not make sense to speak of knowledge unless we grant that there is some *one* that tries to relate himself to the many things in the world. Kant pointed out clearly the inevitable necessity for assuming the unity of the Self as Knower. In his *Critique of Pure Reason* Kant (1781/1966) said:

> During the whole time, while I am conscious of myself, I am conscious of that time as belonging to the unity of myself . . . The identity of my consciousness at different times is therefore a formal condition only of my thoughts and their coherence (p. 259).
>
> For in what we call soul there is a continuous flux, and nothing . . . permanent, except it may be . . . the simple *I* . . . This I or Ego would have to be an intuition, which, being presupposed in all thought (before all experience), might as an intuition *a priori* supply synthetic propositions, if it should be possible to gain any knowledge by pure reason of a thinking being in general (p. 269).

It is important to note that, like all *"a priori"* categories of the mind, the unity of the Self as Knower is purely an assumption accepted as a logical necessity. It is considered an inevitable assumption because, unless we grant such an assumption, we would have to reject the very possibility of knowledge—which is absurd. It is a rational principle without any objectively verifiable basis. Kant's "Pure Ego" is transcendental in the sense of being beyond experience; direct knowledge of Self as subject is considered impossible. William James (1890/1950, Vol. 1, p. 365) rightly pointed out the emptiness of Kant's concept of the Pure Ego and remarked that Kant's Ego is "simply nothing." James also criticized Kant for the ambiguity in his formulation arising from the notion of the Ego as a *condition* for all knowledge on the one hand, and from the implicit view of the Ego as an *agent* who unifies thoughts, on the other hand.

William James's View of Personal Identity

We have noted some of James's criticisms of the Spiritualist, Associationist, and Transcendentalist theories which he had chosen to evaluate as the most important perspectives on the nature of the Pure Ego or the inner principle of the unity and selfsameness of the *I*. Toward the end of his brilliant discussion of these theories, James rejected all of them as inadequate and seemed to be headed for a broad, integrative theory of his own. But, alas, his grand conclusion was summed up in a single sentence: "We may sum up," said James (1890/1950, Vol. 1, p. 371), "by saying that personality implies the incessant presence of two elements, an objective person, known by a passing subjective Thought and recognized as continuing in time." In other words, all that James recognized as a definite conclusion is the two aspects of the self, namely, the self as subject or Knower and the self as whatever is objectively known about him. This conclusion simply asserts the subject-object dichotomy or the "intentional," directed nature of our consciousness. Whatever happened to James's search for a single, selfsame Thinker which he had set out to find in the middle of the diverse Thoughts of the stream of consciousness? Having first made a sharp distinction between the Thinker and his Thought, James finally concluded that such a distinction is unnecessary and that the passing Thought itself must be considered as the Thinker. To quote James's own words:

> For my own part I confess that the moment I become metaphysical and try to define the more, I find the notion of some sort of an *anima mundi* thinking in all of us to be a more promising hypothesis. . .Meanwhile, as *psychologists*, we need not be metaphysical at all. The phenomena are enough, the passing thought itself is the only *verifiable* thinker, and its empirical connection with the brain process is the ultimate known law. (James, 1890/1950, Vol. 1, p. 346. Emphasis original.)

If the passing Thought is supposed to be the only Thinker, then the issue of the unity and selfsameness of the Thinker certainly remains unresolved—in the Jamesian view of psychology, that is. The passing Thought is obviously the most rapidly changing aspect of our subjective life. James's Thinker simply disappears in the mist of the eternal flux of our minds. James, who had criticized Hume for "pouring out the child with the bath" (1890/1950, Vol. 1, p. 352), thus loses himself in the Humean labyrinth. Why did the good James fall into this trap? A couple of answers suggest themselves. First, James was fairly convinced by the

Kantian arguments for a need to assume a selfsame, transcendental Thinker as a basis for the very possibility of knowledge. But he was concerned about the verifiability of the Pure Ego, and it is true that no empirical verification of a transcendental Self is possible unless the continual fluctuations in the thought process are brought to a standstill. Although his later writing (*The Varieties of Religious Experience,* 1902/1958) indicates that James had some knowledge about the "mystical" experiences of Indian Yogis and Vedāntist philosophers, he may not have been aware of the Yogic claim that the direct experience of a selfsame thinker (draṣṭṛ) is possible upon controlling the incessant flow of thoughts in the stream of consciousness. A second reason for his rather abrupt conclusion against the Kantian Pure Ego seems to be his enthusiasm for keeping away from the metaphysical roots of psychology and his eagerness to get on with the business of making psychology a natural science. His interest in the more abstract and subjective aspects of psychology tilted in favor of the newly advancing knowledge of the "brain processes." Along with his conclusions against the method of introspection, this is another example of the powerful effect of the zeitgeist.

Some Directions since William James

Since William James, psychological thinking in the Anglo-American part of the world has been dominated by positivist and empiricist views. The popularity of the behaviorist perspective reflects this trend. Within the behaviorist circles the self was a non-issue just as consciousness was. Although psychologists like Rogers, social psychologists like Muzafer Sherif, and the symbolic interactionists in sociology developed theories of the self, Erik Erikson was perhaps the only one who considered the unity, continuity and selfsameness in personality a crucial issue. In Europe, however, the phenomenologists and existentialists like Husserl and Sartre wrote about this issue. Their views need to be considered at least briefly. Two other trends can also be recognized. One follows the analytical approach of Wittgenstein (1958) which focuses on analyzing what we *mean* when we say "the same person" in common language, and a second trend is concerned with the unity of consciousness in relation to the neurophysiology of the bisected or "split" brain (See Vesey, 1974; Perry, 1975). Since I find these trends too divergent in style and purpose from the Indian perspectives, I shall restrict myself to some views of Husserl and Sartre.

It is impossible to do justice to all the nuances and richness of the writings of Husserl and Sartre (e.g., Husserl, 1933; Sartre, 1936–37/1957) in the limited space available here. I would therefore further restrict this discussion to pointing out a few salient features of their approaches, and to highlighting those aspects that either resemble closely or contrast sharply with the Indian perspectives.

As is well known, Husserl followed Brentano in considering consciousness as always being directed to something. Thus, consciousness is always bipolar, the intending subject being always related to an intended object. Husserl thought of the Ego as an identical pole of all intentional experience. To me what this means is that the Ego is conceived of as the selfsame subject who relates himself to various intended objects one after another. Husserl asserts that the ego is not an empty pole. Although the intentional acts or processes of consciousness such as judging, deciding, willing, and so on vanish quickly, their consequences persist. Thus, the act of deciding may last only for a moment, but a decision once made can last for years—like a firmly held conviction, for instance. The ego thus acquires an abiding property: ". . . from now on I am abidingly the Ego who is thus and so decided." (Husserl, 1933/1977, p. 66). Husserl was certainly aware that we do not make decisions only once and stick to them forever. Our decisions and convictions, like our attitudes and opinions, are only relatively enduring. It is of course true that the process of judging, doubting, repudiating earlier decisions, making new decisions and so on continues in a series of intentional acts. While Kant implied that the transcendental ego was an agent of such acts, Husserl asserted that the ego is not a process or continuity of processes. The ego, he said, "constitutes himself as identical substrate of Ego-properties." Despite alterations in his convictions, the ego manifests "an abiding *style* with a unity of identity throughout all of them: a 'personal character'." (Husserl, 1933/1977, p. 67, emphasis added)

Erikson (1968, p. 50) was thinking along basically the same lines as Husserl when he said that in its subjective aspect ego identity manifests as "the awareness of the fact that there is a selfsameness and continuity to the ego's *synthesizing methods*" (emphasis added). What Erikson means by *synthesis* here is the integration of the present self-images with those abandoned in the past or anticipated for the future. He sees the ego as an organizing agency which tests, selects, and integrates the self-images that are acquired in the course of life (Erikson, 1968, pp. 210–211). Erikson suggests that the sameness of the ego's synthesizing *methods* can be identified in the form of the "style of one's individuality" (1968, p. 50). The similarity between Husserl's and Erikson's views should now be obvious.

Here it is necessary to repeat what I have said before. The problem in considering stylistic features of personality as the basis of selfsameness and continuity in man is twofold: first, it is very difficult to identify or precisely define the "style of one's individuality," and second, what may appear as an enduring stylistic feature (such as the "trait" of boldness, or a style in vocal expression, handwriting, or whatever) may change over a long period of time. While stylistic features of personality are an important aid in identifying a person across space and time, to consider them the basis for selfsameness is to provide a shaky foundation for personal identity.

In his book, *The Transcendence of the Ego*, Sartre (1936–37/1957) criticized the views of Kant as well as those of Husserl. He considered Kant's arguments about the need to postulate an "I" as a condition for the possibility of coherent thought as an insufficient proof for its existence. He would consider such a postulate valid only if based on a direct intuition of the I. He noted that there is no experience of an "I" in spontaneous, unreflective experiences such as the moments when we are involved in contemplating a portrait. In moments of reflective consciousness, the "I" could only be an object of consciousness. Thus, there is no place for the Kantian Self *as Knower* in either reflective or unreflective consciousness according to Sartre's way of thinking. Moreover, he rejects Husserl's view of the ego as a substrate for the unity of consciousness and the view of the "I" as a synthesizing agency that unifies diverse thoughts. If Sartre insists that the ego cannot be considered either as a condition for the unity of consciousness, or as a unifying force of any kind, what role does he grant the ego in his theoretical scheme?

To be able to understand Sartre's view about the ego we must understand the major concern of life as he saw it. To Sartre (1936–37/1957, p. 99) the ceaseless and spontaneous emergence of thoughts in the stream of consciousness was like a "tireless creation of existence of which *we* are not the creators." He notes, to his distress, that ". . . if I *will* to fall asleep, I stay awake; if I *will* not to think of this or that, I think about it *precisely on that account*" (Sartre 1936–37/1957, p. 99). Sartre thus finds himself helpless in coming to grips with this problem of gaining control over one's own state of consciousness. (We have come across this view of Sartre in the excerpt from his novel *Nausea* quoted in Chapter 2.) In *The Transcendence of the Ego*, Sartre describes the "fatality" of the spontaneous flow of thoughts as an anguish, a "dread, absolute and without remedy" (1936–37/1957, p. 102). The ego, according to him, plays a practical role in dealing with this pressing problem of existence. He says: "perhaps the essential role of the ego is to mask from consciousness its very spontaneity" (p. 100).

I am not quite sure what Sartre means by the ego's role in "masking from consciousness its spontaneity." Sartre is by no means easy to understand; one often stumbles over very enigmatic statements while reading his works. Take, for instance, the following sentences in his *Transcendence of the Ego* (Sartre, 1936–37/1957, p. 38) which he writes while criticizing Husserl's view of the ego:

> Now, it is certain that phenomenology does not need to appeal to any such unifying and individualizing *I*. Indeed, consciousness is defined by intentionality. By intentionality consciousness transcends itself. It unifies itself by escaping from itself.

What Sartre perhaps means is that a human being can perceive himself as one object because of his ability to reflect upon the past and future and combine various forms of the *me* as manifestations of one common object. (In drawing this conclusion Sartre resembles James in his approach to the problem of the unity of the self.) Sartre's conclusions become more confusing, however, when he remarks, toward the end of his *Transcendence of the Ego* (Sartre, 1936–37/1957, p. 105), that "It is enough that the *me* be contemporaneous with the World, and that the subject–object duality, which is purely logical, definitively disappear from philosophical preoccupations."

The subject–object dichotomy cannot be dismissed so easily, at least not by someone like Sartre who is committed to the doctrine of intentionality. If intentionality means the directedness of thought, it should be clearly understood that the subject of thoughts (or the underlying "Thinker") must be distinguished from the objects toward which the thoughts are directed. If the intentionality of consciousness is an inescapable fact of life (as Sartre himself seems to believe), then the duality of subject and object can hardly be dismissed as a figment of imagination created by logicians or grammarians for their convenience.

Since a thorough critique of Sartre's views is not possible within the confines of this book, I would rather restrict my comments to certain observations regarding his approach that point to interesting similarities and differences when compared with the Indian views. Note that Sartre does not treat the problem of the ego as a mere puzzle. Although he provides long arguments refuting the views of other philosophers, as is commonly done when writing on philosophical issues; his primary concern is not so much the theoretical solution to the paradox of identity, but the practical concern about how to deal with the runaway spontaneity of the stream of consciousness. In considering the need to deal effectively with one's stream of consciousness and in recognizing the anguish in being tossed endlessly by the constant downpour of new thoughts emerging from somewhere at all times, Sartre's approach is strikingly similar to that of Yoga. However, Sartre's mode of dealing with this common problem is quite different from that of Yoga in both theory and practice.

On the theoretical plane, while Sartre considers the subject–object dichotomy to be merely logical and useless, Yoga considers it necessary to distinguish between the subject (grahītṛ) and object (grāhya). In Vedānta, the distinction between the subject as Knower (jñātṛ) and the object of his knowledge (jñeya) is considered necessary as well as important. Sartre (1936–37/1957, p. 97) suggests that "The ego is not the owner of consciousness; it is the object of consciousness." In this respect, both Yoga and Vedānta hold views exactly opposite to that of Sartre. On the practical plane, we have already noted that while Sartre finds himself helpless in dealing with the downpour of ideas in the stream of consciousness, the yogi claims that the processes of consciousness can be controlled voluntarily so as to bring the stream of consciousness to a standstill. While Sartre would rather immerse himself into the problems of the "World" such as politics, revolution, and war, and forget about the subject–object distinction, the yogi would rather forget about the world with its wars and politics, and come to term with the problem of the self in relation to the world of objects.

In the previous chapter we considered in some detail the practical strategy of Yoga in dealing with the problems of life in general, and those of the stream of consciousness in particular. In the remainder of this chapter we shall examine how the Yogic and Vedāntic systems deal with the problems of self and identity.

The Advaita Vedāntic View of the Self

Anyone who is familiar with the Indian and Western theories of the self would immediately see many differences among them in form and content. The Indian theories, for instance, do not emphasize the social aspects of the self as much as many Western theories do. It is hard perhaps to find any Indian theory which considers self-esteem as important as Rogers does, and there is no Indian parallel to the view of the self as a set of attitudes. But the importance of social roles in the making of a personality, as well as the problems relating to role conflict, have been systematically considered by some Indian thinkers. The epic Ramāyaṇa, for instance, depicts the hero Rāma, his wife Sītā, brother Lakṣmaṇa, and other characters in such a way that their behavior in their respective roles has been considered exemplary by scores of generations. Moreover, there are numerous instances in this epic of role conflict, and ways of resolving them are suggested. Although a fairly sophisticated analysis of the nature of social roles is found in the Rāmāyaṇa and such other sources of the Indian tradition, the Yoga and Vedānta theories of the self do not consider the nature of self systematically in relation to social roles, as modern social psychologists do. The concept of the life cycle is well rooted and well developed in Indian thinking, and there is a popular concept of four "stages" of the life cycle (the four "āśrama"s). Yet, a detailed analysis of developmental changes in self-image, comparable to the Eriksonian model discussed earlier, is not found, as far as I am aware. Given the diversity of the cultural and historical settings in which the Indian and Western theories evolved, such differences among them are not a matter of surprise. What comes as a surprise, however, is the fact that, despite the diversity in their backgrounds and purposes, some Indian and Western theories have recognized common problems relating to the nature of the self.

We have come across the Vedāntic concept of jīva in the previous chapter. The close parallel between James's hierarchy of selves and the Vedāntic view of the five sheaths of the jīva has already been noted. It is this organization of various "selves" or aspects of personality that is associated by the Vedāntists with selfhood in the sense of an "I" as a doer or an agent of actions (kartṛ), and also as an "I" who enjoys pleasures and suffers from pain (bhoktṛ). It is interesting to note further that Vedānta makes a distinction between the self as a "field" (kṣetra) and the self as "Knower of the field" (kṣetrajña) in almost exactly the same way William James distinguished between the self as known and as the knower.[4] Perhaps the most crucial aspect of the Vedāntic approach to the nature of self is what is called a wise discrimination between the permanent and the impermanent aspects of the self (nitya–anitya viveka). What the Vedāntists mean by the discrimination between the permanent and impermanent aspects of the self is pretty much the same as the problem of sameness *versus* change in personality which we have discussed before. When the Vedāntists set out to distinguish between the self as known and the self as knower, they encounter the issue of the unity of the Knower the same way as Kant, James, and other Western thinkers did. Let us examine the Vedāntic views on some of these common problems encountered by both Indian and Western thinkers.

In a relatively minor work on Vedānta called the *Dṛg-Dṛśya Viveka*[5] there is an interesting discussion regarding the distinction between the self as Knower and the self as known. Here is a free translation of the first few verses of this text:

> Form is perceived by the eye which is its perceiver; the eye is perceived by the mind which is its perceiver; the modifications of the mind are known by the Witness who knows them all but is not known in turn.
>
> The eye is able to distinguish between the blue and the yellow, and is also able to perceive as unity [*i.e.*, as a single (ekadhā) category, "form"] the multiplicity of forms such as big and small, long and short.

> The mind is able to cognize the dullness and sharpness of sight and also of the presence and absence of sight because of its ability to put them into a single (ekadhā) category. The same applies to the sensation of sound and touch [implying that the unity of the mind is to be similarly inferred].
>
> It is possible for us to distinguish between doubt and decision, between the state of belief *versus* disbelief, and between feelings of modesty, fear, and others because consciousness (citi) can bring them into a single category.
>
> Consciousness, however, neither grows nor decays; it neither waxes nor wanes. Being self-luminous, consciousness illuminates everything but shines without any aid (*Dṛg-dṛśya Viveka*, 1–5; A. C. Paranjpe, trans.).

Although the form of expression and the style of argument typical of Vedāntic scholars is quite different from that of most Western thinkers, the thrust of their arguments is the same as Kant's thesis, which points to the need for assuming the unity of the self as Knower. As well, the number of objects known may be unlimited, but no object can be comprehended without the unity of consciousness that is the basic condition for the very possibility of knowledge. As we shall see a little later, the Yoga theorists pose their arguments in a still different manner, but finally make the same point.

A discussion of the "wise discrimination between the permanent and the impermanent" appears in several texts of Vedānta. It is pointed out by their authors that all the five sheaths of the jīva, the body, the vital breath which unifies bodily functions, things with which a person identifies himself as me and mine, the various thoughts which he entertains as his own, his feelings of pleasure and pain, and so on—all of these are impermanent. The authors of Vedāntic texts take little trouble in trying to convince their readers that the body, possessions, and all the other things with which the "I" is closely identified are involved in continual change. The various observations and arguments which we encountered in a previous section which point to the changeable character of the bodily self, social self, and the cognitive aspects of the self, seem to be unnecessary for Vedāntists, who often take it for granted that everything that characterizes the jīva is impermanent. According to Vedānta, the only thing that is permanent and unchanging in man (and thus provides a basis for selfsameness) is the Self as Knower. There are many words to represent this principle: sākṣin meaning "the Witness," draṣṭṛ meaning "the Seer," kūṭastha which literally means "unmoving" or "standing on a peak," and, of course, the Ātman or the "real" Self as distinguished from ahaṁkāra or egoism. A concise and lucid account of this concept of the Self as Knower is found in Śaṅkara's well-known work, called the *"Crest-Jewel of Discrimination"* (Vivekacūḍāmaṇi). The following is a short paraphrase of Śaṅkara's ideas, originally expressed in beautiful verses.

> There is something within us which is always the substrate of the conscious feeling of the "I." That something is a witness to the three states of consciousness (wakeful, dream, sleep), and is different from the five sheaths of the jīva. This something knows every thought that passes through the mind, but is not known by them. This inner Self (antarātman) is an eternal principle which is always One and involves an integral experience of bliss (akhaṇḍasukhānubhūtiḥ). This is the Knower of the mind and its modifications, and of the activities of the body and the sense organs. He accompanies all changes and activities like heat in an iron ball, but he neither acts nor is he subject to modifications. This Ātman can be realized by means of a controlled mind (Śaṅkara, c, 127–138; A. C. Paranjpe, trans.).

An important question arises here. If there is within us a principle which is eternal, unitary, and infinitely blissful to its core, why do we always tend to identify ourselves with diverse and continually changing things, and why do we experience misery in life? A typical Vedāntic answer to such a question is somewhat as follows. The root cause of untold miseries of life is the misconceived notion of the self. We take the jīva to be the self and become attached to it. We treat our bodies, possessions, wealth, friends, as well as our ideas about ourselves and the world as if they were going to remain intact for ever. We strive to acquire perishable possessions and then try to protect them because we are afraid of losing them. We feel elated with a new acquisition of a desired object (or friend, idea, etc.), and feel depressed due to its loss. We keep spinning new ideas about ourselves, nourish them, and become wrapped in a world of our own creation—like a moth in a cocoon. We are thus trapped within the boundaries of the self which we have accepted on our own (See Śaṅkara, c, 137).

What, then, is a way out of this trap? The solution to this problem as suggested by Vedānta is the realization of the nature of the Self as Knower. In Vedānta, as in Yoga, the only way to genuinely realize the nature of the self as Knower is to experience the highest state of samādhi. Since the views of Yoga and Vedānta are considerably alike in this respect, we may examine the meaning and significance of their view of self realization after examining some distinctive features of the Yogic view of the self.

Yoga on the Nature of the Self

The Yoga theory makes a distinction between the knower and the known, and it also asserts the unchanging nature of the Self as Knower. Although the conclusions reached by Yoga on the issue of the nature of the Self as Knower are pretty much the same as those of Vedānta, the Yogic approach to this issue is slightly different from that of Vedānta.

Vyāsa, Vācaspati Miśra and other commentators of Patañjali adopt a distinctive view of the nature of knowledge, which should be outlined so that we can understand the typical Yogic approach to the nature of Self as Knower.

When the Yogic scholars refer to the Self as Knower (draṣṭṛ, grahītṛ) they usually imply a broad and general distinction between the subject as a single center of awareness as distinguished from the innumerable objects of knowledge, such as pots and other physical objects, animals, trees, persons or whatever else we may try to know about. The Yogic thinkers do not tend to refer to Self as Knower (kṣetrajña) as distinguished from the Self as Known (kṣetra, *i.e.*, "field," or James's "me") as Vedāntists often do. The Vedāntists, as noted, conceptualize the Self as Known or Self as Object in terms of the jīva. The scholars of the Yoga tradition do not seem to have any use for a concept like jīva, but they do recommend a discrimination between the permanent and the impermanent, insofar as mistaking the unchanging (Seer) for a changeable entity (the power of or the intellect) is viewed in Yoga as being indicative of ignorance (see Patañjali, 2.5). The typical Yogic approach to the issue of sameness *versus* change follows from the Yogic view of what knowledge is and how it is made possible.

According to the Yogic view, knowledge is possible due to the mediation of the citta (or mind) between the Knower (grahītṛ) on the one hand, and the object of knowledge (grāhya) on the other. The citta, with the help of adjuncts such as the senses, has the capacity to be influenced or "colored" (uparañjayati) in such a way as to reflect the characteristics of the object of knowledge. Vijñāna Bhikṣu (4.17) gives the analogy of the way in which molten wax takes the shape of a mold to describe the "shaping" of mental contents in the form of the object of knowledge. This process of shaping of the mind so as to reflect the properties of an object of knowledge takes place in the sphere of the material (jaḍa) Prakṛti. It may be remembered that according to Yoga theory the citta, like the sense organs, is physical or material, and therefore insensate in character. The reflection (pratibiṁba) of objects in the mind is therefore considered unenlightening in itself. To translate this idea into contemporary terms, the Yogic view of the cognitive apparatus is comparable to that of a physical apparatus such as a camera, which can provide a faithful image or a hologram of the original. We cannot say that a camera "knows" the objects it depicts because the facsimile created by such an apparatus lacks the lively and "illuminating" (prakāśa) character of mental images. According to Vācaspati Miśra (4.17), the enlightenment characteristic of what we call knowledge is possible due to the enlivening (cetayamāna) effect of the nonmaterial Puruṣa, which has the quality (or "power") of consciousness (citiśakti) inherent in it.

The Yogic theory thus makes a distinction among three different elements that make knowledge possible. First, there is the sentient principle of the Puruṣa, who is the real Knower, since only he has the enlightening power of consciousness; second, there are the objects in the world to be known; and third, there is the cognitive apparatus of the psyche, which reflects the properties of the objects, on the one hand, and the illuminating character of the Puruṣa, on the other, resulting in the "knowledge" of the object.

Given this view of knowledge, we should be in a position to understand the Yogic perspective on the problem of change *versus* sameness. It is important to note that the cognitive apparatus of the psyche is *capable* of transforming itself so as to reflect various characteristics of the objects of knowledge. This does not mean that appropriate transformation of the psychic apparatus will *always* occur in the presence of an object. Thus, although I may normally be able to find my pencil on the desk, I may fail to "see" it despite its actual presence in front of me. This is because the "mind" may be wandering while I think that I am looking for the pencil. Objects are therefore sometimes known and sometimes not known, depending upon whether the mind changes itself so as to reflect the objects of knowledge, or whether it changes in some other ways as guided by desires and so on. Knowledge of objects occurs intermittently and not in an uninterrupted way. By contrast, the knowledge of eternally changing mental states (or vṛttis) is said to be always possible. Vācaspati Miśra (4.18) points out that whether the mind is in a wandering state, stupefied, occasionally steady, or in a one-pointed state, one is always aware of one's own thoughts. The Puruṣa or the Seer is considered to be the owner of the passing vṛttis and is believed always to be aware of them. From the apparently uninterrupted and continuous character of our awareness, the Yoga theorists infer the unchanging and selfsame character of the Puruṣa or the self as knower.[6]

We may note that the Yogic approach to the conceptualization of an unchanging Puruṣa is somewhat similar to Kant's conceptualization of the Pure Ego, in that both Vyāsa and Kant use an analysis of the nature of knowledge to infer either the selfsameness or the unity of the Self as Knower. Although their specific arguments are different, the thrust of their approach is quite similar.[7] However, there is a clear difference between the Kantian and Yogic approach: For Kant, the unity of the Self as Knower is only a logical inference with no empirical basis, whereas the Yogic system proposes that the nature of the Seer can be verified through the experience of Asaṁprajñāta samādhi. Says Patañjali

(1.2–4): The Seer stays (*i.e.*, is experienced) in his own, natural condition when the thought processes are completely controlled, although he is identified with the vṛtti of the given moment when the thoughts are not so controlled.

We have already discussed the nature of the experience of the Asaṁprajñāta samādhi in the previous chapter. Here we may examine the significance of such an experience in relation to the concept of the self. To put it in the familiar terms of Western psychology, we should note that Patañjali's concept of the vṛtti is much the same as James's notion of the "Thought" as a passing mental event or a pulse of cognitive consciousness, and that the Yogic Seer is much the same as James's "Thinker." Although James initially felt the need to distinguish between a permanent or selfsame Thinker whose Thoughts seem to appear in succession in the stream of consciousness, he finally concluded that the passing "Thought" is the only "Thinker" we need to recognize in psychology. It may be remembered that the main reason for his conclusion was that he could not find any empirical verification of the Thinker (see James, 1890/1950, Vol. 1, p. 370, ff). The yogis, however, claim to have experiential evidence of their postulation of a Seer. Without such a basis for verification, notions like the Self as Knower would remain mere figments of imagination based upon some kind of a word game. Assuming for a moment that Yoga offers a valid method for the empirical verification of something called the Seer or the Self as Knower, does it resolve the paradox of identity? If so, how? An answer to the first question will have to be affirmative. In response to the second question, it may be noted that a yogi who experiences Asaṁprajñāta samādhi has put a stop to the rapid succession of thoughts. The constant flux of the stream of consciousness in which Hume found himself trapped is no longer an intricate and endless labyrinth for a yogi. The self, as the center of awareness, remains unchanged, since the continually emerging thoughts are blocked. Moreover, as noted in the previous chapter, the experience of Asaṁprajñāta samādhi is not characterized by the split between an intending subject and an intended object. It is an "integral" or holistic experience in which the unity of the experiencer is not questioned at all. The self is experienced as the center of awareness, pure and simple, and not as a subject who has directed his consciousness on some intended object. When realized in this form, the unity of the self is not the mere sum of its parts, or even the systematic organization of roles characteristic of a well-integrated personality. The nature of the self as viewed here is undifferentiated consciousness which, as described by the Vedāntic text *Dṛg-dṛśya Viveka* (quoted before), "neither grows nor decays, neither waxes nor wanes." In other words, one who has once realized the self as the Seer can always return to this "real" self to experience it in the same untarnished form. The Seer as viewed by Yoga and Vedānta can satisfactorily account for the unity and selfsameness in man.

We can perhaps grant that during the state of Asaṁprajñāta samādhi one does not experience ongoing change characteristic of wakeful or dreaming states, and that there is nothing to threaten the sense of unity. But, we may say, this is hardly different from the experience of deep sleep in which there is an absence of continual change and diversity of thought. According to Yoga and Vedānta, this is not so, because the samādhi states are much more pleasurable and beneficial than deep sleep. The main consequence of the experience of samādhi states is that it changes the entire pattern of life, leading to lasting happiness in a way that sleep does not. However, even if the samādhi states are immensely more pleasurable than deep sleep, they are short-lived. What, then, happens to the yogi when the samādhi state terminates? If he retains his "psychosocial identity" and carries out the business of his life as usual as we do after waking up from sleep, the so-called basis of unity and sameness provided by the moments of self-realization in Asaṁprajñāta samādhi may be as insignificant for unity and sameness as deep sleep, or perhaps even totally unrelated to self and identity of man.

We have already seen (in the previous chapter) that the experience of Asaṁprajñāta samādhi leads to a gradual "purification" of the stream of consciousness, so that the behavior of a person in the post-samādhi period no longer remains under the control of the cumulative effects of the past. The yogi is gradually "released" from the impelling force of the desires arising from the pleasurable or unpleasant experiences of the past. In his commentary on Patañjali (4.25) Vyāsa explains the implications of the samādhi experience for the transformation of the entire pattern of life during the post-samādhi period of life. Having realized the nature of the self as the Seer, the yogi is no longer concerned about his "self" in the way in which most ordinary people are. He no longer asks the questions "Who am I?"; "How am I doing?"; "What is going to happen to me in the future?" and so on. To put it into typical Western terminology, the continual process of self-examination and of the redefinition of the boundaries of the self ceases when the nature of the Self as Knower is realized. Life is no longer a continual process of changing perspectives on the self and the world. The self-realized person is no longer "becoming" since he has experienced the nature of his "Being"—pure and simple. The transcendental basis of one's psychosocial identity is realized, and the ideal human condition described by Yoga (kaivalya) is attained.

We shall return to the nature of the transformation of the self as viewed by Yoga and Vedānta once again in the next chapter. Meanwhile, we may note that the unity and selfsameness of man as viewed in the Yoga and Vedānta theories is a lot more than the sense of selfsameness and unity experienced by a person normally functioning in society as described by Erikson, in terms of psychosocial identity. Also, the self as Seer as viewed in Yoga and Vedānta is not a mere hypothetical entity conceived like the Kantian "Transcendental Self," out of logical necessity. Realization of the self which occurs in the extraordinary experience of a non-cognitive trance (Asaṁprajñāta samādhi) has specific consequences which amount to a total transformation in the life of the individual who has it. If it did not have such specific consequences, the so-called self-knowledge would be mere verbiage. Says Vyāsa (4.25): "Just as we infer the existence of a seed in the ground by the sprouting of a blade of grass during the rains, we infer that one has attained self-realization when we see someone who is no longer thrilled by joy or led to tears by the rise or fall of his fortunes." Since he has found a steadfast basis for his existence, he no longer needs to redefine his self image in terms of gain or loss, praise or blame.

Notes

1. Study of the "split brain" or the relationship between the bilaterally symmetrical parts of the brain has become a very active area of research over the past decade. Neurophysiologists like Gazzaniga (1970) and Eccles (1965) have been seriously trying to solve the mystery of how the relatively independent and often competing halves of the brain are able to maintain the unity of consciousness. As a result, this field of research is bringing identity back into prominence as a relevant issue. Scholars with such diverse disciplinary backgrounds as neurophysiology and philosophy are getting together. The cross-fertilization of their ideas has the potential for the development of new approaches to old problems. Although this newly emerging field of research is in some respects relevant to the issue of identity, it seems too different from the approaches discussed in this book and so is not being discussed.
2. Says Vidyāraṇya in *Jīvanmukti Viveka:* "It is well-known that unenlightened men, women, and ordinary folks usually praise (praśaṁsā) their own family, kin, friends, one's favorite dieties, and vilify (nindā) the aliens." For an original text and English translation see S. S. Sastri and T. R. S. Ayyangar (eds. and trans.), *Jīvan-Mukti-Viveka of Vidyāraṇya.* Adyar, Madras, Theosophical Publishing House, 1935.
3. M. H. Kuhn and T. S. McPartland (1954) have developed a simple device sometimes called the "Twenty Sentences Test" which asks subjects to write twenty different answers to the same question "Who am I?" This test has been widely used as a convenient instrument in exploring self-images of large numbers of subjects. See Paranjpe (1975) for an example of the use of this test in a longitudinal study of identity formation.
4. The term "field" in this context refers to the "field of operation of the Law of Karma." It is implicit here that everything in man except the "Seer" is ascribed to the domain

of Prakṛti, wherein the Law of Karma reigns supreme. I am thankful to Dr. S. R. Talghatti for bringing this point to my attention.

5. The authorship of the small work (only 46 versus) on Vedānta called the *Dṛg-dṛśya Viveka* is not definitely known. Swāmi Nikhilānanda, who published this work along with an English translation (Mysore: Sri Ramakrishna Ashram, 1931), mentions three names associated with the authorship of this work: Bhāratī Tīrtha, Ānanda Jñāna, and Śaṅkara.
6. sadā jñātāścittavṛttayastatprabhoḥ puruṣasya apariṇāmitvāt. (Patañjali 4.18.) Vyāsa says in his commentary on this aphorism that the unchanging character of the Puruṣa is *inferred* from the fact that mental states are always known to Puruṣa, the "owner" of the mind.
7. In my judgment, Kant's arguments about the need to assume the unity of the Self as Knower as necessary for the very possibility of knowledge are clearer and more powerful than the arguments of the Yogic scholars who conclude likewise. The style or quality of arguments would not matter much if the conclusions were acceptable.

6

OVERVIEW AND PROSPECT

On Consciousness

As we get ready to take an overview of approaches to consciousness, it is necessary to remind ourselves of the cross-cultural nature of our inquiry. The comparison of psychological theories poses the same kind of problems as posed by the comparison of cultures. There is a good reason why the anthropologist Malinowski insisted that every culture must be understood in its own terms. For, if we judged all cultures by the standards of a particular one, we would impose the biases of one culture on the others—which would defeat the whole purpose of comparison. Obviously, we cannot judge behaviorism by Yogic standards and vice-versa. Moreover, social institutions and other aspects of culture are so differentiated that we are faced with the impossible task of having to compare incomparables. Likewise, psychophysiology and Vedānta appear so different that, at least at first glance, it seems pointless to try to compare them.

It is true that Yoga and behaviorism *appear* to have nothing in common. Yet, upon closer examination, the two can be seen as different responses to certain common problems. As noted, the Yogic literature mentions some of the predicaments encountered by the introspectionists of Watson's time—the infinite regress arising from an attempt to examine one's own thought processes, for instance. The unreliability of memories is another common problem mentioned in both Yogic and introspectionist literature concerning the observation of one's own thoughts. Given that Watson turned to the control of behavior as a goal of psychology after concluding that the method of introspection was unworkable, it is

Notes for Chapter 6 are on p. 322.

quite conceivable that someone in the ancient Yogic tradition may have responded similarly in face of the abovementioned problems in introspection. Yoga and behaviorism *are* alike in choosing the control of behavior as opposed to descriptive analysis of conscious content as the goal of their respective enterprises. The main difference between them is that, while Yoga has tried to develop methods for controlling the mind *and* body, Watsonian behaviorism chose to control the body while rejecting the mind altogether.

Many readers find such a comparison of Yoga and behaviorism a mere *tour de force*. The comparison of ideas from ancient Sanskrit texts with those in the works on modern scientific psychology is not an easy task. While suggesting that the yogis as well as the structuralists of Watson's time were involved in introspective observations of consciousness, it is essential to ascertain that both were indeed dealing with the same phenomenon, which we have designated by the label consciousness. The problems in such comparison begin with the need for correct translations. Unless we are quite sure that the terms considered equivalent refer to the same phenomena, the comparison of theories will be deceptive. It is only after careful consideration that I have concluded that the Cartesian "cogito," William James's "Thought," and Patañjali's "vṛtti" are generic terms designed to designate the *same* broad set of mental events such as perceiving, thinking, imagining, remembering, dreaming and the like. Once we establish beyond doubt that two sets of writings are dealing with the same set of phenomena, we can go ahead with a comparative survey of the literature to search for as many equivalent ideas and expressions as possible. Here is a list of ideas commonly found in the psychological literature in English that have been expressed in almost exactly equivalent Sanskrit expressions in the Yoga–Vedānta literature.

Mental events usually involve rapid changes; thoughts are always directed toward objects or, in other words, there is always an implicit subject–object split; mental events leave their impressions behind; such impressions are stored and retrieved, so to speak; the retrieval of impressions usually has cognitive and motivational properties; we tend to seek those objects that have left pleasant impressions and avoid those that have left unpleasant impressions; desires often lead to distortion in the perception of reality; the origin of desires must be traced to past experiences—including some events that may have occurred prior to the birth of the individual, and so on.

That concepts like cogito, thought, and vṛtti originated independently in places continents apart and times centuries apart should be no surprise because, after all, the occurrence of thoughts is a panhuman phenomenon. To say that people in all cultures and in all historical periods think, remember, sleep, dream, and so on may sound trivial. Nevertheless, it is better to start with something that is absolutely and clearly panhuman if we expect to come up with a truly transcultural approach in the end. If we go over the ideas listed in the previous paragraph once again, we can see that they involve some basic assumptions held in common by many psychological theories including Yoga, Vedānta, psychoanalysis, and behaviorism. These ideas do have the character of "folk wisdom," but they cannot be dismissed for being such, just as the panhuman nature of thought processes cannot be considered trivial because it is a commonly known truth. Folk wisdom can be (rather, it often is) the base on which complex theories are built.

Ability to reflect on one's own thought processes is a common human endowment, even as the occurrence of thoughts is a panhuman phenomenon. It is common to find "ordinary" people occasionally reflecting on their own thoughts. However, a serious and systematic use of introspection as a method of exploring various regions of the domain of consciousness is neither common nor easy. The ancient yogis, who must have been tireless explorers of their inner worlds, concluded that it was impossible to grasp the thinker and his thoughts *at the same time.* As noted, Comte arrived at the same conclusion in 19th-century France. Since it seems unlikely that Comte may have come across this idea in an Upaniṣadic or Yogic text, he may be given the credit for independently discovering this principle. Again, as noted, William James uses the metaphor of the stream to describe the flowing character of thought processes, the same way as Vyāsa did more than a millennium before him. Some people may consider this commonality just another example of folk wisdom common to most societies. On the other hand, if we regard the metaphor of the stream and the Comtian conclusion (about the impossibility of observing thoughts and continuing to think at the same time) as small but important steps in the development of systematic theories of consciousness, we may be tempted to trace their historic origins and examine whether they were independently discovered, or transmitted from one place to another.

It is conceivable that James may have "borrowed" the metaphor of the stream directly or indirectly from Yogic sources, because it is known that he was aware of the basic Yogic writings. It is known, for instance, that he encouraged a young scholar (J. H. Woods) in his university to translate the *Yoga Sūtra* of Patañjali (see Riepe, 1968). It would be an interesting exercise in the history of ideas to explore what William James knew about Eastern concepts, and to trace how ideas from ancient sources influenced Western scholars like him. No matter how interesting and legitimate such an exercise may be, I see a rather sensitive aspect of such an inquiry. In this type of cross-cultural research, it is easy to be prompted by a sense of pride in being able to say: "Look, *my* ancestors thought of this before *your* ancestors did." I am tempted to say this because it is my impression that, in the field of Indological studies, Indian scholars have often tried to put the dates of texts as far back in antiquity as possible, and European scholars the opposite. Parochial pride is often as subtle as it is pervasive. I have found that being vigilant about subtle biases wherever they may appear, and trying to guard against one's own parochial biases, is a challenging as well as rewarding aspect of a cross-cultural study such as this one.

Attempting to "deparochialize" approaches to psychological issues is an obvious goal of an undertaking in the field of cross-cultural studies. Yet, attaining this goal is only part of the benefits to be derived from such a study; the main benefit would come from being able to develop broader and more effective theoretical frameworks by combining strong points of diverse origins. Such syncretism is not unheard of in psychology; the work of Roberto Assagioli (1965) is a widely known example, and more recent examples can be cited (e.g., Ikemi, 1979; Ikemi and Ikemi, 1980). The authors just mentioned have tried to combine Eastern and Western therapeutic methods in broad theoretical frameworks. A more systematic effort in this direction must begin with a close examination of the basic theoretical premises of Eastern and Western approaches. If we need to construct a broad, common theoretical framework, it could be built only on the basis of a set of common ideas found in many theories across cultures. The ideas relating to consciousness mentioned earlier in this chapter are good enough to start in this direction.

Ideas such as the constantly changing and object-directed nature of mental events, the storage and retrieval of impressions left behind by them, and others which are found commonly in theories of diverse origins, are admittedly simple rather than profound. The moment we begin to step out of such "common sense" notions into technical terms, we enter the complex web of interconnected concepts which are deeply rooted in philosophical issues. Concepts concerning consciousness, for instance, are inevitably connected with ontological theories concerning the nature of the mind and body. Also, as noted in Chapters 3 and 4, the problems in methodology, as well as those in the practical application of psychological knowledge, are inextricably connected with issues in epistemology and ethics. Issues in the fields of ontology, epistemology and ethics are controversial, to say the least, and together they comprise almost the entire field of philosophy. Idealists and materialists, rationalists and empiricists, those who espouse absolute values and utilitarians have been taking issue with each other for centuries both in India and the West. In psychology, we have partisans of all rival schools of philosophy, and it would be foolish to imagine that solutions to philosophical problems would become easier by simply borrowing insights from other cultures. Nevertheless, psychologists may be able to benefit from borrowed concepts, methodological techniques, and applicational strategies, if they borrow concepts derived from compatible theoretical frameworks, and if the borrowed methods are designed to attain shared goals.

To enable us to combine insights and techniques in a meaningful way, we may begin by identifying simple, commonly shared concepts as we have already done, and then continue to widen the common base by adding as many other closely equivalent concepts as we can find in the literature. We may then move on to roughly equivalent but complementary ideas, and continue our search until we hit upon divergent viewpoints. When we begin to come across more and more viewpoints that seem contradictory and irreconcilable rather than being parallel, we recognize that the different streams must part company. We can then set upon the task of trying to integrate into a common framework whatever ideas and methods may have appeared mutually compatible throughout our comparative survey of the literature.

A strategy for a possible integration of different approaches is more easily laid out than followed, because there are no simple guidelines on the basis of which concepts could be selected and joined together—like pieces of a tinker-toy. Yet, trying to take at least a small step toward the building of an "etic" system is essential, or else we shall never come out of the culturally limiting "emic" systems. In the following pages, I shall try to take a small step in this direction by pointing out several points of convergence in Indian and Western approaches to consciousness, and by suggesting how selected aspects could be put together in a meaningful way. In this process, I shall deal with many concepts which were discussed in Chapters 3 and 4, and add a few which have not been discussed before. In this discussion, I shall first deal with certain issues in the conceptualization of consciousness, and then take up issues relating to the methods of study and the application of knowledge. Again it is necessary to recognize the limitations of a task like this; one must be selective because it is impossible to cover everything. This means that one has to accept some degree of arbitrariness in selecting certain sets of ideas over others. The modest purpose of the exercise is to suggest that a meaningful integration of concepts of diverse origins is indeed possible, and to point to some directions in which a beneficial exchange of ideas can be brought about.

The Concept of Consciousness and Views of Reality

A distinction between mind and matter has been made since ancient times in both the Indian and Western traditions. There have been numerous ways of conceptualizing mind and matter. Of all the Western forms of conceptualization, the Cartesian formulation is clearly the most influential, especially in view of the variety of approaches to the study of consciousness that have arisen against its background. As noted in Chapter 3, the differences among contemporary Western approaches to consciousness are traceable to the positions taken on the mind–body issue as defined in Cartesian terms. Although the Sāṅkhya dualism is not perhaps as important in the history of Indian psychology as Cartesian dualism is in the West, it presents itself as the most relevant candidate for discussion in a comparative study of Indian and Western approaches to consciousness. The Sāṅkhya view of reality is parallel to the Cartesian view in that both views recognize a non-conscious material world in which events are strictly determined by causal laws, in contrast with a separate nonmaterial aspect of reality. Having separated two very different aspects of reality, both forms of dualism are faced with the problem of having to explain the relationship between them. We are not concerned here with either defending or refuting such dualistic conceptions of reality as ontological theories. For our purpose, it is important to tease out only those aspects of the two parallel and complex webs of interconnected concepts which would help us identify the closely equivalent, complementary, or irreconcilable aspects of the Indian and Western approaches to consciousness.

To facilitate such a comparative analysis, I have selected the following three ideas as focal points for discussion: (1) the conceptualization of the mind as a set of processes rather than static entities, (2) the idea that consciousness is a matter of degree as opposed to an all-or-nothing phenomenon exclusively characteristic of the human species, (3) the idea that being conscious is the same as the occurrence of thoughts, thus implying that there is no state of experience in the absense of thoughts. The choice of these points is based on my impression that their discussion will enable us to highlight some of the most crucial aspects of convergence as well as divergence of Indian and Western approaches to consciousness.

The conceptualization of the mind as a set of processes rather than static entities is neither new nor uncommon in the history of Western psychology. In Descartes' own life time, Hobbes viewed thoughts as motions of particles in the brain. Similarly, modern materialists, who follow Hobbes's lead, usually equate mental processes with physicochemical processes in the brain. Outside of the materialist camp, the act psychology of Brentano, functionalism of William James and others, and the symbolic interactionism of G. H. Mead, are prominent instances of theoretical frameworks which clearly emphasize the processual nature of mental events. As noted in Chapter 4, Yoga also emphasizes the processual nature of mental events. This form of conceptualization is important not only because it is common to some Indian and Western theories, but because, as I shall try to show in the subsequent pages, it clears away some tradional trouble spots of the Cartesian dualism. Moreover, the notion of thoughts as processes is implicit in a recent trend of thought in Western philosophy and science which follows the lead of systems theory and cybernetics. It will be useful to discuss several ideas from this trend since they are interestingly similar to the Yogic viewpoint. Before we turn to this new trend, it is necessary to briefly review certain historical developments concerning the Cartesian dualism and see how the new trend relates to these earlier developments.

Descartes' view of the mind as an unextended *substance* is at least partly responsible for promoting the view of thoughts and ideas as static "entities," so to speak, as opposed to events or processes. The notion of substance presents a complex problem in ontology. Here we need not enter into the philosophical ramifications of this issue; we need to be concerned only with its implications for psychology. Once thoughts are viewed as somewhat static entities made of an unextended substance, it becomes difficult to place them in the context of the "real world" of physical objects which we can see, touch and grasp. Such conceptualization gives rise to the question: "How can intangible entities like plans and intentions make physical objects like hands and legs move without *interfering* with the laws of motion?" Such a question brings the mind–body problem into the free will-determinism controversy, which is as complicated as the mind-body problem itself.

When Descartes ascribed freedom of the will to human beings, he was prompted to do so by his theological beliefs and moral concerns. After all, God could not hold men responsible for their actions without giving them the freedom to choose between good and bad courses of action. In order to account for the way in which the soul (equipped with a free will) could make the limbs move, he imagined animal spirits which would carry the soul's messages from the pineal gland near the center of the brain where it was supposed to be located, to the fingers and toes. By the middle of the 19th century, Helmholtz demonstrated that the messages signalled back and forth between the brain and the extremities of the body were electrical in nature. This demonstration was an important landmark in the history of ideas in the West because it laid to rest animal spirits and other super-naturalist and vitalist concepts. It promised that mental phenomena could be *reduced* to physical phenomena. This demonstration led many to conclude that thoughts, intentions and other "phantasms" could not make the limbs move, and thus interfere with the laws of nature. Backed by such a belief, Helmholtz could confidently enunciate the law of conservation of energy.

The work of Helmholtz, along with other similar developments in 19th-century biology and biochemistry, paved the way for the prevalence of reductive explanations in science. The working of the whole organism could be accounted for in terms of the working of the organs; that of the organs in terms of the functions of individual cells; and cells could be reduced to biochemical and electrical phenomena. The revolutionary work of Darwin brought the human organisms into the natural order, and placed them at the apex of a hierarchy of the animal kingdom which starts with the simplest unicellular organism and ranges to the most complex. According to Darwin, the expression of human emotions was a vestige of the species' struggle for survival. Thus, he suggested, we bite our teeth to express anger—like a wolf showing his canine teeth to scare his rivals. Later, James and Lange suggested that we strike first and then feel angry; feeling is not the cause but consequence of action. The feeling of rage was viewed as nothing but the physico-chemical reactions of a fighting body, thus proposing a completely reductive theory of human emotions. These well-known landmarks in the history of psychology trace the march of the reductive approach, a march which continues till the present time.

There can be no doubt whatsoever about the great success of the program of reductionism in not only the natural sciences, but also in the social sciences. Thus, most social phenomena can be explained in terms of the behavior of individual organisms, behavior of organisms in terms of the function of individual cells, and so on down the line till we come to the level of subatomic particles and forces. Accordingly, we have a hierarchy of sciences ranging from psychology and ecology dealing with "molar" and complex phenomena, through biology, cytology, biochemistry and chemistry down to subatomic physics. Each discipline reigns supreme at a given *level* of the hierarchy, and explains a whole entity in terms of parts within its domain. Taken together, the various disciplines offer reductive explanations to account for all types of phenomena. Notwithstanding the meaningfulness of reductive explanations, however, a recent trend of thought suggests that reductionism tells us only a part of the story, because properties of the whole are not completely reducible to those of parts. This point, namely the non-reducibility of the whole to its part, is emphasized by those who take organismic and emergentist positions in biology. The emergentist position suggests that in the course of evolution, *new* properties arise. The new properties *emerge* from a rearrangement of preexistent entities. These new properties may not be explainable in terms of the properties of the preexistent entities, which now form parts of the emergent whole.

The nature of part-whole relationships is discussed in depth in *systems theory*. Systems theory is a conceptual framework relevant to a broad domain of facts covering the subject matter of several disciplines. In this theory, attempt is made to explain the function of the body in terms of the *interdependence* of organs, organs in terms of interdependence of cells, human groups in terms of individual members, and so on. The interdependence of parts, in turn, is explained in terms of the *exchange* of mass, energy and information within and across boundaries of a given system, whether the system is an atom, cell, organism, social group, or any other whole composed of interacting parts.

Cybernetics is a theoretical framework that closely complements the systems approach. It tries to explain how communication networks in mechanical, electrical or neural systems enable the systems to regulate themselves as whole units, and accomplish functions which individual parts cannot perform on their own. It would be useful to briefly mention certain ideas connected with systems theory and cybernetics since I think that these ideas suggest a perspective on consciousness in a way that avoids some of the pitfalls of the Cartesian dualism. Systems theory arranges a broad array of systems in an increasing order of *self-regulation*. At the bottom rung of the systems hierarchy there are relatively closed, mechanical systems such as clockworks and thermostats. A thermostat monitors the rise and fall of temperature and triggers a heating or cooling device in an "appropriate" manner. Homeostatic self regulation of organisms involves increasingly sophisticated mechanisms for monitoring various internal and external conditions, combined with increasing flexibility in regulating the flow of information, mass, and energy within and across system boundaries. Whether in man-made robots, or in products of evolution, the complexity of *feedback loops* designed for information processing must be combined with a matching level of flexibility in response selection so as to ensure increasingly "intelligent" and "purposeful" self regulation.

In animals, a capacity to monitor consequences of past responses is added to the available mechanisms of collecting, storing and retrieving information so as to enable the animal to *learn*. Humans and certain other higher-order species are equipped with an additional feedback loop; they can monitor their monitoring so as to be able to learn how to learn. Further, humans are markedly ahead of other species in their ability to use symbols, rather than mere signs, in communicating with each other. On the basis of the above observations, it makes sense to view human thought processes and cognitive functions at the pinnacle of the hierarchy of the increasingly complex forms of information processing which starts with robotic levels, and rises through organic and human psychological levels.

Over the past decade, more and more psychological processes are being interpreted in systems and cybernetic terms with high levels of theoretical rigor. For instance, W. T. Powers (1973), a systems engineer, has tried to show how learning and perception can be explained in terms of system principles on which the underlying neural mechanisms operate. Piaget (1967/1971) shows how human cognitive processes are systematically related to organismic self-regulative functions. Stanley Milgram (1974) has tried to explain complex cognitive processes involved in obedience to authority on the basis of cybernetic principles.

Systems theory establishes a continuum of mechanical, organic and psychological functions. It is no longer necessary to view the world as divided between mind, thought, and consciousness on the one hand, and non-conscious matter on the other, as Descartes did. We can now say that the thermostat "takes notice" of rising temperatures, or that a wolf "minds" its position in the pecking order of the pack, without anthropomorphizing the machine or the animal. Lower levels of consciousness can be attributed to animals without violating Lloyd Morgan's Canon, because the bases of their "awareness" can be explained parsimoniously within the systems framework. To speak of the mind is not to place a "ghost in the machine," or to believe in a vitalist principle; we follow Helmholtz in interpreting the mental functions in terms of the forces of nature without adopting a totally reductive approach. What appears as "freedom of the will" is but a higher form of self-regulation; self-regulation in humans violates no such law of nature as the law of conservation of energy.

Systems theory has an advantage over the theories of Leibniz and Fechner in bridging the gap between the conscious and the non-conscious, the mental and the physical. Unlike the theories of these thinkers of the past, who either created imaginary entities like monads, or invented mathematical laws governing the mind–matter relationship, the systems theory places a long series of systems at various levels of complexity between the diverse domains of mind and matter. Since systems at various levels differ only slightly in degrees of complexity or self-regulation, they link the "black and white" of Cartesian duality like slightly varying shades of gray. Nevertheless, the General Systems Theory of James Miller (1965) and others faces a major problem in that it lacks a general principle that will help explain the relationships across the hierarchically graded levels of systems. We may now note some recent developments in theory building which may help solve this problem.

Once we agree that it makes sense to view the world in levels of system organization ranging from closed to open systems and from simple to complex, we must show how these different levels are *connected* with one another. The reductionist principle, which is widely supported in the scientific community, suggests that changes in parts, or lower level systems, lead to changes in higher level systems. We may explain, for instance, how the lowering of the blood-sugar level in cells triggers appropriate mechanisms in the brain so as to cause an organism to seek food. In offering such reductive explanations, we assume that there is a causal chain starting with events at the subatomic level, and working its way through atomic, molecular, cellular, and organic levels of organization all the way up to the macrocosm—whether the macrocosm be the ecology of the earth, or the totality of psychological events. Such a chain of "upward causation" operating from the microcosm to the macrocosm is often taken for granted. Obviously, if emergentism is to be accounted for, an additional causal principle must be introduced into the picture. D. T. Campbell (1974) has suggested the principle of "downward causation" to represent a reverse causal chain which would work from the whole to parts, from the macrocosm to the microcosm. He states the principle of downward causation as follows: ". . . the laws of higher level . . . system determine in part the distribution of lower-level events and substances" (Campbell, 1974, p. 180).

The philosopher Karl Popper gives the following example to illustrate the principle of downward causation. The governor of a steam engine, a macroscopic structure, regulates the flow of steam molecules, an event in the microscopic structure (Popper and Eccles, 1977, p. 19). Several other examples of such regulation through "negative feedback" can be cited. In cybernetics, we find numerous examples of mechanical, electrical, and neural systems that can effectively use the feedback principle so as to attain high levels of self-regulation for the system as a whole. Such examples show how the functions of a system as a whole can manifest emergent properties without violating any laws of nature. Moreover, such examples also show that the emergent properties are not causally impotent insofar as they exert a regulative influence over events and entities at lower levels. The implication of this to the mind–body problem should be clear. Thoughts, which are regarded as functions of the brain as a whole, even by arch materialists all the way from Hobbes to Armstrong (1968), are not mere epiphenomenal end-products of a long causal chain that starts at the subatomic level; they are emergent functions that can effectively influence the body and its activities. Contemporary Western philosophers like Popper, as well as neuroscientists like Eccles (1974) and Sperry (1979), have taken similar positions on the mind–body problem.

The attribution of causal potency to mental processes is made plausible by interpreting them as *information-exchange processes*. Modern computer technology has demonstrated that complex forms of information can be reduced to as simple a physical event as the starting and stopping of the flow of electrical current in a circuit. Information, reduced in this manner, can be stored, retrieved, reorganized, and put into action by computers and computer-directed robots. The newly emerging discipline called "artificial intelligence" tries to show how methods of information processing can be placed in a continuum of mechanical, electronic, biological and psychological levels. We may grant that mechanically stored information may never be considered equivalent to human knowledge, and also that the most sophisticated computers lack the creativity characteristic of human brains. Nevertheless, information processing, which once appeared to be as elusive and mysterious as Descartes' animal spirits, can now be taken to be as "real" as electronic computers. The development of such ideas has far-reaching implications. It can radically alter the view of reality acceptable to persons trained in modern sciences. Signs of such change have already begun to appear.

A change in views of reality based on recent ideas about information processing is reflected in the work of David Bakan (1974). He has cogently argued that "information itself has a reality quite on a par with physical reality," and has cited support for such a view from the work of several well-known scientists including Leo Szilard, Erwin Schrodinger, and several others. He suggests that it is necessary to grant "ontic status" to all information processes, including those which manifest themselves in human thinking.

It is neither possible nor necessary for us to examine all of Bakan's arguments. Bakan is not the only one to propose that mental events be considered a piece of the world. The philosopher Karl Popper is another well-known author who has expressed similar views. He has offered an elaborate set of arguments to show that scientific knowledge has causal potency in that knowledge of the laws of nature enables us to bring about changes in the world of "real" or tangible objects. Like Bakan,

Popper places mental events or consciousness on a par with objects and events in the physical world (see Popper and Eccles, 1977). Further, he proposes a broad view of the world divided into three interacting levels which he refers to as "cosmic evolutionary stages." The first level of *World I* is comprised of physico-chemical and biological entities ranging from simple elements such as hydrogen and helium, through heavier elements and molecules, to complex living organisms. *World II* is the world of subjective experience, i.e., of sentience or animal consciousness, as well as human consciousness. *World III* involves the products of the human mind, such as human language, theories of self and death, as well as the works of art, science and technology.

Popper's world view, described above in a most schematic form, is based on a thorough and critical analysis of the long history of ideas concerning mind and body in the Western tradition starting from the early Greek philosophers to the most recent advances in the natural sciences. The reason for mentioning Popper's views here is not because I wish to discuss them in detail, but because I wish to point out interesting similarities and contrasts between Popper's world view and the world view of the Sāṅkhya system. Let me first note certain general points of similarity between the Popperian and Sāṅkhya models. Popper's *World I* is comprised of physical objects including chemical elements as well as bodies of organisms. This domain roughly corresponds with *tamas*, the aspect of Prakṛti characterized by heaviness and inertia. Popper assigns human as well as animal consciousness to *World II*, while the Sāṅkhyas assign events in the domain of consciousness to primarily the active aspect of Prakṛti, namely *rajas*. Further, Popper's *World III* includes aspects of human knowledge such as theories of science and abstract ideas in various forms of art, while the Sāṅkhyas assign the illuminating character of knowledge to the "light" aspect of Prakṛti, namely *sattva*. Moreover, events in the three worlds of Popper are considered capable of causal interaction, even as the Sāṅkhyas view the three aspects of Prakṛti as being involved in continual interaction. What is suggested here is of course a rough correspondence between Popperian and Sāṅkhya world views, and not close equivalence, for there are obvious dissimilarities. For instance, while the Sāṅkhyas seem to assign mass and energy to two different strands of Prakṛti, no such division is implied in Popper's scheme. Many more differences between them could be easily pointed out. After all, given the great diversity in the sociohistoric backgrounds, the two systems can be expected to be different in many ways. So, instead of continuing to point out other more or less obvious differences, it would be useful to note some additional points of convergence between the Popperian and other recent

Western approaches to consciousness on the one hand, and some relevant aspects of the Sāṅkhya-Yoga theory on the other.

Yoga avoids substantialism and the associated view of thoughts as unextended static entities just as Popper does. We may recall that an emphasis on the processual nature of mental events is explicit in Yoga, and the same is true in many Western approaches ranging from Brentano to Bakan. Although the Cartesian split between man and brute is widely rejected under the influence of the Darwinian revolution, the Cartesian view that consciousness is an exclusive feature of human beings still lingers in Western psychology. Notwithstanding the popularity of notions like the threshold of awareness and subliminal perception which imply lower levels of awareness in humans, the concept of levels of consciousness graded across animal kingdom is not yet widely accepted. In other words, consciousness is generally viewed as an all-or-nothing phenomenon in modern Western psychology. By contrast, a continuum of levels of consciousness is implicit in the Sāṅkhya-Yoga theory. Note, for instance, that the root "cit" from which the Sanskrit word citta (i.e. mind, or "that which is conscious") is derived, has the following connotations: to take note of, to attend to, to aim at, perceive, cognize, understand, comprehend, know, or reflect. (See Monier-Williams's *Sanskrit–English Dictionary*.)

These shades of the meanings of the term "cit" imply the conception of consciousness as a matter of levels rather than an all-or-nothing phenomenon. This connotation is clearly reflected in the usage of the related term "cetana" which refers to all living or sentient creatures as opposed to insentient (acetana) objects. In contrast to the implicit conceptualization of the levels of consciousness reflected in the Yogic usage of terms like "cit" and "cetana," the term sentience, which refers to a "lower" level of consciousness characteristic of animals, has gone almost completely out of circulation in the vocabulary of English-speaking psychologists. Perhaps Lloyd Morgan's canon, which asked us to refrain from the anthropomorphic fallacy of attributing intentions and plans to animals, has outlived its usefulness. It is now necessary to recognize that there is nothing wrong if we attribute sentience, or lower levels of consciousness, to animals. This will be consistent with the acceptance of a continuum of information processing across species suggested by the cybernetic model.

It is interesting that certain basic ideas of systems theory are found in Yoga. For instance, Yogic theory makes a clear distinction between parts (avayava) and the whole (avayavin). Vācaspati Miśra (1.43) points out that, although an object as a whole (such as a water jar) is identical with the parts (atoms) of which it is composed, it has some properties (e.g., its capacity to contain water) which are different from those of its parts. Thus, Yoga clearly accepts the view that the whole has emergent properties which are not reducible to those of parts. It is of course true that the more specific analytical concepts of systems theory and cybernetics, such as feedback, system boundaries, transaction of mass, information and energy across boundaries, and so on cannot be found in Yoga. Nevertheless, another crucial principle of cybernetics, namely self-regulation, is certainly implicit in the practice of Yoga.

Yogic practices enable us to regulate the inhalation, exhalation, and other input–output functions of the bodily system. As is well known, Haṭha yogis can attain a voluntary control over the regulatory functions of the autonomic nervous system, and keep their bodies working efficiently like fine-tuned machines. While Haṭha Yoga helps enhance self-regulation of the body, Rāja Yoga aims at voluntary regulation of the mind. If thought processes, as information processes, can be considered crucial aspects of the self-regulative functions of the mind-brain system, Yoga suggests itself as a method for establishing a total voluntary control of the cybernetic mechanisms which the mind–brain system has at its disposal.

Seen this way, Yoga can be viewed as a method of self-regulation par excellence. As we shall see in a later section of this chapter, it is difficult to find a close parallel to the Yogic technique of the voluntary regulation of thought processes in the West. Before we turn to a separate discussion of methods of study and techniques of control of mental processes, however, it is necessary to note a matter of difference in the conceptualization of consciousness which flows from the attainment of a total control over the emergence and disappearance of thoughts in the mind with the use of Yogic methods. As noted in Chapter 4, Yoga claims that one continues to experience after the flow of thoughts is completely arrested. What is experienced then is the "no-thought zone" of consciousness. It is designated by the concepts of Asaṁprajñāta Samādhi and Nirvikalpa Samādhi in Yoga and Vedānta respectively.

Although it is difficult to find a clear recognition and conceptualization of the trans-cognitive aspects of consciousness in modern Western philosophical and psychological writings, it is possible to find similar ideas in the old mystical writings. A medieval English mystical text called *The Cloud of Unknowing* written by an unknown author, for instance, suggests that one can know God by removing the cloud of unknowing (see Progoff, 1957). What this means, I think, is that one attains enlightening trans-cognitive states when the ongoing thought processes are set aside, so to speak. I believe that more closely parallel approaches to the "no thought zone" may be found if we compare the writings of Eastern and Western mystics. Since the attainment of the trans-cognitive states is closely associated with (although not entirely dependent on) the methods of the control of thought processes, we shall return to this issue in a later section devoted to the methods of dealing with one's own thought processes. Before closing this discussion of the concepts of consciousness and views of reality, we may note that, given the numerous points of convergence between Yogic conceptualization and certain modern viewpoints just discussed, Yoga need not appear to be totally outlandish to those who adopt modern Western perspectives. One can begin with the modern systems framework and cross over to the Yogic approach as a method of acquiring the highest level of self regulation. On the other hand, one may begin with the Yogic system and adopt several concepts of systems theory and cybernetics to help understand the nature of mechanisms underlying the various practices of Haṭha Yoga. On the basis of the above discussion, one can be assured that there is a solid core of commonly shared *basic* concepts to serve as a bridge for a cross-cultural exchange of ideas.

On Exploring the Domain of Consciousness

The ability to reflect on one's own thoughts is a common human endowment, and it is usual to find "ordinary" people introspecting now and then. However, a serious use of systematic methods of exploring the various regions of the domain of consciousness is neither common nor easy. As noted, the impossibility of observing one's thoughts, and continuing to think *at the same time,* poses a difficulty in introspection, and this difficulty has been noted by several Eastern as well as Western thinkers. In my judgment, a person simply cannot divide the stream of consciousness into two parts so that one observes while other thinks simultaneously. This is an *inevitable* conclusion.

Given this inherent difficulty in introspection, John Stuart Mill was right in asking us to substitute retrospection in descriptive studies of conscious content. Although the method of retrospection suffers from inaccurate recall and other deficiencies, it is nevertheless useful in generating phenomenological data. As well, Boring (1953) was right in concluding that retrospective observation has been widely practiced in its various forms in American psychology. That this was done despite Watson's vigorous attacks against introspection, speaks for the overall usefulness of the retrospective mode of "inner observation." Three rather distinct approaches to the observation, description, and analysis of the contents of consciousness can be identified. The *first* type is the Titchenerian approach which aims at the identification of the "elements" of consciousness. The *second* approach aims at interpretation of the hidden meanings of thoughts, dreams and fantasies so as to unearth the troublesome desires buried into the unconscious. The *third* approach, which may be called the hermeneutic type, aims at determining which one of the given or possible interpretations of the phenomenal world may be the "correct" one. These approaches were discussed in Chapter 3, indicating their development in the history of Western psychology. Now let us examine how these methods of description and analysis relate to the Yogic and Vedāntic approaches to consciousness.

Neither the Yogis nor the Vedāntists may have ever tried to identify the basic elements of conscious content, or to discover the laws of their combination, using the *experimental* methods devised by Wundt, Titchener or the psychologists of the Würzberg school. Nevertheless, the Yogic concept of *tanmātra*, which refers to five elemental constituents of conscious content corresponding to the five senses, suggests that the Yogis and the structuralists arrived at the same conclusions regarding the constituents of conscious content. The recognition of elements of conscious content corresponding to the five senses is an obviously simple "common sense" notion which hardly merits recognition as an instance of independent discovery. After all, the basic sensory endowments are common to the entire human species. So, it is not surprising that the thinkers of ancient India, as well as their counterparts in Greece, recognized the fivefold nature of sensory experience, and proposed "scientific" models based on five elements of nature (fire, water, air etc.), one corresponding with each sensory modality. In contrast with the ancients, the introspectionists of Würzberg and Cornell Universities started with 19th-century chemistry as their model, and expected to find a larger number of elements of consciousness—perhaps like the elements in Mendelejeff's Periodic Table. Now in the late 20th century, it is widely recognized that notions of mental chemistry were misguided. Quantitative analysis of conscious content, guided by the hope of finding basic elements and the laws of their combination, is now a dead issue in psychology.

Nevertheless, quantitative analysis of conscious content is far from extinct; in fact it has staged a clear comeback on the stage of American psychology. Numerous articles in several volumes would testify to the change in this direction (Pope and Singer, 1978; Klinger, 1981). Interestingly, it is in connection with this trend that a possibility of meaningful combining Yogic concepts with "Western" quantitative methods arises. To illustrate, let us consider the Yogic claim that during the course of the dhāraṇā and dhyāna stages of meditation, the stream of consciousness is slowed down and becomes more homogenous in content (see

Chapter 4). What this means is that fewer units of thought and imagery now emerge in and disappear from the stream of consciousness in a unit of time than in previous stages of meditation. Also, the contents of consciousness are more like one another in the higher stages of meditation than in the lower. This claim is testable if the units of conscious content are properly defined, and if subjects are trained to identify and report them. Some attempts at the development of appropriate techniques useful for such purpose have already been reported (e.g., Pope and Singer, 1978). Such attempts, if successful, could not only be used to verify the Yogic claims, but may also be useful for meditators in monitoring their performance. Space does not allow us to examine the methodological issues involved in such studies in light of the current literature. It must be emphasized, however, that a *meaningful* convergence of typical "Eastern" concepts and "Western" methods is indeed possible in this field.

The possibility of combining the *second* type of approach to the analysis of conscious content, namely the symbolic interpretation to help identify the repressed desires, does not seem to be as clear and straightforward as the previous illustration. As noted in Chapter 4, some of the Vedāntic interpretations of contents of dreams are strikingly similar to the psychoanalytic interpretations of dream content, in that Vedāntists also recognize their wish-fulfilling nature. Yet, there is no clear statement of, or emphasis on, the unconscious in Yoga or Vedānta in a manner comparable to psychoanalysis. Besides, there is a fundamental difference between the Yoga–Vedānta and psychoanalytic approaches to the sating of desires. A spiritual seeker, who follows a Yogic or Vedāntic path, may wish to be able to cope with his passions as much as a spiritually uninclined person would. But I do not know whether he or she would benefit from a Freudian or Jungian analysis to help in this task in a manner consistent with his or her goals. There is no doubt that the psychoanalytic approach would be (and is) found useful for appropriate cases in the Indian cultural milieu, if the purpose is to relieve the "patient" of troublesome repression of desires. How far the psychoanalytic concepts and methods are cross-culturally applicable is an interesting question which cannot be examined within the scope of the present work. The incompatibility of psychoanalytic versus Yoga–Vedāntic approach to the interpretation of conscious content derives from the differences in their overall goals and strategies, not from a disagreement regarding the distorting effect of desires on the contents of consciousness.

The *third*, hermeneutic approach to the interpretation of conscious content is compatible with the basic principles of Yoga in that Yoga implicitly recognizes the "meaning-bestowal function" of the acts of consciousness. Similarly, a basic assumption of phenomenology, namely that views of reality are "constructed" by the acts of consciousness, is also consistent with the Vedānta philosophy. This assumption is implicit, for instance, in the Vedāntic view that the phenomenal world is a world of "names and forms" (nāma-rūpa)—meaning that it is based on organization of experience into forms or gestalts, and on attaching verbal labels to them. As such, most phenomenological and cognitive approaches are *in principle* consistent with the Vedāntic approach. However, there are basic differences between the contributions of the Indian and Western theories which adopt a constructivist approach. Thus, the Gestalt theorists have explored the domain of consciousness so as to formulate the rules governing form perception, and Piaget tells us how various modes of cognitive construction emerge and operate in the course of human development. Since I see no parallel developments of this sort in Indian psychology, such Western specialties could meaningfully complement those Indian viewpoints (such as Vedānta) which have similar theoretical underpinnings.

Here one may say: "What sense does it make to try to complement the Vedāntist theory with the laws of perceptual organization, cognitive construction, and the techniques of hermeneutic phenomenology, since the Vedāntists consider cognition of the world only illusory (mithyā)? In response it may be said that for a Vedāntist, cognitive constructions are illusory *only* when seen from the level of the absolute knowledge (parā vidyā) which is attained in the state of Nirvikalpa Samādhi. That state is attained only when one *deconstructs* the phenomenal experience of the world, and attains the transcognitive state of consciousness. However, as noted, one stays in such states only for short periods of time; the most common mode of being-in-the-world *does* require sharing a socially constructed reality. This shared reality is a *practical* reality (aparā sattā), so to speak, as opposed to the "absolute" reality which is experienced through cognitive deconstruction. So long as one is within the realm of the practical reality of day-to-day affairs, it is necessary to check whether one's constructions are properly matched with those of others with whom we interact. At this practical level, the methods of hermeneutic phenomenology are not at all inconsistent with Vedānta. It is important to remember that Vedānta does recognize *both* absolute and practical realities, although the former is placed at a higher level.

The notion of an absolute level of reality attainable through the experience of transcognitive states of consciousness presents the most difficult issue in an East–West encounter in psychology. As noted, the validation of claims to the "knowledge" of this level of reality is based on the experience which is attainable through the total deconstruction of one's cognitive framework. Such transcognitive experiences are by definition *beyond* the scope of a socially constructed reality, which must be supported by interpersonal verification. For those psychologists who adopt the contemporary Western models, any proposition unsupported by public verification is an anathema. There is no doubt that public verifiability of propositions is an inevitable and useful component of the enterprise of science. Constructing and testing models of reality is, after all, the business of scientists. It would be foolish to deny the value of adopting a natural science approach to psychology including a positivist epistemology associated with this approach. The issue is whether public verifiability and other such aspects of a "scientific" approach are applicable to *all* areas of psychology. It should be clear that, in any method of exploring consciousness, reliance on a subject's "private" judgment is inevitable. In my view, the philosopher Baier's arguments (quoted before) concerning the need to grant a final epistemic authority to the subject with regard to his or her "private experiences" such as pain, are irrefutable. Moreover, for the validation of judgments concerning the transcognitive experiences, we have not only to depend on the subject's epistemic authority, but have to step out of the socially constructed reality. For those who are committed to making psychology a natural science, and thus insist on public verifiability, even exploring the domain of consciousness must be suspect. Obviously, any reference to trance-cognitive states is beyond the scope of psychology if we wish to restrict our scope to the methods and goals of natural science.

On Dealing with Thought Processes: Techniques and their Uses

Since the occurrence of thoughts is a panhuman phenomenon, the question "How do I deal with my thoughts?" must be faced in all cultures. Normally, one does not expect everyone to ask himself this question because thoughts are always directed to objects—so one is concerned with the objects of thought rather than the thinking process itself. Even when one becomes concerned with thoughts as such, the usual and natural tendency is to allow them to drift. Waking thoughts tend to flow endlessly and the chain rarely breaks—except when one falls asleep, or becomes unconscious due to shock or other unusual conditions. Nevertheless, it is quite conceivable that countless people throughout history and across the world may have tried to deliberately break the chain of thoughts or stop thinking. Those who try to control their thought processes in meditation usually find that this apparently simple task is not easy to accomplish. It is common to find persons who find themselves unable to stop their thought processes despite training even when trying hard to do so. It is quite possible, therefore, that although innumerable persons may have spontaneously tried to face up to their thoughts and avert their emergence, many of these people have felt as helpless as the hero of Sartre's *Nausea* (see the extensive quote from Sartre's novel in Chapter 2).

Someone, somewhere, in the ancient history of India, seems to have tackled the runaway "stream" of consciousness like taking a bull by the horns—and taming it. It appears to me that that the person who did this shared the experience with other people, and they shared theirs with still others, and so on. After several generations, a *technique* was developed for effectively dealing with the stream of thoughts. Indeed the Yogic techniques may have developed over tens of generations in which each generation passed new insights as well as old ones to the next generation. Such an evolutionistic view of the origin of Yoga makes sense to me, although it may not be readily acceptable to many contemporary followers of the Yogic tradition.[1] The claim that the stream of thought can be gradually attenuated to a point of near stop through deliberate and systematic effort is a distinctive feature of psychological theories of Indian origin. Likewise, the discovery of the "no thought zone" of consciousness is perhaps the most important contribution of Indian psychology. That similar ideas and practices are found in Chinese, Japanese and other Eastern systems of psychology is not surprising because, as is well known, ideas concerning such matters travelled throughout the East with Buddhist monks, philosophers, and other travellers. That such ideas were transmitted does not mean, of course, that they were uniformly known or universally accepted all over the East. There are marked differences in some of the techniques of meditation developed by the various sects of Hinduism, Jainism, Buddhism, and other religions. This, too, makes sense insofar as a combination of creative minds and distinct student-teacher chains has led to specialization of theory and practice in distinct directions. It is my impression that, although the techniques of different schools or sects are highly varied, the concept of a "no-thought zone" of consciousness (or the recognition of various aspects of the samādhi-type experience), and a positive value attached to such "transcendental" states of consciousness, are widely shared features of Eastern psychological thought.

How does the Western tradition compare with the Eastern traditions in this respect? As far as the usual sources of the history of Western philosophy and psychology are concerned, it is difficult to find explicit references to states of consciousness beyond thought, or to specific methods of dealing with the stream of consciousness so as to retard or stop the course of its flow. The closest we get is Husserl's reductive phenomenology. The "bracketing" technique of reductive phenomenology involves an attempt to "hold on" to certain contents of consciousness, so to speak. As noted, Husserl used expressions like "putting out of action" the acts of consciousness, and wrote about a valuable personal transformation resulting from the practice of phenomenological reduction (see Chapter 4). These aspects of reductive phenomenology resemble Yogic concepts and methods. It would have been possible for Husserl to borrow from the Indian approaches to consciousness since several German universities in his time had accomplished Indologists who were conversant with Sanskrit literature and Indian philosophy. However, there are no references to Indian sources in Husserl's writings. Besides, Quentin Lauer, who is well acquainted with Husserl's published and unpublished writings, has mentioned in an editorial comment that Husserl knew little or nothing about Eastern thought (see Husserl, 1936/1965, p. 171). As such, the similarities between Husserl's ideas and methods and those of Yoga may be attributed to independent discovery. It is true that Husserl's published works have no *clear* account of the "no thought zone" of consciousness comparable to Yogic accounts of samādhi, and his techniques of controlling the stream of consciousness are less developed than those of Yoga.[2] Having said this, I must admit that it is unfair to expect that the accomplishments of a single individual's work of a lifetime should equal the cumulative accomplishments of several generations. Given that Husserl did not benefit from traditionally developed expertise with regard to the control of the stream of consciousness, his accomplishments were indeed remarkable.

It is not difficult to appreciate that a complex system such as Yoga, being a product of a specific chain of teachers and students, is a unique product of a particular cultural tradition. Against this background, what can we say about the states such as *samādhi* which the Yogic techniques are designed to acquire? Are the samādhi experiences attainable only by those who have benefitted from the Yogic or similar other cultural legacy? According to Patañjali (1.18–19), the samādhi experiences are attainable not only by those who learn the techniques of Yoga, but also by some persons without any training or even effort. Moreover, according to Vedānta, what is experienced by the Self in Nirvikalpa samādhi is, after all, its original state. One does not realize it as long as one clings to mistaken notions of the self and remains attached to the same. As soon as the mistaken notions of the self and its attachments with the phenomenal world are removed, the real self must shine forth in the "Fourth" state of consciousness. If this is correct, then the experience of states such as samādhi must be a natural (although rather rare) psychological phenomenon occurring in all cultures. Why, then, are accounts of experiences like samādhi so rare to find in Western philosophical and psychological literature?

As suggested before, references to transcendental states of consciousness are not difficult to find in the Western mystical writings, although they are not very common in most historical accounts of the Western philosophy and psychology. In the previous section, a mention was made of a medieval English text called *The Cloud of Unknowing*. In this text it is suggested that an enlightening state is attained when the clouds of thought are removed. Closer parallels between Eastern and Western views of trans-cognitive states of consciousness can be found if we compare writings on mystical experience from various cultures. Thus, mystical experiences have been considered ineffable or impossible to describe, and also as being ecstatic and blissful, in Western as well as Eastern writings. They have also been associated with other exalting characteristics such as truth-bearing character, or a capacity to establish a direct communion with God or Reality. Such characterization of mystical experiences is generally consistent with Yogic and Vedāntic accounts of the samādhi experience. Many scholars have written on various aspects of both Eastern and Western mysticism. (Otto, 1932; Ranade, 1933; Zaehner, 1957; Scharfstein, 1973; Staal, 1975; Stace, 1960). Their writings point to many similarities in the accounts of mystical experience given by persons of diverse religions and cultural backgrounds through millennia. Comparative studies of mysticism is a rich, challenging and complex field of study. A comparative study of mystical experience is obviously quite consistent with the present study, but space does not permit me to include it within the scope of the present work.

On the Nature of the Self

Before discussing the similarities and differences in the Eastern and Western theories of the self, it is necessary to deal with certain extratheoretical factors relevant to this topic. The most important extratheoretical factor which is often associated with the study of the self is a personal concern. No other topic in psychology may be a matter of such direct personal concern as the self. This concern may be as casual and superficial as an occasional narcissistic desire to have a look at one's "mirror image," or may be a serious matter of deep emotional involvement and existential concern. Adolescents are often quite serious in asking themselves the question "Who am I?" Indeed the answers which the adolescent finds in response to this question may have long-term effects on his or her life. However, the typical adolescent's inquiry rarely transcends the concern over finding a suitable niche in the society, a common task for the adolescent stage of the life cycle. A more serious interest in the inquiry into the nature of the self at a deeper level than is common among adolescents is reflected in certain well-known autobiographical and literary writings such as St. Augustine's *Confessions*, and the writings of existential philosophers like Camus, Dostoevsky, Sartre, and others. The existential quest for the self portrayed in such writings is generally centered around a deeply personal need for arriving at a coherent set of values or a meaning of life.

The Indian philosophical writings, such as those of Vedānta, reflect a deeply personal existential concern similar to that reflected in modern existentialist literature. Although many Vedāntic texts are scholarly works written in a didactic style, and despite the fact that they usually involve endless arguments based on hair-splitting logic, the personal nature of the inquiry is never lost sight of. Such specifically personal concern is often lacking in the contemporary Western psychological writings on the self. Moreover, modern psychological writings convey a cultivated sense of impersonality even when they pertain to the self. Such an impersonal stance reflects the objectivist and positivist temper of the zeitgeist of modern Western psychology.

Another important extratheoretical factor which has deeply influenced the Indian as well as Western views of the self pertains to the models of the ideal human condition which have guided their inquiry. The typical Indian and Western views of the ideal human condition were discussed toward the end of Chapter 2, and we shall return to the same issue later in this chapter. Suffice it to note here that, by and large, the Indian theories have usually cherished the saint as their ideal, while the hero seems to be the ideal of many modern Western psychological theories. This difference in the Indian and Western theories is reflected in the popularity of the concept of self-realization in the former tradition and of self-actualization models in the latter. We shall return to this issue in a later section of this chapter.

With regards to theoretical issues, reference may be made to Gordon and Gergen (1968) who have suggested that the following dilemmas appear again and again throughout the literature on the self published in the English language: The self as (1) fact versus construct, (2) structure versus process, (3) subject versus object and, (4) single versus multiple. I think that it will be useful to discuss these dilemmas not only because they refer to important theoretical issues, but because they would provide us with relevant and important dimensions on which to compare the Indian and Western views of the self. In the remainder of this section, therefore, I shall try to discuss these issues and also indicate how the extratheoretical factors just noted influence certain theoretical considerations.

1. The Self as Fact versus Construct. Gordon and Gergen (1968, p. 2), have clarified that the word fact as used by them implies the view of the self as "an existing entity or actuality." They add that this implies that the self is an "individual's material possession" with "substantive properties locatable in time and space." The logical opposite of this is the view of the self as an artifact, a hypothetical construct designed to explain certain facts rather than being a fact itself. Gordon and Gergen (1968, p. 3) point out that most (Western) psychologists use the term self in the sense of a construct rather than a fact. It can be easily seen that the implicit issue here is the distinction between the real and the unreal. It is implied that anything which is not solid, like an object you can hold or see or grasp by directly touching it, cannot be real. Since the self is not real in this sense, it follows that it must be a mere figment of imagination. Another implication in the fact-construct dichotomy is that it reflects the mind-matter dichotomy. Since only material entities are considered real, such things as images of the self must be "epiphenomena." An epiphenomenalist view of the mind and the self is dominant in contemporary psychology, although Bakan, Popper and others have begun to suggest that mental events are not causally impotent. At any rate, users of such concepts as the self must ascribe to them at least some causal potency, or else they must abandon their use. The psychologist Hebb recognized this when he remarked that "The self is a fantasy all right, but a *real* fantasy, with effects on human behavior" (Hebb, 1960, p. 741). Obviously, anyone who accepts Hebb's position cannot be a materialist or an epiphenomenalist.

How does the Yogic and Vedāntic views of the self compare in light of the fact versus construct dilemma? The Yogic concept of Puruṣa as well as the Vedāntic concept of Ātman fall into neither of these categories. The self, conceived as Puruṣa or Ātman, is neither a tangible object, nor a mental entity such as an image or even "a real fantasy" which has "effects on behavior" to use Hebb's expression. Both Yoga and Vedānta assert the existence of the self somewhat in the sense in which Descartes asserted it, i.e., by recognizing that we cannot deny the existence of the thinker without self contradiction. Moreover, the Yogic and Vedāntic views consider the trans-cognitive experience, which occurs when all thinking and doubting is stopped, as *the* criterion of reality, self evident and indubitable. Thus, both types of ontic statuses which are implied in the terms fact and construct do not apply to the Yogic and Vedāntic views of the self.

2. The Self as Structure versus Process. As noted by Gordon and Gergen (1968, p. 5–6), the notion of structure involves a mechanical metaphor. It implies the analogy of the arrangement in space of relatively stable and unchanging parts. Sherif's view of the self as a systematic *organization* of attitudes, and Erikson's concept of identity as a *configuration* of roles, are examples of the use of the metaphor of structure in relation to the self. Gordon and Gergen rightly point out that the metaphor of structure makes sense when dealing with the stability of the individual over time and across circumstances. In contrast, the metaphor of process conveys movement or change, and is suitable when dealing with the changing aspects of the self. William James alludes to the metaphor of process when he suggests that the "I" is the same as the ongoing thought at any moment of time, thus implying that the images of the self keep changing with the ongoing cognitive processes. In the same vein, Erikson speaks of the identity formation process as involving a continual redefinition of the images of the self and their reorganization, although he recognizes a (presumably unchanging) transcendental "I" which underlies this process. Gordon and Gergen (1968, p. 6) point out that it seems necessary to use *both* the structure and process metaphors to designate the contrasting yet complementary aspects of the self, namely stability and change.

The Vedāntic view of the jīva, or the individual, as a set of concentric layers or sheaths, is an obvious example of the use of the structure metaphor. The Yogic notion of vṛtti, as noted, is a close parallel of the Jamesian concept of thought processes. However, it is important to note that these Indian theories insist that the structure of the jīva as well as the processual vṛttis are characteristic of the *non-self*. Moreover, they insist that it is a great mistake to equate the real self with either the structured jīva, or with the ongoing thought processes—although the self usually *appears* to be identified with them. The crux of the matter here is that both Yoga and Vedānta view the real self as being not only different from the changing images of oneself, but also different from the relatively stable characteristics of personality. The rejection by Yoga and Vedānta of the structure as well as process metaphors in relation to the real self is based on the distinctive positions taken by them on the dilemma of sameness versus change. Since this dilemma is inextricately associated with the issue of self as single versus multiple, both these dilemmas will be discussed together in a separate section to follow.

3. The Self as Subject versus Object. The distinction between the self as subject versus self as object is an important distinction, but the use of these terms is rather unfortunate since they are sometimes taken in a linguistic sense, i.e., as designating components of a sentence. Taken in this sense, the distinction is often dismissed as an artifact of language. In my view, it would be better to use the terms "knower" and "known" instead of "subject" and "object" so as to clearly delineate the dilemma involved in this issue. Taken this way, this issue bring us directly to philosophy—rather, to the most crucial problem of epistemology. The credit for forcefully arguing for the need to understand and appreciate the self as knower in Western philosophy goes to Kant. As noted in the previous chapter, Kant pointed out that refusal to accept the existence of the self as knower is to deny the very possibility of knowledge.

We may briefly recapitulate the points raised in relation to this issue in Chapter 5. Both Yoga and Vedānta conclude that it is necessary to accept the existence of the self as knower as Kant did, although their arguments in support of this conclusion are somewhat different from Kant's. Also, both Yoga and Vedānta escape James's criticism of the Kantian position. We may recall that one of James's criticisms of Kant involved the observation that the Kantian concept of the Pure Ego is ambiguous. The Pure Ego is considered a necessary condition for the possibility of knowledge and also a synthesizer of the manifold data into unified wholes. Obviously, it cannot be something active and changing, like an organizer of information, as well as something passive—like an unchanging backdrop of experience—at the same time. In Vedānta, this ambiguity is avoided by ascribing the synthetic function to an agency or an "inner instrument" (antaḥkaraṇa) which is considered to be separate from the unchanging and passive witness, the Ātman. The Yogic theory avoids this problem in much the same way.

Again we may ask: "Are we not playing a mere word-game by suggesting the separation between the self as agency that accomplishes cognitive synthesis on the one hand, and an unchanging backdrop for awareness on the other?" Such delineation of concepts cannot be dismissed as a word-game if we accept the need for conceptual frameworks and choose among alternative frameworks on the basis of their internal consistency and unambiguity. I, for one, would prefer the Vedāntic conceptualization over Kantian Pure Ego since the former avoids the ambiguity of the latter. However, what is even more important than this conceptual issue is the *verifiability* of the claims concerning the nature of the self as knower offered by the Indian perspectives. It is possible for anyone to actually try out the suggested modes of verification (e.g., stopping the thought processes as suggested by Yoga) if one is serious enough, and settle the issue on the basis of one's own experience. It is of course possible that one may find the suggested methods unworkable, or, even after mastering the suggested methods, one may find that they fail to deliver the promised results. Even if we are not prepared to take the trouble involved in such verification, we will have to admit that the Yoga–Vedānta propositions about the self as knower are at least potentially verifiable, while the Kantian formulation precludes verification even in principle.

A contemporary psychologist may say that all this is philosophy; what is there in subject–object distinction as far as psychology is concerned? For the psychologist, it is a question of choice as to how far one should go in the realm of subjectivity. Most contemporary Western psychologists who take a phenomenological approach are generally interested in the individual's subjective view of the world and of himself. However, a focus on the images of the self or cognitive representations, definitions, evaluations and the like, refer to self as object. They represent James's "Me," not the "I." To speak of the self as subject is to focus on *the very basis* of subjectivity. In other words, the "I" refers to the subject pole of intentional experience. Thus, if I say "I am a human being, intelligent, compassionate"—or whatever, all these characterizations stand at the object pole and not the subject pole of my experience. Husserl tried to grapple with this subject pole of intentional experience. It is my impression that, as far as contemporary Western psychology goes, even phenomenological and existential psychologists are reluctant to take the self as subject as seriously as Husserl did. By contrast, the Advaita Vedāntic approach takes the self as subject most seriously. The Vedāntists ask us to focus attention on the "I," the very center of awareness. Here I do not mean to suggest a mere philosophical analysis, which we have discussed before, but a program for a psychological investigation and for a transformation of one's own personality. This program asks us to grapple with the very basis of our subjectivity, and to make it the foundation of our existence. Such a program for exploration and change—call it meditation, if you will—has been introduced into Western psychology only recently, and that largely as an Eastern import. (I do not mean to say that there are no Western disciplines of meditation, but only that when modern Western psychologists refer to meditation, they seem to mean the Eastern practices.) Here again we are faced with a cross-cultural issue. Where and how does this import fit in the context of contemporary Western psychology—especially psychotherapy? We shall examine this issue in a later section on Eastern psychologies in the Western world.

4. Self as Single versus Multiple. The dilemma of the self as single versus multiple is concerned with the problem of having to unite the diverse and numerous "selves" associated with the various social roles into single whole. Since the perceptions and definitions of the self must change with the passage of time, the changing images must also be linked through some form of continuity so as to forge them into a single whole. Thus, the dilemma of change versus sameness is the same as the dilemma of single versus multiple seen over a period of time. Unity, continuity and sameness of personality present a set of inextricably connected issues which are collectively referred to as the *problem of identity*. As noted, to say that something has changed and has yet remained the same is a paradox which presents itself as a *puzzle* when seen from a purely theoretical level. However, the issue of unity and sameness is not a mere puzzle which can be left to those who have an itch for brain teasers; it poses as a *practical problem* for individuals in dealing with themselves and with others. As noted in the previous chapter, the practical problem has various aspects. It may be as simple and informal as recognizing an old friend who has changed in many ways over decades, or a bit more formal one as in establishing one's eligibility to borrow books or to cross an international boundary by producing documentary proofs, or a much more serious one as in identifying a criminal. In contrast to these *interpersonal* and social situations where the identity of a person is an issue, there are *intrapersonal* problems concerned with the unity and sameness. Resolving conflict of loyalties and coping with rapid bodily changes (as in adolescence) are examples of intrapersonal aspects of the identity issue. Besides being a theoretical as well as a practical problem manifesting itself in various forms, the issue of change versus sameness is concerned with *values*. Take the following questions, for instance. Why is it important to be concerned with the issue of sameness versus change in the first place? Do we not consider certain types of changes in a person to be more desirable than other changes? Do we not like to preserve certain aspects of ourselves? Why? All these questions are clearly concerned with values.

From what was said in the previous paragraph, it should be clear that the dilemma of self as single versus multiple is a complex and multifaceted issue which is at once a puzzle, a practical problem, and also an issue concerned with values. Although some aspects of this issue have already been discussed at length in the previous chapter, it will be useful to take another look so as to examine the influence of values on theoretical positions, since such differences in values set one school of psychology apart from another.

To begin with, we may note that the practical aspects of the identity problem in the social context are relatively easier to deal with. Recognizing an individual even after a gap of thirty years does not usually pose any great difficulty because, despite major changes, the individual's appearance or style continues to be so nearly unchanged as to provide a clue to selfsameness. The establishing of identity in the legal context is quite important since a mistaken identity may bring a life sentence to an innocent suspect. Fortunately, cases of mistaken identity are relatively rare, and jurisprudence demands that the suspect be given the benefit of the doubt if the identity of the wrongdoer is not clearly established. In the ordinary day-to-day situations, the problem of identity does not prove to be a very difficult puzzle to solve. Wittgenstein (quoted in Vesey, 1974, pp. 104–105) was right in pointing out that the *ordinary* use of the word person involves a "composite" use, which means that it refers to a loose conglomerate of characteristics or things such that we can pick and choose those which are appropriate to the occasion. Thus, there is no contradiction involved in saying that the competent scientist with whom I was just speaking is the same person as the average-looking student whom I met some thirty years ago. We can argue along the same lines and recognize that the ordinary use of the first person singular pronoun "I" also involves a composite use which not only allows, but even requires, us to mean different things appropriate to the occasion. Nevertheless, does this mean that I should be satisfied with a similarly composite and, shall we say, "fuzzy" meaning of the term "I" even when I ask myself the question "Who am I?" in a deeply existential or philosophical sense?

It is true that the concerns which lead a person to ask himself or herself the question "Who am I?" are not the same or equally serious at all times, and therefore different answers are satisfactory depending on the level of seriousness of the inquirer and the context of inquiry. Under ordinary circumstances, most of us are rather casual about the identity issue, and accept a loose conceptualization of the self. James was right when he said that ". . . the identity found by the *I* in it's *me* is only a loosely construed thing." But this is true only at the *ordinary* level which Wittgenstein was referring to (see James, 1890/1950, Vol. 1, p. 372; more fully quoted in the previous chapter). It follows, therefore, that most people when asked "Who are you?" tend to give a list of self-definitions, role categories, or personal characteristics which are only loosely put together. Yet, even "ordinary" adolescents who ask themselves the question "Who am I?" are often quite serious in asking this; they tend to seek a sense of unity among various abandoned and anticipated images of the self organized around a reasonably meaningful theme. Nevertheless, the dominant concerns of the youth are *mastering* the tasks relevant to the middle phase of life, namely, finding a suitable niche in the society, coping with rapid changes which threaten continuity from inside (such as bodily changes) and outside (changing society and expectations from others), and so on. As Erikson rightly points out, the sense of identity gained through a successful resolution of the dilemmas of growth to adulthood is mainly a sense of *stability*. It is derived from the confidence in one's abilities to cope with the challenges of change.

It is interesting to note that Gordon and Gergen (1968, p. 6), in their discussion of the dilemma of the self as single versus multiple consider stability "an important counterpart of singularity." As noted by Erikson, a sense of identity is not gained and maintained once and for all; it is continually threatened, occasionally lost, and usually restored without great difficulty. Most "normal" adults have adequate levels of ability to cope with changes in an "average expectable environment" (to use an ego-psychoanalytic term) and are thereby able to maintain a sense of stability throughout adulthood and old age. Those who do not have adequate levels of coping would benefit from psychological counselling, and contemporary psychologists are developing numerous techniques for therapy relevant at various levels of deficit in coping.

Let us forget for a moment those persons who have difficulties in coping with the changes and challenges of life, and consider those who are reasonably successful in life, need no special help in coping, and are looking for a more intrinsically satisfying and stable basis for their selfhood. Among some persons of this category, the quest for the nature of the self is usually much different from the typical adolescent quest for identity. Such persons may ask themselves the question "Who am I?" not in the sense "Where do I belong?" as many adolescents do, but in the sense "What is the best in me which I must preserve at any cost?" or "Is there something which can provide an absolutely firm basis for my selfhood?" There are, of course, some psychologists who would say that psychologists, as scientists, have nothing to do with these latter types of issues; science cannot deal with absolute principles or with values. They would rather assign such issues to philosophy and religion and restrict the scope of psychology to whatever fits the natural science model. However, others, who do not wish to confine their view of psychology in this manner, must take up the identity issue at a deeper philosophical level without shying away from values and ideals.

It is clear that modern Western psychology has not considered the identity issue as an important issue. In fact, Erikson is perhaps the only prominent Western psychologist who has taken the identity issue seriously, although contemporary Western philosophers continue to display an active interest in it (Vesey, 1974; Perry, 1975). As noted in the previous chapter, Erikson (1968, p. 135) suggests that "there is in fact in each individual an 'I,' an observing centre of awareness" which transcends what he has called psychosocial identity. I think that Erikson's view of the "I" is not much different from Kant's transcendental ego—

except that Erikson avoids the ambiguity in the Kantian position by separating the "center of awareness" from the ego, and by assigning the synthetic and integrative functions to the latter. Nevertheless, Erikson's "I," being nothing but a center of awareness, is as empty and inconsequential as the Kantian ego. The problem here is not philosophical or epistemological, i.e., concerned with the logic of postulation or its verification, but psychological in the sense of offering help or guidance for an individual's quest for identity at levels higher than finding or maintaining a sense of psychosocial identity. It is in relation to such a higher level of existential awareness that the Indian approaches can claim to offer some help.

As noted in the previous chapter, both Yoga and Vedānta take the identity issue not as a mere puzzle to be solved with the use of logic, but as a serious problem concerning human existence itself. For them, the quest for identity is part of a program for the transformation of personality which aims at working out a life style based on an unfailing principle of selfsameness. What Yoga and Vedānta claim is that the experience of pure consciousness can provide an absolutely firm basis for one's selfhood. Since the experience of pure consciousness is said to provide a lasting sense of fulfilment, it can be taken as a key to progress toward "positive mental health." This position can be expected to lead to a relevant program of "therapy"—if by therapy we mean a program for improving the human condition to the highest degree possible. Thus, the identity issue, as treated in the Indian tradition can be seen as a way of bridging the gap between philosophy, human spiritual needs, and the enterprise of psychology. It is difficult to find a similar connection between philosophy and psychology in the Western intellectual tradition.

Here again Husserl comes closest to the Indian approach in that, starting with the Kantian notion of the Pure Ego, he tried to trace its basis in "pure subjectivity." Moreover, as noted in Chapter 4, Husserl's program of reductive phenomenology not only involves an attempt to "put out of action" the acts of consciousness, but is also expected to bring about a valuable existential transformation of the individual. Indeed, Husserl's discovery of the "existential transformation" following from the practice of phenomenological reduction could have been expected to lead to a psychological theory and a "therapeutic" technique to help attain higher levels of fulfilment. If such a technique did indeed develop, I have no doubt that it would closely parallel the techniques of Yoga. Although the direct and indirect influence of Husserl (and his protégé, Heidegger) has in fact led to phenomenological and existential approaches to psychology and psychotherapy, the direction of such influence is much different from the Yogic approach.

To suggest that reductive phenomenology would have led to something like Yoga is to engage in pure speculation. Nevertheless, it would be instructive to speculate on the reasons why the development of Husserl's ideas followed a particular course in history. More specifically we may ask: "why was Husserl's lead in the development of reductive phenomenology not followed even by his own best student?" For an answer to such a question we must examine the sociocultural milieu in which Husserl's ideas developed. Husserl was working in an academic community which expected its members to engage in activities like philosophical thinking, debating and publishing. Academics are by no means expected to bring about an existential transformation in themselves or in others. It is possible that Husserl may have found that the "existential gains" which follow after the phenomenological reduction are extremely valuable, but he found no better place for them in his writings than a brief mention in a casual footnote! I wonder if he would have found a better place for his "meditations" in a monastery. After all, his own teacher Brentano had escaped the restrictive atmosphere of organized religion and taken refuge in the relatively more permissive academia. Husserl could have hardly turned to psychology for any possible practical "applications" of his techniques either, because the academic psychology of his days had adopted a natural science model—which he almost hated. Thus, for want of a supportive sociocultural milieu, further development of reductive phenomenology stopped in Husserl's own lifetime. Later, his own junior colleague, Heidegger, was to inspire the application of phenomenological principles to psychology and psychotherapy, but the direction of the influence of Heideggerian hermeneutics was bound to be much different from that of the reductive approach.

As noted, hermeneutic phenomenology can effectively deal with the perceptions of the objective world, and with the self as object. Also, in its psychoanalytical version, "hermeneutics" or interpretations of conscious content can enable us to deal with the unconscious. However, it provides us no leads to the self as subject, or into its inner core, the transcognitive zones of consciousness. It should be clear from the previous discussion, that reductive phenomenology had already demonstrated that it could help in grappling with self as subject, and it has great potential for providing further leads into the region of pure subjectivity. Obviously, this potential was not fully realized.

Methods of hermeneutic phenomenology can help clarify one's position in the socially constructed reality, and thus help solve problems in coping with practical problems in daily life. In the sociocultural milieu in which Husserl and Heidegger worked, there was place for a psychology which would help individuals in coping with the problems of the so-called "real" world, and not for a psychology which would help attain higher levels of fulfillment or spiritual goals. As I shall try to show in the following section, the influence of the phenomenological approach has manifest itself in the development of methods for enhancing "self-actualization," an ideal which was fully entrenched in the Western cultures. In contrast, thinkers of the Yogic and Vedāntic traditions, who were dealing with problems similar to those that Husserl had, helped develop techniques of "self-realization"—which is an ideal cherished by Eastern cultures.

Self-Actualization and Self-Realization: Alternative Models for the Transformation of Personality

It is but natural that a discussion of the nature of self and of the quest for identity should return to issues concerning human nature and views of the ideal human condition. This is inevitable because the identity issue cannot be separated from our views of what human beings are by nature, and what they can be at their best. Again, as noted in the introductory section of Chapter 2, there are obvious cultural differences in approaches to these issues. Given the great diversity of opinions in both the Indian and Western traditions, it is not easy to decide which themes dominate the respective traditions in these matters. With the admission of some arbitrariness, I would repeat that, in my view, self-realization and self-actualization are dominant themes of Indian and Western traditions which have deeply influenced the views of identity and personality development in the respective traditions. Let me explain why it is so.

Let us take once again the Eriksonian view of identity. Although Erikson recognizes that there is a transcendental "I" which provides a basis for the unity and sameness of a human being, the entire course of the life cycle is viewed as a continual process of adaptation to changes forced upon us from the inside and the outside. In the Eriksonian model of man, an incessant drive toward growth is implicitly taken for granted as a natural characteristic of human nature. This view is similar to the motion of self-actualization which is prominent in the writings of Maslow, Rogers, and many other Western psychologists. As pointed out in Chapter 2, self-actualization implies the actualization of *potentials* or abilities as they become manifest in accomplishments in science, technology, art, sports, or other human pursuits. A self-actualizing person masters certain tasks, pursues excellence, and works toward success. This is consistent with Erikson's emphasis, following Freud's, on love and *work* as major concerns of human beings. The ideal here is the hero, a person who is at the top of one field or another (Coan, 1977).[3] A related but secondary ideal is the sage—an ideal popular since the ancient Greeks and reflected in contemporary Western psychology in many ways, such as in the value of a dispassionate pursuit of knowledge ("value-free" science), or in Erikson's emphasis on wisdom as a virtue, for instance.

When I say that the hero and the sage are ideals implicit in Western psychology, I do not mean that they represent the entire range of values relevant to Western psychology, nor do I mean that pursuit of excellence or the value of work are absent in India. What I mean to point out here is the two-way relationship between the dominant values of culture and the concepts of psychology. While psychological concepts are molded by the dominant values of the society of their origin, the teaching of such concepts, and the practice of therapeutic techniques based on them, in turn strengthen the same values in the culture. In my view, the Indian approaches to psychology cherish the saint the most, and place the sage and the hero next in order. In contrast, the Western traditions of psychology have cherished the hero the most, placed the sage next, and have almost nothing to do with the saint. Let me try to explain how this difference in ideals manifests itself in the theory and practice of psychology.

In Western psychology, emphasis on self-actualization implies that a mature person is seen as constantly striving for higher and higher levels of accomplishment and excellence. Thus, the Maslowian Third Force in psychology has promoted "growth groups" to help enhance continued growth of personality through the realization of a person's latent potentials. Thus, the "human potential movement" tries to bring out the best in man by encouraging the expression of abilities in the performance of various types of work. In this model, life is seen as a continual process of *becoming*, a process where change is not simply accepted, but a change for better (usually in the sense of higher and higher accomplishments in various worldly pursuits) is highly cherished. Note also that in this process, one is explicitly or implicitly setting goals for the future which are worthwhile within a certain framework of values. One strives hard to reach these goals. If the goals are found to be beyond reach, one must either switch to other goals which are not beyond reach, or else feel frustrated and hopeless. If the goals are reached, new and higher goals must be set and one must continue striving toward them—or else face stagnation and boredom. In either case, the process of "becoming" is a process where one has an "ideal self" which is different from the "real self" as Carl Rogers has put it. This means that one always tries to become something *different* from what one is. If this is true, then the following points suggest themselves as implications of the self-actualization model.

First, there is always a certain level of dissatisfaction in the process of self-actualization, since at any given time, one has never reached the point where one should have been. Well, it is true that dissatisfaction with the current state of affairs (or "relative deprivation") is the key to progress, but paradoxically, continued dissatisfaction is the *price* of progress. Second, the process of becoming is such that images of the self and perspectives on the world must always keep changing. Although there is much to enjoy in the changing and widening of vistas, it is nevertheless an unending journey because the horizons keep receding just as rapidly as one chases them. One is forever starting, but never arriving. Finally, we may ask: does one "find oneself" in this process? The answer must be no, because the eyes are always set on becoming something one is not.

The Vedāntists argue along these lines and conclude that self-actualization is not the correct way of knowing the true nature of the self, or of seeking genuine and lasting happiness for that matter. What, then, is the correct way? According to Vedānta, the correct way involves making a "wise discrimination" between self and the non-self. This, in turn, involves learning to distinguish between the permanent and the impermanent, and focusing on that which remains unchanged within us throughout the life cycle. As noted, there is nothing in a human being that remains unchanged through the life cycle except the "I," the center of awareness.

The critical issue here is to see *what* remains the same throughout the human life span. This type of a question does not appeal to many contemporary psychologists and philosophers. The philosopher Popper has remarked, for instance, that the question "What is the self?" is not worth asking (see Popper and Eccles, 1977, p. 100). In his opinion, "What is X?" type of questions are always connected with the idea of essences; they lead to a discussion of the meaning of words, and simply "degenerate into verbalism." Perhaps Popper's observations make sense if understood within the Western intellectual tradition, but I do not think that they are applicable to the Indian approaches to the self. As noted, the Yoga–Vedānta claim is that the knowledge of the Self is not a matter of mere logical inference or of making an unverifiable postulate. The correct answer to the question "What is Self?" is based on a special type of experience which is verifiable through suggested means, and also has predictable behavioral consequences. In fact, the Vedāntists often point out that mere understanding of the arguments concerning the self and the non-self is not enough. Rather, it is common in the Indian tradition to look down upon mere scholarship and verbal knowledge unaccompanied by self-realization and by behavior consistent with genuine self-realization.

Let us now recapitulate the basic arguments of Yoga which explain why the Yogic answer to the question "What is Self" does not lead to mere verbiage. According to Yoga, experience of the real self is based on a transcognitive samādhi experience. As noted, positive consequences of the samādhi experience are expected to manifest themselves after the attainment of even the preliminary stages of samādhi. The samādhi experiences can be said to be "positively reinforcing" in the sense that one tends to seek more and more of the same. However, the desirable quality of these experiences is rooted in an inexhaustible source of inner calm and peace. Being independent of any object of pleasure, they do not set a person upon an incessant pursuit of objects of pleasure. As a person seeks and discovers an inner calm, the cumulative force of the ordinary reinforcements of the past is attenuated. Over a period of time, the yogi is released from the burden of the past so that the effects of the past reinforcement can no longer dictate the direction of his thought and behavior. Thus, a yogi is able to enjoy genuine freedom.

The Vedāntists give a somewhat different account of how and why self-realization through samādhi experience leads to a total transformation of the individual's personality. Instead of giving a discursive summary of the Vedāntic arguments, let me present a poetic account in the words of the 17th century saint-poet Tukārām:

> Tinier than an atom,
> yet vast like the skies
> so is the self, realizes Tukārām.
>
> Body, the very basis of
> the world—a mere illusion—
> is transcended
> as if swallowed by itself.
>
> The triad of
> the knower, knowable, and knowledge
> is transcended;
> a light is lit within.
>
> Now, says Tukārām,
> what is left in life
> is only for others.
> (Tukārām, 1973, 993; A. C. Paranjpe, trans.).

This poetic expression of self realization certainly has a "mystical" quality. However, a close examination of the poem would help explain the meaning. Thus, the first stanza mainly asserts that the self is unextended. If we accept, like Descartes, that the self is not identifiable with anything extended, it follows that it could be either like a tiny point without dimensions (a *center* of awareness), or unbounded (like the skies). This means that the "I" could be both tiny and vast at the same time! Except for the use of the paradox, what the "mystic" says is not different from the familiar Cartesian notion of the unextended character of the self. However, the second stanza says something much different from what Descartes or James would have us believe. Unlike these Western philosophers, Vedāntists like Tukārām assert that the Self is neither the thinker nor his thoughts, but the ability to experience which continues to be with us throughout our lives. Such realization dissolves the identification of the "I" with the body, or with the Jamesian "material self." This type of a realization is illuminating without being cognitive. But why should such a mystical experience lead to an altruistic note (living for others) in the end as suggested in the last stanza? The reason may be explained with the help of another poem by Tukārām.

> I saw my death with my own eyes,
> and what a spectacle it was!
>
> The skies were filled with joy
> bringing boundless fulfilment.
>
> Once I was infused with pride.
> Now that the pride is abandoned,
> a bountiful joy is here to stay.
> (Tukārām, 1973, 2669; A. C. Paranjpe, trans.).

Well, this poem would seem to be even more puzzling than the previous one. How could anyone witness his own death? Obviously, what the poet means by the death of his self is the definite end of his *egoism*. If the only basis of our selfsameness is a center of awareness, any and all definitions of the self which lead to a prideful attachment to a body, a name, family, kith and kin, ideology, reputation, or whatever must be *ultimately* misguided. Since no aspects of my psychosocial identity are based on anything permanent or of *absolute* value, they cannot provide me with a lasting sense of genuine fulfilment. Therefore, instead of clinging to particular psychosocial self-definitions, I should retract my identifications from anything and everything (physical or social) which is subject to change. Such a conclusion has obviously stupendous implications for a life in society.

This implies first of all that one must reject all attachments with the "me" and the "mine"—whether it be property, occupation, family, kith and kin, country, or whatever. This, in turn, implies becoming totally selfless. It does not of course mean that one has to lose the capacity to love anyone. It simply means that one does not identify oneself exclusively with a particular social sphere which one has chosen to call one's own. There is no special circle called the "we" with which the "I" is identified, as opposed to a separate entity called the "they." As such, the "they" do not invoke fear, anger, malice or hatred, nor does a "thou" invoke jealousy or a threat of competition.

All this, one may say, is pure idealism. Since it is common experience that having to discard anything with which one is identified heart-and-soul is extremely painful, we may dismiss all this as either unrealizable poetic idealism, or as simply the outlook of one unfit to live in society. In fact many contemporaries of Tukārām called him a fool because he neglected his wife and his grocery business as he went on helping the poor and guiding the spiritually inclined. There are, of course, millions of people over the centuries who have read his poetry and biography and have recognized him as a truly selfless person of unlimited compassion—a saint.

Saintliness is obviously a value and guiding principle for the philosophy and psychology of Vedānta. For those of us in modern psychology who have imbibed the values of survival, adaptation, achievement, or even self-realization, just the mention of saintliness would appear to be either impracticable idealism, or simply the intrusion of some religious mumbo-jumbo. To say the least, the Vedāntic view of self-realization may be said to be an escapist view that asks us to withdraw ourselves from the struggle for success and the striving for excellence. As suggested earlier, it may also be called a "sour grapes" attitude. The Vedāntists of course claim that the inner calm and blissfulness of self-realization is much more valuable and deeply fulfilling than mastery of the world. Although some Vedāntists retreat from the rough-and-tumble of the practical life and seek sanctuary in a monastery, there are others who accept a "normal" life style involving an active participation in family, workforce, and community. The realization of the self as the unchanging center of awareness does not necessarily imply forsaking the usual social obligations, nor does the "death of the self" mean a loss of the capacity to play the usual social roles. What it means is the cultivation of a sense of detachment in one's mode of being-in-the-world, or a sense of being in the world, but not of it. This way, one continues to function in the day-to-day activities without hankering for power, name or fame. For a person who has realized the true self in the Vedāntic sense of the term, there is no "ideal" to be realized, no goals to be striven for. The process of "Becoming" ends when the true nature of "Being" is realized. The true self continues to provide not only a firm basis for a robust and flexible empirical self relevant to the practical life, but also an inner source of calm and bliss.

Again, are we supposed to accept this as an article of faith? No, says the Vedāntist, because the claims pertaining to the nature of self-realization are experientially verifiable, and the procedures for verification are described in detail. There does not seem to be a substantial difference between the Yogic descriptions of self-realized persons (those who have attained kaivalya) and their Vedāntic counterparts (the jīvanmukta). However, there are clear differences in the prescriptions given by the two approaches for attaining such exalted states. By and large, the yogis stress a program of mind-control or "concentrative meditation," while the Vedāntists stress a serious, continual and arduous examination ("mindful meditation") of the self with a stress on what is permanent and basic to one's identity. Neither of these schools claim quick success in attaining such high ideals. Do they have enough credibility so that they can at least be considered worth a try?

Credibility of psychological models depends on several aspects of the entire sociocultural milieu which may help support (or destroy) that credibility. There are numerous aspects of the Indian culture which support the credibility of Yoga and Vedānta: myths, legends, biographies of saints, epics, stories, temples, idols, festivals, sermons, poems, songs, phrases and sayings and so on. The most powerful supports for the credibility of such models are the actual examples of self-realized persons in everyday life. Although such great examples as Rāmakṛṣṇa Paramahaṁsa and Ramaṇa Maharṣi are rare, there are always less-well-known examples, or at least saintly persons who are close to such ideals, in various regions of India in every generation. The most unmistakable signs of progress toward self-realization are loss of egoism, and genuine, Christ-like compassion for all beings. Besides, there are various behavioral manifestations of inner calm, tranquility and evenness of temperament among those who are well ahead on the path to self-realization.

The principles and practices of psychology influenced by a cultural background and milieu that displays and fosters such distinctive ideals is bound to be itself distinctive. Although certain sections of the Indian and Western societies have emphasized effective adaptation, self-actualization, self-realization and other such values, and have thereby led to the development of distinctive approaches to psychology, they cannot (and have not) *monopolize(d)* such ideals. To put it simply, there are innumerable people in India who need behavior therapy, and there are many others who strive for self-actualization. At the same time, there are Westerners who aspire to self-realization in the Vedāntic sense. The needs and conditions of people in any society vary widely, and so do temperaments of psychologists. As such, there is a wide scope for an "import and export" of specialized approaches to suit the special needs of individuals—researchers, therapists, and patients. In the following section, we shall examine certain problems in a cultural exchange of specialized approaches.

On Cross-Cultural Exchange in Psychology: Problems and Prospects

Much of contemporary psychology in India today is either a direct copy of Western models, or a locally adapted minor variation of the same. The overwhelming influence of Western models is easily ascribed to the colonial influence; it is hardly surprising if people are impressed by many aspects of the dominant culture. It is of course not true that the Indians were given to blind emulation of the British; the British influence was not so overwhelming in the fields of religion, philosophy and classical music, fields in which there were highly established and even growing local traditions. Why, then, were the Indians so prone to accept uncritically the Western models in psychology? Several reasons can be suggested. *First,* modern Western psychology entered the Indian scene as a "science," a field in which the Europeans had clearly established superiority. Those who were trained in the imported models began to equate psychology with an implicit natural science model. Since the psychological concepts of native origin could not fit this model, they could hardly be recognized as having any relevance to what the university professors called psychology. *Second,* classical problems of general psychology, such as reaction time, psychophysics, sensation, perception, learning, and memory could be studied without much regard to the cultural context. Therefore, there was little or no problem in uncritically accepting concepts and methods in this field of study. *Third,* academic psychologists have tended to define problems in the same way as the imported textbooks define them, rather than starting with problems faced in their own individual or collective lives. It seems to me that the value-free and impersonal stance of behavioristically oriented experimental psychology was so dominant in the Indian academic scene that few dared choose to study problems as they arose from daily living in Indian society. *Fourth,* although Freud's ideas were introduced into India quite early, they have not taken root in either the academic or medical fields. I cannot say whether this is due to the limitations of the psychoanalytical model in terms of its cross-cultural applicability, or to the prohibitive costs of psychoanalytic therapy. Clinical counselling and psychotherapy based on Western models did become available here and there. But the high costs of counselling have restricted the practice of clinical psychology to a limited field of, shall I say, a rather Westernized urban elite. Of course there is such a thing as psychiatry in India, but it is largely confined to custodial care for acute psychotics in overpopulated mental hospitals. The restrictive hospital settings could hardly be congenial for Indian psychiatry to be concerned with problems of a wider scope. As far as studies in personality are concerned, there have been numerous attempts to adopt aptitude and personality tests to the Indian cultural context, but such attempts are largely restricted to the level of test items and the development of local norms for test scores. Attempts to develop new theoretical frameworks, or even to deal with basic conceptual models, are relatively rare.

Over the years, however, there has been some change in this situation. As the colonial mentality is gradually fading, there is increasing confidence in looking into the native intellectual tradition for perspectives on psychological issues. Some recent books on Indian psychology were mentioned early in the first chapter. We now have the *Journal of Indian Psychology,* which is not an Indian journal of Western psychology, but a journal that emphasizes ideas of Indian origin. In India, there is a rich cultural legacy to which one can turn for insights into the human psyche. *First,* there is a rich and varied philosophical literature, two major epics, mythology, Tāntric and other sectarian writings, and so on. *Second,* for concepts in psychopathology, one can turn to Āyurveda, the indigenous system of medicine which is alive and growing in popularity. There is some recent work in the field (*e.g.,* Gupta, 1977; Weiss, 1978) but more work is needed. *Third,* it would be useful to examine the relevance of traditional healing practices, such as various methods of inducing trance states and other "shamanist" techniques, in terms of their psychological significance. Some recent research indicates that there is a sort of psychological counselling associated with practice of astrology in India.[4] More ethnopsychiatric field work would indicate how the Indian culture has developed methods of offering help to those who suffer from psychological problems.[5] Finally, it is necessary to conduct a very close study of the interpersonal encounters between the Guru and his disciple which are intended to enhance the spiritual well-being of the disciple and offer him help in the process of self-realization. We shall have more about this later on.

Despite the several indications which show that the Indian psychologists have started to return to their intellectual legacy, there are some strong reservations against doing so. Let me indicate some of the reservations against returning to the traditional psychological thought of Indian origin which were expressed to me by psychologists in India. One reservation arose from the concern for maintaining a universalist stance. This is a genuine concern, and any mention of regional origins of ideas arouses suspicions of parochial pride and ethnocentrism. All I can say is that one should not be fooled by the apparently universalistic stance of modern psychology in the name of "science." One cannot bury one's head in the sand and refuse to look to various cultures for their valuable insights and alternative models. I need not say more on this toward the end of this book because the reader may not have even touched this book if he or she was convinced that the opposite was true!

Another reservation is specific to the psychology of Yoga and Vedānta. It is argued that these traditional perspectives are not relevant in view of the important problems which Indian society is facing today. A related concern is expressed thus: "What good is Yoga or Vedānta for the common man?" In response I would say that certainly Yoga and Vedānta have little or nothing to offer by way of directly trying to solve pressing contemporary problems such as poverty, corruption, prejudice, regionalism, casteism, or class conflict. In fact, I think that the Yoga enthusiasts who recommend daily meditation as a panacea for all the social problems including urban crime and war are as misguided as are the learning theorists who think of the schedules of reinforcements as the royal road to a utopian world. I also think that Yoga and Vedānta focus on individualism of sorts—although they offer programs that would liberate individuals from their narrow loyalties. As to concerns for the "common man," I would say that pointing a finger at the problems of the common man is to unnecessarily sidetrack the usefulness of self-realization models for those who need and deserve them. One cannot reject the relevance of psychology for special purposes in the name of the so-called "common man." Otherwise, we should have to reject the relevance of psychology to minorities with special needs—the epileptic, the retarded, or the gifted—because none of them represent the common man. Besides, Vedānta has been translated into simple language by saints and by devotional cults across India in a way that makes sense to the poor and the illiterate. Yoga, Vedānta, Jainism and other systems have survived through millennia, and do continue to be useful to innumerable "common" men and women not only in India but also to some small groups of people elsewhere in the world. At any rate, the merits or demerits of any system must be judged in relation to the range of problems it is designed to solve.

Turning now to the entry of Indian concepts into the Western world, we may first note that reference has already been made (in Chapter 1) to William James's acquaintance with the Indian approach to religious experience, to Jung's views on Eastern concepts, and to the early psychophysiological studies of Yogic meditation. Such early examples indicate the sporadic interest of a few scholarly persons focussed on specific concepts or phenomena. From the 1960s, however, an academic or scholarly interest in Indian psychological concepts has become more widespread and broadly based. For better or for worse, it has been concomitant with—or often loosely associated with—the popularity of Eastern religions in Europe and the United States. This popular interest was part of a sociohistoric context and a cultural milieu associated with numerous events and persons: the troubled youth scene, the beatniks of Europe, and the Vietnam-war protestors in the U.S.; Aldous Huxley's interest in soma—the legendary elixir of ancient India; Timothy Leary, LSD, and the "drug cults," the Beatles and their Indian guru; Ravi Shankar and his sitar; the chanting of "Hare Krishna" on the streets; advertisements in local newspapers asking us to enroll in Mahesh Yogi's TM classes, and so on. Certainly, these various aspects of the Western cultural scene in the 'sixties and the 'seventies have done much to popularize the idea of Yoga, meditation, guru, karma and other concepts associated with Indian psychology. During the 'sixties and the 'seventies many Indian gurus took to jet travel around the world, trying to carry ancient wisdom to international audiences. Also, many Westerners have taken trips to India, some in search of drugs, and others seeking guidance from wise Indian gurus in their secluded ashrams. Some serious psychologists have been to India to learn about Yoga and meditation. While the cultural exchange on this scene must have done much in the way of promoting better understanding among peoples, the "pop" character of much of the East–West exchange has extracted its price—in terms of "bastardization" of concepts like karma, for instance. In a book called *Karma Cola,* Gita Mehta (1980) has poked fun at the emptiness of the crosscultural encounters under "Guru Industries, Inc."

The faddish popularity of Yoga and meditation is bound to wear off. The fashionable and trendy attraction for Eastern religions seems to have already begun to decline. Quite possibly, however, the cultural exchange of the post-World War II era has sown the seeds of interest in Eastern concepts among a small minority of serious-minded psychologists in the U.S. and Europe. Already there are signs of increasing recognition of concepts of Indian origin in a growing body of North American literature on consciousness. In my judgment, closer East–West cooperation may be expected in the near future in the use of Yogic and Zen techniques in the treatment of psychosomatic disorders in combination with Western techniques. Several researchers in Japan have been working in this field (Goyeche, 1977; Ishikawa, Kikuchi and Morita, 1977; Sasaki, 1981). The concept of self-realization is of great relevance to Western psychologists interested in positive mental health, growth of human potentials, self-actualization and other related concepts. It seems to me that introducing the *methods* of self-realization in the field of contemporary Western psychology is even more problematic than communicating the *concept* of self-realization to Western psychologists. To be able to appreciate the nature of problems in this field of cultural exchange, we must once again examine the distinctive *institutional frameworks* which are necessary to support distinctive approaches to psychology.

Clinical psychology originated in Western societies in the medical context. Although clinical psychologists are still second-class citizens to the medical establishment, they are by and large bound by the same ethical code as the medical practitioners. Although specific conventions, values, and laws governing the doctor-patient relationship are different from country to country, the roles of the therapist and the client are similarly structured in much of the Western world. Asian countries by and large seem to be following the same Western model, including the beginning of medical training with the Hippocratic Oath—a legacy of Greek civilization. In this model, the medical doctor, and likewise the psychologist, is a *professional* who offers his services to the client in return for a fee. The training, certification and the disciplining of nonprofessional conduct are handled primarily by the regional or national *associations* which are supposed to operate democratically within the framework of legislation which protects and controls the practice of the professions. The patient or the client normally respects and trusts the practitioners' expertise and judgment, and is usually aware of his own rights and responsibilities as patient. Like all other social roles, the doctor and patient roles are sets of reciprocal expectations structured within the framework of consensually supported beliefs and values.

Beliefs and values concerning health and health-care are clearer and better defined in the medical field than in the field of mental health. Although abortion and euthanasia are highly controversial issues in contemporary North America, the issues involve more polarization than confusion. By contrast, issues concerning values and goals of psychotherapy are characterized more by confusion than by polarization. Obviously, there is great diversity of opinion among psychologists as to what mental health really means, and there is a good deal of confusion as to what it means as far as the public is concerned. While most people know what to expect from a doctor, and while nobody is generally concerned about possible value differences between oneself and one's doctor, the same is not (and cannot be) true among persons who seek psychological (as opposed to medical) help. This is particularly true in relation to positive mental health, self-actualization and similar other concerns. Note that the role in North American society of a T-group trainer or that of the leader of an encounter group is less well defined than that of a psychoanalyst, and much less clear than that of a medical doctor. There are problems concerning not only the qualifications and certification of such "trainers", "leaders" and "facilitators," but also concerning the values that should govern their behavior.

It is in this gray zone of the promoters of positive mental health and instructors in the art of self-actualization that the role of the Indian guru is being introduced. Such introduction only adds confusion to the already murky waters. The concept of guru originated in a much different sociocultural context than the contemporary Western social context, and it is by no means easy to fit it into the latter context. It is my observation that in the Western society, the concept of guru is often grossly misunderstood. I think, therefore, that it is necessary to say a few simple things about the concept of guru which are generally taken for granted by those who are raised in the Indian culture. The word guru literally means a teacher, and although it is used in many Indian languages to refer to any teacher including a school teacher, it has a special meaning and significance in the context of spiritual development (adhyātma). A guru is not a title conferred by any institution; he or she is not a priest, a healer, or a therapist. A guru is a guide chosen by a spiritual aspirant. It is a popular and conventional belief in India that it is impossible to attain spiritual enlightenment or self-realization without the guidance of a teacher who is himself or herself enlightened. It appears that early Vedāntic writings do not emphasize the role of the guru as much as later writings do. Patañjali does not say much about this subject, and there is nothing in his aphorisms which suggests that Yogic practices cannot be undertaken without the help of a guru. Nevertheless, the place of a guru is considered so high that a popular and oft-chanted prayer says the guru is identical with the trinity—the gods of creation, maintenance, and destruction of the universe!

Obviously, the guru is the most important and revered person in an aspirant's life. Only your guru knows what is good for you. The guru commands total obedience once a person accepts him as his guide. It is not considered easy to find the right guru; he or she must be worthy of highest respect, and his or her spiritual merit must be unquestionable. Much is written on how to identify the right person to be chosen as a guru, and biographies of aspirants are full of accounts of their long and difficult searches for a guru, searches that usually involve chasing any and every person who may be reputed to be a great soul. Yet, the tradition holds that it is futile to go out looking for a guru because, it is said, the appropriate person will come looking for you as soon as you are ready to receive proper advice. In the traditional world view, every spiritual seeker is destined to meet his or her guru when the time is right; it is just the way the cosmic order is supposed to work!

Given this intricate belief system, the guru–disciple relationship can be seen as being culturally unique. It has no counterpart that I know of in the Western cultures. To say the least, the role of the guru is unlike that of a professional psychotherapist in many ways. The guru may be said to be a therapist of sorts only in the sense that he is a person who helps improve one's state from a less satisfactory condition to a more satisfactory one. However, the guru cannot be seen as a professional psychologist who offers his services to those who pay for his time and expertise. The question of payment is too mundane to interfere with a process of guidance which is built into a cosmic order! One cannot enter into a contractual relationship with one's guru. You surrender everything to him, and he will tell you what you should do; he has only your interests at heart. This may sound very authoritarian to the Western ears, but we must remember that it is the disciple who chooses the guru. It is of course true that many unsuspecting religious aspirants around the world have played into the hands of greedy charlatans promising nirvana. But here we are talking about a careful choice of an enlightened guide, not a blind following. An enlightened person who is fit to be your guru must be a self-realized person who has cast off all selfishness. If I have made a mistake in choosing my guide, I have no one to blame but myself.

Against the background of what has just been said, it should be clear that it is by no means easy to fit the role of the guru within the framework of the systems of Western psychology. It should now be easy to understand why many knowledgeable persons are suspicious about programs like Transcendental Meditation which are said to have worked out a fee schedule for everything they offer from ordinary initiation to instruction on how to levitate. Does this mean that an Indian-style guru has no place in the Western world? Not so. Concepts like self-realization may be relevant to persons of all types of culture, and personal interactions which facilitate progress toward it are relevant and possible wherever there is a desire for it.

Notes

1. All kinds of mythical accounts of the origin of Yoga are popular among the Yogis. One myth, for instance, is that Matsyendranāth, a legendary yogi, learned the doctrine of Yoga as it was recited by Lord Śiva to Goddess Pārvati on the seashore. George Weston Briggs (1938/1973) has described in detail how various historical accounts of the teacher–student chains are often mixed with legends and myths. The typical Indian tolerance for mixing history, myth and legend is aversive to the Western temperament.
2. For a systematic comparison of Husserl and Yoga, see Sinari (1965) and Puligandla (1970).
3. R. W. Coan (1977) has suggested that the hero, sage, saint and the artist are the ideals which have often provided guiding models for various Eastern and Western theories of psychology. I have benefitted from Coan's discussion of the role of such ideals in shaping psychological theory and practice.
4. Judy Pugh's doctoral thesis at the University of Chicago has made interesting observations about the counseling component of the astrologers' interactions with their clients.
5. See Sudhir Kakar's *Shamans, mystics and doctors* (New York: Knopf, 1982) for an interesting account of indigenous psychotherapeutic practices of India.

GLOSSARY

Note: Many of the terms explained below have different meanings in different systems and contexts. Only those meanings relevant to the concerns of this book are given here.

abhiniveśa An urge for survival or for self-preservation. Sometimes also translated as "love for life" or "lust for life."

ādhibhautika Generally it means "derived from or pertaining to the elements or matter." This adjective is often used to designate knowledge pertaining to nature—such as scientific knowledge—or to typify suffering arising from material causes, such as fire, falling objects, and so on.

ādhidaivika Relating to, or proceeding from gods or spirits. This adjective is often used to designate knowledge of deities—such as that in theology—or to typify suffering arising from deities, spirits, ghosts, or other "mysterious" causes.

adhyātma Literally, "relating to the self or spirit." In general, the term is used to refer to everything which belongs to the "spiritual" aspects of life—those pertaining to spiritual upliftment, self-realization, self-knowledge and so on.

adhyātmika Literally, relating to the self or the soul. When this adjective is used to describe types of suffering, it refers to that arising from internal, mental or "spiritual" reasons—everything which contrasts āhibhautika and adhyātmika explained above.

Advaita Vedānta Advaita literally means the state of being non-dual. Advaita Vedānta is a branch of the Vedānta school of philosophy which holds that the individual soul (Ātman) is one and the same as Brahman, the single, ubiquitous principle of reality.

āgama Generally, it refers to knowledge—percepts, doctrines—handed down by tradition, particularly by the scriptures. In the context of Yoga, it refers to mental activities leading to cognitions which are deemed valid on the basis of verbal testimony of trustworthy persons.

ahaṁkāra Awareness of oneself, or of individuality; egoism.

ānanda Bliss.

antaḥkaraṇa Inner instrument. In Vedānta, it refers to the active element of the mind as opposed to Ātman, the passive "witness."

aparā vidyā Vedāntic term for knowledge of the phenomenal world as distinguished from the ultimate knowledge of "parā vidyā," which is attainable in the state of Nirvikalpa samādhi.

asaṁprajñāta samādhi A trans-cognitive state of consciousness in which one is conscious without being conscious *of* anything. This state contrasts with the saṁprajñāta variety of states characterized by various levels of cognition or awareness of something.

āsana Literally, posture. Patañjali has recommended a stable and comfortable posture as a third important aid to Yoga.

asmitā Egoism.

āśrama (1) A hermitage or an abode of ascetics. (2) One of the four stages of the life cycle recommended in the Hindu tradition. The four stages are: the student, the householder, a stage of semi-retirement to prepare for renunciation of worldly affairs, and a final stage of complete renunciation of worldly affairs for fully devoting to God or the pursuit of self-realization.

ātman Vedāntic term for the Self.

avidyā Avidyā means nescience or ignorance. This term is often used to refer to a particular type of "ignorance," namely that arising from mistaken notions of the self.

Bhagavad-Gītā The *Bhagavad-Gītā* or "Divine Song" is a section of the epic *Mahābhārata* in which Lord Kṛṣṇa exhorts the warrior Arjuna to fight a holy war. The popularity of this text derives in part from its succinct account of the major philosophical issues discussed in the Upaniṣadic texts and other earlier sources of Indian philosophy.

Bhakti Yoga Path to liberation of the soul, or self-realization through devotion to God.

bhoktṛ One who experiences—enjoys or suffers.

Brahman A Vedāntic concept which refers to the single, ubiquitous, formless, and essentially indescribable principle which is said to pervade the universe. In approximate terms, it is often described as having three main qualities, namely, Being, Consciousness, and Bliss.

buddhi Generally, it means intellect or the power of comprehension, reasoning and so on. In Sāṅkhya philosophy, the term "buddhi" and its equivalent "mahat" refer to an initial product of Prakṛti in the course of its evolution. In Vedānta, buddhi or "intellect" is recognized as part of the inner instrument (antaḥkaraṇa) which is involved in willing, or in determining a course of action.

cit Sentience, or capacity to be conscious at any level, from the lowest to the highest.

citta A Yogic concept roughly equivalent to "mind" or "psyche." It is primarily the seat of all experiences, and also the repository of the residual effects or impressions left behind by all experiences and actions of the past.

cittanadī Literally, "mind-river." Vyāsa uses this expression to describe the flowing character of mental events just as James uses the metaphor "stream of consciousness."

citta vṛtti Activities of the mind (citta), or processes of consciousness, such as thinking, imagining, recollecting and so on.

dhāraṇā Usually translated as "contemplation." Technically, it means the "binding" or "holding" of the processes of consciousness to a particular "place", that is, concentrating thought processes onto a particular object of thought by initially focusing attention on the tip of the nose, or any other object, for instance. This is described by Patañjali as a step in the course of restraining the processes of consciousness.

dharma (1) The word "dharma" has many different connotations such as prescribed conduct, duty, justice, virtue, morality, religion, religious merit, and so on. It also means fulfilling one's obligations to family, society, teachers and so on. Taken in this sense, "dharma" is commonly considered one of the four goals of life along with acquiring wealth or power (artha), fulfilling sexual desire (kāma), and liberating the soul (mokṣa). (2) In Yogic theory, the term "dharma" is used to refer to *properties* of objects as opposed to their substrate or substance (dharmin).

dhyāna Holding on to a particular thought, idea, or image so that the contents of the stream of consciousness become homogenous. This is considered by Patañjali as a step in the gradual restraint of the processes of consciousness leading to the state(s) of samādhi.

draṣṭṛ The "seer," that is, Self-as-percipient.

duḥkha Pain, suffering, or misery.

Gītā Short name for the *Bhagavad-Gītā*. (See above.)

grahaṇa The means of cognition, such as the sense organs.

grahītṛ Self as subject or self-as-knower.

grāhya An object of cognition or of knowledge.

guṇa Quality, aspect, or component. Sāṅkhya theory assumes three interacting aspects or "strands" of Prakṛti, namely, sattva, rajas and tamas.

Haṭha Yoga A form of Yoga that specializes in physical aspects of Yoga, such as postures.

jāgṛti The wakeful state of consciousness. One of the four major states of consciousness recognized by Vedānta. The other three states are suṣupti or sleep, svapna or dream, and turīyā or the "Fourth."

jīva Literally, a living being. As used in Vedānta, it refers to an individual organism, or "personality."

jīvanmukta One who has attained liberation of the soul, and has thus emancipated, while still alive, from the liability of future births and of all suffering therein. A jīvanmukta is a saintly person with infinite compassion for all forms of life. Such a person manifests an ideal condition of human existence highly cherished in the Indian cultural tradition.

Jñāna Yoga The path of knowledge as a means to the attainment of self-realization or liberation of the soul.

kaivalya Literally, kaivalya means a "state of being by oneself." It usually means the separation of Puruṣa or the individual soul from its attachments with objects in the "material" world of Prakṛti. Since the individual's attachments with the worldly objects are believed to be the root of all actions, one is said to attain liberation from the perceptual chain of action and it's consequences by becoming completely detached from all objects of experience in the state of samādhi. Kaivalya can be said to be the Sāṅkhya-Yoga equivalent of mokṣa (or mukti), nirvana (nirvāṇa), or liberation of the soul.

kāma Sexual desire, lust.

karma Literally, karma means action. In most philosophical systems of Indian origin, it is believed that all human actions, like any other events in nature, must be followed by their lawful consequences.

karmāśaya The totality of the residual effects of past experiences and behavior.

karmavipāka "Ripening of actions," whereby residual effects of past experiences and behaviors "fructify" — like seeds germinating under appropriate conditions—leading to appropriate new experiences and behaviors.

Karma Yoga A path to the attainment of liberation of the soul or self-realization by means of a dispassionate pursuit of duty regardless of the fruits of one's action.

kleśa Pain, affliction, or suffering arising from disease.

kriyā yoga Practical aspect of Yoga involving eight parts or "limbs" such as the prescribed restraints, observances, postures and so on.

manana Reflection. In Vedānta, it refers to deeply contemplating the conclusions of Vedāntic philosophy as a means to self-realization.

manas Mind.

māyā This term refers to the Vedāntic concept of the "Primeval (basic or fundamental) Illusion." It is suggested that the phenomenal world, or the world as we see it, is illusory when viewed from the vantage point of the ultimate reality, which is the qualityless Brahman.

mokṣa Literally, it means liberation. Generally, mokṣa refers to the liberation of the self from its entrapment in saṁsāra, the perpetual cycle of birth and death. Since the origin of this cycle is traced to the misconceived notions of the self and to the endless chain of egoistic actions and their consequences, self-realization is suggested as the chief means to liberation.

mukti Same as mokṣa or liberation explained above.

nididhyāsana The repeated and persistent contemplation of the conclusions of the Vedāntic philosophy as a means to self-realization.

nidrā Sleep.

nirbīja samādhi The "seedless" samādhi as opposed to the sabīja type of samādhi described below.

nirvāṇa Literally, it means calmed, quieted or extinguished. The term usually refers to the state of perfect calm, repose or bliss resulting from the absolute extinction of all desires. It is often used synonymously with other terms such as kaivalya, mokṣa and mukti which describe an ideal human condition.

nirvicāra samādhi In the nirvicāra type of samādhi, the cognition of an object becomes completely identified with the object so as to "lose itself" in the process, so to speak.

nirvikalpa samādhi A state of consciousness in which one transcends the duality of the subject and the object of experience.

nirvitarka samādhi This state is said to be attained when memories involving the associative meanings relating to the object of cognition acquired through socially learned verbal conventions are eliminated from consciousness, and a cognition of only the most essential aspects of the object of attention are retained in consciousness.

niyama A set of observances like cleanliness, contentment, ascetic self-control and others recommended by Patañjali as a second set of aids to Yoga.

parā vidyā The ultimate form of knowledge attained in the nirvikalpa samādhi. Vedānta distinguishes this type of knowledge from the knowledge of the phenomenal world, or "aparā vidyā."

Prakṛti One of the two ontological categories which constitute reality according to the Sāṅkhya philosophy. This principle refers to the "material" aspect of reality in contrast to the sentient principle, which manifests itself in the form of the innumerable Puruṣas or "souls."

pramāṇa Generally, in philosophical contexts, pramāṇa means an instrument or means of knowledge. However, as used by Patañjali, the term pramāṇa refers to a set of mental events or processes of consciousness which involve valid cognition. In other words, pramāna means "a mental state reflecting external reality without distortion."

prāṇāyāma Breathing exercises recommended by Patañjali as a fourth aid to Yoga.

pratyakṣa Literally, present before the eyes. As a philosophical term, it refers to direct perception or observation as an epistemic principle or a means of validating propositions. In Yoga, "pratyakṣa" refers to mental activities leading to valid cognition on the basis of direct perception.

pratyāhāra Withdrawing of the senses from their objects (e.g., stop allowing the eyes from looking at one object after another, or ears from listening to various sounds, etc.) recommended by Patañjali as a primary step leading to the restraint of the processes of consciousness.

pratyaya In the context of Yoga, the term "pratyaya" seems to refer primarily to images, ideas, and other such "contents of consciousness."

Puruṣa One of the two ontological categories which constitute reality according to the Sāṅkhya philosophy. This principle manifests itself in the form of innumerable "souls" that reside in all kinds of living creatures. The sentient Puruṣa stands in contrast with Prakṛti, which refers to the "material" aspect of reality.

rajas One of three guṇas or "strands" of Prakṛti, or the material world, as conceptualized in the Sāṅkhya philosophy. Rajas is characterized primarily by activity or energy; sattva and tamas are the other two strands.

Rāja Yoga Name usually assigned to Yoga as described by Patañjali. It contrasts with Hatha Yoga in emphasizing controlling the mind rather than the body.

sabīja samādhi Sabīja literally means "with a seed." Sabīja samādhi refers to a category of four samādhi states (savitarka, nirvitarka, savicāra, and nirvicāra) which are considered to be "with seeds" because they depend upon external, perceptible objects to which consciousness is directed.

sākṣin Literally, witness. In Vedānta, it refers to the Self as an uninvolved witness, as opposed to a self which is egoistically attached to objects in the world.

samādhi A set of hierarchically ordered states of consciousness characterized by an increasing degree of modification of the cognitive and other aspects of consciousness.

saṁnyāsin One who has entered the fourth stage of the life cycle recommended in Hinduism so as to renounce worldly affairs for fully devoting to God or the pursuit of self-realization (see āśrama, above).

saṁprajñāta samādhi All samādhi states which are characterized by cognition are included in this category. It is implied that in these states consciousness is directed either toward external objects, or to the means of their awareness, namely sensory experience, or to the subject of awareness. This category contrasts with the asaṁprajñāta or trans-cognitive type of samādhi, a state in which one is conscious, but not conscious *of* anything.

saṁsāra The eternal cycle of birth and death, a cycle in which individual souls are said to be trapped. Although everyone experiences pleasure as well as pain, the balance of samsāra is generally believed to be negative because what is initially viewed as pleasure also often leads to some kind of pain. Ignorance about the true nature of self is often suggested as the cause of saṁsāra, and consequently, self-realization is considered a means to liberation from it.

saṁskāra Residual effects or impressions left behind by all types of mental and physical activity. These impressions are said to be "stored" in the psyche, and are believed to have the potential for reappearing in the form of experiences and behaviors similar to those that caused them.

sānanda samādhi Literally, a samādhi state characterized by bliss. One is said to attain this state of samādhi when attention is withdrawn from the object of cognition, and is focused entirely on the sensory elements of consciousness.

Sāṅkhya Name of an ancient school of Indian philosophy known for its dualistic ontological doctrine. The philosophy of Yoga is very close to Sāṅkhya, the main difference between them being that the former is theistic while the latter is atheistic.

sāsmitā samādhi Sāsmitā samādhi is a samādhi state with awareness of "I am"—a state in which consciousness is focused on the subject of awareness rather than on an external object, or on the means of cognition, such as sensory experience.

sat "Being," having an existence, or real.

sattva One of the three guṇas or "strands" of Prakṛti, or the "material" world, as conceptualized in the Sāṅkhya philosophy. Sattva is characterized by lightness, illumination, and subtlety. Rajas and tamas are the other two strands.

savicāra samādhi Having focused upon only the most essential aspects of the object of attention in the preceding stage, called the nirvitarka samādhi, a yogi moves to the comprehension of object's finer aspects in its spatiotemporal context, so as to arrive at the savicāra samādhi state.

savikalpa samādhi A type of samādhi experience in which one has not transcended the subject–object duality.

savitarka samādhi Literally, a samādhi state characterized by conjecture or reasoning. It is a primary level of samādhi state, or a highly steady cognitive state in which the word, its connotative meaning, and the denotative meaning are indiscriminately fused.

siddhi Special powers such as levitation, the knowledge of past and future events, and others which are said to accrue to a yogi at a certain stage of his or her progress. In general, such powers are considered impediments in reaching the true goal of Yoga which is samādhi, or kaivalya, that is, the isolation of Puruṣa or the soul from its attachments with the world of Prakṛti.

smṛti Literally, recollection of memory. Patañjali considers remembering as a category of the processes of consciousness characterized by the "not dropping off" of what is once experienced.

śravaṇa Literally, listening. In Vedānta, it refers to the learning the non-dualist conclusions of the Vedāntic philosophy as a first step toward self-realization.

śreyas Something intrinsically desirable and better—as opposed to things that are merely pleasurable (preyas). Sometimes the term "śreyas" also refers to liberation of the soul through self-realization as the highest and most desirable thing in life.

sthitaprajña One whose intellect is stable. This term designates the ideal human condition characterized by inner calm and equanimity as described in the *Bhagavad-Gītā*.

suṣupti Deep, dreamless sleep as a state of consciousness. One of the four major states of consciousness recognized by Vedānta. The other three states are jāgṛti (wakeful), svapna (dream), and turīyā or the "Fourth."

sūtra Literally, a thread. In the context of literature, it means an aphorism, a short sentence or a concisely stated rule. It also refers to a work or a manual consisting of such rules hanging together like interwoven threads.

svapna Dream as a state of consciousness. One of the four major states of consciousness recognized by Vedānta. The other three are jagṛti (wakeful), suṣupti (sleep), and turīyā or the "Fourth State."

tamas One of the three guṇas or "strands" or Prakṛti, or the material world, as conceptualized in the Sāṅkhya philosophy. Tamas is characterized by heaviness, inertia, and darkness. Sattva and rajas are the other two strands.

tanmātra Subtle elemental particles which are assumed to be constituents of the contents of conscious and also of the natural objects.

Tāntric Pertaining to "Tantras", that is, to texts and/or traditional practices (often viewed as esoteric and "mystical" in character) which are designed to attain spiritual experiences as well as worldly goals.

titikṣā Enduring hardships, or ascetic self-control (as a means to self-realization).

turīyā avasthā Literally, the "Fourth State" of consciousness. So named in the Vedānta philosophy to indicate its unique, transcognitive nature in contrast with three other "ordinary" states, namely, jagṛti or wakeful, svapna or dream, suṣupti or sleep. The experience of this state is said to bring self-realization.

Upaniṣad A group of ancient Sanskrit texts generally devoted to the discussion of philosophical issues.

vairāgya A sense of non-attachment or non-ego involvement with the worldly life.

vāsanā Vāsanās are general propensities generated by saṁskāras or "impressions" left behind by experience of the past, usually by experiences form a period preceding birth in the present life cycle. In this sense, the concept of vāsanā closely resembles the concept of "drives" of biological origin.

Veda The Vedas are ancient scriptural texts of the Hindus. There are four major texts: the Ṛg Veda, Yajurveda, Atharva Veda and Sāma Veda.

Vedānta A system of philosophy which is said to have been developed through the Upaniṣadic texts toward the later period of the development of the Vedic literature.

vikalpa A category of the processes of consciousness involved in imagining or in cognitive construction. In contrast with the other categories of mental events such as pramāṇa (valid cognition) and viparyaya (distorted cognition), vikalpa can be said to be "a process of consciousness characterized by doubt or indetermination."

viparyaya Processes of consciousness involved in incorrect cognition or in the experience of illusions, such as the experience of seeing two moons.

vṛtti A process of consciousness or a mental event of any of the following categories: cognitive processes such as perceiving and thinking which involve valid cognition, cognitive processes (such as having illusory perceptions) which involve erroneous or distorted cognitions, imagining and constructing, sleeping, and recollecting.

vyutthāna Activated or aroused states of the mind as distinguished from the states of samādhi in which mental activities or processes of consciousness are restrained.

yama Restraints on behavior, such as abstaining from inflicting injuries, speaking lies, stealing, being lustful or avaricious, and the like recommended by Patañjali as the first of the eight aids to Yoga.

Yoga Sūtra Name of Patañjali's work consisting of a set of aphorisms.

REFERENCES

Abeles, M., & Schilder, P. Psychogenic loss of personal identity. *Archives of Neurology and Psychiatry*, 1935, *34*, 587–604.

Adler, A. [*The neurotic constitution: Outline of a comparative individual psychology and psychotherapy*] (B. Glueck & J. E. Lind, Eds. and trans.) Freeport, N.Y.: Books for Libraries Press, 1972. (Originally published, 1926.)

Adorno, T. W., Frenkel-Brunswik, E., Levinson, D. J., & Sanford, R. N. *The authoritatian personality*. New York: Harper, 1950.

Akhilananda, S. *Hindu psychology*. London: George Allen & Unwin; 1948.

Akhilananda, S. *Mental Health and Hindu psychology*. London: George Allen & Unwin, 1952.

Allport, G. W. The ego in contemporary psychology. *Psychological Review*, 1943, *50*, 451–478.

Allport, G. W. *The individual and his religion*. New York: Macmillan, 1950.

Allport, G. W. *The nature of prejudice*. New York: Doubleday/Anchor, 1958.

Allport, G. W. The open system in personality theory. *Journal of Abnormal and Social Psychology*, 1960, *61*, 301–310.

Allport, G. W. The historical background of modern social psychology. In G. Lindzey & E. Aronson (Eds.), *The handbook of social psychology* (2nd ed.) (Vol. 1). Reading, Mass.: Addison Wesley, 1968.

Anand, B. K., Chhina, G. S., & Singh, B. Some aspects of electroencephalographic studies in yogis. *EEG and Clinical Neurophysiology*, 1961, *13*, 452–456.

Angyal, A. *Foundation for a science of personality*. New York: Commonwealth Fund, 1941.

Aristotle. [De anima.] In W. D. Ross (Ed.), *The works of Aristotle* (Vol. 3) (J. A. Smith, trans.). Oxford: Clarendon Press, 1931.

Armstrong, D. M. *A materialist theory of the mind*. London: Routledge & Kegan Paul, 1968.

Asch, S. *Social psychology*. New York: Prentice-Hall, 1952.

Aserinsky, E. & Kleitman, N. Regularly occurring periods of eye motility and concomitant phenomena during sleep. *Science*, 1953, *118*, 273–274.

Assagioli, R. *Psychosynthesis: a manual of principles and techniques*. Harmondsworth: Penguin, 1965.

Bagchi, B. K., & Wenger, M. A. Electro-physiological correlates of some Yogi exercises. In J. Kamiya, N. E. Miller, D. Shapiro & J. Stoyva (Eds.) *Biofeedback and self-control: An Aldine reader on the regulation of bodily processes and consciousness*. Chicago: Aldine/Atherton, 1971. (Reprinted from *EEG and Neurophysiology*, 1957, Supplement 7.)

Baier, K. Smart on sensations. *Australian Journal of Philosophy*, 1962, *40*, 57–68.

Bakan, D. *Sigmund Freud and the Jewish mystical tradition*. Princeton: D. Van Nostrand, 1958.

Bakan, D. The mystery–mastery complex in contemporary psychology. *American Psychologist*, 1965, *20*, 186–191.

Bakan, D. *The duality of human existence*. Chicago: Rand McNally, 1966.

Bakan, D. Mind, matter and the separate reality of information. *Philosophy of the Social Sciences*, 1974, *4*, 1–15.

Barber, B., & Hirsch, W. (Eds.) *The sociology of science*. New York: Free Press of Glencoe, 1962.

Barnes, B. (Ed.) *Sociology of science*. Harmondsworth: Penguin, 1972.

Barrett, W. *Irrational man: a study in existential philosophy*. Garden City: Doubleday, 1958.

Behanan, K. T. *Yoga: a scientific evaluation*. New York: Dover, 1964. (Originally published, 1937.)

Benedict, R. Continuities and discontinuities in cultural conditioning. *Psychiatry*, 1938, *1*, 161–167.

Bentham, J. *An introduction to the principles of morals and legislation*. New York: Hafner, 1948. (Originally published, 1789.)

Berger, R. J., & Oswald, I. Eye movements during active and passive dreams. *Science*, 1962, *137*, 601.

Berry, J. W. On cross-cultural comparability. *International Journal of Psychology*, 1969, *4*, 119–128.

Bhagavad-Gītā (S. Radhakrishanan, Ed. and trans.) New York: Harper & Row, 1973.

Bharati, A. *The light at the center: context and pretext of modern mysticism*. Santa Barbara: Ross-Erikson, 1976.

Bhikṣu, V. Yogavārtika. In S. N. Miśra (Ed.) *Pātañjalayogadarśanam vācaspatimiśra-viracita tattvavaiśāradī vijñānabhikṣu-kṛta yogavārtikavibhūṣita vyāsabhāṣya-sametam*. Varanasi, India: Bharatiya Vidya Prakashan, 1971.

Bhoja. *Pātañjalayogasūtram bhojadevakṛta rājamārtaṅḍavṛttisametam*. (R. Bhattacharya, Ed.) Varanasi, India: Bharatiya Vidya Prakashan, 1969.

Binswanger, L. [Insanity as life-historical phenomena and as mental disease: the case of Ilse.] In R. May, E. Angel, & H. F. Ellenberger (Eds.), *Existence*. New York: Basic Books, 1958(a).

Binswanger, L. [The case of Ellen West.] In R. May, E. Angel & H. F. Ellenberger (Eds.), *Existence*. New York: Basic Books, 1958(b).

Binswanger, L. [*Being-in-the-world: selected papers of Ludwig Binswanger*.] (J. Needleman, trans.) New York: Basic Books, 1963.

Boring, E. G. *A history of experimental psychology* (2nd ed.). New York: Prentice-Hall, 1950.

Boring, E. G. A history of introspection. *Psychological Bulletin*, 1953, *50*, 169–189.

Brett, G. S. *Brett's history of psychology*. (Abridged and rev. ed.) (R. S. Peters, Ed.). Cambridge, Mass.: M.I.T. Press, 1962. (Originally published, 1912.)

Briggs, G. W. *Gorakhnāth and the Kānphaṭā Yogis*. Varanasi, India: Motilal Banarsidass, 1973. (Originally published, 1938.)

Briskman, L. B. Is a Kuhnian Analysis applicable to psychology? *Science Studies*, 1972, *2*, 87–97.

Brosse, T. A psychophysiological study. *Main Currents in Modern Thought*, 1946, *4*, 77–84.

Brown, B. Recognition of aspects of consciousness through association with EEG Alpha activity represented by a light signal. *Psychophysiology*, 1970, *6*, 442–452.

Brown, B. Awareness of EEG-subjective activity relationships detected within a closed feedback system. *Psychophysiology*, 1971, *7*, 451–464.

Brown, R. *Social Psychology*. New York: Free Press, 1965.
Buber, M. *Between man and man*. New York: Macmillan, 1965. (Originally published, 1947.)
Buss, A. R. The emerging field of the sociology of psychological knowledge. *American Psychologist*, 1975, *30*, 988–1002.
Buss, A. R. Galton and the birth of differential psychology and eugenics: social, political and economic forces. *Journal of the History of the Behavioral Sciences*, 1976, *12*, 47–58.
Campbell, D. T. Ethnocentrism and other altruistic motives. In D. Levine (Ed.), *Nebraska Symposium on Motivation* (Vol. 13). Lincoln: University of Nebraska Press, 1965.
Campbell, D. T. "Downward causation" in hierarchically organized biological systems. In F. J. Ayala & T. Dobzhansky (Eds.), *Studies in the philosophy of biology: reduction and related problems*. Berkeley: University of California Press, 1974.
Camus, A. [*The outsider*.] (S. Gilbert, trans.). London: Hamish Hamilton, 1967. (First published, 1946.)
Camus, A. [*The myth of Sysiphus and other essays*.] (J. O'Brien, trans.) New York: Knopf, 1969. (Originally published, 1955.)
Carnap, R. [Psychology in physical language.] (G. Schick, trans.) In A. J. Ayer (Ed.), *Logical positivism*. New York: Free Press, 1959. (Originally published in *Erkenntnis*, III, 1932–33)
The cloud of unknowing. I. Progoff (Ed. and trans.) New York: Dell, 1957.
Coan, R. W. *Hero, artist, sage, or saint*. New York: Columbia University Press, 1977.
Comte, A. [*Introduction to positive philosophy*.] (F. Ferré, Ed. and trans.). New York: Bobbs-Merrill, 1970. (Originally published, 1830.)
Cooley, C. H. *Human nature and the social order*. New York: Schocken, 1964. (Originally published, 1902.)
Coster, G. *Yoga and Western psychology: a comparison*. New York: Harper & Row, 1972. (Originally published, 1934.)
Crutchfield, R. S. Conformity and character. *American Psychologist*, 1955, *10*, 191–198.
Curtis, J. E., & Petras, J. W. (Eds.) *The sociology of knowledge: a reader*. New York: Praeger, 1970.
Darwin, C. *On the origin of species*. Cambridge, Mass.: Harvard University Press, 1966. (Originally published, 1859.)
Dasgupta, S. N. *A history of Indian philosophy*. (2 vols.) Cambridge: Cambridge University Press, 1922.
Dasgupta, S. N. *Yoga as philosophy and religion*. New York: Gordon Press, Krishna Press, 1974.(Originally published, 1924.)
Delgado. J. M. R. *Physical control of mind: toward a psychocivilized society* New York: Harper & Row, 1969.
Dement, W., & Kleitman, N. The relation of eye movements during sleep to dream activity: an objective method for the study of dreaming. *Journal of Experimental Psychology*, 1957, *53*, 339–346.
Descartes, R. *L'Homme*. In C. Adam & P. Tannery (Eds.). *Oeuvres de Descartes*, Vol. 11 Paris: Librairie Philosophique J. Vrin, 1967. (Originally published, 1664.)
Dollard, J., & Miller, N. E. *Personality and psychotherapy: an analysis in terms of learning, thinking, and culture*. New York: McGraw Hill, 1950.
Dṛg-dṛśya Viveka. S. Nikhilananda (Ed. and trans.) Mysore, India: Sri Ramakrishna Asrama, 1931.
Eccles, J. C. *The neurophysiological basis of mind*. Oxford: Clarendon Press, 1953.
Eccles, J. C. *The brain and the unity of conscious experience*. Cambridge: Cambridge University Press, 1965.

Eccles, J. C. Cerebral activity and consciousness. In F. J. Ayala & T. Dobzhansky (Eds.), *Studies in the philosophy of biology: reduction and related problems.* Berkeley: University of California Press, 1974.

Efron, R. Biology without consciousness—and its consequences. *Perspectives in Biology and Medicine,* 1967, *11,* 9–36.

Elms, A. The crisis of confidence in social psychology. *American Psychologist,* 1975, *30,* 967–976.

Erikson, E. H. The problem of ego-identity. *Journal of the American Psychoanalytic Association,* 1956, *4,* 56–121.

Erikson, E. H. *Identity, youth and crisis.* New York: Norton, 1968.

Feigl, H. *The "mental" and the "physical": the essay and a postscript.* Minneapolis: University of Minnesota Press, 1967. (The "essay" originally published, 1958.)

Fellows, E. W. Happiness: a survey of research. *Journal of Humanistic Psychology,* 1966, *6,* 17–30.

Festinger, L. A theory of social comparison process. *Human Relations,* 1954, *7,* 117–140.

Festinger, L. *A theory of cognitive dissonance.* Stanford: Stanford University Press, 1957.

Fink, E. [The phenomenological philosophy of Edmund Husserl and contemporary criticism.] In R. O. Elveton (Ed. and trans.), *The phenomenology of Husserl: selected critical readings.* Chicago: Quadrangle, 1970. (Originally published, 1933.)

Freud, S. [Analysis of a phobia in a five-year-old boy.] In J. Strachey (Ed.) *The standard edition of the complete psychological works of Sigmund Freud* (Vol. 10). London: Hogarth, 1962. (Originally published, 1909.)

Freud, S. [The future of an illusion.] In J. Strachey (Ed.) *The standard edition of the complete psychological works of Sigmund Freud* (Vol. 21). London: Hogarth, 1961. (Originally published, 1927.)

Freud, S. [Civilizaton and its discontents.] In J. Strachey (Ed.) *The standard edition of the complete psychological works of Sigmund Freud* (Vol. 21). London: Hogarth, 1961. (Originally published, 1930.)

Freud, S. [An outline of psychoanalysis.] In J. Strachey (Ed.) *The standard edition of the complete psychological works of Sigmund Freud* (Vol. 23). London: Hogarth, 1964. (Originally published,1940.)

Gazzaniga, M. S. *The bisected brain.* New York: Appleton-Century-Crofts, 1970.

Gergen, K. J. Social psychology as history. *Journal of Personality and Social Psychology,* 1973, *26,* 309–320.

Globus, G. G., Maxwell, G., & Savodnik, I. (Eds.) *Consciousness and the brain: a scientific and philosophical inquiry.* New York: Plenum, 1976.

Goldschmidt, W. *Comparative functionalism.* Berkeley: University of California Press, 1966.

Goldstein, K. *The organism: a holistic approach to biology derived from pathological data in man.* Boston: Beacon Press, 1963. (Originally published, 1939.)

Gordon, C., & Gergen, K. J. (Eds.) *Self in social interaction.* New York: Wiley, 1968.

Goyeche, J. R. M. Yoga: clinical observations. In *Proceedings: The Fourth Congress of the International College of Psychosomatic Medicine.* Kyoto, Japan: 1977.

Gupta, S. P. *Psychopathology in Indian medicine (Āyurveda) with special reference to its philosophical bases.* Aligarh, India: Ajaya Publishers, 1977.

Haeckel, E. [*The riddle of the universe at the close of the nineteenth century.*] (J. McCabe, trans.) Grosse Pointe, Mich.: Scholarly Press, 1968. (Originally published, 1900.)

Hebb, D. O. The American revolution. *American Psychologist,* 1960, *15,* 735–745.

Heidegger, M. [*Being and time.*] (J. Macquarrie & E. Robinson, trans.) New York: Harper, 1962. (Originally published, 1927.)

Hempel, C. G. [The logical analysis of psychology] In H. Feigl & W. Sellars (Eds.) *Readings in philosophical analysis*. New York: Appleton-Century-Crofts, 1949. (Originally published, 1935.)

Hiriyanna, M. *Outlines of Indian philosophy*. London: George Allen & Unwin, 1932.

Hobbes, T. *Leviathan*. Oxford: Clarendon Press, 1962. (Originally published, 1651.)

Hogan, R. Theoretical egocentrism and the problem of compliance. *American Psychologist*, 1975, *30*, 533–540.

Hook, S. (Ed.) *Determinism and freedom in the age of modern science*. New York: Collier Books, 1958.

Hook, S. (Ed.) *Dimensions of mind: a symposium*. New York: New York University Press, 1960.

Hume, D. A treatise of human nature. In T. H. Green, & T. H. Grose (Eds.), *David Hume: The philosophical works* (4 vols.) Germany: Scientia Verlag Aalen, 1964. (Originally published, 1886.)

Hume, R. E. (Trans.) *The thirteen principal Upanishads* (2nd ed.). London: Oxford University Press, 1931.

Husserl, E. [*Ideas: general introduction to phenomenology*.] (W. R. Boyce-Gibson, trans.) New York: Collier Books, 1962. (Originally published, 1913.)

Husserl, E. [*Cartesian meditations: an introduction to phenomenology*.] (D. Cairns, trans.) The Hague: Martinus Nijhoff, 1977. (Originally published, 1933.)

Husserl, E. [*Phenomenology and the crisis of philosophy*.] (Q. Lauer, Ed. and trans.) New York: Harper, 1965. (Originally published, 1936.)

Ikemi, Y. Eastern and Western approaches to self-regulation: similarities and differences. *Canadian Journal of Psychiatry*, 1979, *24*, 471–480.

Ikemi, Y., & Ikemi, A. *A new model for integrating occidental and Oriental approaches to psychosomatic medicine*. Paper presented at the Fifth International Conference of the International Association of Cross-Cultural Psychology. Bhubaneswar, India: December, 1980.

Ishikawa, H., Kikuchi, T., & Morita, Y. Integrated Yoga therapy and cybernetics. *Proceedings: the Fourth Congress of the International College of Psychosomatic Medicine*. Kyoto, Japan: 1977.

Jahoda, M. The meaning of psychological health. *Social Casework*, 1953, *34*, 349–354.

Jahoda, M. Toward a social psychology of mental health. In A. M. Rose (Ed.), *Mental health and mental disorder*. New York: W. W. Norton, 1955.

James, W. *The principles of psychology* (2 vols.). New York: Dover, 1950. (Originally published, 1890.)

James, W. *Varieties of religious experience*. New York: New American Library, 1958. (Originally published, 1902.)

John, E. Roy. *Mechanisms of memory*. New York: Academic Press, 1967.

Jones, W. T. *A history of Western philosophy* (4 vols.) (2nd ed.). New York: Harcourt, Brace & World, 1969.

Joshi, K. S. *Yoga and personality*. Allahabad: Udayana Publications, 1967.

Jung, C. G. Psychological commentary on the "Tibetan Book of the Great Liberation." In H. Read, & M. Fordham (Eds.), *The collected works of C. G. Jung* (Bollingen Series, Vol. 11). New York: Pantheon, 1958. (Original in English, 1939.)

Kakar, S. *Shamans, mystics, and doctors*. New York: Knopf, 1982.

Kamiya, J. Operant control of EEG alpha rhythm and some of its reported effects on consciousness. In C. T. Tart (Ed.), *Altered states of consciousness* (2nd ed.). Garden City, New York: Doubleday, 1972.

Kant, I. [*Critique of pure reason*] (F. Max Müller, trans.) Garden City, N.Y.: Doubleday/Anchor Books, 1966. (Originally published, 1781.)

Karczmar, A. G., & Eccles, J. C. (Eds.) *Brain and human behavior.* New York: Springer - Verlag, 1972.

Karṇāṭak, V. *Vyākhyākāron kī dṛṣṭi se pātañjalayogasūtra kā samīkṣātmaka adhyayana.* Varanasi, India: Kasi Hindu Visvavidyalaya, 1974.

Kasamatsu, A. & Hirai, T. An electroencephalographic study of Zen meditation (Zazen). In C. T. Tart (Ed.) *Altered states of consciousness* (2nd ed.). Garden City, N.Y.: Doubleday, 1972.

Kelly, G. A. *The psychology of personal constructs.* New York: Norton, 1955.

Kety, S. S. A biologist examines the mind and behavior. *Science,* 1960, *132,* 1861–1870.

Kleitman, N. *Sleep and wakefulness* (Rev. ed.) Chicago: University of Chicgo Press, 1963.

Klinger, E. (Ed.) *Imagery* (3 vols.) New York: Plenum, 1981.

Kluckhohn, C. Universal categories of culture. In A. L. Kroeber (Ed.), *Anthropology today: an encyclopedic inventory,* Chicago: University of Chicago Press, 1953.

Kluckhohn, C., & Murray, H. A. Personality formation: the determinants. In C. Kluckhohn, H. A. Murray, & D. M. Schneider (Eds.) *Personality in nature, society and culture* (Rev. ed.). New York: Knopf, 1953.

Kluckhohn, F. R. Dominant and variant value orientations. In C. Kluckhohn, H. A. Murray, & D. M. Schneider (Eds.), *Personality in nature, society and culture* (Rev. ed.) New York: Knopf, 1953.

Koch, S. Psychology and emerging conceptions of knowledge as unitary. In T. W. Wann (Ed.) *Behaviorism and phenomenology: contrasting bases for modern psychology.* Chicago: University of Chicago Press, 1964.

Koestler, A. *Ghost in the machine.* New York: Macmillan, 1967.

Kohlberg, L. From is to ought: How to commit the naturalist fallacy and get away with it in the study of moral development. In T. Mischel (Ed.), *Cognitive development and epistemology.* New York: Academic Press, 1971.

Krebs, D. Altruism: an examination of the concept and a review of the literature. *Psychological Bulletin,* 1970, *73,* 258–302.

Kuhn, M. H., & McPartland, T. S. An empirical investigation of self-attitudes. *American Sociological Review,* 1954, *19,* 68–76.

Kuhn, T. S. *The structure of scientific revolutions* (2nd ed.). Chicago: University of Chicago Press, 1970.

Kulkarni, T. R. *Upanishads and Yoga: an empirical approach to the understanding.* Bombay: Bharatiya Vidya Bhavan, 1972.

Laing, R. D. *The divided self: an existential study in sanity and madness.* London: Tavistock, 1960.

Lauer, Q. *Phenomenology: its genesis and prospect.* New York: Harper, 1965. (Originally published, 1958.)

Levine, R., Chein, I., & Murphy, G. The relation of the intensity of a need to the amount of perceptual distortion: a preliminary report. *Journal of Psychology,* 1942, *13,* 283–293.

LeVine, R. A., & Campbell, D. T. *Ethnocentrism: theories of conflict, ethnic attitudes, and group behavior.* New York: Wiley, 1972.

Lipsey, M. W. Psychology: preparadigmatic, postparadigmatic, or misparadigmatic? *Science Studies,* 1974, *4,* 406–410.

Lipton, S. Dissociated personality: a case report. *Psychiatric Quarterly,* 1943, *17,* 35–56.

Locke, J. Of human understanding. In *The works of John Locke* (10 vols.). Germany: Scientia Verlag Aalen, 1963. (Originally published, 1823.)

Malinowksi, B. *Sex and repression in savage society.* London: Routledge & Kegan Paul, 1953. (Originally published, 1927.)

Mannheim, K. [*Ideology and utopia: an introduction to the sociology of knowledge.*] (L. Wirth & E. Shils, trans.) New York: Harcourt, Brace & World, 1936. (Originally published, 1929.)

Manusmṛti. [The laws of Manu.] (G. Bühler, trans.) In F. Max Müller (Ed.) *The sacred books of the East* (Vol. 25). Oxford, England: Clarendon Press, 1886.

Maslow, A. *Religions, values and peak experiences.* New York: Viking Press, 1970. (Originally published, 1964.)

Maslow, A. *Motivation and Personality* (2nd ed.). New York: Harper & Row, 1970.

McClelland, D. C. *The achieving society.* Princeton: Van Nostrand, 1961.

McClelland, D. C., Atkinson, J. W., Clark, R. A. & Lowell, E. L. *The achievement motive.* New York: Appleton-Century, 1953.

Mead, G. H. *Mind, self and society: from standpoint of a social behaviorist.* Chicago: University of Chicago Press, 1934.

Mead, M. *Coming of age in Samoa.* New York: Dell, 1968. (Originally published, 1928.)

Mehta, G. *Karma cola.* Madras, India: Macmillan, 1980.

Merton, R. K. *The sociology of science: theoretical and empirical investigations.* Chicago: University of Chicago Press, 1973.

Meyer, M. *Psychology of the other-one* (2nd ed.). Columbia, Missouri: Missouri Book Company, 1922.

Milgram, S. Behavioral study of obedience. *Journal of Abnormal and Social Psychology,* 1963, *67,* 371–378.

Milgram, S. *Obedience to authority: an experimental view.* New York: Harper & Row, 1974.

Mill, J. S. On liberty. In M. Warnock (Ed.), *Utilitarianism, On Liberty, Essay on Bentham.* Cleveland, Ohio: The World Publishing Company, Meridian Books, 1962. (Originally published, 1859.)

Mill, J. S. Utilitarianism. In M. Warnock (Ed.), *Utilitarianism, On Liberty, Essay on Bentham.* Cleveland, Ohio: The World Publishing Company, Meridian Books, 1962. (Originally published, 1863.)

Miller, J. G. Living systems. *Behavioral Science,* 1965, *10,* (special issue).

Miller, N. E. The frustration-aggression hypothesis. *Psychological Review,* 1941, *48,* 337–342.

Mischel, T. (Ed.) *Cognitive development and epistemology.* New York: Academic Press, 1971.

Miśra, V. Pātañjalayogasūtra ṭīkā. In *Pātañjalayogasūtrāṇi.* Ānandāśrama Sanskrit series, No. 47. Pune, India: Anandashram, 1978.

Murphy, G., & Murphy, L. B. (Eds.). *Asian psychology.* New York: Basic Books, 1968.

Neumann, J. von, & Morgenstern, O. *Theory of games and economic behavior* (3rd ed.). Princeton, N.J.: Princeton University Press, 1953.

Nowlis, D. P., & Kamiya, J. The control of electroencephalographic alpha rhythms through auditory feedback and the associated mental activity. *Psychophysiology,* 1970, *6,* 476–484.

O'Connor, J. (Ed.) *Modern materialism: readings in mind-body identity.* New York: Harcourt, Brace & World, 1969.

Orne, M. T. On the social psychology of the psychological experiment, with particular reference to demand characteristics and their implications. *American Psychologist,* 1962, *17,* 776–783.

Ornstein, R. E. *The psychology of consciousness.* San Francisco: W. H. Freeman, 1972.

Osgood, C. E., & Tannenbaum, P. H. The principle of congruity in the prediction of attitude change. *Psychological Review,* 1955, *62,* 42–55.

Otto, R. [*Mysticism East and West: a comparative analysis of the nature of mysticism.*] (B. L. Bracey and R. C. Payne, trans.). New York: Macmillan, 1932.

Palermo, D. S. Is a scientific revolution taking place in psychology? *Science Studies,* 1971, *1,* 135–155.

Paranjpe, A. C. *In search of identity*. New York: Halsted Press/Wiley, 1975.

Patañjali. Yoga-sūtra. In Ānandāśrama Sanskrit Series, No 47. *Pātañjalayogasūtrāṇi*. Pune, India: Anandashram, 1978.

Perry, J. (Ed.) *Personal identity*. Berkeley: University of California Press, 1975.

Piaget, J. [*Biology and knowledge: an essay on the relations between organic regulations and cognitive processes*.] (B. Walsh, trans.) Chicago: University of Chicago Press, 1971. (Originally published, 1967.)

Piliavin, I. M., Rodin, J., & Piliavin, J. A. Good Samaritanism: an underground phenomenon. *Journal of Personality and Social Psychology*, 1969, *13*,289–299.

Place, U. T. Is consciousness a brain process? *British Journal of Psychology*, 1956, *47*, 44–51.

Plotkin, W. B. On the self-regulation of the occipetal alpha rhythm: control strategies, states of consciousness and the role of psysiological feedback. *Journal of Experimental Psychology: General*, 1976, *105*, 66–99.

Pope, K. S., & Singer, J. L. *The stream of consciousness: scientific investigations into the flow of human experience*. New York: Plenum Press, 1978.

Popper, K. R. The sociology of knowledge. In K. R. Popper. *Open society and its enemies*. (2nd ed.) (Vol. 2). New York: Harper & Row, 1967. (Originally published, 1945.)

Popper, K. R., & Eccles, J. C. *The self and its brain: an argument for interactionism*. New York: Springer Verlag, 1977.

Powers, W. T. *Behavior: the control of perception*. Chicago: Aldine, 1973.

Prasada, R. (Trans.). *Patañjali's Yoga Sūtras with the commentary of Vyāsa and the gloss of Vācaspati Miśra*. In B. D. Basu (Ed.), *Sacred books of the Hindus* (Vol. 4). New York: AMS Press, 1974. (Originally published, 1912.)

Pribram, K. *Languages of the brain: experimental paradoxes and principles of neuropsychology*. Englewood Cliffs, N.J.: Prentice-Hall, 1971.

Prince, M. *The dissolution of a personality: a biographical study in abnormal psychology* (2nd ed.). London: Longmans, Green, 1905.

Progoff, I. (Ed. and trans.) *The cloud of unknowing*. New York: Dell, 1957.

Pugh, J. F. Person and experience: the astrological system of North India. Unpublished doctoral dissertation, Department of Anthropology, University of Chicago, 1981.

Puligandla, R. Phenomenological reduction and Yogic meditation. *Philosophy East and West*, 1970, *20*, 19–33.

Radhakrishnan, S. *The Hindu view of life*. New York: Macmillan, 1969. (Originally published, 1926.)

Radhakrishnan, S. *Indian philosophy* (2nd ed.) (2 vols.). London: George Allen & Unwin, 1929.

Raja, C. K. *The Sāṅkhya Kārikā of Īśvarakṛṣṇa: a philosopher's exposition*. Hoshiyarpur, India: V. V. Research Institute, 1963.

Ramachandra Rao, S. K. *Development of psychological thought in India*. Mysore: Kavyalaya Publishers, 1962.

Ranade, R. D. *Indian mysticism: mysticism in Maharashtra*. Pune, India: Aryabhushan Press, 1933.

Rapoport, A. *Two-person game theory*. Ann Arbor, Mich.: University of Michigan press, 1966.

Remmling, G. W. (Ed.) *Toward the sociology of knowledge: origin and development of a sociological thought style*. New York: Humanities Press, 1973.

Ricoeur, P. [*The conflict of interpretations: essays in hermeneutics*.] (D. Ihde, Ed.) Evanston, Ill.: Northwestern University Press, 1974.

Riepe, D. A note on William James and Indian philosophy. *Philosophy and Phenomenoligical Research*, 1968, *28*, 587–590.

Riesman D. *The lonely crowd: a study of the changing American character*. New Haven: Yale University Press, 1950.
Rogers, C. R. *Client-centered therapy: its current practice, implications and theory*. Boston: Houghton Mifflin, 1951.
Rogers, C. R. A theory of therapy, personality and interpersonal relationships as developed in the client-centered framework. In S. Koch (Ed.), *Psychology: A study of a science* (Vol. 3). New York: McGraw-Hill, 1959.
Rosenthal, R. *Experimental effects in behavioral research*. New York: Appleton-Century-Crofts, 1966.
Russell, B. *Mysticism and logic and other essays*. London: Longmans, Green, 1921.
Russell, B. *Religion and science*. London: Oxford University Press, 1935a.
Russell, B. *Sceptical essays*. London: Unwin, 1935b.
Russell, B. *History of Western philosophy*. New York: Simon & Schuster, 1945.
Ryle, G. *The concept of mind*. Harmondsworth: Penguin, 1949.
Sadānanda. Vedāntasāra. In G. A. Jacob (Ed.), The Vedāntasāra of Sadānanda with the commentaries of Nṛsiṁhasarasvati and Rāmatīrtha. Bombay, India: Panduranga Javaji, 1925.
Safaya, R. *Indian psychology: a critical and historical analysis of the psychological speculations in Indian philosophical literature*. New Delhi: Munshiram Manoharlal, 1976.
Śaṅkara. *Vivekacūḍāmaṇi*. (S. Madhavananda, trans.) Calcutta, India: Advaita Ashrama, 1921. (c)
Śaṅkara. *Pātañjalayogasūtrabhāṣyavivaraṇam* (P. S. R. Sastri, & S. R. K. Sastri, Eds.) Madras, India: Government Oriental Manuscripts Library, 1952. (a)
Śaṅkara. *Śrīmadbhagavad-Gītā Śāṅkarabhāṣya hindī-anuvāda-sahita* (8th Ed.) (Harikṛṣṇa Dāsa Goyandakā, trans.). Gorakhpur, India; Gita Press, Saṁvat 2010 (1953 A.D.). (d)
Śaṅkara. Bādarāyaṇa brahmasūtra śāṅkarabhāṣya. In V. M. Apte (Trans.), *Bādarāyaṇa's Brahmasūtras with Śaṅkarācārya's commentary*. Bombay: Popular Book Depot, 1960. (b)
Sartre, J. P. [*The transcendence of the ego: an existential theory of consciousness*.] (F. Williams & R. Kirkpatrick, trans.) New York: Noonday Press, 1957. (Originally published, 1936–37.).
Sartre, J. P. [*Nausea*.] (L. Alexander, trans.) New York: New Directions. 1964, (Originally published, 1938.)
Sartre, J. P. [*Being and nothingness*.] (H. E. Barnes, trans.) New York: Washington Square Press, 1966. (Originally published, 1943.)
Sasaki, Y. *Zen and psychosomatic medicine*. Paper presented at the Sixth World Congress of the International College of Psychosomatic Medicine. Montreal, Canada, 1981.
Scharfstein, B-A. *Mystical experience*. Baltimore: Penguin, 1974. (Originally published, 1973.)
Scheler, M. [On the positivistic philosophy of the history of knowledge and its Law of Three Stages.] In J. E. Curtis, & J. W. Petras (Eds.), *The sociology of knowledge*. New York: Praeger, 1970. (Date of original publication unknown.)
Shubik, M. (Ed.) *Game theory and related approaches to social behavior: selections*. New York: Wiley, 1964.
Sinari, R. The method of phenomenological reduction and Yoga. *Philosophy East and West*, 1965, *15*, 217–228.
Sinha, D. Integration of modern psychology with Indian thought. *Journal of Humanistic Psychology*, 1965, *5*, 6–17.
Skinner, B. F. *Walden Two*. (New ed. with a new preface). New York: Macmillan, 1969. (Originally published, 1948.)
Skinner, B. F. *Science and human behavior*. New York: Macmillan, 1953.
Skinner, B. F. Behaviorism at fifty. In T. W. Wann (Ed.), *Behaviorism and phenomenology: contrasting bases for modern psychology*. Chicago: University of Chicago Press, 1964.

Skinner, B. F. *About behaviorism*. New York: Knopf, 1974.

Smart, J. J. C. Sensations and brain processes. In V. C. Chappel (Ed.), *The philosophy of mind*. Englewood Cliffs, N.J.: Prentice-Hall, 1962.

Sperry, R. W. Mental phenomena as causal determinants in brain function. In G. G. Globus, G. Maxwell, & I. Savodnik (Eds.), *Consciousness and the brain: A scientific and philosophical inquiry*. New York: Plenum Press, 1976.

Sperry, R. W. Consciousness, free will and personal identity. In D. A. Oakley, & H. C. Plotkin (Eds.), *Brain, behavior and evolution*. London: Methuen, 1979.

Spiegelberg, H. *The phenomenological movement: a historical introduction* (2 vols.) (2nd ed.). The Hague: Martinus Nijhoff, 1965.

Spiegelberg, H. *Phenomenology in psychology and psychiatry: a historical introduction*. Evanston, Ill.: Northwestern University Press, 1972.

Spiegelberg, H. *Doing phenomenology: essays on and in phenomenology*. The Hague: Martinus Nijhoff, 1975.

Staal, F. *Exploring mysticism*. Harmondsworth: Penguin, 1975.

Stace, W. T. *Mysticism and philosophy*. New York: J. B. Lippincott, 1960.

Stevenson, R. L. Strange case of Dr. Jekyll and Mr. Hyde. In *The works of Robert Louis Stevenson* (Valima ed., Vol. 7). London: Heinemann, 1922.

Stoyva, J., & Kamiya, J. Electrophysiological studies of dreaming as the prototype of a new strategy in the study of consciousness. *Psychological Review*, 1968, *75*, 192-205.

Sumner, W. G. *Folkways*. New York: New American Library, 1960. (Originally published, 1906.)

Tart, C. (Ed.) *Altered states of consciousness* (2nd ed.). Garden City, N.Y.: Doubleday/Anchor Books, 1972. (First edition, 1969.)

Tart, C. (Ed.) *Transpersonal psychologies*. New York: Harper & Row, 1975.

Thigpen, C. H., & Cleckley, H. A case of multiple personality. *Journal of Abnormal and Social Psychology*, 1954, *49*, 135–151.

Thoreau, D. Walden; or, life in the woods. In P. V. D. Stern (Ed.), *The annotated Walden*. New York: Clarkson N. Potter, 1970. (Originally published, 1854.)

Thorndike, E. L. Animal intelligence: an experimental study of the associative process in animals. *Psychological Review*, 1898, *5*, (Monograph Supplement No. 8), 551–553.

Tilak, B. G. *Śrīmadbhagavadgītārahasya athavā karmayogaśāstra* (7th Marathi ed.). Pune, India: J. S. Titak, 1956. (Originally published, 1915.)

Tilak, B. G. [*Śrīmadbhagavadgītarahasya or Karma-Yoga-Śāstra.*] (B. S. Sukthankar, trans.) (3rd ed.) Pune, India: Tilak Brothers, 1971. (Originally published in Marathi in 1915.)

Titchener, E. B. *Lectures on the experimental psychology of the thought process*. Ann Arbor, Mich.: University Microfils, 1967. (Originally published, 1909.)

Tukārām. *Śrītukārāmbāvāncyā abhaṅgāncī gāthā*. Bombay: Government Central Press, 1973.

Uttal, W. R. *The psychobiology of sensory coding*. New York: Harper & Row, 1973.

Uttal, W. R. *The psycholobiology of mind*. Hillsdale, N.J.: Laurence Erlbaum Associates, 1978.

Vesey, G. *Personal identity: a philosophical analysis*. Ithaca, N.Y.: Cornell University Press, 1974.

Vidyāraṇya. *Jīvanmuktiviveka*. In S. S. Sastri and T. R. S. Ayyangar (Eds. & trans.), *Jīvanmuktiviveka of Vidyāraṇya*. Adyar, Madras, India, 1935.

Vyāsa. Pātañjalayogasūtrabhāṣya. In Ānandāśrama Sanskrit Series, No. 47. *Pātañjalayogasūtrāṇi*. Pune, India: Anandashram, 1978.

Wallace, R. K. *The phsyiological effects of transcendental meditaion*. Los Angeles: Students' International Meditation Society, 1970.

Walsh, D. H. Interactive effects of alpha feedback and instructional set of subjective set. *Psychophysiology*, 1974, *11*, 428–435.

Wann, T. W. (Ed.) *Behaviorism and phenomenology: contrasting bases for modern psychology.* Chicago: University of Chicago Press, 1964.

Warren, N. Is a scientific revolution taking place in psychology?—Doubts and reservations. *Science Studies,* 1971, *1,* 407–411.

Watson, J. B. Psychology as the behaviorist views it. *Psychological Review,* 1913, *20,* 158–177.

Watson, R. I. *The great psychologists* (4th ed.). Philadelphia: Lippincott, 1978.

Weber, M. [*The Protestant ethic and the spirit of capitalism.*] (T. Parsons, trans.). New York: Charles Scribner's Sons, 1958. (Originally published, 1904–5.)

Weimer, W. B., & Palermo, D. S. Paradigms and natural science in psychology. *Science Studies,* 1973, *3,* 211–244.

Weiss, M. G. Critical study of "unmāda" in the early Sanskrit medical literature: an analysis of Āyurvedic psychiatry with respect to present-day diagnostic concepts. (Doctoral dissertation, University of Pennsylvania, 1977). *Dissertation Abstracts International,* 1978, *38,* (11), 6880A. (University Microfilms, No. DDK 78-06655)

Wenger, M. A., Bagchi, B. K., & Anand, B. K. Experiments in India on "voluntary" control of heart and pulse. In J. Kamiya, N. E. Miller, D. Shapiro, & J. Stoyva (Eds.), *Biofeedback and self-control: an Aldine reader on the regulation of bodily processes and consciousness.* Chicago: Aldine/Atherton, 1971. (Reprinted from *Circulation,* 1961, *24.*)

White, R. W. Motivation reconsidered: the concept of competence. *Psychological Review,* 1959, *66,* 297–334.

Whyte, W. H. *The Organization man.* New York: Simon and Schuster, 1956.

Wittgenstein, L. *The blue and brown books.* Oxford, England: Basil Blackwell, 1958.

Wolman, B. Does psychology need its own philosophy of science? *American Psychologist,* 1971, *26,* 877–886.

Woods, J. H. *The Yoga-system of Patañjali.* Delhi: Motilal Banarsidass, 1972. (Originally published, 1914.)

Woodworth, R. S., & Schlosberg, H. *Experimental Psychology.* New York: Holt, Rinehart & Winston, 1954.

Wundt, W. [*Outlines of psychology.*] (C. H. Judd, trans.) New York: Gustav E. Stechert, 1897.

Zaehner, R. C. *Mysticism: sacred and profane.* Oxford: Clarendon Press, 1957.

AUTHOR INDEX

SUBJECT INDEX

Abhiniveśa, 76
Ādhibhautika, 36, 86
Ādhidaivika, 36, 86
Adhyātma, 5, 30
Adhyātmika, 36–37, 86–87
Advaita Vedānta, 4, 63, 175
  basic concepts, 210–217
  views of consciousness, 215*ff*
  view of the self, 265–268
Aggression, 90
Alpha states, 13, 150–155
Altered states of consciousness. *See* Samādhi; Consciousness
Altruism, 75, 77
Androidology, 136
Animism, 59
Anxiety, 90, 188
Asmitā, 76–77
Associationism
  Hume, 257
  role of continuity, 257–259
Assumptions
  basis of discussions, 57
  about the human condition, 85*ff*
  about human nature, 69*ff*
  of lawfulness, 64
  of rationality, 78*ff*
  universe as a cosmos, 59*ff*
Ātman, 5, 37, 213–214, 256
Attitudes, Indian and Western
  toward nature, 66*ff*
Autism, 83
Āyurveda, 5, 316

Becoming. *See* Self-actualization
Behaviorism, 23, 34, 67, 91, 131–134, 184, 258, 275*ff*
  approach to consciousness, 129*ff*
  models and therapy, 96–98
Behavior modification (therapy), 156, 314
Bias, of theorists, 50–52
Biofeedback, 13, 150–153, 156
Brahman, 61
  as principle of Vedānta, 211, 220
  realization of, 226
  as self, 213
Brain–mind relationships, 144–157
Breathing
  Yoga exercises, 12, 107, 187
Buddhism (Buddha), 4, 30, 31, 58, 61, 85, 175, 295
  Tibetan, 16
  Zen, 13, 16, 150

Caste system, 59
Catholicism, 5, 19, 20, 22
Christianity, 30, 58
Citta, 177, 215, 288
Clinical psychology. *See* Psychotherapy
Cognition
  in Piaget, 208–209
  in Yoga, 178, 198–199, 204–205, 209
Cognitive dissonance, 78
Concept formation, 197
Congruity, 78